ON THE TIP OF MY TONGUE

ON THE TIP OF MY TONGUE

*Questions, Facts, Curiosities,
and Games of a Quizzical Nature*

DAVID GENTLE

BLOOMSBURY

Published by Bloomsbury USA, New York

ISBN-13: 978-1-60751-277-6

Typeset by Hewer Text UK Ltd, Edinburgh
Printed in the United States of America

Dear Reader,

Welcome to *On the Tip of My Tongue*, a user-friendly, interactive, and indispensable quiz book. It contains numerous quizzes* and games†
for you to play as you navigate through a world of curiosity‡ and trivia. Use this book exactly as you wish: read and play it by yourself, or lock horns with friends and family in gentle, or perhaps zealous, competition. Play the games as suggested or create new ones of your own; dive straight into the solutions§ or resist their allure and give your brain a workout instead. Whatever you do, have fun with this book—even if you find the answer¶ is, as you will no doubt say, "On the Tip of My Tongue."

---

* Quizzes start on page 1. The objective of some quizzes is to name items from a list, others to answer questions related to a particular topic. The target figures provided may be used as a yardstick, a goal, or an indication of difficulty.
† Games start on page 351.
‡ Footnotes are provided throughout this book to supply additional information, to help clarify a question or solution, or to illuminate disputes or ambiguities that may exist in the content.
§ The solutions start on page 203.
¶ While great care has been taken in assembling the content of this book, it is possible that factual inaccuracies may have crept in either through the passage of time (the Browns finally win the Super Bowl), through disputed or debatable subject material (is the Nile really longer than the Amazon?), or through simple . . . ahem. Please send any comments or ideas you have to comments@onthetipofmytongue.co.uk

This book is dedicated to Kate and Zac with love.

I would like to thank the following people for their advice, efforts or enthusiasm:

Andrew Walsh, Charles Beach, Emily Walton, Gordon Wise, Helen Miller, James Hollands, Jenny Parrott, Jon Hampson, Jonathan Derwent, Kate Derwent, Mark Littlewood, Mary Instone, Mike Jones, Neil Peplow, Pam Gentle, Peter Gentle, Sarah Morris, Sophie White, Sarah Hall, Holly Roberts, Miles Doyle, Todd Sievers, Elizabeth Peters, Benjamin Adams, Andrew Chappell, and especially Kate Gentle.

CONTENTS

QUIZZES

"Go to your bosom, knock there,
and ask your heart what it doth know."

William Shakespeare

FIRST LINES OF POPULAR NOVELS I Identify the novels or works of literature* that have these opening lines. If you wish, name the authors as well. The solutions are on page 327. [**Target: 8 correct answers**]

1. "In a hole in the ground there lived a hobbit."
2. "One day when Pooh Bear had nothing else to do, he thought he would do something, so he went round to Piglet's house to see what Piglet was doing."
3. "It is a truth universally acknowledged, that a single man in possession of a good fortune, must be in want of a wife."
4. "It was the best of times, it was the worst of times, it was the age of wisdom, it was the age of foolishness, it was the epoch of belief, it was the epoch of incredulity, it was the season of Light, it was the season of Darkness, it was the spring of hope, it was the winter of despair . . ."
5. "Once there were four children whose names were Peter, Susan, Edmund and Lucy."
6. "You don't know about me without you have read a book by the name of *The Adventures of Tom Sawyer*, but that ain't no matter."
7. "I looked at my notes and I didn't like them. I'd spent three days at U.S. Robots and might as well have spent them at home with the Encyclopedia Tellurica."
8. "It was a bright cold day in April, and the clocks were striking thirteen."
9. "A wide plain, where the broadening Floss hurries on between its green banks to the sea and the loving tide, rushing to meet it, checks its passage with an impetuous embrace."
10. "Last night I dreamt I went to Manderley again."
11. "Many years later, as he faced the firing squad, Colonel Aureliano Buendia was to remember that distant afternoon when his father took him to discover ice."
12. "'Christmas won't be Christmas without any presents,' grumbled Jo, lying on the rug."

---

* A candidate for the first recorded novel is *The Education of Cyrus*, written in the fourth century B.C. by Xenophon, a Greek soldier and philosopher. It is a fictional account of the education of King Cyrus II of Persia (who effectively founded the Persian Empire after becoming King in 559 B.C.).

13. "Dr. Iannis had enjoyed a satisfactory day in which none of his patients had died or got any worse."

14. "Emma Woodhouse, handsome, clever, and rich, with a comfortable home and happy disposition, seemed to unite some of the best blessings of existence; and had lived nearly twenty-one years in the world with very little to distress or vex her."

15. "Where's Papa going with that ax?" said Fern to her mother as they were setting the table for breakfast.

16. "1801—I have just returned from a visit to my landlord—the solitary neighbour that I shall be troubled with."

17. "Like the brief doomed flare of exploding suns that registers dimly on blind men's eyes, the beginning of the horror passed almost unnoticed; in the shriek of what followed, in fact, was forgotten and perhaps not connected to the horror at all."

18. "The Time Traveller (for so it will be convenient to speak of him) was expounding a recondite matter to us."

19. "The boy with fair hair lowered himself down the last few feet of rock and began to pick his way toward the lagoon."

20. "The drought had lasted now for ten million years, and the reign of the terrible lizards had long since ended."

21. "Renowned curator Jacques Saunière staggered through the vaulted archway of the museum's Grand Gallery."

22. "Samuel Spade's jaw was long and bony, his chin a jutting v under the more flexible v of his mouth."

23. "There were 117 psychoanalysts on the Pan Am flight to Vienna and I'd been treated by at least six of them."

24. "It was a dark and stormy night; the rain fell in torrents, except at occasional intervals, when it was checked by a violent gust of wind which swept up the streets (for it is in London that our scene lies), rattling along the house-tops, and fiercely agitating the scanty flame of the lamps that struggled against the darkness."

TRIPLE CROWN Which *three* races make up the Triple Crown? The solution is on page 225. [Target: 3]

BRONTË SISTERS Name the *three* Brontë sisters. Turn to page 205 for the solution. [Target: 3]

FILMS AND THEIR STARS I Identify the films from these selected cast members and the date of release. Find the solutions on page 328. [Target: 10]

1. Leonardo DiCaprio, Kate Winslet (1997)
2. Harrison Ford, Carrie Fisher, Alec Guinness, Peter Cushing (1977)
3. Sean Connery, Ursula Andress, Joseph Wiseman (1962)
4. Marilyn Monroe, Jack Lemmon, Tony Curtis (1959)
5. Janet Leigh, Anthony Perkins (1960)
6. Katharine Ross, Robert Redford, Paul Newman (1969)
7. Helen Hunt, Jack Nicholson (1997)
8. Debra Winger, Richard Gere (1982)
9. Audrey Hepburn, George Peppard (1961)
10. Colin Farrell, Angelina Jolie, Val Kilmer, Anthony Hopkins (2004)
11. Thandie Newton, Matt Dillon, Sandra Bullock (2006)
12. Charlton Heston, Roddy McDowall (1968)
13. Paul Giamatti, Thomas Haden Church, Virginia Madsen, Sandra Oh (2004)
14. Tom Hanks, Edward Burns, Giovanni Ribisi, Matt Damon, Vin Diesel (1998)
15. Frances McDormand, William H. Macy, Steve Buscemi (1996)
16. Steve Guttenberg, Mickey Rourke, Kevin Bacon* (1982)
17. Spencer Tracy, Sidney Poitier, Katharine Hepburn (1967)
18. Greg Kinnear, Toni Collette, Steve Carell, Alan Arkin (2006)
19. Amy Madigan, Ray Liotta, Burt Lancaster, Kevin Costner (1989)
20. Danny DeVito, Annette Bening, Michael J. Fox, Pierce Brosnan, Glenn Close, Jack Nicholson (1996)
21. Dustin Hoffman, Steve McQueen (1973)

---

* Kevin Bacon is the subject of a game called "Six Degrees of Kevin Bacon," the aim of which is to link another actor to Bacon by common film appearances with other actors in the fewest number of steps. Taking Sylvester Stallone, for example, Stallone appeared in *Cliffhanger* with John Lithgow; Lithgow was in *Footloose* with Bacon, giving two steps. The name derives from the fact that it is always seems possible to link Kevin Bacon with any other actor in six steps or fewer. In fact, for any well-known actor it is possible to get to Bacon in no more than two steps. Computer scientists at the University of Virginia have allocated Bacon Numbers to all credited actors and actresses. Kevin Bacon has a Bacon Number of 0; 1,806 actors have a Bacon Number of 1 (Bacon's various co-stars); and 145,024 actors have a Bacon Number of 2.

22.   George C. Scott, Peter Sellers (1963)
23.   David Bowie, Barbara Hershey, Harvey Keitel, Willem
      Dafoe (1988)
24.   Elizabeth Taylor, Richard Burton, George Segal (1966)

PRIMARY COLORS Name the *three* traditional primary colors.
Turn to page 272 for the solution. [**Target: 3**]

NEWTON'S LAWS OF MOTION List Newton's *three* laws of
motion. You will find the solution on page 291. [**Target: 1**]

NOTORIOUS SHIPS I Identify the renowned vessels* from the
descriptions that follow. Turn to page 308 for the solutions.
[**Target: 8**]

1.   White Star liner sunk by an iceberg on her maiden voyage in
      1912 with the loss of 1,500 lives.
2.   Greenpeace ship sunk by French agents in Auckland Harbour
      in 1985.
3.   Subject to a mutiny in 1789 when Fletcher Christian set
      Captain William Bligh and eighteen crew adrift in the Pacific.
4.   Nelson's flagship at the Battle of Trafalgar.
5.   Found adrift and deserted in the Atlantic between Portugal and
      the Azores in 1872.
6.   Capsized ocean liner of the eponymous 1972 disaster movie
      starring Gene Hackman.
7.   The large transatlantic passenger liner built by Cunard in 1968.
8.   Ship on which Drake circumnavigated the world in 1580.
9.   Fictional British naval vessel of the eponymous Gilbert and
      Sullivan opera.
10.   Passenger liner sunk by a German torpedo in 1915 with the
      loss of 1,200 lives.

---

* In the eighteenth century it was common practice for cargo ships to be overloaded
by their owners, ever hopeful of collecting insurance payouts should they sink. To
lessen the prevalence of these "coffin ships," Samuel Plimsoll's successful campaign
brought about the Merchant Shipping Act in Britain in 1875, a piece of legislation
which ensured all ships were marked with a line on the hull to indicate the limit of
the waterline under full load.

11. Vessel on which James Cook explored the Southern Hemisphere between 1768 and 1771.
12. Legendary phantom ship, the subject of Richard Wagner's 1843 opera.
13. Vessel captained by Robert Fitzroy, from which Charles Darwin collected evidence for *On the Origin of Species*.
14. Vessel featuring in the eponymous 1951 film starring Humphrey Bogart and Katharine Hepburn.
15. The world's first nuclear-powered aircraft carrier.
16. German battleship of the Second World War, and sister ship of the Bismarck; sunk off the Norwegian coast in 1944.
17. Wooden raft on which Thor Heyerdahl crossed the Pacific in 1947.
18. Submarine featuring in *Twenty Thousand Leagues Under the Sea* by Jules Verne.
19. U.S. Navy aircraft carrier, sunk in the Battle of Midway.
20. Jacques Cousteau's exploration vessel.
21. Confederate ironclad battleship that was the nemesis of the U.S.S. *Monitor* at the Battle of Hampton Roads.
22. Japanese warship commissioned in 1941 and the largest battleship ever constructed.
23. Quint's fishing boat in *Jaws*.
24. Munitions ship involved in the collision that led to the Halifax Explosion in 1917 in Halifax, Nova Scotia, killing 2,000 people.*

MUSKETEERS List the *three* title characters from *The Three Musketeers*. The solution is on page 328. [**Target: 3**]

TEAMS WINNING FIVE SUPER BOWLS Name the *three* teams to have won the Super Bowl on five occasions. Find the solution on page 205. [**Target: 3**]

LINKED MISCELLANY I In this quiz, the solutions are linked by a connecting theme. Evaluate the clues and deduce the connection. The solutions are on page 205. [**Target: 6**]

1. Who starred in *Wayne's World*, *Austin Powers*, and *Shrek*?

---

* The Halifax Explosion was the largest man-made explosion until the advent of nuclear weapons.

2. Who has a sister called Sally Brown and a best friend called Linus?
3. Who wrote the *Hunchback of Notre Dame* and *Les Miserables*?
4. During which month do All Saints Day, All Souls Day, and Veterans Day fall?
5. What name, meaning "snowy range" in Spanish, is given to the mountains that run between California and Nevada?
6. Which Asian country is the seventh largest country in the world by area?
7. What single unit of weight is the equivalent of 2.2 lb?
8. Which word describes both a radioactive particle consisting of two protons and two neutrons, and a dominant male?
9. Which film* starring Greta Garbo, John Barrymore, and Joan Crawford won the Academy Award for Best Picture in 1932?
10. What was discovered by Wilhelm Röntgen in 1895?

CREW OF APOLLO 11 Name the *three* members of the crew of Apollo 11. Turn to page 246 for the solution. [**Target: 3**]

TRIANGLES Name the *three* types of triangle (as classified by the length of their sides).† You can find the solution on page 272. [**Target: 2**]

CAPITAL CITIES I Identify the countries that have these capital cities. The solutions are on page 291. [**Target: 10**]

1.	Bangkok	2.	Seoul
3.	Helsinki	4.	Prague
5.	Sofia	6.	Addis Ababa
7.	Nairobi	8.	Tripoli
9.	Sarajevo	10.	Harare
11.	Colombo	12.	Rangoon
13.	Baku	14.	Kiev
15.	Pyongyang	16.	Abu Dhabi
17.	Nassau	18.	Dhaka‡

---

* The film is bookended by the line ". . . People come and go. Nothing ever happens."
† Triangles may also be defined by their internal angles. These are known as the right-angle triangle (with one 90° angle), the obtuse-angle triangle (one angle that is greater than 90°), and the acute-angle triangle (all three angles less than 90°).
‡ Note the spelling differs from Dakar in Senegal.

19.	Yerevan	20.	Kinshasa
21.	San José	22.	Astana
23.	Podgorica	24.	Ouagadougou

STOOGES List the *three* Stooges. The solution can be found on page 309. [**Target: 2**]

SONS OF ADAM AND EVE Name the *three** sons of Adam and Eve. Turn to page 328 for the solution. [**Target: 2**]

WIT AND WISDOM I The following quotations are attributed to either Winston Churchill or Oscar Wilde† or Mark Twain. Identify the correct author of each quotation. The solutions are on page 205. [**Target: 18**]

1. "I have nothing to declare but my genius."
2. ". . . and you, madam, are ugly. But in the morning I shall be sober."
3. "I can resist anything but temptation."
4. "The report of my death was an exaggeration."
5. "It is better to keep your mouth closed and let people think you are a fool than to open it and remove all doubt."
6. "There is only one thing in the world worse than being talked about, and that is not being talked about."
7. "I have taken more out of alcohol than alcohol has taken out of me."
8. "A classic is something that everybody wants to have read and nobody wants to read."
9. "This is the sort of English up with which I will not put."
10. "Work is the curse of the drinking classes."
11. "He hadn't a single redeeming vice."
12. "I am ready to meet my Maker. Whether my Maker is prepared for the great ordeal of meeting me is another matter."

---

* Only three sons are named in Genesis although the text states there were many more sons and daughters. According to the Bible, Adam lived to the age of 930.
† It is apocryphal that Oscar Wilde's dying words were, "Either that wallpaper goes—or I do."

13. "Truth is more of a stranger than fiction."
14. "He has all the virtues I dislike and none of the vices I admire."
15. "I must decline your invitation owing to a subsequent engagement."
16. "Man is the only animal that blushes. Or needs to."
17. "A modest man, who has much to be modest about."
18. "If you tell the truth you don't have to remember anything."
19. "I am not young enough to know everything."
20. "I am always ready to learn although I do not always like being taught."
21. "Familiarity breeds contempt—and children."
22. "It has been said that democracy is the worst form of government except all the others that have been tried."
23. "America is the only country to go from barbarism to decadence without civilization in between."
24. "Men stumble over the truth from time to time, but most pick themselves up and hurry off as if nothing happened."

COMPONENTS OF THE MIND What are the *three* components of the mind as proposed by Sigmund Freud? Find the solution on page 225. [**Target: 2**]

BONES OF THE EAR Name the *three* bones* of the middle ear. Turn to page 246 for the solution. [**Target: 2**]

MISCELLANY I These questions are of a miscellaneous nature. The solutions can be found on page 272. [**Target: 10**]

1. Where did the Wright brothers make the first successful powered flight in 1903?
2. How is the Jewish Day of Atonement better known?
3. How many times does the letter "p" occur in the first line of the tongue-twister about Peter Piper?
4. Which is the only common chemical compund to expand when it freezes?
5. Which country's name means "The Savior"?

---

* The bones of the middle ear are collectively known as ossicles.

6. How many of Snow White's seven dwarfs had beards?
7. Which two elements are liquid at room temperature?
8. Which amendment to the American constitution protects witnesses from self-incrimination?
9. Who wrote *Tosca*?
10. In the northern hemisphere, does water drain clockwise or counter-clockwise?
11. What morbid coincidence links Mama Cass and Keith Moon?
12. What is known in France as "mercredi des Cendres"?
13. In which film did the song "Moon River" originally appear?
14. Which composer conducted a performance of one of his works in Wanamaker's department store in New York in 1904?
15. In which sport do competing teams try to travel backwards and in opposite directions?
16. What was the first National Park in the U.S.?
17. Where is the official residence of the First Lord of the Treasury?
18. After the White House, what is the most visited home in the U.S.?
19. A mother and father have five sons. Each son has one sister. How many people are there in this family?
20. Which 1949 novel was originally titled *The Last Man in Europe*?
21. How many feet are in a mile?
22. Which note does an orchestra tune up to?
23. What average speed did the winning car of the Indianapolis 500 exceed for the first time in 1925?
24. A man jumps from a bridge into a river and swims for a kilometer upstream. At exactly one kilometer, he passes a bottle floating in the river. He continues swimming in the same direction for half an hour and then turns around and swims back towards the bridge. The man and the bottle arrive at the bridge at the same time. If the man has been swimming at a constant speed, how fast is the river flowing?

GHOSTS VISITING EBENEZER SCROOGE Name the *four* ghosts who visited Ebenezer Scrooge in *A Christmas Carol.* Turn to page 292 for the solution. [**Target: 4**]

GOLF MAJORS List the *four* major golf* tournaments. The solution is on page 309. [**Target: 4**]

CELEBRITY BABY NAMES Name the celebrity parent(s) of these children. Note that the same celebrity parents may feature in the solutions to more than one of these questions. Look for the solutions on page 246. [**Target: 10**]

1.	Brooklyn	2.	Coco Riley
3.	Zowie	4.	Jermajesty
5.	Prince Michael	6.	Lourdes
7.	Apple	8.	Moon Unit
9.	Moxie CrimeFighter	10.	Rocco
11.	Sean Preston	12.	Levon Green
13.	Hopper Jack	14.	Shiloh Nouvel
15.	Roman Zelman	16.	Dweezil
17.	Moses Amadeus	18.	Tallulah Pine
19.	Scout LaRue	20.	Pilot Inspektor
21.	Misty Kyd	22.	Elijah Bob Patricius Guggi Q
23.	Sage Moonblood	24.	Speck Wildhorse

OFFICIAL RESIDENCES What are the *four* official residences of the United States of America? Turn to page 205 for the solution [**Target: 3**]

THE MONKEES Name the *four* members of the Monkees. The solution is on page 225. [**Target: 3**]

---

* Golf originated in Scotland in the fifteenth century. It is thought to have descended from the games of Kolven (from Holland) and Chole (from Belgium), which involved players chasing a pebble around a course with a stick. The Scots gave the game its defining characteristic by adding a hole and making this the objective of the game. Golf became so popular in Scotland that King James II (of Scotland) banned the sport in 1457 to prevent military training being neglected. Many of his subjects defied the ban, continuing to play the sport on dunes and beaches around the coastline on courses they called "links." The game was adopted in the rest of Britain under the patronage of James I (formerly James VI of Scotland) from where it was exported to North America and then the rest of the world. There are now many thousands of courses worldwide with their own unique characteristics. The longest hole in the world, at 909 yards, is the (par 7) 7th hole of the Sano Course at the Satsuki Golf Club in Japan; the world's largest bunker is Hell's Half Acre on the 585-yard 7th hole of the Pine Valley Course in New Jersey.

FIRST LINES OF POP SONGS I Deduce the titles of these songs from the first lines presented. (The year each song was a hit is supplied to assist you.) For advanced play, also name the performers. Turn to page 246 for the solutions. [**Target: 10**]

1. "Sometimes it's hard to be a woman." (1975)
2. "And now, the end is near." (1969)
3. "You walked into the party like you were walking onto a yacht." (1973)
4. "There's nothing you can do that can't be done." (1967)
5. "Good-bye to you my trusted friend, we've known each other since we were nine or ten." (1974)
6. "I bet you're wondering how I knew." (1969)
7. "Look, if you had one shot, or one opportunity to seize everything you ever wanted." (2002)
8. "Today is gonna be the day that they're gonna throw it back to you." (1995)
9. "When I'm feeling blue, all I have to do is take a look at you." (1988)
10. "Risin' up back on the street, did my time took my chances." (1982)
11. "Fire in the disco." (2003)
12. "You don't have to be beautiful to turn me on." (1986)
13. "Almost heaven, West Virginia, Blue Ridge Mountains, Shenandoah River." (1972)
14. "You keep saying you've got something for me." (1966)
15. "Born down in a dead man's town, the first kick I took was when I hit the ground." (1985)
16. "I know I stand in line until you think you have the time to spend an evening with me." (1967)
17. "All the old paintings on the tomb." (1986)
18. "I was born in the wagon of a travelling show, my mama used to dance for the money they'd throw." (1971)
19. "Kick it!" (1987)
20. "The Mississippi Delta was shining like a national guitar." (1986)
21. "Sometimes you're better off dead, there's a gun in your hand, it's pointing at your head." (1986)
22. "Look into my eyes, you will see what you mean to me." (1991)
23. "When I was young, it seemed that life was so wonderful, a miracle." (1970)
24. "Please allow me to introduce myself." (1968)

13

TEA PARTY IN WONDERLAND Name the *four* attendees at the Mad Tea Party in *Alice's Adventures in Wonderland*. Find the solution on page 273. [**Target: 4**]

U2 List the *four* members of U2. Turn to page 292 for the solution. [**Target: 3**]

CHARACTERS IN LITERATURE I Identify the works of literature in which these characters appear. For advanced play, also name the authors. The solutions are on page 309. [**Target: 10**]

1.	Bilbo Baggins	2.	Rhett Butler
3.	Elizabeth Bennet	4.	Captain Nemo
5.	Jim Hawkins	6.	John Clayton, Lord Greystoke
7.	Captain Yossarian	8.	Daniel Cleaver
9.	Edmond Dantès	10.	Sancho Panza
11.	Blanche DuBois	12.	Benjamin Braddock
13.	Mr. Willoughby	14.	John the Savage
15.	Anne Elliot	16.	Dorothea Brooke
17.	William of Baskerville	18.	Nick Carraway
19.	Abel Magwitch	20.	Agatha Trunchbull
21.	Becky Sharp	22.	The Mock Turtle
23.	Ignatius J. Reilly	24.	John Blackthorne

GRAND SLAM TENNIS TOURNAMENTS Name the *four* Grand Slam tennis* tournaments. The solution is on page 329. [**Target: 4**]

---

* The game of tennis owes its existence to two quite different nineteenth-century inventions. In 1839, Charles Goodyear discovered the process for creating vulcanized rubber, enabling the material to be commercially usable for the first time (before Goodyear's invention, rubber would get too soft when warm and be too brittle in the cold). Nineteen years earlier, Gloucester engineer Edward Beard Budding had the notion that the cloth-trimming machines he had designed could be adapted to cut grass, a hugely labor-intensive process at the time, giving rise to the lawnmower. When, in 1874, Major Walter Wingfield invented the game of lawn tennis (which he originally named "Sphairistikè"), it featured rubber balls that would bounce on the neatly mowed lawns of England's wealthy classes and became an immediate success.

MONOPOLY STATIONS Which four stations are found on the standard Monopoly board?* Find the solution on page 206.
[Target: 4]

ADVERTISING SLOGANS I† Name the products that were being marketed with these slogans. Turn to page 225 for the solutions.
[Target: 16]

1. "Because you're worth it"
2. "They're grrreat!"
3. "Put a tiger in your tank"
4. "The milk chocolate melts in your mouth, not in your hand"
5. "Eat fresh!"
6. "Finger lickin' good!"
7. "It's everywhere you want to be"
8. "Leave the driving to us"
9. "Fly the friendly skies"
10. "Imagination at work"
11. "Nobody doesn't like . . . _____"
12. "The happiest place on earth"
13. "Just for the taste of it"
14. "Tastes so good cats ask for it by name"
15. "Bank of opportunity"
16. "Get N or get out"
17. "The longer lasting snack"
18. "Connecting people"
19. "Top breeders recommend it"
20. "Welcome to the human network"
21. "Something special in the air"
22. "The daily diary of the American dream"
23. "Does it make sense to jump out of a warm bed into a cold cereal?"
24. "See America at see level"

---

* The original Atlantic City version.

† Adverts date back to Roman times and have even been found in the ruins of Pompeii; advertising as we would recognize it first emerged with the rise of popular media, and particularly as the newspapers of the seventeenth and eighteenth centuries began to enjoy wide circulation. A candidate for the first nationally memorable slogan to appear was Lord Kitchener's "Your Country Needs You" on the British Army recruitment poster campaign at the onset of the First World War.

BLOOD GROUPS Name the *four* blood groups. Find the solution on page 247. [**Target: 4**]

STATES AT FOUR CORNERS MONUMENT Name the *four* states which intersect at Four Corners Monument. The solution is on page 273. [**Target: 3**]

RECENT HISTORY I Identify each of these years by the clues provided. Turn to page 292 for the solutions. [**Target: 10**]

1.   An international group of volunteers travels to Iraq to act as human shields in an attempt to avert an invasion; the space shuttle Columbia disintegrates during re-entry, killing all seven crew members; Iraq is invaded by coalition forces and Saddam Hussein is overthrown; Arnold Schwarzenegger is elected as Governor of California; Concorde makes its last commercial flight; Michael Jackson is arrested on charges of child molestation.

2.   U.S. vice president Dick Cheney accidentally shoots his friend Harry Whittington; Slobodan Milosevic commits suicide in his cell during his trial for war crimes; Pluto is demoted in status to a "Dwarf Planet"; North Korea claims to have conducted a nuclear test; Saddam Hussein is executed in Baghdad; Warren Buffet donates $30 billion to the Bill and Melinda Gates Foundation.

3.   Hong Kong is transferred to Chinese sovereignty; Princess Diana is killed in a car crash in Paris, her funeral watched by one billion people worldwide; Mother Theresa dies in Calcutta; O. J. Simpson is found liable for murder in a civil case and ordered to pay $35 million in damages; comet Hale-Bopp passes close to earth; *Harry Potter and the Philosopher's Stone* is published; the Green Bay Packers win the Super Bowl for the first time since 1967.

4.   Atomic bombs are detonated on Hiroshima and Nagasaki; the Allied leadership meets at the Potsdam conference in Germany; Auschwitz is liberated; the Japanese surrender is taken on board the U.S.S *Missouri*, ending the Second World War; Franklin D. Roosevelt is inaugurated as American president for an unprecedented fourth time; the United Nations and the Arab League are formed.

5. The world's population exceeds 6 billion for the first time; *Star Wars Episode I: The Phantom Menace* is released; a plane piloted by John F. Kennedy Jr. crashes off the coast of Martha's Vineyard, killing him, his wife, Carolyn Bessette Kennedy, and her sister Lauren Bessette; Wayne Greztky is inducted into the Hockey Hall of Fame; Vladamir Putin succeeds Boris Yeltsin as Russian president.

6. Gas escapes from the Union Carbide plant in Bhopal, in India, killing 2,000 and poisoning 200,000 people; Indira Gandhi is assassinated by Sikh extremists angered by the storming of the Golden Temple; the Soviet Union boycotts the Los Angeles Olympics; *Miami Vice* airs for the first time; Apple releases the Macintosh computer, a ground-breaking Orwellian ad for the product is aired just once in the third quarter of the Super Bowl; Ronald Reagan defeats Walter F. Mondale in the U.S. presidential election.

7. Republican forces surrender, ending the Spanish Civil War; Germany occupies Czechoslovakia and Poland; Britain and France declare war on Germany; Russia invades Finland and the Baltic States; the Graf Spee is scuttled after the Battle of the River Plate; *The Grapes of Wrath* is published by John Steinbeck; *The Wizard of Oz* and *Gone with the Wind* both premiere; LaGuardia Airport opens in New York City.

8. The space shuttle Challenger explodes shortly after takeoff; the Chernobyl nuclear power plant melts down; America bombs Libya in response to terrorist attacks; Mikhail Gorbachev campaigns for "Glasnost" and "Perestroika"; Prince Andrew marries Sarah Ferguson; the centennial of the Statue of Liberty is celebrated; Mike Tyson wins his first title fight to become the youngest heavyweight champion in history.

9. Bill Clinton is inaugurated as U.S. president; six people are killed in a bomb attack on the World Trade Center; "I Will Always Love You" by Whitney Houston spends its fourteenth week at number one; Mosaic, the first popular Web browser, is released; *The Late Show with David Letterman* airs for the first time on CBS; *Jurassic Park* is released.

10. Concorde enters regular passenger service; Israeli commandos storm a hijacked plane at Entebbe in Uganda and rescue the hostages; Mao Tse-tung dies; the first Cray-1 supercomputer is

installed; the Teton Dam in Idaho collapses, killing 11 people and causing $300 million of damage; The United States Bicentennial is celebrated; Gerald Ford beats Ronald Reagan for the Republican presidential nomination; Nadia Comaneci scores a perfect 10 at the Montreal Olympics, the first time in Olympic gymnastics this has ever been achieved.*

11. Idi Amin seizes power in Uganda; Jim Morrison dies in Paris; Apollo 15 astronauts ride in the Lunar Rover on the moon; Stanley Kubrick directs *A Clockwork Orange*; Charles Manson receives the death sentence[†] in Los Angeles; a man calling himself Dan Cooper jumps with $200,000 of ransom money from a highjacked Boeing 727 over Washington state and is never seen again.

12. Martin Luther King Jr. makes his "I have a dream" speech; ZIP[‡] codes are introduced; a volcanic eruption creates the island of Surtsey; Valentina Tereshkova becomes the first woman in space; *Dr. No*, the first James Bond film, opens in the United States; John F. Kennedy is assassinated in Dallas.

13. Bolsheviks murder Tsar Nicholas II and his family; Russia withdraws from the First World War; Allied forces are victorious at the Battle of Amiens, which has a decisive impact on the outcome of war; the First World War ends with the signing of the Armistice on November 11; an influenza pandemic kills 26 million people worldwide; time zones and daylight saving time are formally introduced in the United States by Congress.

14. Iraq launches SCUD missiles at Israel; Operation Desert Storm liberates Kuwait; Los Angeles police are videotaped beating Rodney King; Soviet president Mikhail Gorbachev is imprisoned for three days in a coup by communist hardliners; Boris Yeltsin becomes Russian president; the USSR collapses and the Warsaw Pact is dissolved; Freddie Mercury dies of AIDS; Nirvana releases *Nevermind*.

15. Mikhail Gorbachev becomes leader of the Soviet Union; Ronald Reagan is sworn in for his second term as U.S.

---

* The scoreboard was not equipped to display "10.0"—the perfect scores were displayed as "1.0s."

† Manson's sentence was commuted to life imprisonment the following year when California (temporarily) abolished the death penalty.

‡ Zone Improvement Plan.

president; Coca-Cola reintroduce their original formula after the disastrous introduction of New Coke; Live Aid concerts take place in London and Philadelphia; the Greenpeace vessel the *Rainbow Warrior* is sunk by French agents in Auckland Harbour.

16. British and Commonwealth forces are repelled by the Turks at Gallipoli; the *Lusitania* is torpedoed and sunk by a German U-boat; the German army uses chlorine gas at the Second Battle of Ypres; Babe Ruth hits his first home run; the foundation stone of the Lincoln Memorial is laid.

17. The Six Day War occurs in the Middle East; Che Guevara is captured and executed; Apollo 1 catches fire on the launch pad, killing three astronauts*; San Francisco experiences the Summer of Love; the Beatles release *Sgt. Pepper's Lonely Hearts Club Band*; Elvis Presley and Priscilla Beaulieu marry in Las Vegas; theoretical physicist John Wheeler coins the term "black hole."

18. The PLO is founded; the Civil Rights Act is signed in the U.S., outlawing discrimination on grounds of race, religion, sex, or nationality; the Beatles top the charts with "I Want To Hold Your Hand"; the Warren Commission delivers its report on the Kennedy assassination and concludes that Lee Harvey Oswald acted alone; Martin Luther King Jr. receives the Nobel Peace Prize.

19. Richard Nixon announces his resignation as U.S. president; Haile Selassie is deposed in Ethiopia; Patty Hearst controversially participates in the robbery of a San Francisco bank, while a hostage of the Symbionese Liberation Army; Muhammad Ali and George Foreman fight the "Rumble in the Jungle" in Zaire, Ali wins in eight rounds; after fighting for thirty years, Hiroo Onoda, a Japanese army officer, surrenders in the Philippines.†

20. Albert Einstein publishes his *General Theory of Relativity*; German and British fleets engage in the Battle of Jutland; the Battle of the Somme takes place with unprecedented loss of

---

* Gus Grissom, Ed White, and Roger Chaffee.

† When he was discovered, Onoda refused to surrender unless he was ordered to by a superior officer. The Japanese government duly located Onoda's wartime commanding officer, Major Taniguchi (by then a shopkeeper) and flew him to the Philippines to order Onoda to give up his arms. Onoda was officially pardoned by Ferdinand Marcos for the numerous civilians he had killed in the intervening years.

life; Rasputin* is assassinated in Moscow; Woodrow Wilson is re-elected; David Lloyd George becomes British prime minister; Monet paints the Water Lilies series.

21. The Warsaw Pact is established; Juan Perón is ousted by a military coup in Argentina; the first McDonald's restaurant opens in Des Plaines, Illinois; the Soviet Union officially announces the end of the war with Germany; Bill Haley and His Comets top the charts with "Rock Around the Clock."

22. Dwight D. Eisenhower is sworn in for a second term; Sputnik I is launched; civil rights violence takes place in Little Rock, Arkansas, as black students are prevented from enrolling in high school; the U.S. and USSR successfully test ICBMs; Elvis Presley moves into Graceland; Toyota exports the first Land Cruisers to the U.S.

23. The Treaty of Versailles is signed, placing harsh post-war terms on Germany; the League of Nations is founded; the Eighteenth Amendment is passed, establishing Prohibition; Alcock and Brown fly the Atlantic; British forces massacre 379 demonstrators in Amritsar; the Grand Canyon is established as a national park.

24. Japan annexes Korea; in Britain, Edward VII dies and is succeeded by George V; the Union of South Africa is founded; Halley's Comet is photographed for the first time; Theodore Roosevelt rides in an airplane, the first president to do so.

ROOSEVELT'S FOUR FREEDOMS Recall if you can Roosevelt's *Four* Freedoms.† Find the solution on page 310. [**Target: 3**]

CLASSICAL COLUMNS Name the *four* types of column of classical architecture. The solution is on page 329. [**Target: 3**]

---

* Grigori Rasputin was a faith healer who played a role in the downfall of the Romanov dynasty. Tsarina Alexandra (the wife of Tsar Nicholas II) invited Rasputin to help her hemophiliac son, the Tsarevich Alexei. Under Rasputin's treatments Alexei's condition seemed to improve and consequently so did the healer's standing in the court. As his reputation increased, so Rasputin indulged himself in an ever more scandalous personal life, which revolved around St. Petersburg society ladies, prostitutes, and heavy drinking. During the First World War, the (German) Tsarina's relationship with Rasputin was a cause of much suspicion, with many Russians believing Rasputin to be a spy, and this heaped yet more pressure on the already unpopular Romanovs. In an attempt to rectify the situation, Prince Felix Yusupov and the Tsar's cousin, Grand Duke Dmitri Pavlovitch Romanov, murdered Rasputin.
† Roosevelt referred to the freedoms in the State of the Union address in January 1941.

MISCELLANY II These questions are of a miscellaneous nature. Turn to page 206 for the solutions. [**Target:** 12]

1. What is the freezing point of water in degrees Kelvin?
2. Which U.S. state is the first alphabetically?
3. What does G.I. stand for?
4. Armand Zildjian is associated with which type of musical instrument?
5. A man says "Everything I say is false." Is he telling the truth?
6. What song did Otis Redding write while staying on a houseboat on Waldo Pier in Sausalito, California, in 1967?
7. Which state takes its name from a word meaning "snow covered"?
8. What are the first three words in the Bible?
9. What type of gemstone was in Diana Spencer's engagement ring?
10. Who was the victim of the world's first live televised murder?
11. Who, upon splitting with her partner, famously said, "At least I can wear high heels now"?
12. Which two letters are worth the most in a game of Scrabble?
13. On a standard dartboard, what is the lowest number that cannot be scored with a single dart?
14. Which playwright was killed during a brawl in a Deptford tavern in 1593?
15. Which well-known fictional vessel was originally going to be called the U.S.S. *Yorktown*?
16. Which is the only muscle in the human body anchored only at one end?
17. Which Sanskrit phrase may be translated literally as "love discourse"?
18. Who granted a pardon to Richard Nixon for his role in the Watergate scandal?
19. What links the words "charm" and "yam"?
20. Which American state flag features the Pole Star and the Great Bear on a blue background?
21. In Greek mythology, who solved the riddle of the Sphinx?
22. What links the words "scissors," "shorts," and "doldrums"?
23. Of the three Triple Crown races, which is the longest?
24. The power ballad "All By Myself," written in 1976 by Eric Carmen and popularized by Céline Dion in 1996, is based on a classical piece by which composer?

ASSASSINATED U.S. PRESIDENTS Name the *four* presidents of the United States who have died in office as a result of assassinations. Find the solution on page 226. [**Target:** 3]

BOY BANDS Name the boy bands from these clues. Turn to page 273 for the solutions. [**Target: 10**]

1. Jackie, Tito, Jermaine, Marlon, Michael
2. Wanya, Michael, Shawn, Nathan
3. Micky, Davy, Michael, Peter
4. Alan, Donny, Merrill, Jay, Wayne
5. Barry, Maurice, Robin
6. JC, Justin, Chris, Joey, James
7. Donnie, Jordan, Jon, Danny, Joe
8. Nick, Howie, Brian, AJ, Kevin
9. Bobby, Ralph, Michael, Ricky, Ronnie
10. Omari, Dreux, DeMario, Jarell
11. George, Andrew
12. Joe, Ron, Terry, Otis, G.C.
13. Bryan, Mark, Kevin, Sam
14. Les, Eric, Woody, Alan, Derek
15. Nick, John, Roger, Andy, Simon
16. Bryan, Shane, Mark, Nicky, Kian
17. Gary, Mark, Robbie, Jason, Howard
18. Ronan, Stephen, Mikey, Shane, Keith
19. Jeff, Eric, Ray, Felipe, Alex, David
20. Andre, Brian, Christopher, Jason
21. Brian, Brandon, Kyle, Richard
22. Isaac, Taylor, Zac
23. Tony, Jamie, Delious, Alfred
24. Quinnes, Daron, Marvin, Michael

THE GOLDEN GIRLS Name the *four* main characters in *The Golden Girls*. Turn to page 310 for the solution. [**Target: 4**]

HOBBIES AND PROFESSIONS I Describe these hobbies and professions.* Find the solutions on page 329. [**Target: 8**]

---

* The word "hobby" derives from "hobby horse," a term appearing in the sixteenth century to describe a child's toy riding horse. In the seventeenth century this took on the meaning of a pastime, with the connecting notion of it being an activity that led to nothing. "Profession" is an older word, appearing around the thirteenth century to refer to the declaration of vows on entering a religious order. By the sixteenth century, the meaning had expanded closer to its current sense of an occupation that "one professes" to be skilled in.

1.	Origamist	2.	Chandler
3.	Philatelist	4.	Wainwright
5.	Apiarist	6.	Broderer
7.	Roughneck	8.	Sommelier
9.	Mercer	10.	Founder
11.	Charcutier	12.	Jobber
13.	Tanner	14.	Bowyer
15.	Stringer	16.	Campanologist
17.	Cooper	18.	Lepidopterist
19.	Arborist	20.	Numismatist
21.	Assayer	22.	Cartophilist
23.	Chapman	24.	Almoner

TELETUBBIES List the *four* Teletubbies. The solution is on page 206. [**Target: 4**]

AMERICAN STATES BEGINNING WITH "I" Name the *four* U.S. states that begin with the letter "I." Turn to page 226 for the solution. [**Target: 4**]

LINKED MISCELLANY II The solutions to these questions are linked by a connecting theme. Evaluate the clues and deduce the connection. The solution is on page 247. [**Target: 5**]

1. Which classic song was first recorded in the U.S. by Louis Armstrong in 1954, was a Billboard Hot 100 number one for Bobby Darin in 1959, was recorded as a duet by Frank Sinatra and Dean Martin, and earned Ella Fitzgerald a Grammy when in a 1961 performance in Berlin she improvised new lyrics, having forgotten the words?
2. Who had hits with "I Can't Go for That" and "Maneater"?
3. Which toxic, metallic element has an atomic number of 82?
4. What is the nickname of the U.S. Special Forces?
5. How is albumen better known?
6. What institution was founded in 1800 by an Act of Congress which allowed funds of $5,000 for the purchase of books?
7. Where do the San Francisco 49ers play their home games?
8. What is the name of the chemical agent used by the Germans at the Battle of Ypres in 1917 and by Saddam Hussein in 1988?
9. What was Pete Sampras's nickname?
10. Who starred in *Lost in Translation* and *Girl with a Pearl Earring*?

PAC-MAN GHOSTS List the *four* ghosts in the game of Pac-Man. Turn to page 273 for the solution. [**Target: 1**]

MAJOR ACCOUNTING FIRMS Name the *four* major global auditors. The solution is on page 292. [**Target: 3**]

NICKNAMES OF PEOPLE I Identify the people who have been given these nicknames. The solutions can be found on page 310. [**Target: 12**]

1.	Jackie O	2.	Hanoi Jane
3.	The Maid of Orleans	4.	The Body
5.	Old Blood and Guts	6.	Flo Jo
7.	Mahatma	8.	Wilt the Stilt
9.	The Governator	10.	The Italian Stallion
11.	Scarface	12.	Superbrat
13.	The Sultan of Swat	14.	Marky Mark
15.	Mr. Mojo Risin'	16.	Bird
17.	The Louisville Lip	18.	Duke
19.	Marvellous	20.	Judge Dread
21.	Calamity Jane	22.	The Divine Miss M
23.	The Refrigerator	24.	Lady Day

BIG FOUR TROPHIES Name the *four* major trophies of U.S. sports. Turn to page 329 for the solution. [**Target: 4**]

BONES OF THE LEG List the *four* bones found in the human leg (exclude bones found in the foot from your response). The solution is on page 206. [**Target: 3**]

INFORMATION SUPPLIED BY PRISONERS OF WAR Identify the only *four* pieces of information that, under provision of the Third Geneva Convention, a prisoner of war can be required to supply. Turn to page 248 for the solution. [**Target: 4**]

HOUSES AT HOGWARTS Name the *four* houses at Hogwarts (from the *Harry Potter* stories). Find the solution on page 273. [**Target: 3**]

MISCELLANY III These questions are of a miscellaneous nature. The solutions are on page 292. [**Target: 10**]

1. Which 1928 novel by a British author became a bestseller in the U.S. in 1959, the year a ban on it was lifted?

2. 90210, 90211, and 90212 are ZIP codes in which U.S. town?

3. The opera *Die Zauberflöte* is better known as what?

4. In which part of a living cell is DNA found?

5. Logically, which body feature was not possessed by either Adam or Eve?

6. In a street of one hundred houses numbered one through one hundred, how many number nines are there?

7. In which sport is the Vince Lombardi Trophy awarded?

8. What film starring Al Jolson is considered to be the first talking film?

9. The name for which animal comes from Malay and means "man of the woods"?

10. Who was the financial beneficiary of the Louisiana Purchase of 1803?

11. What is the name of Dr. Seuss's egg-hatching elephant?

12. In medicine, how is the laryngeal prominence more commonly known?

13. Which of the United States is furthest west?

14. What was the title of the hit duet between Roberta Flack and Peabo Bryson?

15. In which river was Jesus baptized?

16. What color was Moby-Dick?

17. In Beatrix Potter's book, what type of animal was Mr. Jeremy Fisher?

18. What is a perfect score in a game of tenpin bowling?

19. What was commissioned by Sir Benjamin Hall in London in 1838?

20. What are "First," "Middle," "Morning," "Forenoon," "Afternoon," "First Dog," and "Last Dog"?

21. Who wrote "You'll Never Walk Alone"?

22. Which twelve-letter word contains six alternate letter "a's"?

23. Which country did America attempt to invade in the War of 1812?

24. Some apes were playing tug-of-war. When three baboons played two chimpanzees, the game was a draw. When three gorillas played against four chimpanzees, the game also ended in a draw. If two gorillas played five baboons, which side, if any, would win?

BEAUTY PAGEANTS List the four major international beauty pageants. Turn to page 310 for the solution. [**Target: 3**]

LED ZEPPELIN Name the *four* members of Led Zeppelin. Look for the solutions on page 329. [**Target: 3**]

EVENTS IN HISTORY I Identify the century in which each of these events in history* took place (be even more precise and attempt the year if you wish). Find the solutions on page 206. [**Target: 10**]

1. Great Fire of London.
2. Florence Nightingale founds her nursing school at St. Thomas' Hospital, London.
3. Completion of the Domesday Book.
4. American Declaration of Independence.
5. Defeat of Napoleon Bonaparte at Waterloo.
6. Publication of the *Communist Manifesto*.
7. Defeat of George Custer at the Battle of Little Big Horn.
8. The Black Death first arrives in Europe.
9. Beginning of the English Civil War.
10. Henry VIII breaks with Rome.
11. English defeat the French at Agincourt.
12. Declaration of Papal infallibility.
13. Accession of William of Orange in the Glorious Revolution.
14. Magna Carta signed at Runnymede.

---

* Although there had been chroniclers before him, Herodotus is known as the "father of history" for being the first person to record events with the objective of trying to understand human behavior and learn from it. In the fifth century B.C. Herodotus wrote about the Persian invasion of Greece and described his work as a "historia"—a Greek word meaning "learning by enquiry," from which the modern connotation is derived.

15. Pilgrims reach New England on the *Mayflower*.
16. Scots defeat the English at Bannockburn.
17. King Harold victorious at the Battle of Stamford Bridge.
18. Act of Union unites England and Scotland.
19. Fall of Constantinople to the Turks.
20. St. Augustine lands in Britain.
21. Arrival of Arab arithmetical notation in Europe.
22. Genghis Khan begins Mongol conquest of Asia.
23. Muhammad begins dictation of the Koran.
24. Beginning of the Hundred Years' War between England and France.

COMMONWEALTH STATES Name the *four* U.S. states which term themselves "Commonwealths." The solution is on page 000. [Target: 3]

LITTLE WOMEN List the *four* eponymous characters of Louisa May Alcott's novel. Turn to page 248 for the solution. [Target: 3]

ASTRONOMERS, MATHEMATICIANS, AND PHYSICISTS

Identify the scientists* from the clues presented. Find the solutions on page 274. [Target: 10]

1. German theoretical physicist whose *General Theory of Relativity* defined the relationship between energy, matter, time, space, and gravity.
2. Lucasian professor at Cambridge University who revolutionized the sciences of math and physics by defining gravitation and the laws of motion, which he published in his work *Philosophiae Naturalis Principia Mathematica* in 1687.

---

* In antiquity, classical scholars would study and master a variety of subjects (and often all of the known subjects). To them, the fields that we now call theology, philosophy, and astrology were no less "scientific" than the disciplines that we term natural sciences. A feature of the classical scientific method was its reliance on intuition; sometimes this led to brilliant insights but classical scholars were also guilty of turning out errors which could last for centuries (famously Ptolemy's model of the solar system). The modern scientific method of deduction from observation was first proposed by the philosopher Francis Bacon in his *Novum Organum*   *cont'd over*

3. Greek mathematician who famously discovered the principles of density and buoyancy while taking a bath (proclaiming, "Eureka!" meaning, "I have it!").

4. Polish astronomer who challenged Ptolemy's view of the universe and proposed a heliocentric model of the solar system, published in 1543 as *De Revolutionibus Orbium Coelestium* ("On the Revolution of Celestial Spheres"), thereby upsetting the establishment and particularly the Catholic church.

5. Italian astronomer who was the first person to use a telescope to observe the night sky and discover, among other things, the moons of Jupiter and the rings of Saturn.

6. American astronomer who was the first to observe galaxies beyond the Milky Way, who discovered the expansion of the universe and derived a law to describe it, and gave his name to the space telescope launched by NASA in 1990.

7. British astronomer who discovered the comet that now bears his name, correctly observing its seventy-six-year orbit and predicting its reappearance in 1758 (after his death).

8. Greek mathematician who deduced that the sum of the squares of the sides of a right-angled triangle is equal to the square of the hypotenuse.

---

cont'd (meaning "True Suggestions for the Interpretation of Nature") of 1620. The title page of this work contained a picture of a ship passing the Pillars of Hercules; in Greek mythology this marked the edge of the world. Carefully chosen to upset the establishment, the image made the emphatic point that ancient learning had now become a limiting factor from which man had to break free for his quest for knowledge and betterment to continue. The seventeenth century marked a real turning point in the history of scientific investigation with the subjective fields of philosophy and astrology departing forever to be replaced by the specialized disciplines of astronomy, physics, medicine, and the multitude of other subjects that are studied today. When, in 1663, Henry Lucas created the Lucasian Chair of Mathematics at Cambridge University, he insisted that the professorship should not be held by anyone who was active in the church. Charles II was even persuaded to pass legislation excusing holders of the post from taking holy orders (a requirement for all Cambridge professors at the time). These events, which presumably horrified churchmen of the time, seem to have been foreseen centuries earlier by St. Augustine when he wrote: "The good Christian should beware of mathematicians, and all those who make empty prophecies. The danger already exists that the mathematicians have made a covenant with the devil to darken the spirit and to confine man in the bonds of Hell."

9. Austrian physicist who discovered the apparent shift in frequency and wavelength that occurs as the source of a wave moves nearer or further from the observer, accounting, for example, for the change in pitch of a fire engine siren as it passes or the red shift in light emitted from stars that are travelling away from the earth.

10. French mathematician and philosopher who invented the system of coordinates influential in the development of modern calculus and who famously wrote, "I think, therefore I am."

11. British mathematician and Second World War cryptologist who made a large contribution towards the modern concept of electronic computing and whose insights led to the development of Colossus (in 1945), the first programmable digital electronic computer.

12. Austrian physicist who made significant contributions to quantum theory and famously illustrated its counterintuitive nature with a thought experiment featuring a cat.

13. British nurse whose work with public health data led to advancements in the field of statistics; she was the first person to illustrate data using a pie chart.

14. British physicist who discovered the concept of electromagnetic induction and built the first dynamo; he founded the Christmas lectures for young people at the Royal Institution that bears his name.

15. Greek mathematician and "father of geometry" whose work *Elements* (*c.* 300 B.C.) defined the rudiments of geometry and the properties of numbers.

16. German physicist whose work on thermodynamics (black body radiation) led to the development of quantum theory.

17. British mathematician and Lucasian Professor who designed the first programmable computer, a mechanical device called a difference engine, which was never completed.

18. German physicist who worked on quantum theory and in 1927 originated the "uncertainty principle": that at any given instant it is possible either to know the direction an electron is travelling in or the position of the electron, but never both at the same time.

19. French physicist and mathematician who clarified the concepts of pressure and vacuum and gave his name to a unit of pressure.

20. German-born astronomer who discovered Uranus and was given the title King's Astronomer by George III.

21. Greek astronomer who formulated the geocentric model of the universe in the second century (in a work called *Almagest*, meaning "The Great Treatise"), which was accepted until the sixteenth century.

22. British physicist (born in New Zealand) who discovered alpha and beta radiation and in 1911 deduced that atomic structure must include a dense nucleus at its center.

23. Danish physicist who combined quantum theory with the concept of atomic structure and proposed in 1913 the modern model of atomic structure with electrons orbiting a nucleus.

24. British physicist and contemporary of Isaac Newton and Christopher Wren who discovered the law of elasticity, which describes the relationship between tension and elasticity in a spring.

AMERICAN STATES BEGINNING WITH "A" List the *four* American states whose names begin with the letter "A." The solution is on page 293. [**Target: 4**]

CLASSICAL ELEMENTS Name the *four* classical elements. Find the solution on page 310. [**Target: 4**]

SPORTS GOVERNING BODIES I Identify the sports represented by these sporting governing bodies. Go to page 329 for the solutions. [**Target: 12**]

1.	MCC	2.	FIFA
3.	PGA	4.	WBO
5.	NHL	6.	TCCB
7.	FIA	8.	IAAF
9.	WBA	10.	CONCACAF
11.	BAGA	12.	AELTC
13.	NBA	14.	IIHF
15.	FIS	16.	ITF

17.	FIM	18.	BDO
19.	FIBA	20.	ITTF
21.	WPBSA	22.	WWSU
23.	FIG	24.	WKF

CHARACTERISTICS OF DIAMONDS
List the *four* "c's" used to describe the characteristics of diamonds. Find the solution on page 206. [Target: 3]

HORSEMEN OF THE APOCALYPSE
Name the *Four* Horsemen of the Apocalypse. You can find the solution on page 226. [Target: 4]

ADVERTISING SLOGANS II
Identify the products that were promoted using these advertising slogans.* Look for the solution on page 248. [Target: 12]

1. "You better run for the border"
2. "The best a man can get"
3. "Be all you can be"
4. "WASSSSSUP?!"
5. "Two all-beef patties, special sauce, lettuce, cheese, pickles, onions on a sesame seed bun"
6. "The real thing"

---

* The cigarette manufacturer Philip Morris introduced the Marlboro brand of cigarette in 1924. The brand was one of the first to have a filter and as such was deliberately targeted at female smokers; it was launched with the slogan "Mild as May." The brand did poorly until the 1950s when reports linking smoking with health problems first began to appear. Many smokers switched to filtered cigarettes, perceived to be lower risk, but Marlboro with their feminine image had a problem in attracting new consumers. The company rectified this by launching a series of adverts featuring a range of masculine characters, one of which, a cattle rancher, would endure as the Marlboro Man; it became the most recognizable advert in history. In the eight months after the advert was first introduced, sales of Marlboro increased by 5,000%. In 1990, Wayne McLaren, one of the models who had portrayed the Marlboro Man, was diagnosed with lung cancer. McLaren, a lifelong smoker, devoted the last years of his life to anti-smoking campaigns, even lobbying Philip Morris at a shareholders meeting to voluntarily restrict their advertising. Wayne McLaren died in 1992 at the age of fifty-one. The same year, Marlboro became the number one cigarette brand in the world, with a market value of $32 billion; it was the ultimate example of the effectiveness of advertising.

7. "Nothing comes between me and my _____"
8. "Have you driven a _____ lately?"
9. "We're number two. We try harder."
10. "Obey your thirst"
11. "Have you met life today?"
12. "The choice of a new generation"
13. "Buy it. Sell it. Love it."
14. "Have it your way"
15. "The pursuit of perfection"
16. "Human energy"
17. "Solutions for a small planet"
18. "Challenge everything"
19. "We keep your promises"
20. "Let your fingers do the walking"
21. "Impossible is nothing"
22. "Do more, feel better, live longer"
23. "I dreamed I went shopping in my _____"
24. "If man were meant to fly, God would have lowered the fares"

WILL & GRACE Recall the *four* starring actors in *Will & Grace*. The solution is on page 274. [**Target: 3**]

FAMILY HOMINIDAE Name the *four* members of the family Hominidae (apes). Find the solution on page 293. [**Target: 4**]

ENTREPRENEURS I Identify the companies most associated with these entrepreneurs.* Turn to page 310 for the solutions. [**Target: 12**]

1. Victor Kiam
2. Tom Anderson
3. Richard Branson

---

* To qualify to be called a true entrepreneur usually requires the achievement of something above and beyond simple commercial success. Businessmen and businesswomen stand out as entrepreneurs largely because of: (i) their creation of a large amount of wealth; (ii) their rapid accumulation of wealth, usually in less than five years; (iii) their acceptance of ventures with a very high level of risk; and (iv) their ability to innovate, either in their products or their business processes.

4. Steve Jobs and Steve Wozniak
5. Ben Cohen and Jerry Greenfield
6. Louis B. Mayer
7. Paul Allen
8. Jerry Yang and David Filo
9. Robert Woodruff
10. Jeff Bezos
11. Akio Morita
12. Ingvar Kamprad
13. Howard Schultz
14. Scott McNealy
15. Allen Lane
16. George Eastman
17. Jorma Jaakko Ollila
18. Ray Kroc
19. Phil Knight
20. Sergey Brin and Larry Page
21. Pierre Omidyar
22. William Durant
23. Samuel Walton
24. Larry Ellison

FACES OF MOUNT RUSHMORE List the *four* American presidents honored at the Mount Rushmore National Memorial. Find the solution on page 330. [**Target: 3**]

EVANGELISTS Name the *four* biblical evangelists (Gospel writers). The solution is on page 206. [**Target: 4**]

MISCELLANY IV These questions are of a miscellaneous nature. Go to page 226 for the solutions. [**Target: 10**]

1. What new technique was pioneered by Dick Fosbury at the Mexico City Olympics in 1968?
2. Who wrote *The Strange Case of Dr. Jekyll and Mr. Hyde*?
3. Which two countries fought the Pastry War ("La Guerra de los Pasteles") of 1838?
4. Which computing-related word is derived from the words "picture element"?

5. Which fabric is most closely associated with athletes, superheroes, and glam rock bands?
6. Of which native American tribe was Geronimo a member?
7. How many stars are on the New Zealand flag?
8. Which letters of the alphabet have a "tittle"?
9. How many time zones are there in China?
10. After a successful libel action against a British newspaper, which entertainer famously said he "cried all the way to the bank"?
11. Which element has an atomic number of one?
12. What type of food was nicknamed "goober peas" in the Civil War?
13. Which U.S. state contains 75% of the country's land over 10,000 feet elevation?
14. Who was the first poet to be buried in Poets' Corner in Westminster Abbey?
15. Within a standard domino set, how many blocks are there (given that each block is unique)?
16. Who was the first president of the French Fifth Republic?
17. Who initiated the New Deal in 1933?
18. What was the number of the mobile hospital unit Hawkeye Pierce and Hot Lips Houlihan belonged to on TV's *M*A*S*H*?
19. What did soccer referees get for the first time in 1970?
20. Which author's given names were John Ronald Reuel?
21. What is the angle in degrees between the hands of a clock when the time is ten minutes to one?
22. Which sea does the Danube flow into?
23. Which 1950 film was the first non-animated Disney film?
24. In a group of men and horses there are twenty-two heads and seventy-two feet. How many of the group are horses and how many are men?

BATMEN Recall the *five* actors to have played the role of Batman in feature films. Look for the solution on page 248. [**Target: 4**]

NORDIC COUNCIL Name the *five* members of the Nordic Council. The solution is on page 274. [**Target: 5**]

MEANINGS OF PLACE NAMES Identify the places from the clues provided. Turn to page 293 for the solutions. [**Target: 10**]

1. South American city meaning "river of January"
2. English county, formerly "East Saxony"
3. Country meaning "land of silver"
4. Canadian province meaning "New Scotland"
5. North American city meaning "red stick"
6. African city, name derives from "South Western Townships"
7. Country meaning "rich coast"
8. African city meaning "white house"
9. Caribbean town meaning "rich harbour"
10. New York district deriving its name from "south of Houston Street"
11. Country meaning "black mountain"
12. Irish city meaning "monastery"
13. African city meaning "three towns"
14. Mountain range meaning "snowy range"
15. Country meaning "white Russia"
16. Country meaning "lion mountains"
17. African city meaning "fountain of flowers"
18. Indian state meaning "land of kings"
19. London district named from a hunting cry
20. U.S. state meaning "place of the gods"
21. North American city meaning "the fertile valleys"
22. African city meaning "lakes"
23. North American city meaning "royal mountain"
24. Caribbean island meaning "bearded"

TRAVELING WILBURYS Name the *five* Traveling Wilburys. Find the solution on page 310. [**Target: 5**]

POSITIONS IN A BASKETBALL TEAM Name the *five* positions in a basketball team. The solution is on page 330. [**Target: 4**]

FILMS AND THEIR STARS II Identify the films from these selected cast members and the date of release. Look for the solutions on page 206. [**Target: 10**]

1. Uma Thurman, John Travolta, Samuel L. Jackson (1995)
2. Dustin Hoffman, Meryl Streep (1979)
3. Tom Hanks, Audrey Tautou, Ian McKellen, Jean Reno (2006)
4. Martin Sheen, Charlie Sheen, Michael Douglas (1987)
5. Sean Young, Rutger Hauer, Harrison Ford (1982)
6. Kevin Bacon, Ed Harris, Tom Hanks (1995)
7. Robin Williams, Matt Damon, Ben Affleck, Minnie Driver (1997)
8. Matt Damon, Brian Cox, Clive Owen (2002)
9. Dennis Hopper, Natalie Wood, James Dean (1955)
10. Edward Norton, Brad Pitt, Helena Bonham Carter (1999)
11. Lily Tomlin, Dolly Parton, Jane Fonda (1980)
12. Lori Singer, John Lithgow, Kevin Bacon (1984)
13. Jack Nicholson, Faye Dunaway, Roman Polanski (1974)
14. Dirk Bogarde, James Caan, Michael Caine, Sean Connery, Denholm Elliott, Elliott Gould, Edward Fox, Gene Hackman, Anthony Hopkins, Laurence Olivier, Robert Redford, Hardy Krüger, Ryan O'Neal (1977)
15. Nicole Kidman, Julianne Moore, Meryl Streep (2002)
16. Peter Ustinov, Farrah Fawcett, Jenny Agutter, Michael York (1976)
17. Dakota Blue Richards, Nicole Kidman, Daniel Craig, Ian McKellen, Eva Green (2007)
18. Angela Lansbury, Mickey Rooney, Elizabeth Taylor (1945)
19. Humphrey Bogart, Katharine Hepburn, Robert Morley (1951)
20. Henry Travers, Donna Reed, James Stewart (1946)
21. Roy Scheider, Donald Sutherland, Jane Fonda (1971)
22. Kevin Kline, Joan Allen, Tobey Maguire, Christina Ricci, Elijah Wood, Sigourney Weaver (1997)
23. Charlize Theron, Woody Harrelson, Frances McDormand (2006)
24. Jim Carrey, Kate Winslet, Elijah Wood (2004)

UNITED NATIONS SECURITY COUNCIL Name the *five* permanent* members of the United Nations Security Council. The solution is on page 227. [**Target: 5**]

EVENTS OF THE MODERN PENTATHLON List the *five* events of the modern pentathlon. Find the solution on page 248. [**Target: 5**]

---

* The Security Council has five permanent members and ten temporary members. The ten temporary seats are voted on by the United Nations General Assembly and held for two years.

LINKED MISCELLANY III The solutions to these questions are linked by a connecting theme. Evaluate the clues and deduce the connection. The solution is on page 275. [**Target: 6**]

1. Which film, the first of a popular franchise, was the highest grossing film of 1981?
2. Which character was Randy Jones in Village People?
3. How is the Act of Congress which came into law on October 26, 2001, as a result of the September 11 terror attacks, commonly known?
4. Who was famously known as the "Hardest Working Man in Show Business"?
5. Which common metal alloy contains iron and carbon?
6. What was James Dean's last film, posthumously released in 1956?
7. How was Richard I of England more commonly known?
8. Who meets at a Papal Conclave?
9. Which line of latitude forms the border between the U.S. and Canada from Minnesota to Washington?
10. How are the members of the Delphinidae and Platanistoidea families better known?

NEW YORK CITY BOROUGHS List the *five* boroughs of New York City. Turn to page 293 for the solution. [**Target: 4**]

SPICE GIRLS Name the *five* Spice Girls (real names rather than nicknames). Go to page 311 for the solution. [**Target: 4**]

HOLY PLACES Identify the religion associated with each of these holy places.* The solutions are on page 330. [**Target: 10**]

---

* The world's most popular religion is Christianity, with around 2 billion adherents. Christianity and Islam (the second most popular religion with around 1.2 billion followers) are both derivations of Judaism; all three share beliefs in the biblical patriarch Abraham and are sometimes described as "desert monotheism." Judaism dates from around 2000 B.C., Christianity from around A.D. Islam first appeared in the Arabian Peninsula at the beginning of the seventh century. The oldest religion in the world, however, is Hinduism, which has been practiced for nearly 5,000 years. Most religions have geographical sites associated with them that are held to be sacred, often at locations where important events in the evolution of the religion took place.

1. Church of the Nativity (Bethlehem)
2. The Vatican
3. Mecca (Saudi Arabia)
4. Nazareth (Israel)
5. Canterbury (UK)
6. Lourdes (France)
7. Medina (Saudi Arabia)
8. Salt Lake City (U.S.A.)
9. Amritsar (India)
10. Mount Sinai (Egypt)
11. Mount Fuji (Japan)
12. The Western Wall (Jerusalem)
13. The Dome of the Rock (Jerusalem)
14. River Ganges (India)
15. Istanbul (Turkey)
16. Bodh Gaya (India)
17. Varanasi (India)
18. Potala Palace (Tibet)
19. The Holy Sepulchre (Jerusalem)
20. Mount Athos (Greece)
21. Mount Tai Shan (China)
22. Church of St. Mary of Zion (Ethiopia)
23. Palitana (India)
24. Kusinara (India)

JACKSON 5 Name the *five* members of the Jackson 5. Turn to page 207 for the solution. [**Target: 3**]

HOUSE OF TUDOR Identify the *five* Tudor monarchs. Go to page 227 for the solution. [**Target: 4**]

AIRPORT CODES I Name the cities that are served by these airports, from their three-letter IATA codes.* The solutions are on page 248. [**Target: 14**]

---

* The International Air Transport Association (IATA) is responsible for defining and allocating three-letter codes to airports that are used for flight reservations, flight information, and baggage handling.

1.	LGW	2.	JFK
3.	LAX	4.	HKG
5.	MEX	6.	BOS
7.	DFW	8.	PHL
9.	CDG	10.	BKK
11.	DTW	12.	AMS
13.	HNL	14.	BOM
15.	SFO	16.	AKL
17.	LAS	18.	SEA
19.	ORD	20.	JNB
21.	SVO	22.	SXF
23.	DBX	24.	NRT

MARX BROTHERS List the *five* Marx brothers. Find the solution on page 275. [**Target: 4**]

COMMITTEE OF FIVE Name the *five* members of the Committee of Five who drafted the United States Declaration of Independence. The solution is on page 293. [**Target: 4**]

MISCELLANY V Supply the correct answers to the miscellaneous questions presented. Go to page 311 for the solutions. [**Target: 12**]

1. What does SAT stand for?
2. The name of which film star is an anagram of "Old West Action"?
3. In Britain, by what name are the Yeomen of the Guard better known?
4. What are White House staff referring to when they use the acronym "FLOTUS"?
5. What color is the maple leaf on the Canadian flag?
6. Who wrote the *Just So Stories*?
7. Who published *A Compendious Dictionary of the English Language* in 1806?
8. Which is the only marsupial native to North America?
9. Which literary work features a pig and a turkey as well as the eponymous animal and bird?
10. Which lawyer never lost a case in *The Flintstones*?
11. Which outlaw was killed by his cousin, Bob Ford, in order to claim a reward?

12. Which country has its map on its national flag?

13. Which baseball team was the first to wear numbers on their shirts in 1928?

14. A man spends a fifth of the money in his wallet. He then spends a fifth of the money remaining. He spends $36 in total. How much money was in his wallet to begin with?

15. What did Ismail Pasha, the Viceroy of Egypt, sell to the United Kingdom for £400,000 in 1885?

16. Which vitamin does the body get from sunshine?

17. What were "Little Boy" and "Fat Man"?

18. What is the only anagram of the word "Monday"?

19. Who was the Captain of the *Pequod*?

20. What was the town of Salem named after?

21. The winner of the Louis Vuitton Cup is eligible to compete in which sporting contest?

22. What was agreed by the Connecticut Compromise?

23. A paragon is a unit used to measure what?

24. A wooden block measures 4 cm × 7 cm × 11 cm and is painted orange on the outside. The block is cut into 308 cubes measuring 1 cm × 1 cm × 1 cm. How many of these cubes have orange paint on them?

NOVELS BY F. SCOTT FITZGERALD Name the *five* novels written by F. Scott Fitzgerald. Turn to page 330 for the solution. [**Target:** 2]

RAT PACK Recall the *five* members of the Rat Pack. The solution is on page 207. [**Target:** 4]

CATCHPHRASES I Identify the people or characters associated with these catchphrases.* Go to page 227 for the solutions. [**Target:** 12]

---

* A phrase that becomes associated with a particular person or fictional character, usually through its repetition. Catchphrases are particularly loved by comedy writers as they give their characters a trademark by which they can easily be identified. It is a device that has been found to greatly increase the popularity of comedy shows when used effectively.

1. "D'oh!"
2. "Live long and prosper."
3. "I'll be back."
4. "What's up, doc?"
5. "Here's Johnny!"
6. "I love it when a plan comes together."
7. "Who loves ya, baby?"
8. "How you doin'?"
9. "Come on down!"
10. "There's just one more thing."
11. "Heh heh."
12. "Sit on it!"
13. "Dyn-o-mite."
14. "Yada, yada, yada."
15. "Howdilly doodily."
16. "Norm!"
17. "Tell me what you don't like about yourself."
18. "Don't make me angry . . ."
19. "Book 'em, Danno."
20. "Let's be careful out there."
21. "Respect my authority!"
22. "You rang?"
23. "Just the facts, ma'am . . ."
24. "Sock it to me!"

BONES OF THE SHOULDER AND ARM List the *five* bones of the arm (excluding the bones of the wrist and the hand). The solution is on page 248. [**Target: 3**]

PLATONIC SOLIDS Identify the *five* Platonic Solids. Turn to page 275 for the solution. [**Target: 2**]

EVENTS IN HISTORY II Identify the century in which each of these historical events took place (be even more precise and attempt the year if you wish). Find the solutions on page 293. [**Target: 10**]

1. George Washington becomes the first American president.
2. The Gunpowder Plot is foiled.

3. Napoleon Bonaparte invades Russia.
4. The Battle of Trafalgar.
5. The Roman Conquest of Britain.
6. Mutiny on the *Bounty*.
7. The Boston Tea Party.
8. Abolition of slavery in the British Empire.
9. Isaac Newton publishes *Principia*.
10. Leonardo da Vinci paints the *Mona Lisa*.
11. Mary Queen of Scots is executed.
12. The British East India Company is founded.
13. The last Western Roman Emperor is deposed.
14. Charles I is executed.
15. Oliver Cromwell becomes Lord Protector of England.
16. The storming of the Bastille.
17. Cortes begins conquest of the Aztecs.
18. Pompeii is destroyed by the eruption of Mount Vesuvius.
19. Building of Hadrian's Wall commences.
20. Joan of Arc burned at Rouen.
21. Alfred the Great defeats the Danes at Edington.
22. Defeat of British revolt under Boadicea.
23. Westminster Abbey is consecrated.
24. Constantine unites the Roman Empire.

DISNEY THEME PARKS Name the *five* Disney theme parks in the world. Look for the solution on page 311. [Target: 4]

OLYMPIC RINGS Identify the *five* colors of the rings* of the Olympic flag. You can find the solution on page 330. [Target: 5]

CAPITAL CITIES II Name the capital cities of each of these countries. The solutions are on page 207. [Target: 12]

---

* The Olympic flag was introduced at the 1920 Olympics in Antwerp. The five rings represent the five (populated) continents of the world. At the end of the closing ceremony of each Olympics, the Olympic flag is handed from the mayor of the host city to the president of the IOC, who then presents it to the mayor of the next host city. This is known as the Antwerp Ceremony.

1.	Sweden	2.	India
3.	Brazil	4.	Sudan
5.	Cambodia	6.	Vietnam
7.	Iceland	8.	Venezuela
9.	Algeria	10.	Saudi Arabia
11.	Romania	12.	Peru
13.	Canada	14.	Uzbekistan
15.	Nigeria	16.	Malaysia
17.	Belarus	18.	Cyprus
19.	Indonesia	20.	Liberia
21.	Jordan	22.	Turkmenistan
23.	Malawi	24.	Lesotho

PRESIDENTS WITH BEARDS Name the *five* U.S. presidents who had beards during their time in office. Look to page 227 for the solution. [**Target: 3**]

HOLLYWOOD FILM STUDIOS List the *five* prominent studios of the Golden Age of Hollywood. You will find the solution on page 248. [**Target: 4**]

OLOGIES I Describe the objectives of these fields of study. Turn to page 275 for the solutions. [**Target: 10**]

1.	Ornithology	2.	Genealogy
3.	Meteorology	4.	Neurology
5.	Apiology	6.	Dermatology
7.	Cosmology	8.	Campanology
9.	Gerontology	10.	Phonology
11.	Rhinology	12.	Chronology
13.	Pathology	14.	Cardiology
15.	Hematology	16.	Lithology
17.	Entomology	18.	Cytology
19.	Dendrology	20.	Cetology
21.	Oology	22.	Formicology
23.	Dactylology	24.	Exobiology

PILLARS OF ISLAM Name (or describe) the *five* Pillars of Islam. The solution is on page 293. [**Target: 3**]

ATMOSPHERIC LAYERS Name the *five* major layers of the earth's atmosphere. Turn to page 311 to find the solution. [Target: 3]

BATTLES I Identify the wars in which each of these battles* was fought. Note that some may share the same answer. Look for the solutions on page 330. [Target: 10]

1.	Gettysburg	2.	Midway
3.	Bunker Hill	4.	Iwo Jima
5.	Hamburger Hill	6.	Alamo
7.	Yorktown	8.	Hastings
9.	Antietam	10.	Somme
11.	Shiloh	12.	Balaclava
13.	Chancellorsville	14.	Princeton
15.	Leningrad	16.	Lexington and Concord
17.	Agincourt	18.	Fort Sumter
19.	Jutland	20.	Salamis
21.	Marston Moor	22.	Plassey
23.	Issus	24.	Orleans

BOOKS OF MOSES Name the *five* Books of Moses†; that is, the first five books of the Hebrew Bible or the Christian Old Testament. The solution is on page 207. [Target: 3]

---

* Pyrrhus (318 B.C.–272 B.C.) was the King of Epirus, an area of northwestern Greece, and was revered as the greatest military commander of his day. History remembers him for the Battle of Asculum (279 B.C.), a massive battle for its time, fought in southeast Italy against the Romans, led by Publius Decius Mus. Roman tactics and the terrain of the battlefield, spread as it was across hills and woods, prevented Pyrrhus from using his elephant cavalry effectively (which was usually decisive) and although he ended the battle in the ascendancy it was after the loss of 3,500 of his own men and 6,000 Romans. He gave his name to the term "pyrrhic victory"—a victory that is won at a high cost—from a quote attributed to him on the battlefield. When congratulated on the result Pyrrhus replied: "One more such victory and I will be undone."

† The Five Books of Moses are known as the "Pentateuch." It is traditionally believed that these five books were written by Moses.

HALOGENS List the *five* halogens; that is, the elements found in Group VII of the periodic table. You can find the solution on page 227. [**Target: 3**]

MISCELLANY VI These questions are of a miscellaneous nature. The solutions can be found on page 249. [**Target: 10**]

1. Which famous harbor city does Sugarloaf Mountain overlook?
2. Adrenaline is produced by the adrenal glands, located where in the body?
3. Which landmark stands on the Champ de Mars in Paris?
4. In which U.S. city was a World Series game interrupted by an earthquake?
5. Which is the only planet not named after a god?
6. Which Hollywood actress is an anagram of the word "Germany"?
7. What type of car is associated with Lady Creighton-Ward?
8. In which country is the Masai Mara game reserve?
9. What is the cube root of 1,728?
10. What breed of dog was Snoopy?
11. What was patented by Ezra Warner in 1858, forty-eight years after tin cans first appeared?
12. How is Severe Acute Respiratory Syndrome better known?
13. How long would a 2-kilowatt electrical appliance need to run to expend a kilowatt-hour of energy?
14. Who won the popular vote in the 2000 U.S. presidential election?
15. King Charles I was the last British monarch to be admitted into which building (in 1642)?
16. Which two constraints govern the height and width of modern U.S. battleships?
17. Who wrote *Crime and Punishment*?
18. Which three South American countries does the equator cross?
19. The eruption of Vesuvius in A.D. 79 destroyed which two cities?
20. What links the Mediterranean Sea and *The Hobbit*?
21. Which model of car became in 1997, and remains today, the bestselling design in history?
22. What links Thomas "Boston" Corbett and Jack Ruby?

23. How many clubs can a player carry in professional golf?

24. It takes two farm laborers eight days to plow a field. One is lazy and one is hardworking. The hardworking laborer would take twelve days to plow it on his own. How many days would the lazy farm laborer take to plow the field if he were to work on his own?

TASTES Name the *five* tastes to which the human tongue is responsive. Turn to page 275 for the solution. [**Target: 4**]

"CIVILIZED" TRIBES Recall the *five* Native American tribes who came to be labelled "civilized"* by white settlers. Find the solution on page 294. [**Target: 2**]

PSEUDONYMS I Identify the pseudonyms† by which these people are famously known. Find the solutions on page 311. [**Target: 14**]

1. David Solberg
2. Andrés Arturo García Menéndez
3. Marshall Bruce Mathers III

---

* The label derived from the willingness of the tribes to cooperate with settlers and adopt their customs. The homelands of the five tribes originally were in the southeastern United States, but under the Indian Relocation Act of 1830, they were forced to relocate west of the Mississippi to land in present-day Oklahoma. The tribes were recognized as dependent domestic nations and each had a written constitution, a government, and a legislature.

† A pseudonym is a fabricated name adopted by an individual and used instead of their given name. The word pseudonym itself can go under many different assumed names: moniker, nickname, sobriquet, epithet, appellation, alias, nom de plume, and alter ego, to name a few. The suffix "-onym" comes from Greek, meaning "name" and crops up in words that are used to describe other words. Heteronyms are words that are spelled the same but have different meanings with different pronunciations. For example, pasty (meaning either pale-looking or a meat pie), record (a list or to write down), desert (a dry place or to abandon), intermediate (in-between or to intervene). Conversely, homonyms are words that have different spellings and meanings but are pronounced the same way. For example, berth and birth, gorilla and guerrilla, mints and mince, tacks and tax, yoke and yolk, cited, sited, and sighted. More unusually, contronyms are words that have contradictory meanings. Examples of these are cleave (meaning to split apart or to cling to), sanction (to approve or to penalise), transparent (easily seen or invisible). Rarer still are capitonyms, words that change their pronunciation when capitalized; for example, polish/Polish, job/Job, nice/Nice, reading/Reading, and tangier/Tangier.

4. Eric Clapp
5. Norman Cook
6. Jean-Claude van Varenberg
7. Norma Jean Baker
8. Curtis Jackson
9. Eldrick Woods
10. Nicholas Coppola
11. Allen Konigsberg
12. Eleanor Gow
13. Frederick Austerlitz
14. Georgios Panaylotou
15. Marion Morrison
16. Sealhenry Samuel
17. Annie Mae Bullock
18. George Ivan Morrison
19. Marvin Aday
20. Robert Zimmerman
21. William Cody
22. Archibald Leach
23. Shawn Corey Carter
24. Pablo Ruiz

THE A-TEAM Name the *five* original characters in the A-Team.*
The solution is on page 331. [**Target: 4**]

BIG GAME Try to name the Big Five Game, the *five* African
animals regarded by hunters as the most difficult to hunt on foot.
Look for the solution on page 207. [**Target: 4**]

FILMS AND THEIR STARS III Identify these films according to
the selected cast members and the date of release provided. Find the
solutions on page 227. [**Target: 14**]

---

* Each episode began with the following voice-over: "Ten years ago, a crack
commando unit was sent to prison by a military court for a crime they didn't
commit. These men promptly escaped from a maximum security stockade to the Los
Angeles underground. Today, still wanted by the government, they survive as soldiers
of fortune. If you have a problem, if no one else can help, and if you can find them,
maybe you can hire . . . the A-Team."

1. Marlon Brando, Al Pacino, James Caan, Robert Duvall (1972)
2. Ian Holm, Sean Bean, Orlando Bloom, Ian McKellen (2001)
3. Liam Neeson, Ben Kingsley, Ralph Fiennes (1993)
4. Denholm Elliot, Jamie Lee Curtis, Dan Aykroyd, Eddie Murphy (1983)
5. Ingrid Bergman, Peter Lorre, Sidney Greenstreet, Humphrey Bogart (1942)
6. Kim Basinger, Kevin Spacey, Russell Crowe, Guy Pearce (1997)
7. Morgan Freeman, Jessica Tandy (1989)
8. Jodie Foster, Kelly McGillis (1988)
9. Bruce Cabot, Robert Armstrong, Fay Wray (1933)
10. Jack Hawkins, Alec Guinness, Omar Sharif, Peter O'Toole (1962)
11. Sean Connery, Christian Slater (1986)
12. Albert Finney, Julia Roberts (1999)
13. Cate Blanchett, Gwyneth Paltrow, Matt Damon, Jude Law (1999)
14. Clint Eastwood, Hilary Swank, Morgan Freeman (2004)
15. Steve McQueen, Faye Dunaway (1968)
16. Tim Robbins, Sean Penn, Kevin Bacon, Laurence Fishburne (2003)
17. Suzanna Hamilton, Richard Burton, John Hurt (1984)
18. Edward Norton, Courtney Love, Woody Harrelson (1996)
19. Alan Rickman, Hugh Grant, Emma Thompson, Kate Winslet (1995)
20. Raymond Burr, Grace Kelly, James Stewart (1954)
21. Joaquin Phoenix, Reese Witherspoon (2005)
22. Jessica Tandy, Kathy Bates (1991)
23. Bob Hoskins, Michael Palin, Jonathan Pryce, Robert De Niro (1985)
24. Don Cheadle, Sophie Okonedo, Nick Nolte, Joaquin Phoenix (2004)

ELEMENTS WITH FOUR-LETTER NAMES List the *five* elements that have four-letter names. Turn to page 275 for the solution. [**Target: 3**]

LINKED MISCELLANY IV Answer these questions and deduce the connection that links them. Look for the solution on page 294. [**Target: 5**]

1. At which venue did Mohammad Ali fight Joe Frazier on March 8, 1971, in what was billed as the "Fight of the Century"?
2. Which Rogers and Hammerstein musical features the songs "Oh What a Beautiful Morning" and "The Surrey with the Fringe On Top"?
3. What is the title of the fifth *Harry Potter* novel?
4. Which supersonic passenger aircraft was operational from 1976 until it was retired in 2003?
5. Where were the ancient Olympic Games held?
6. Which supermodel was a former Miss Denmark and Victoria's Secret Angel and appeared with Chris Isaak in the video for "Wicked Game"?
7. Which German statesman oversaw the unification of Germany in 1871, becoming the first Chancellor of the German Reich and earning the nickname "the Iron Chancellor"?
8. Which shuttle was the first to go into space?
9. What is used by conductors, majorettes, and relay runners?
10. Who wrote letters to the Romans, the Corinthians, the Galatians, and the Thessalonians?

GREAT LAKES List the *five* Great Lakes (of North America). Turn to page 312 for the solution. [**Target: 4**]

TIME ZONES Name the *six* time zones in the United States. The answers are on page 331. [**Target: 5**]

SINGERS AND BACKERS I Complete the names of these groups by naming the singer (most closely associated with the backing band). Find the solutions on page 207. [**Target: 10**]

1. _____ and the Pacemakers
2. _____ and the Shadows
3. _____ and the Blockheads
4. _____ and the Banshees

5. _____ and Wings
6. _____ and the Range
7. _____ and the Medics
8. _____ and Cockney Rebel
9. _____ and the Vandellas
10. _____ and the Attractions
11. _____ and the Blackhearts
12. _____ and the Revolution
13. _____ and the Waves
14. _____ and the Four Seasons
15. _____ and Crazy Horse
16. _____ and the Drells
17. _____ and the Heywoods
18. _____ and the Zodiacs
19. _____ with the Jordanaires
20. _____ and the Bluenotes
21. _____ and the Medicine Show
22. _____ and the Hurricanes
23. _____ and the Dinosaurs
24. _____ and the Hotrods

ORIGINAL SIX Name the *six* teams who were members of the NHL from 1942 until its expansion in 1967. You can find the solution on page 228. [**Target: 3**]

MENTAL DISORDERS Identify the mental disorders* from the clues provided. Find the solutions on page 275. [**Target: 10**]

1. An inability to sleep.
2. A compulsion to steal.
3. An eating disorder characterized by voluntary starvation.
4. An inability to remember.

---

* The *Diagnostic and Statistical Manual of Mental Disorders* (*DSM-IV*) categorizes mental illnesses into thirteen groups according to their common symptoms. These include psychotic disorders (where perception of reality is distorted), cognitive disorders (where the normal cognitive function of the brain becomes limited), mood disorders (affecting the emotional state of the sufferer), anxiety disorders (such as phobias), impulse control disorders (where sufferers are unable to suppress strong compulsions), and personality disorders (categorized by serious behavioral changes).

5. An eating disorder characterized by alternately binge eating and vomiting.
6. An experience of overwhelming sadness or complete lack of emotion or energy.
7. A tendency towards extravagant behavior and a need to capture the attention of others, often by exposing oneself.
8. An abnormal and excessive need or desire in women for sexual intercourse.
9. An anxiety disorder caused by exposure to extreme mental or physical stress in which symptoms will not typically appear until three months or more after the event.
10. A compulsion to light fires.
11. An inability to separate real from unreal experiences with sufferers typically experiencing both "positive" symptoms (in addition to abnormal behavior such as delusions and hallucinations) and "negative" symptoms (a lack or decline in normal behavior such as attention deficit or a lack of energy); historically regarded as a "split personality."
12. A progressive decline in cognitive function, normally as a result of aging.
13. A disorder in which sufferers experience involuntary, sudden, rapid, recurrent vocalizations.
14. A fear caused by a specific object or situation, exposure to which provokes an anxiety response.
15. A fear of disease and a conviction that one is suffering from an illness.
16. An experience of grandiose delusions of power, wealth, or fame.
17. An excessive feeling of sleepiness and need for daytime sleep even after adequate sleep at night.
18. A psychological response often seen in hostage situations where the hostage shows loyalty towards their captor.
19. A personality disorder characterized by passive resistance (such as forgetfulness, procrastination, inefficiency, and negative attitude) to acceptable social or occupational performance.
20. An anxiety disorder in which sufferers experience obsessions and/or compulsions that are time-consuming and interfere with their normal routine.
21. A disorder in which sufferers experience delusions such as inflated self-power or of persecution by others.

22. A mood disorder in which sufferers are given to inflated self-esteem, hyperactivity, elation, decreased need for sleep, and accelerated thought and speech.

23. A disorder in which sufferers fabricate medical symptoms in order to be subjected to medical tests and procedures.

24. A disorder in which parents fabricate symptoms in their children, thereby subjecting them to unnecessary medical tests and procedures.

NOBLE GASES Name the *six* noble (or inert) gases. Find the solution on page 294. [**Target: 4**]

VOCAL RANGES Name the *six* standard classifications of vocal range. Turn to page 312 for the solution. [**Target: 4**]

MISCELLANY VII Answer the miscellaneous questions posed below. Go to page 331 for the solutions. [**Target: 12**]

1. According to the sea shanty in *Treasure Island*, how many men are "on a dead man's chest"?

2. Traditionally, on which playing card in a deck is the card maker's trademark?

3. Which American president is associated with jelly beans?

4. What name is given to the bending of light as it passes from one medium to another?

5. Who plays Grace in *Will & Grace*?

6. The performance of which Olympian in 1988 led to the IOC instituting a rule that Olympic hopefuls must have placed in either the top 30% or the top fifty competitors of an international event to qualify for the Games?

7. What is a pangram?

8. How did the blues musician Robert Johnson, according to the legend which is often associated with him, achieve his talent?

9. Which is the only letter of the alphabet that does not appear in any of the names of the fifty American states?

10. What was most notable about the presidency of William Henry Harrison?

11. What was the first foreign capital city to be occupied by American forces?

12. Since Roman times, which year has so far been the longest to write out in Roman numerals?
13. A museum dedicated to which type of food is located in Pontedassio, Italy?
14. How is the practice of chiromancy better known?
15. What links the words "almost" and "biopsy"?
16. Which British lake contains the largest volume of water?
17. Hibernia was the Roman name for which modern-day country?
18. Which chemical caused hatters to go mad?
19. Where were the Pillars of Hercules?
20. Which South American country is named after an Italian city?
21. Which Hollywood actress made her first film appearance playing a little girl called Gertie?
22. Which German line lay opposite the French Maginot Line?
23. What was high school student Britney Gallivan able to do twelve times in 2001 which until then scientists and mathematicians had believed could only be done eight times?
24. A man is walking home with his dog at a steady four miles per hour. With six miles to go the dog is let off the leash and runs all the way home at six miles per hour. The dog immediately turns and runs back to the man at the same speed, and upon meeting him it turns and runs home again. It continues to run back and forth at the same speed until the man reaches home. What distance has the dog run since being let off the leash?

NEW ENGLAND STATES List the *six* American states that constitute New England. The solution is on page 207. [**Target: 5**]

NUTRIENTS List the *six* nutrients required to sustain a healthy life.* Find the solution on page 228. [**Target: 4**]

FIRST LINES OF POPULAR NOVELS II Identify the novels that have these opening lines. For advanced play, name the authors as well. Go to page 249 for the solutions. [**Target: 8**]

1. "129lbs. (but post-Christmas), alcohol units 14 (but effectively covers 2 days as 4 hours of party was on New Year's Day), cigarettes 22, calories 5,424."

---

* Sometimes water is also included in this list, being an essential part of diet.

2. "Call me Ishmael."

3. "Scarlett O'Hara was not beautiful, but men seldom realized it when caught by her charm as the Tarleton twins were."

4. "Mr. and Mrs. Dursley, of number four, Privet Drive, were proud to say that they were perfectly normal, thank you very much."

5. "Mr. Sherlock Holmes, who was usually very late in the mornings, save upon those not infrequent occasions when he stayed up all night, was seated at the breakfast table."

6. "Marley was dead: to begin with. There is no doubt whatever about that."

7. "At a village of La Mancha, whose name I do not wish to remember, there lived a little while ago one of those gentlemen who are wont to keep a lance in the rack, an old buckler, a lean horse and a swift greyhound."

8. "Happy families are all alike; every unhappy family is unhappy in its own way."

9. "James Bond, with two double bourbons inside him, sat in the final departure lounge of Miami Airport and thought about life and death."

10. "Rosemary and Guy Woodhouse had signed a lease on a five-room apartment in a geometric white house on First Avenue when they received word, from a woman named Mrs. Cortez, that a four-room apartment in Bramford had become available."

11. "No one would have believed, in the last years of the nineteenth century, that this world was being watched keenly and closely by intelligences greater than man's and yet as mortal as his own; that as men busied themselves about their various concerns they were scrutinized and studied, perhaps almost as narrowly as a man with a microscope might scrutinize the transient creatures that swarm and multiply in a drop of water."

12. "All this happened, more or less."

13. "There was no possibility of taking a walk that day."

14. "Tom!"

15. "You will rejoice to hear that no disaster has accompanied the commencement of an enterprise which you have regarded with such evil forebodings."

16. "The past is a foreign country; they do things differently there."

17. "Ba-room, ba-room, ba-room, baripity, baripity, baripity, baripity—Good."

18. "3 May. Bistritz.—Left Munich at 8:35 P.M., on 1st May, arriving at Vienna early next morning; should have arrived at 6:46, but the train was an hour late. Buda-Pesth seems a wonderful place, from the glimpse which I got of it from the train and the little I could walk through the streets."

19. "It was a pleasure to burn."

20. "A few miles south of Soledad, the Salinas River drops in close to the hill-side bank and runs deep and green."

21. "In my younger and more vulnerable years my father gave me some advice that I've been turning over in my mind ever since."

22. "He was an old man who fished alone in a skiff in the Gulf Stream and he had gone eighty-four days now without taking a fish."

23. "Ages ago, Alex, Allen and Alva arrived at Antibes, and Alva allowing all, allowing anyone, against Alex's admonition, against Allen's angry assertion: another African amusement . . . anyhow, as all argued, an awesome African army assembled and arduously advanced against an African anthill, assiduously annihilating ant after ant, and afterward, Alex astonishingly accuses Albert as also accepting Africa's antipodal ant annexation."

24. "It was love at first sight."

FRIENDS Name the *six* actors who played the title characters in *Friends.* Turn to page 276 for the solution. [**Target: 6**]

MOON LANDINGS List the *six* Apollo missions that landed men on the moon. Look for the solution on page 294. [**Target: 5**]

CURRENCIES Identify the countries where you might spend these currencies.* The solutions are on page 312. [**Target: 7**]

1.	Rouble	2.	Yen
3.	Rupee	4.	Baht

---

* The most popular currency in the world is the U.S. dollar, with an estimated $700 billion in circulation, two-thirds of which are thought to be held outside of the United States. Countries that produce their own dollar currencies include Australia, Barbados, the Bahamas, Belize, Bermuda, Brunei, Canada, the Cayman Islands, Fiji, Guyana, Hong Kong, Jamaica, Liberia, Namibia, New Zealand, Singapore, the Solomon Islands, Suriname, Taiwan, Trinidad and Tobago, and Zimbabwe.

5.	Shekel	6.	Rand
7.	Boliviano	8.	Zloty
9.	Lira	10.	Real
11.	Rupiah	12.	Krona
13.	Krone	14.	Yuan
15.	Bolivar	16.	Quetzal
17.	Won	18.	Lek
19.	Sucre	20.	Lat
21.	Dirham	22.	Colon
23.	Nuevo Sol	24.	Todrog

VILLAGE PEOPLE List the characters played by the *six* members of Village People. Find the solution on page 331. [**Target: 6**]

ENGLISH ROMANTIC POETS Name the *six* poets central to the English Romantic movement, sometimes known as the "Big Six." The solution is on page 207. [**Target: 4**]

DANCES Identify the dances* according to the clues provided. You can find the solutions on page 228. [**Target: 12**]

1. Caribbean dance in which dancers pass under a low bar.
2. Rock 'n' roll dance of the 1960s popularized by Chubby Checker.
3. Solo dance of Arabic origin performed by a woman and featuring improvisational gyration of the whole body and especially the stomach.
4. Spanish dance performed usually by a solo woman involving fast hand-clapping and stamping and accompanied by guitar and castanets.
5. Boisterous music-hall dance performed by a chorus line, originating in Algeria in the 1830s and popularized in Parisian clubs such as the Moulin Rouge.

---

* In 1928, a Hungarian named Rudolf von Laban came up with an unwieldy system of notation that enabled dance movements to be written down for the first time. He called it Labanotation. His system has a staff, similar to musical notation, onto which symbols are placed relating to body parts, and an indication of the length of duration of movement, the direction of movement, and the intensity of the movement.

6. Erotic dance, usually a striptease, performed in private to a seated patron.

7. Latin American dance consisting of three steps and a kick in repetition usually performed by a long line of people.

8. Quadruple-time ballroom dance combining long and short steps in the tempo "slow-quick-quick-slow"; named after a New York vaudeville performer called Harry Fox.

9. Emotionally charged Argentinian ballroom dance characterized by long gliding steps and sudden staccato movements.

10. Spanish ballroom dance in which double steps are taken in fast 2/4 time; the name means "two step" in Spanish and the actions mimic a bullfight.

11. Popular Latin American dance combining Latin rhythms with rock; the name means "sauce" in Spanish.

12. Moderately slow Spanish dance set in triple time and performed solo or by a couple; popularized by the composer Maurice Ravel in 1928.

13. A lively and energetic Brazilian dance in 2/4 time; the popular dance at the Rio carnival.

14. Brazilian musical and dance style with jazz roots popularized in Rio de Janeiro in the 1950s; its name translates as "new beat."

15. Folk dance usually in 6/8 time and particularly associated with Ireland.

16. Traditional Mexican dance in which sombreros feature prominently.

17. Fast foxtrot named after a town in South Carolina which became popular in New York in the 1920s.

18. Ritualized traditional dance performed in the Hawaiian islands.

19. European ballroom dance in 3/4 time that emerged in Vienna in the 1780s.

20. Punjabi dance, performed by Indian men often at social occasions to rhythmic accompaniment by a dohl (drum) and chimta (percussion); the term is now more associated with a type of contemporary dance music played in nightclubs.

21. Latin American ballroom dance in which steps are made on the beat with one leg slightly dragging as if to give the appearance of having a limp.

22. Slow and romantic Cuban dance performed in 8/8 time. Similar to salsa, it first appeared in the 1920s and is now a popular ballroom dance.

23. Fast, rhythmic and erotic Brazilian dance popularized in the 1980s in which couples dance with touching hips.

24. Bohemian dance, popular in the nineteenth century, comprising three steps and a hop to fast 2/4 time.

QUARTERBACK CLASS OF '83 Name the *six* quarterbacks who are known as the Class of '83.* Look to page 250 for the solution. [**Target: 4**]

NOBEL PRIZES Identify the *six* fields of accomplishment for which Nobel Prizes are awarded. The solution is on page 276. [**Target: 6**]

CAPITAL CITIES III Identify the capital city of each country. Find the solutions on page 294. [**Target: 10**]

1.	Australia	2.	Norway
3.	Poland	4.	Egypt
5.	Portugal	6.	Argentina
7.	Chile	8.	Turkey
9.	Colombia	10.	Cuba
11.	Ecuador	12.	Tunisia
13.	Taiwan	14.	El Salvador
15.	Albania	16.	Serbia
17.	Uruguay	18.	Slovakia
19.	Latvia	20.	Senegal
21.	Georgia	22.	Tajikistan
23.	Madagascar	24.	Liechtenstein

STATES OF MATTER Name the *six* states of matter.† The solution is on page 312. [**Target: 4**]

MONTY PYTHON Identify the *six* members of *Monty Python's Flying Circus.* Go to page 331 for the solution. [**Target: 6**]

---

* The six quarterbacks were first-round draft picks of the 1983 draft. Of the six, four have played in the Super Bowl and three have been inducted into the Pro Football Hall of Fame.

† Scientific theory is constantly evolving. These six states of matter are currently accepted by most but not all of the scientific community.

COOKING TERMS I Identify each cooking* term from the clues provided. The solutions can be found on page 207. [**Target:** 10]

1. From Mexico, minced beef with tomato, beans, and chilli.
2. Flat, wide sheets of pasta and an Italian dish in which they are commonly used.
3. Greek dish of minced lamb and layers of potato and aubergine baked with white sauce and cheese.
4. Traditional Spanish dish of rice, chicken, and seafood, flavored with saffron.
5. Mexican relish made from tomatoes, onions, chillies, and coriander.
6. From Russia, a small pancake often served with caviar and sour cream.
7. Italian term for small pasta-like dumplings made from potato.
8. North African wheat and semolina mixture formed into tiny pellets.
9. A stuffed pizza folded over and baked.
10. A slice of meat (usually veal) that has been beaten thin and fried in breadcrumbs.
11. French term for "juice," usually applied to the juices from a roast meat.
12. Italian term for an appetizer (literally "before the meal").
13. Dried fish from India or Bangladesh that is crumbled and sprinkled over curry dishes.
14. French term for a small young chicken, sometimes called a "spring chicken."
15. Pasta tubes with diagonally cut ends.

---

* The Anglo-Saxons were not renowned for their culinary flair, a fact possibly reflected in their language. In Old English there was no distinction between an animal and the food that comes from it. (This is also true of modern German, where words like "Rindfleisch" [literally "cow flesh"] and "Schweinefleisch" ["pig flesh"] are used for beef and pork.) We left it to the French, a country more passionate about their food, to give us our words for beef, pork, veal, mutton, and so on, words which arrived with the Normans in 1066 (it is also notable that in medieval times, although many people worked with animals, few could afford to eat meat; those who could were in the main the French-speaking ruling classes). It is indicative of the culinary sophistication of the French that so many cooking terms have come to us from France; while the English boiled and roasted the French blanched and sautéed.

16. Italian term for thin strips of ham such as Parma ham.
17. North African stew which takes its name from the earthenware pot with a distinctive conical lid in which it is cooked.
18. Prunes wrapped in bacon.
19. French term for fruit cooked in a light sugary syrup (more liquid in consistency than jam), which may be served hot or cold.
20. French term meaning "in pastry."
21. A cooked mixture of flour and butter used as a basis for any sauce.
22. French term usually applied to preparation of shellfish (especially mussels) meaning "cooked in white wine and shallots."
23. Italian cold dessert similar to crème caramel, meaning "cooked cream."
24. Provençal mayonnaise made with plenty of garlic.

TEXAN GOVERNMENTS Name the *six* historical governments of Texas.* Find the solution on page 228. [**Target: 6**]

WOODWIND INSTRUMENTS Name the *six* instruments commonly found in the woodwind section of an orchestra. Turn to page 250 for the solution. [**Target: 6**]

MISCELLANY VIII Answer these miscellaneous questions. Go to page 276 for the solutions. [**Target: 10**]

1. Who in Greek mythology fell in love with his own reflection?
2. Which U.S. state has the largest economy?
3. The *Encyclopaedia Galactica* is the chief rival to which other book?
4. Who founded the Church of England?
5. Which private eye operated out of a trailer on Malibu Beach?
6. What film role links Carl Weathers, Dolph Ludgren, and Mr. T?

---

* Six different flags have been flown over Texas in its history.

7. If Air Force One is the U.S. president's plane, what is Marine One?

8. What material is named after a French phrase meaning "cloth of the king"?

9. What sport was originally known as "battledore and shuttlecock"?

10. In medicine, what does the term "vascular" refer to?

11. How many square inches are in a square foot?

12. On which island were American marines famously photographed raising the U.S. flag over Mount Suribachi in February 1945?

13. What are the surnames of Romeo and Juliet?

14. What line from "Bohemian Rhapsody" was also the title of a hit single by Abba?

15. How is *La Gioconda* better known?

16. What is the name of a female cat?

17. Which lost city was discovered by Hiram Bingham III in 1911?

18. Where is the Space Needle?

19. What was the first Hollywood film shown on TV after the U.S. movie industry ended its ban and started selling television rights to its films in late 1955?

20. Which Scottish clan, often accused of collusion with the English, murdered members of the MacDonald clan in the Massacre of Glencoe?

21. Which famous battle was fought on Breed's Hill in June 1775?

22. Which U.S. president coined the term "the silent majority"?

23. Which city has the highest number of residents born outside its parent country?

24. What links the words "trollied," "wronged," and "sponged"?

NFL TEAMS YET TO REACH THE SUPER BOWL Name the *six* teams in the NFL who have yet to appear in a Super Bowl. The solution is on page 294. [**Target: 4**]

NOVELS BY JANE AUSTEN Name the *six* novels written by Jane Austen. Go to page 312 for the solution. [**Target: 4**]

FOREIGN WORDS AND PHRASES I
Identify the foreign word or phrase from the description provided. Each word or phrase is in common use in English but has been loaned from another language.* Find the solutions on page 332. [**Target: 12**]

1. Already seen (French)
2. A school for the very young (German)
3. Nothing (Arabic)
4. A human-like machine (Czech)
5. An important person, especially in the media (Hindi)
6. The intellectual social class (Russian)
7. A duty levied on goods (Arabic)
8. Dread and anxiety (German)
9. An annually published book of information (Arabic)
10. The good life (Italian)
11. A low house, literally "house in the Bengal style" (Hindi)
12. A rich and powerful businessman (Japanese)
13. A priest, teacher, mentor, or expert (Hindi)
14. In relation to, literally "face-to-face" (French)
15. Forbidden (German)
16. To behave in a servile manner; to go along with the wishes of another (Chinese)
17. A great yield of riches (Spanish)
18. A lookalike (German)

---

* English has a vocabulary much larger than any other language. It is estimated that the English language has in the region of 600,000 words (in comparison, German has around 180,000 and French has around 100,000). Most English speakers know a fraction of these; a well-educated person will have on average a vocabulary of around 25,000 words, less than 5% of the total. English has a propensity to borrow words from other languages and has done so with an enthusiasm unmatched by any other language. The language derives from three main sources. Shorter, commonplace words tend to come from Old English, introduced by the Anglo-Saxons and used by the common people. Literary words tend to come from French, arriving with the Normans and being used initially by the wealthy and the ruling classes. Intellectual words typically come from classical Latin and Greek and started arriving during the Renaissance, driven by the acceleration in learning which has continued since. In selecting a word, an English speaker is therefore unique in that he usually has available a choice of at least three words. For example, one may think (Anglo-Saxon), ponder (French), or cogitate (Latin); a monarch may be kingly (Anglo-Saxon), royal (French), or regal (Latin); one may seek freedom (Anglo-Saxon), liberty (French), or autonomy (Greek).

19. An enthusiastic amateur (Spanish)
20. A platform from which a candidate speaks prior to an election (Norwegian)
21. Vulgarity, tastelessness, or ostentation, literally "worthless art" (German)
22. A potential danger (Arabic)
23. Elevated wasteland (Russian)
24. Literally "the king has died." (Arabic)

WEAPONS IN CLUE Recall the *six* murder weapons featured in the game of Clue.* The solution is on page 208. [**Target: 6**]

WIVES OF HENRY VIII Recall the *six* wives of Henry VIII. Turn to page 228 for the solution. [**Target: 6**]

SUPERMAJORS Try to name the *six* major global oil companies. Find the solution on page 312. [**Target: 5**]

TAGLINES OF POPULAR FILMS I Identify the films[†] from the clues provided. The solutions are on page 250. [**Target: 14**]

---

* Anthony E. Pratt, a solicitor's clerk from Birmingham, invented Clue (known in the UK as Cluedo) as a means of escaping boredom during air raids in the war. Pratt and his wife, Elva (who designed the board), presented the game in 1946 to Waddingtons, who liked what they saw and released the game in 1949.

† Two French brothers, Auguste and Louis Lumière, are credited with the invention of cinema. They introduced their new device, the cinematograph at a screening on December 28, 1895, in the basement lounge of the Grand Café on the Boulevard des Capucines in Paris. The brothers showed ten short films, lasting only twenty minutes in total, of subjects ranging from people walking along a boulevard to a train pulling into a station. Although their subject matter was a touch mundane, the effect on their audience was striking; the train sequence in particular caused panic among a section of the audience who believed the train was about to crash through the screen. Ironically, the two French inventors never thought their idea would take off. Perhaps feeling that people would tire of watching everyday scenes, the brothers couldn't anticipate the application of their technology to creative storytelling and the multi-billion-dollar film industry that the cinematograph would spawn. "The cinema is an invention without a future," Louis Lumière once said.

1. "A long time ago in a galaxy far, far away . . ."(1977)
2. "Life is like a box of chocolates—you never know what you're gonna get." (1994)
3. "Seven deadly sins. Seven ways to die." (1995)
4. "If he were any cooler, he'd still be frozen, baby!" (1997)
5. "First dance. First love. The time of your life." (1987)
6. "She brought a small town to its feet and a huge corporation to its knees." (2000)
7. "The greatest picture in the history of entertainment." (1939)
8. "They were seven—and they fought like seven hundred!" (1960)
9. "Expect the Impossible." (1996)
10. "An adventure 65 million years in the making." (1993)
11. "They changed her diapers. She changed their lives." (1987)
12. "Feel its fury." (2000)
13. "First comes love. Then comes the interrogation." (2000)
14. "Not every gift is a blessing." (1999)
15. "The mission is a man." (1998)
16. "Make your last breath count." (1996)
17. "Fear can hold you prisoner. Hope can set you free." (1994)
18. "Paul Sheldon used to write for a living. Now, he's writing to stay alive." (1990)
19. "Music was his passion. Survival was his masterpiece." (2002)
20. "Reality is a thing of the past." (1999)
21. "Get ready for rush hour." (1994)
22. "She's a blessing . . . in disguise." (1993)
23. "Love is a force of nature." (2005)
24. "Catch it." (1977)

BEACH BOYS List the *seven* core members of the Beach Boys (who were inducted into the Rock and Roll Hall of Fame in 1988). The solution is on page 276. [**Target: 3**]

SEVEN SUMMITS Name the highest peaks in each of the *seven* continents and which make up the Seven Summits* mountaineering challenge. The solution is on page 247. [**Target: 3**]

---

* As postulated by Reinhold Messner.

NOVELS BY GEORGE ELIOT List the *seven* novels penned by George Eliot. The solution is on page 249. [**Target: 4**]

ACTORS IN *CASABLANCA* Name the *seven* actors playing the lead roles in *Casablanca*. Turn to page 294 for the solution. [**Target: 4**]

LINKED MISCELLANY V In the course of answering these questions, deduce the connection that links them. Look for the solution on page 313. [**Target: 5**]

1. Which is the largest species of penguin?
2. What name have scientists given to a woman who is believed to have lived about 140,000 years ago and who is defined as the matrilineal most recent common ancestor for all currently living humans?
3. What name is given to a military unit which numbers about thirty to fifty men divided into four squads and typically is the smallest unit that is led by a commissioned officer?
4. What song does the computer HAL sing in *2001: A Space Odyssey* just before it is disconnected?
5. Which cult 1970s series starring Lee Majors led to a spin-off show starring Lindsay Wagner?
6. Which is the second largest continent in the world in terms of both area and population?
7. Whom did Kirstie Alley play in *Cheers*?
8. Who had hits with "Hard to Say I'm Sorry," "Hard Habit to Break," and "You're the Inspiration"?
9. What is the largest city in Morocco?
10. Which American general led the Third Army in Normandy following the D-Day landings?

HARRY POTTER NOVELS Name the *seven Harry Potter* novels in the series by J. K. Rowling. Find the solution on page 332. [**Target: 6**]

SYMBOLS IN ROMAN NUMERALS List the *seven* letters that are used to represent figures in Roman numerals. The solution is on page 208. [**Target: 7**]

FRUIT AND VEGETABLES Name the fruit or vegetable from the varieties listed. Go to page 228 for the solutions. [**Target:** 7]

1. Admiral, Golden Wonder, Jersey Royal, King Edward, Maris Piper
2. Parson Brown, Washington Navel, Seville, Jaffa
3. Laxton's Superb, Rome Beauty, York Imperial, Cox's Orange Pippin, Bramley
4. Riesling, Almeria, Syrah, Zinfandel, Muscat
5. Bird's Eye, Scotch Bonnet, Hungarian Hot Wax, Jalapeño, Ring of Fire
6. Blewits, Chestnut, Oyster, Shitake, White Cap
7. Green Zebra, Liberty Belle, Plum, Red Alert, Cherry
8. Bordeaux, Claret, Purple Sprouting, White Sprouting, Wok Brocc
9. Buttercrunch, Little Gem, Lizzie, Saladin, Cos
10. Laxton's Cropper, Victoria, Warwickshire Drooper, Damson, Green Gage
11. Derby Day, Spring Hero, Wong Bok, Tatsoi, Savoy
12. Black Beauty, Long Purple, Mini Finger, Tres Hative de Barbentane, Violetta di Firenza
13. Bolthardy, Carillon, Crimson Globe, Egyptian Turnip Rooted, Red Ace
14. Burpless Tasty Green, Long Maraicher, Muncher, Slice King, Tokyo Slicer
15. Dobies All Rounder, Marshall's Giant Fenglobe, Pearl Pickler, Spring, Red Baron
16. Feltham First, Histon Mini, Kelvedon Wonder, Little Marvel, Meteor
17. Amsterdam Forcing, Autumn King, Figaro, Long Red Surrey, Regulus Imperial
18. Bedford-Fillbasket, Brilliant, Cambridge No. 5, Half Tall, Noisette
19. Black Republic, Black Tartarian, Maraschino, Morello, Napoleon
20. Avonresister, Gladiator, Half Long Guernsey, Tender and True, White Gem
21. Baboon, Escondido, Lisbon, Meyer, Sicilian
22. Cavendish, Green, Red, Lady Finger, Golden Beauty
23. Burgundy, Duncan, Marsh, Ruby Red, Star Ruby
24. Anjou, Bartlett, Conference, Josephine de Malines, Louise Bonne de Jersey

SPACE SHUTTLES Name the *seven* NASA space shuttles. The solution is on page 250. [**Target: 5**]

FIFA WORLD CUP WINNERS Recall the *seven* countries to have won the Football World Cup.* Find the solution on page 276. [**Target: 5**]

QUOTATIONS FROM SHAKESPEARE I Name the plays of Shakespeare† from which these quotations are taken. (Note that the same play may be the solution to more than one quotation.) If you wish, also name the character who is quoted. Go to page 295 for the solutions. [**Target: 12**]

1. "To be, or not to be; that is the question"
2. "Double, double, toil and trouble / Fire burn, and cauldron bubble"
3. "A horse! a horse! my kingdom for a horse!"
4. "Something is rotten in the state of Denmark"

---

* The Football World Cup was the brainchild of Jules Rimet, who was president of the World Football Federation from 1921 to 1954. Rimet organized the first World Cup tournament in 1930, and on July 13 it kicked off with France beating Mexico 4–1.

† Shakespeare's literary output was extraordinary, both in terms of quantity and quality, and few would doubt his status as the greatest English-language writer. But he has perhaps made an even greater contribution to the English language itself, inventing around 2,000 new English words, many of which are in everyday use. Words attributed to Shakespeare include: alligator, bandit, barefaced, bedroom, besmirch, bloodstained, bump, castigate, cold-blooded, courtship, critical, dwindle, employer, equivocal, elbow, excitement, excellent, eyesore, football, frugal, gloomy, glow, gossip, hoodwinked, lackluster, leapfrog, lonely, luggage, majestic, manager, mimic, moonbeam, monumental, negotiate, obscene, outbreak, radiance, shooting star, shudder, submerged, tranquil, undress, watchdog, and zany. Shakespeare coined an equally large number of phrases. For example: a sorry sight, all that glitters is not gold, as good luck would have it, bated breath, the be-all and the end-all, brave new world, break the ice, budge an inch, cold comfort, dead as a doornail, devil incarnate, eaten me out of house and home, elbow room, faint-hearted, fair play, fancy-free, fool's paradise, foregone conclusion, foul play, full circle, good riddance, heart of gold, high time, improbable fiction, in a pickle, in my mind's eye, into thin air, laughingstock, give short shrift, milk of human kindness, more in sorrow than in anger, naked truth, neither a borrower nor a lender be, not slept one wink, one fell swoop, own flesh and blood, pitched battle, play fast and loose, pound of flesh, rhyme and reason, sea change, seen better days, send packing, set my teeth on edge, shuffle off this mortal coil, spotless reputation, too much of a good thing, tower of strength, wear my heart upon my sleeve, wild goose chase.

5. "If music be the food of love, play on"
6. "Beware the Ides of March"
7. "And gentlemen in England now abed / Shall think themselves accursed they were not here, / And hold their manhoods cheap whiles any speaks / That fought with us upon Saint Crispin's day"
8. "Lord, what fools these mortals be!"
9. "When we have shuffled off this mortal coil"
10. "Where's my serpent of old Nile?"
11. "Is this a dagger which I see before me?
12. "Goodnight, sweet prince, / And a flight of angels sing thee to thy rest"
13. "We few, we happy few, we band of brothers"
14. "Parting is such sweet sorrow"
15. "How sharper than a serpent's tooth it is / To have a thankless child?"
16. "We are such stuff / As dreams are made on"
17. "Some are born great . . . / Some achieve greatness . . . / And some have greatness thrust upon them"
18. "Thus with a kiss I die"
19. "I am a man / More sinned against than sinning"
20. "If you prick us do we not bleed? If you tickle us do we not laugh? If you poison us do we not die? And if you wrong us shall we not revenge?"
21. "I must be cruel only to be kind"
22. "Things that love night, love not such nights as this"
23. "Many a good hanging prevents a bad marriage"
24. "All the world's a stage / And all the men and women merely players"

AFRICAN COUNTRIES BEGINNING WITH "M" Name the *seven* African countries that begin with the letter "M." The solution is on page 313. [**Target:** 5]

DWARFS List the *Seven* dwarfs. Turn to page 332 for the solution. [**Target:** 6]

MISCELLANY IX These questions are of a miscellaneous nature. Find the solutions on page 208. [**Target:** 12]

1. Which drug is named after the Greek god of dreams?
2. The *1812 Overture* contains passages of the national anthems of which two countries?
3. Which abbreviation for an imperial unit comes from a sign of the zodiac?
4. Who was the first person to reach the South Pole?
5. What is the oldest letter in the alphabet?
6. From which animal does cashmere wool come?
7. Which well-known film title is an anagram of "Con Bites the Male Flesh"?
8. Which small breed of dog is named after a Mexican state?
9. After Paris, which is the next largest French-speaking city?
10. Which play by Shakespeare has a title that is also a proverb?
11. The cortex and medulla are parts of which human organ?
12. Which artist wore a diving suit to the opening of an exhibition at London's New Burlington Gallery in 1936?
13. What were the first names of the characters played by John Travolta and Olivia Newton-John in *Grease*?
14. What word is used in fencing to acknowledge a valid hit?
15. In the "Scopes Monkey Trial" of 1925, what was John Scopes charged with?
16. Who played Jessica Fletcher in a long-running TV series?
17. Which country has the world's largest Muslim population?
18. A woman is twelve years old plus half her age. How old is she?
19. Which musical instrument takes its name from the Greek meaning "wooden sound"?
20. How is Barbara Millicent Roberts better known?
21. Followers of which religion assemble at what is the largest gathering of people anywhere in the world?
22. Who was the first president to have a telephone on his desk at the White House?
23. Canaletto was best known for his paintings of Venice and which other city?
24. Which number is equal to six times the sum of its digits?

SOVIET COMMUNIST PARTY LEADERS Name the *seven* people to have led the Soviet Communist Party. The solution is on page 229. [Target: 6]

CITIES OF HAMPTON ROADS Name the *seven* cities of
Hampton Roads. Look for the solution on page 250. [**Target: 4**]

ANIMAL ADJECTIVES Identify the animal that is described by
each adjective. Turn to page 276 for the solutions. [**Target: 10**]

1.	Equine	2.	Leonine
3.	Avian	4.	Zebrine
5.	Simian	6.	Bovine
7.	Piscine	8.	Porcine
9.	Taurine	10.	Delphine
11.	Ostracine	12.	Ursine
13.	Apian	14.	Caprine
15.	Cervine	16.	Hircine
17.	Lupine	18.	Murine
19.	Ovine	20.	Vespine
21.	Leporine	22.	Vulpine
23.	Anserine	24.	Columbine

CATHOLIC SACRAMENTS Name the *seven* Catholic Sacraments.
Find the solution on page 295. [**Target: 4**]

WONDERS OF THE ANCIENT WORLD Name the *Seven*
Wonders of the Ancient World. The solution is on page 313. [**Target: 5**]

HOBBIES AND PROFESSIONS II Describe these hobbies and
professions. Find the solutions on page 332. [**Target: 8**]

1.	Topiarist	2.	Haberdasher
3.	Vintner	4.	Hosier
5.	Barista	6.	Ham
7.	Draper	8.	Equerry
9.	Milliner	10.	Artificer
11.	Pedagogue	12.	Bibliopole
13.	Subaltern	14.	Fletcher
15.	Farrier	16.	Stenographer
17.	Wrangler	18.	Horologist
19.	Cartomancer	20.	Funambulist
21.	Phillumenist	22.	Ecdysiast
23.	Costermonger	24.	Prestidigitator

DEADLY SINS Name the *Seven* Deadly Sins.* Turn to page 208 for the solution. [**Target: 6**]

MOST OSCAR-NOMINATED ACTRESSES Name the *seven* actresses who have received seven or more Oscar† nominations in their careers. You can find the solution on page 229. [**Target: 3**]

EPONYMOUS AIRPORTS Identify the cities that are served by airports named after these people. Go to page 251 for the solutions. [**Target: 14**]

1.	John F. Kennedy	2.	Charles de Gaulle
3.	Leonardo da Vinci	4.	John Lennon
5.	Ayatollah Khomeini	6.	Indira Gandhi
7.	Louis Armstrong	8.	Marco Polo
9.	Mustafa Kemal Ataturk	10.	David Ben-Gurion
11.	Galileo Galilei	12.	Wolfgang Amadeus Mozart
13.	Edward O'Hare	14.	Pierre Trudeau
15.	Ronald Reagan	16.	George H. W. Bush
17.	Benito Juárez	18.	Abraham Lincoln
19.	Bob Hope	20.	Edward Lawrence Logan
21.	Frédéric Chopin	22.	Jomo Kenyatta
23.	Mother Theresa	24.	Yasser Arafat

---

* The Seven Deadly Sins is not a concept found in the Bible but is attributable to Pope Gregory the Great in the sixth century A.D. The concept was popularized by Dante in *The Divine Comedy* and by many artists of the fourteenth century and since.

† The Academy of Motion Picture Arts and Sciences was founded in 1927 and annually hosts the world's most prestigious artistic awards ceremony. Winners are chosen according to an annual vote of all members, which is carried out in the utmost secrecy. Until the envelopes are opened, only two people know the results of the vote (the two assigned accountants from Price Waterhouse) and the counting of votes is performed by six assistants who are given random selections from each category. Two sets of winning envelopes are sealed in a safe and on the day of the awards ceremony are driven to the location by two different routes. They arrive two hours before the ceremony and are guarded until they are ready to be given to the presenters.

EVENTS IN THE HEPTATHLON Name the *seven* events of the heptathlon. Find the solution on page 277. [**Target:** 5]

MERCURY SEVEN Recall the *seven* original astronauts of the U.S. space program, known as the Mercury Seven.* Turn to page 295 for the solution. [**Target:** 5]

FIRST LINES OF POP SONGS II Deduce the titles of these songs from the first lines below. (The year each song was a hit in the UK is given.) For advanced play, name the performers as well. You will find the solutions on page 313. [**Target:** 12]

1. "There's a lady who's sure all that glitters is gold." (1971)
2. "I remember when, I remember, I remember when I lost my mind." (2006)
3. "We skipped the light fandango." (1967)
4. "Some people call me the space cowboy." (1973)
5. "As I walk through the valley of the shadow of death." (1995)
6. "It's close to midnight and something evil's lurking in the dark." (1983)
7. "Please, please, tell me now." (1983)
8. "They say we're young and we don't know." (1965)
9. "I'm coming up." (2002)
10. "And you may find yourself living in a shotgun shack." (1981)
11. "I met a gin-soaked bar-room queen in Memphis." (1969)
12. "Yes! So crazy right now." (2003)
13. "You were working as a waitress in a cocktail bar when I met you." (1981)
14. "Hello? Is there anybody in there?" (1979)
15. "I heard you on the wireless back in '52." (1979)
16. "Well my friends the time has come to raise the roof and have some fun." (1983)
17. "Well, I don't know why I came here tonight." (1973)
18. "Now there's a backstreet lover that is always undercover." (1986)
19. "Children behave, that's what they say when we're together." (1987)

---

* The Mercury Seven were the subject of *The Right Stuff* by Tom Wolfe and the film of the same name.

72

20. "See the stone set in your eyes." (1987)
21. "Every night I grab some money and I go down to the bar." (1981)
22. "Who's gonna tell you when it's too late?" (1984)
23. "You were my sun, you were my earth." (2003)
24. "I met a devil woman, she took my heart away." (1974)

CATHOLIC CHURCH HIERARCHY List the *seven* ranks of the clerical hierarchy of the Roman Catholic church. Turn to page 332 for the solution. [**Target: 5**]

VIRTUES Name the *Seven* Virtues (counterparts to the Seven Deadly Sins). Look for the solution on page 208. [**Target: 4**]

CHRONICLES OF NARNIA Name the seven books by C. S. Lewis which make up the series of the Chronicles of Narnia. Turn to page 314 for the solution. [**Target: 4**]

FIRST LINES OF POPULAR NOVELS III Identify the novels from these first lines. For advanced play, name the authors as well. The solutions are on page 229. [**Target: 10**]

1. "All children, except one, grow up."
2. "Dorothy lived in the midst of the great Kansas prairies, with Uncle Henry, who was a farmer, and Aunt Em, who was the farmer's wife."
3. "Garp's mother, Jenny Fields, was arrested in Boston in 1942 for wounding a man in a movie theater."
4. "Mr. Phileas Fogg lived, in 1872, at No. 7, Savile Row, Burlington Gardens, the house in which Sheridan died in 1814."
5. "Once upon a time there were four little Rabbits, and their names were—Flopsy, Mopsy, Cotton-tail, and Peter."
6. "A squat grey building of only thirty-four stories. Over the main entrance the words, CENTRAL LONDON HATCHERY AND CONDITIONING CENTRE, and, in a shield, the World State's motto, COMMUNITY, IDENTITY, STABILITY."
7. "By now the other warriors, those that had escaped head-long ruin by the sea or in a battle, were safely home."

8. "It was three hundred forty-eight years, six months, and nineteen days ago today that the citizens of Paris were awakened by the pealing of all the bells in the triple precincts of the City, the University and the Town."

9. "Miss Brooke had that kind of beauty which seems to be thrown into relief by poor dress."

10. "My father's family name being Pirrip, and my Christian name Philip, my infant tongue could make of both names nothing longer or more explicit than Pip."

11. "The great fish moved silently through the night water, propelled by short sweeps of its crescent tail."

12. "Vaughan died yesterday in his last car-crash."

13. "These two very old people are the father and mother of Mr. Bucket."

14. "When Mrs. Frederick C. Little's second son arrived, everybody noticed that he was not much bigger than a mouse."

15. "As Gregor Samsa awoke one morning from uneasy dreams he found himself transformed in his bed into a gigantic insect."

16. "Lyra and her daemon moved through the darkening Hall, taking care to keep to one side, out of sight of the kitchen."

17. "Amerigo Bonasera sat in New York Criminal Court Number 3 and waited for justice; vengeance on the men who had so cruelly hurt his daughter, who had tried to dishonour her."

18. "Except for the Marabar Caves—and they are twenty miles off—the city of Chandrapore presents nothing extraordinary."

19. "It was seven o'clock of a very warm evening in the Seeonee hills when Father Wolf woke up from his day's rest, scratched himself, yawned, and spread out his paws one after the other to get rid of the sleepy feeling in their tips."

20. "You better not never tell nobody but God."

21. "It was a feature peculiar to the colonial wars of North America, that the toils and dangers of the wilderness were to be encountered before the adverse hosts could meet."

22. "When he was nearly thirteen, my brother Jem got his arm badly broken at the elbow."

23. "At half-past six on a Friday evening in January, Lincoln International Airport, Illinois, was functioning, though with difficulty."

24. "The *Nellie*, a cruising yawl, swung to her anchor without a flutter of the sails, and was at rest."

LIBERAL ARTS List the *seven* Liberal Arts.* The solution is on page 251. [**Target: 2**]

NOVELS BY E. M. FORSTER Name the *seven* novels by E. M. Forster. You will find the solution on page 292. [**Target: 3**]

SEVEN SEAS List the *seven* seas. Find the solution on page 277. [**Target: 5**]

MISCELLANY X Answer these questions of a miscellaneous nature. Turn to page 295 for the solutions. [**Target: 12**]

1. Who wrote the words, "All animals are equal but some animals are more equal than others"?
2. Which company was known until 1924 as the Computing Tabulating Recording Company?
3. A drawer contains ten red socks and ten blue socks. Without looking, how many socks would have to be picked to be absolutely sure of having a pair of red socks?
4. Which medical condition takes its name from the French word for "yellow"?
5. What honor was actress Joanne Woodward the first person to receive?
6. Which word, meaning "to destroy," is derived from the Roman practice of punishing mutinies by killing every tenth person?
7. *The Rime of the Ancient Mariner* is told at what social gathering?
8. Which technological innovation was first constructed in 1942 on a racquets court at the University of Chicago?
9. What does the *Mona Lisa* have on her left hand?
10. What is the lightest gas?
11. How many letters are there in the Greek alphabet?
12. Which muscle in the human body is capable of exerting the greatest force?

---

* The Liberal Arts of antiquity describe the pursuit of knowledge by free men, as distinct from activities carried out by working men such as trades or crafts (the servile arts). The Liberal Arts represented the intellectual capital of the social élite, those people who did not have to work for a living.

13. Which nation were the winners of the inaugural baseball world cup in 1938?

14. Which artistic movement were Goya, Munch, and Van Gogh said to belong to?

15. In which city was the Declaration of Independence signed in 1776?

16. What name was given to the attack by North Vietnamese forces in January 1968?

17. When was the Jules Rimet Trophy last awarded?

18. The word used to describe bulk, unsolicited e-mail is thought to derive from a sketch by which comedy performers?

19. Who was shot by Denis "Sonny" O'Neill in County Cork in 1922?

20. On which day of the year are the most personal calls made in the U.S.?

21. How many points are there on a Maltese Cross?

22. Enovid 10, in 1957, was the first publically available of which type of drug?

23. Which was the first film that Alfred Hitchcock made in Hollywood and the only one of his films to win a Best Picture Oscar?

24. A snail is at the bottom of a well. The well is thirty feet deep. The snail can climb three feet during the day, but always slides back two feet during the night. How long will it take the snail to reach the top of the well?

FRAT PACK Name the *seven* actors who make up a group known as the Frat Pack.* Find the solution on page 251. [**Target: 5**]

WONDERS OF THE NATURAL WORLD Name the *seven* wonders of the natural world. Find the solution on page 314. [**Target: 3**]

COUNTRIES IN CENTRAL AMERICA Name the *seven* countries in Central America.† Turn to page 333 for the solution. [**Target: 6**]

---

* Frat Pack films include *Meet the Parents*, *The Royal Tenenbaums*, *Starsky and Hutch*, *Anchorman*, and *The Wedding Crashers*.
† Note that Mexico is technically part of North America.

AIRPORT CODES II Identify the cities that are served by these airports from the three-letter IATA codes listed. The solutions are on page 208. [**Target: 12**]

1.	LHR	2.	MIA
3.	ATL	4.	SYD
5.	EWR	6.	MAD
7.	ZRH	8.	IAD
9.	FRA	10.	PEK
11.	SIN	12.	MSP
13.	CPH	14.	DUB
15.	DEN	16.	HAV
17.	PHX	18.	FLL
19.	GIG	20.	IAH
21.	MCO	22.	FCO
23.	CLT	24.	YYZ

CHARACTERISTICS OF LIVING THINGS Identify the *seven* characteristics common to all living things. Turn to page 229 for the solution. [**Target: 5**]

ROAD PICTURES Try to name the *seven* pictures in the *Road to . . .* comedy film series.* Find the solution on page 251. [**Target: 4**]

BRITISHISMS I For each of these words, supply the equivalent word or words that would be used in Britain.† Look for the solutions on page 277. [**Target: 8**]

---

* The series starred Bing Crosby, Bob Hope, and Dorothy Lamour.

† As early as the start of the eighteenth century, British commentators were noting a divergence in the language either side of the Atlantic and making disparaging remarks about how Americans were misusing the mother tongue. Ironically, many of the differences could be accounted for by changes to the language in Britain rather than in America. Words such as "trash" (rubbish), "fall" (autumn), "loan" (instead of lend), and "gotten" (got) are all found in Shakespeare but have since fallen out of use in Britain. Shakespearian English is in many respects closer to American English than it is to English (UK). English in America differs still further because of its acceptance of words from the indigenous population (such as canoe, barbecue, savannah, hickory) and also from Spanish colonists (canyon, ranch, stampede). There has been no pattern or logic to the way the language has developed in each of the two countries, a fact that led Bill Bryson to once observe: "How else could the American Postal Service deliver the mail when in Britain the Royal Mail delivers the post?"

1.	Apartment	2.	Pants
3.	French fries	4.	Fall
5.	Diaper	6.	Attorney
7.	ZIP Code	8.	Cookie
9.	Eggplant	10.	Flashlight
11.	Jell-O	12.	Purse
13.	Station wagon	14.	Trunk
15.	Wrench	16.	Drugstore
17.	Robe	18.	Windshield
19.	Sedan	20.	Realtor
21.	Hickey	22.	Valise
23.	Vaudeville*	24.	Kerosene

NOVELS BY THE BRONTË SISTERS Recall the titles of the *seven* novels† written by the Brontë sisters. Find the solution on page 295. [**Target: 3**]

SIGNS OF AGING Name the *Seven* Signs of Aging identified by the Oil of Olay advertising campaign. Turn to page 314 for the solution. [**Target: 3**]

LINKED MISCELLANY VI Answer these questions and deduce the theme that links them. Look for the solutions on page 333. [**Target: 6**]

---

* The word describes the variety shows of the nineteenth and early twentieth centuries. It is thought to derive from an area of France, Val de Vire, with a reputation for songs and entertainment. The term proper first appears in 1840 with the opening of the Vaudeville Theatre in Boston.

† In the nineteenth century novels were being published in greater numbers than ever before. Often they were serialized in newspapers and magazines, which were becoming increasingly popular, giving the public real access to literature for the first time. Unlike the romantic adventures of the previous century (such as Defoe's *Robinson Crusoe* or Swift's *Gulliver's Travels*), they tended to be grounded in the social reality of the times and largely reflected the morals and aspirations of the middle classes, who were now the most prolific writers. Reflecting the social changes taking place, literature by female writers rose to prominence for the first time in history, particularly the works of Jane Austen, Louisa May Alcott, the Brontë sisters, and George Eliot.

1. What is the most populous city in Ohio?
2. What brand of underwear did Mark Wahlberg advertise in the 1990s?
3. Which 1995 film was directed by Clint Eastwood and starred Eastwood alongside Meryl Streep?
4. Which cartoon strip was created by Jim Davis?
5. Which global American pharmaceutical company has products which include Tylenol, Neutrogena, and Band-Aid?
6. Which novel by James Joyce was published in 1922 and relates the events of single day in Dublin?
7. Which popular CBS sitcom running from 1970 to 1977 centered on Mary Richards, a single woman in her thirties?
8. Who had hits with "In the Midnight Hour," "Land of 1,000 Dances," and "Mustang Sally"?
9. Who was married to James Dougherty, Joe DiMaggio, and Arthur Miller?
10. Which biblical figure is regarded as the patriarch of the Israelites?

CLASSICAL PLANETS Name the *seven* classical planets (celestial bodies that appear in classical astrology, alchemy, etc.). Find the solution on page 208. [**Target: 5**]

THE MAGNIFICENT SEVEN List the *seven* actors who played the title roles in the 1960 film. Turn to page 229 for the solution. [**Target: 4**]

NICKNAMES OF PRESIDENTS Identify the presidents according to these nicknames. You will find the solutions on page 251. [**Target: 12**]

1. Tricky Dickie
2. Ike
3. Teflon Bill
4. The Peanut Farmer
5. Old Read My Lips
6. The Gipper
7. L.B.J.
8. Give 'Em Hell Harry
9. Jack
10. The Liberator
11. The Father of His Country

12. The Great Engineer
13. The Father of the Declaration of Independence
14. Teddy
15. The Accidental President
16. Old Zack
17. The Velcro President
18. The New Dealer
19. Silent Cal
20. The Professor
21. The Father of the Constitution
22. The American Caesar
23. The Preacher President
24. The Hangman of Buffalo

COUNTRIES ENDING WITH " ~ STAN" Name the *seven* countries with names which end in "~stan."* Go to page 277 for the solution. [**Target: 4**]

COLORS OF THE VISIBLE SPECTRUM Name the *seven* colors of the visible spectrum of light. The solution is on page 296. [**Target: 7**]

CHARACTERS IN LITERATURE II Identify the works of literature that feature these characters. For advanced play, name the authors as well. You will find the solutions on page 314. [**Target: 8**]

1.	Ebenezer Scrooge	2.	Big Brother
3.	Tess Durbeyfield	4.	Henry Higgins
5.	Jean Brodie	6.	Mr. Rochester
7.	Emma Woodhouse	8.	Edwin Drood
9.	Atticus Finch	10.	Fitzwilliam Darcy
11.	Napoleon the Pig	12.	Lucy Honeychurch
13.	Jack Aubrey	14.	Ben Gunn
15.	Holly Golightly	16.	Tom Ripley
17.	Dolores Haze	18.	Lyra Belacqua
19.	Wilkins Micawber	20.	Natasha Rostova
21.	Arthur "Boo" Radley	22.	Widow Douglas
23.	Count Vronsky	24.	Gussie Fink-Nottle

---

* "Stan" is the Persian word for country.

TAXONOMY OF LIVING THINGS List the *seven* hierarchical categories into which living things are classified. Turn to page 333 for the solution. [**Target: 3**]

NEW WONDERS OF THE WORLD List the *seven* historic sites which have been voted as the New Seven Wonders of the World.* Find the solution on page 209. [**Target: 4**]

MISCELLANY XI Answer these questions of a miscellaneous nature. Go to page 230 for the solutions. [**Target: 10**]

1. Who famously suggested his epitaph should be "I'll be right back?"
2. Which country begins with the letter "O"?
3. Who were Juanito in 1970, Gauchito in 1978, Striker in 1994, and Footix in 1998?
4. Cleopatra's four children were fathered by which two men?
5. How many hurdles does a competitor jump in the men's 110m hurdles race?
6. "Voices rant on" is an anagram of which twelve-letter word?
7. Which sport features in the NATO phonetic alphabet?
8. How many people went onto Noah's Ark?
9. Pulmonology is associated with the study of diseases of which organ?
10. In which direction do tidal bores travel, upstream or downstream?
11. Specifically, who made the first powered flight at Kitty Hawk on December 17, 1903?
12. What is the smallest U.S. state by area?
13. In which UK cathedral is the Whispering Gallery?
14. Which president was served by three different vice presidents during his period of office?
15. What is the literal translation of the Latin phrase "lapsus linguae"?
16. What does the F7 key do in Microsoft Word?
17. How is the aurora australis better known?
18. What instrument did Glenn Miller play?

---

* A Swiss initiative by the corporation called the New Open World Corporation, which announced the results in 2007. The Great Pyramid, the only remaining wonder from the original Seven Wonders of the World is included in the list in an honorary position as an eighth wonder.

19. Which actor held the highest rank in the U.S. armed forces for an entertainer?
20. In which film does the character Popeye Doyle first appear?
21. A farmer keeps a number of geese and a number of pigs. If there are thirty-two eyes and forty-six legs, how many pigs and how many geese are there?
22. Whom did *Forbes* name as the highest-earning dead celebrity in 2007?
23. Whose footsteps, according to legend, along with a blue ox called Babe, created Minnesota's thousands of lakes?
24. Two days ago I was fifteen years old. Next year I will be eighteen years old. What is today's date, and when is my birthday?

BASEBALL TEAMS YET TO WIN THE WORLD SERIES
Name the *eight* Major League Baseball teams which have yet to win the World Series. The solution may be found on page 251. [**Target: 6**]

STATES CROSSED BY ROUTE 66
Name the *eight* states which Route 66 passed through. Find the solution on page 278. [**Target: 6**]

BRAT PACK
Name the *eight* members of the Brat Pack.* The solution is on page 277. [**Target: 5**]

SPORTS GOVERNING BODIES II
Identify the sports represented by these governing bodies. Go to page 296 for the solutions. [**Target: 14**]

1.	FA	2.	WBC
3.	UEFA	4.	USPGA
5.	NFL	6.	RFU
7.	IOC	8.	IRB
9.	ICC	10.	IRFB
11.	LPGA	12.	RYA
13.	RL	14.	CONMEBOL
15.	LTA	16.	IJF
17.	FIH	18.	IBA
19.	ISA	20.	WBB

---

* The Brat Pack was a group of young actors and actresses who appeared together in the 1980s, mainly in teen-oriented films. Brat Pack films include *The Breakfast Club* (1985), *St. Elmo's Fire* (1985), *Weird Science* (1985), *About Last Night* (1986), *Pretty in Pink* (1986), and *The Lost Boys* (1987).

21. IWF 22. FIDE
23. FIVB 24. TWIF

IVY LEAGUE Name the *eight* Ivy League institutions. Turn to page 315 for the solution. [**Target: 4**]

PRESIDENTS WHO DIED IN OFFICE Name the *eight* U.S. presidents who died while they were in office. Find the solution on page 333. [**Target: 5**]

FIRST LINES OF POP SONGS III Identify the titles of these songs from the first lines below. (The year each song was a hit in the UK is given.) For advanced play, name the performers as well. Turn to page 209 for the solutions. [**Target: 12**]

1. "Right about now." (1998)
2. "I believe the children are our future." (1986)
3. "Why do birds suddenly appear?" (1970)
4. "Strumming my pain with his fingers, singing my life with his words." (1973)
5. "Now look at them yo-yo's that's the way you do it." (1985)
6. "Dearly beloved we're gathered here today to get through this thing called life." (1985)
7. "What you want, baby I got." (1967)
8. "One, two, three, four, five, everybody in the car, so come on let's ride." (1999)
9. "I make it alone." (1980)
10. "Poor old Johnny Ray." (1982)
11. "I am just a poor boy though my story's seldom told." (1969)
12. "Yo listen up here's a story about a little guy that lives in a blue world." (1999)
13. "Very superstitious writings on the wall." (1973)
14. "I feel so extraordinary something's got a hold on me." (1987)
15. "There must be some kind of way out of here." (1968)
16. "Holly came from Miami FLA." (1973)
17. "The problem is all inside your head, she said to me." (1975)
18. "Does she walk? Does she talk? Does she come complete?" (1982)
19. "Move yourself, you always live your life." (1983)
20. "Who knows what tomorrow brings?" (1983)

21. "You never close your eyes any more when I kiss your lips." (1965)
22. "I get up, and nothing gets me down." (1984)
23. "On your mark, ready, set, let's go." (1998)
24. "She's got a smile that it seems to me." (1988)

WARSAW PACT Name the *eight* nations which were signatories of the Warsaw Pact.* Find the solution on page 230. [**Target: 6**]

GOLF SCORES Recall the *eight* names that are commonly given to the scores from a hole in golf. Look for the solution on page 252. [**Target: 7**]

INNOVATIONS I Identify the technical innovations† which were created by these individuals or organizations. Turn to page 277 for the solutions. [**Target: 12**]

1. Alexander Graham Bell (1876)
2. Orville and Wilbur Wright (1903)
3. Johannes Gutenberg (1455)
4. Charles Macintosh (1823)
5. Guglielmo Marconi (1901)
6. Sony (1979)
7. John Boyd Dunlop (1888)
8. Linus Yale (1848)
9. IBM (1981)

---

* The Warsaw Pact was drafted by Russian president Nikita Khrushchev in response to the formation of NATO and it was signed in Warsaw in 1955. Although during the Cold War, East and West never came into direct conflict, the Warsaw Pact often had to use military force to crush uprisings in member states (notably in Hungary in 1956 and Czechoslovakia in 1968). The Soviet policy towards the member countries was ominously stated in the so-called Brezhnev Doctrine: "When forces that are hostile to socialism try to turn the development of some socialist country towards capitalism, it becomes not only a problem of the country concerned, but a common problem and concern of all socialist countries."

† An innovation may be described as an invention or process for which a practical use or application has been found. It is often said that necessity is the mother of invention, which goes some way to explaining the huge leaps in technology that are produced during periods of warfare (for example, radar, modern computing, atomic energy, rocket technology, and the jet engine were all advanced by the Second World War). But this is not always the case. It is noteworthy that the parachute was invented some 300 years before the first powered flight.

10. James Watt (1769)
11. Michael Faraday (1831)
12. Alfred Nobel (1863)
13. Nikolaus Otto (1876)
14. Charles Pathé (1909)
15. Nestlé (1937)
16. Jacques and Joseph Montgolfier (1783)
17. Christiaan Barnard (1967)
18. Alessandro Volta (1800)
19. Joseph Lister (1867)
20. Otto Frisch, Niels Bohr, and Rudolf Peierls (1939)
21. Frank Whittle (1937)
22. Christopher Cockerell (1959)
23. The Roslin Institute (1997)
24. Gabriel Fallopius (1560)

STATES BEGINNING WITH "M" Name the *eight* states in the U.S. which begin with the letter "M." The solution is on page 296. [**Target: 8**]

RESERVOIR DOGS Name the *eight* characters in the film *Reservoir Dogs*. You will find the solution on page 315. [**Target: 6**]

FOOTBALL OFFICIALS Name the *eight* types of referee who officiate at NFL games. The solution is on page 252. [**Target: 4**]

QUOTATIONS FROM POPULAR FILMS I Identify the films from which these quotations* are taken. (The date of the film is provided.) Look for the solutions on page 333. [**Target: 12**]

---

* "Bond. James Bond" is a likely candidate for the most memorable film quotation of all time and a phrase that would be recognizable to the estimated 3 billion people that the Bond franchise has reached. The line was first used in *Dr. No* (1962) to introduce the character of Bond (played by Sean Connery) to cinema audiences. Bond is in a casino playing baccarat with Sylvie Trench (played by Eunice Gayson, the first Bond girl). Director Terence Young set the scene up with Connery's back to the camera. When Bond is addressed by Trench, his face is seen for the first time as he lights a cigarette and introduces himself:

James Bond: I admire your courage, Miss . . . ?
Sylvia Trench: Trench. Sylvia Trench. I admire your luck, Mr . . . ?
James Bond: Bond. James Bond.

1. "Escape is not his plan. I must face him. Alone." (1977)
2. "A census taker once tried to test me. I ate his liver, with some fava beans and a nice Chianti . . ." (1991)
3. "At my signal, unleash hell." (2000)
4. "If my calculations are correct, when this baby hits eighty-eight miles per hour you're gonna see some serious shit." (1985)
5. "I remember the days of Sputnik and Yuri Gagarin, when the world trembled at the sound of our rockets. Now they will tremble again, at our silence." (1990)
6. "Your ego is writing checks your body can't cash." (1986)
7. "Look at that! Look how she moves! It's just like Jell-O on springs." (1959)
8. "Stupid is as stupid does." (1994)
9. "Pay no attention to the man behind the curtain . . ." (1939)
10. "Don't worry, princess. I used to be afraid of the dark until . . . No, wait. I'm still afraid of the dark." (2001)
11. "I'm sorry I ate your fish, OK?" (1988)
12. "Your clothes, give them to me." (1984)
13. "It's a very difficult job and the only way to get through is we all work together as a team. And that means you do everything I say." (1969)
14. "Is it safe?" (1976)
15. "You're crazy. You oughta be locked up. You, too. Two hundred and fifty guys just walking down the road, just like that?" (1963)
16. "Failure is not an option." (1995)
17. "Me? I'm dishonest, and a dishonest man you can always trust to be dishonest. Honestly." (2003)
18. "I want you to hit me as hard as you can." (1999)
19. "One minute you're defending the whole galaxy, and, suddenly, you find yourself sucking down Darjeeling with Marie Antoinette and her little sister." (1995)
20. "The man is the head, but the woman is the neck. And she can turn the head any way she wants." (2002)
21. "I was born a poor black child." (1979)
22. "She's so deliciously low. So horribly dirty." (1964)
23. "I feel like I've been in a coma for the past twenty years. And I'm just now waking up." (1999)
24. "I'm walking here! I'm walking here!" (1969)

PLANETS List the *eight* planets in the solar system. Find the solution on page 209. [**Target: 8**]

REINDEER Name the *nine* reindeer that belong to Santa Claus. The solution is on page 230. [**Target: 4**]

QUOTATIONS FROM SHAKESPEARE II Identify the plays of Shakespeare* from which these quotations are taken. (Note the same play may be the solution to more than one quotation.) If you wish, also name the character who is quoted. Go to page 252 for the solutions. [**Target: 12**]

1. "Et tu, Bruté?"
2. "Cry, 'God for Harry! England and Saint George!'"
3. "Now is the winter of our discontent / Made glorious summer by this son of York"
4. "Friends, Romans, countrymen, lend me your ears"
5. "A pair of star-cross'd lovers take their life"
6. "We will have rings, and things, and fine array / And kiss me Kate, we will be married o' Sunday"
7. "O beware, my lord, of jealousy: / It is a green-eyed monster which doth mock the meat it feeds on"
8. "A sad tale's best for winter"
9. "A plague o' both your houses"
10. "Once more unto the breach, dear friends, once more"
11. "But soft! What light through yonder window breaks?"

---

* *Macbeth*, one of Shakespeare's best-known plays, tells the story of the eponymous king who ruled Scotland from 1040 until 1057. In the play, Macbeth, encouraged by his devious and ambitious wife and the predictions of three witches, murders Duncan and becomes King in his place. Having gained the throne, Macbeth becomes increasingly paranoid, committing further crimes against those he believes are plotting against him. He eventually receives his comeuppance at the hands of Macduff, and Malcolm (Duncan's son) is proclaimed King. As always, Shakespeare took small liberties with historical accuracy, wise, as he was, to the political sensibilities of the time and, more important, to make a better story. There is no evidence to suggest Macbeth was a particularly bad man (nor that Duncan was a particularly strong or wise king as the play portrays him; the historical evidence is that he was weak and ineffective). Duncan was killed in battle rather than in cold blood and although Malcolm did defeat Macbeth in the Battle of Dunsinnan in 1054, it was Malcolm not Macduff who killed Macbeth and actually in battle at Lumphanan in 1057. This is, however, academic given *Macbeth*'s status as one of the greatest plays ever written.

12. "A woman moved is like a fountain troubled, / Muddy, ill-seeming, thick, bereft of beauty"
13. "Yet who would have thought the old man to have had so much blood in him?"
14. "Murder most foul, as in the best it is"
15. "By the pricking of my thumbs, / Something wicked this way comes"
16. "You call me misbeliever, cut-throat, dog, / And spit upon my Jewish gabardine"
17. "The course of true love never did run smooth"
18. "The lady doth protest too much, methinks"
19. "All that glitters is not gold"
20. "I know a bank where the wild thyme blows / Where oxlips and the nodding violet grows / Quite over canopied with luscious woodbine / With sweet musk-roses and with eglantine"
21. "But I will wear my heart upon my sleeve, for daws to peck at"
22. "What's in a name? That which we call a rose / By any other word would smell as sweet"
23. "Very tragical mirth"
24. "This blessed plot, this earth, this realm, this England"

BASEBALL FIELDING POSITIONS Recall the *nine* fielding positions in baseball. Look for the solution on page 296. [**Target: 7**]

MISCELLANY XII Answer these questions of a miscellaneous nature. You will find the solutions on page 315. [**Target: 14**]

1. What word means "favoring of relatives or friends"?
2. What links gazpacho with revenge?
3. Which famous building, completed in 1648, contains the tomb of Queen Mumtaz Mahal?
4. Which of the Great Lakes is at the lowest elevation?
5. What links Uriah Heep and Claudia Schiffer?
6. How many sides does a standard pencil have?
7. "Tossed Salad and Scrambled Eggs" is the closing tune to which long-running comedy?
8. If your geographical position were 0° latitude, 0° longitude, where in the world would you be?
9. Where was the body of George Mallory found in 1999, seventy-five years after his death?

10. What does the acronym "SALT," when related to U.S. diplomacy, stand for?

11. Which honor has been accorded once to Neil Amstrong and Winston Churchill, twice to Dwight D. Eisenhower and John Glenn, and seven times to the New York Yankees?

12. Which state is the first the see the sun rise?

13. What was equal to $79 million in 1791, zero in 1835, and $9 trillion in 2007?

14. Which literary character had a housekeeper called Mrs. Hudson?

15. "W" is the symbol for which chemical element?

16. Who would normally carry a crosier?

17. What film role links Telly Savalas, Donald Pleasance, Max Von Sydow, and Charles Gray?

18. Who was the first Soviet leader to have been born after the 1917 revolution?

19. Which main character dies in *Harry Potter and the Half-Blood Prince*?

20. In which war were the battles of Bunker Hill and Brandywine Creek fought?

21. You have two hourglass timers; one runs for exactly two minutes, the other for exactly five minutes. Using only these devices, how could you time an egg to cook for exactly three minutes?

22. Which type of beans are used to make baked beans?

23. The Hindu god Ganesha is depicted with the head of which animal?

24. A woman goes into four shops. In each shop she pays an entry fee of $1, spends half of her money, and on the way out puts $1 in the charity box. After leaving the fourth shop she has no money left. How much money did she begin with?

COUNTRIES ENDING WITH " ~ LAND" Name the *nine* sovereign countries in the world whose names end in "-land." Find the solution on page 334. [**Target:** 7]

BOOKS BY GEORGE ORWELL Name the *nine* books written by George Orwell.* Go to page 209 for the solution. [**Target:** 3]

RECENT HISTORY II Identify the correct year from each of these clues. Go to page 230 for the solution. [**Target:** 10]

---

* George Orwell was the pen name of Eric Arthur Blair.

---

1.   Concorde* crashes in Paris and all Concorde flights are immediately suspended; the Russian submarine, the *Kursk*, sinks in the Barents Sea; George W. Bush controversially wins the presidential election, the result coming down to disputed votes in Florida; *American Beauty* wins the Oscar for Best Picture; Microsoft releases Windows Me; the New York Yankees win the World Series, defeating the New York Mets in the first postseason Subway Series in forty-four years; Hillary Clinton is elected to the United States Senate.

2.   Crown Prince Dipendra murders his father and other members of the Nepalese royal family before killing himself; U.S. and UK forces overthrow the Taliban in Afghanistan; Apple releases the iPod; Enron files for bankruptcy; *The Fellowship of the Ring* film is released; Google patents the PageRank search algorithm†; 3,000 people are killed in the 9/11 terrorist attacks on the World Trade Center and the Pentagon.

3.   Al-Qaeda bombs U.S. embassies in Nairobi and Dar es Salam, killing 224 people; Bill Clinton is challenged with impeachment over his affair with Monica Lewinsky; the number of AIDS sufferers reaches 33 million worldwide; *Titanic* wins eleven Oscars and becomes the highest-ever grossing film; the U.S. Department of Justice files an antitrust case against Microsoft; smoking is banned in California bars and restaurants; the Denver Broncos become the first AFC team to win the Super Bowl in fourteen years; the merger of Exxon and Mobil is announced.

4.   O. J. Simpson is found not guilty of murder; Timothy McVeigh bombs an Oklahoma government building, killing 168 people; Princess Diana talks candidly about her marriage in a television interview; Steve Fossett becomes the first person to cross the Pacific Ocean in a balloon; Drew Barrymore "flashes" David Letterman live on his talk show; 25,000 people attend a memorial to Jerry Garcia in Golden Gate Park.

---

* The Paris crash saw Concorde jump from being statistically the safest aircraft in the world (with no fatal accidents in thirty years—a single incident of a blown tire in 1979) to one of the most dangerous, due to the relatively low number of flights it had made (less than 100,000). This, combined with the 2001 terror attacks, which depressed the airline industry, led to the retirement of Concorde in 2003, leaving jet-setters at the mercy of no-frills travel.

† PageRank is an innovative means of assessing the importance of a web page by assigning a numerical weighting according to how many pages are linked to it.

5.   Deep Blue, an IBM computer, beats Garry Kasparov at a game of chess; beach volleyball debuts as an Olympic sport; eight climbers die in bad weather on Mount Everest; the Prince and Princess of Wales divorce; Bill Clinton is elected for a second term; Mariah Carey and Boyz II Men spend their sixteenth week at number one with "One Sweet Day"*; Muhammad Ali lights the Olympic Torch at the summer Olympics in Atlanta.

6.   The Camp David Accords between Egypt and Israel is brokered by President Jimmy Carter; Sid Vicious murders Nancy Spungen in a New York hotel; the *Amoco Cadiz* runs aground off the coast of Brittany, creating the biggest oil spill to date (at the time); Cardinal Karol Wojtya becomes Pope John Paul II, the first Polish pope; John Belushi and Dan Aykroyd perform as the Blues Brothers on *Saturday Night Live* for the first time; *Grease* premieres in the U.S.

7.   Apollo 11 astronauts Neil Armstrong and Buzz Aldrin are the first men to set foot on the moon; El Salvador and Honduras go to war over a soccer match; the Woodstock music festival takes place; John Lennon and Yoko Ono marry and spend their honeymoon in a "bed-in" to promote peace; Richard Nixon is sworn in as president; the Battle of Hamburger Hill is fought in Vietnam.

8.   Palestinian terrorists murder eleven Israeli athletes at the Munich Olympics; the Watergate building is burgled in Washington; the Bloody Sunday shootings take place in Northern Ireland; Jane Fonda tours North Vietnam; the pocket calculator is introduced; Richard Nixon visits China; *The French Connection* wins the Oscar for Best Picture; Bobby Fischer defeats Boris Spassky to become world chess champion.

9.   Allied forces land in Normandy on D-Day; a German counteroffensive takes place, resulting in the Battle of the Bulge; the Siege of Leningrad is finally relieved by Russian forces; the Bretton Woods conference takes place to establish a framework for postwar economic development; Rome and Paris are liberated; Anne Frank and her family are discovered in hiding by the Gestapo.

10.   President Reagan admits the Iran Contra affair; West German pilot Mathias Rust lands a private plane in Red Square in Moscow; Klaus Barbie is sentenced to life imprisonment for war crimes; *The Simpsons* airs for the first time on the *Tracey Ullman*

---

* The longest of any recording.

Show, *Three Men and a Baby* is the year's top-grossing film; the New York Giants defeat the Denver Broncos in Super Bowl XXI.

11. Nelson Mandela becomes president of South Africa; the Channel Tunnel opens; *Schindler's List**wins seven Oscars; Ayrton Senna is killed at the San Marino Grand Prix; the North American Free Trade Agreement (NAFTA) comes into being; the Buffalo Bills lose their fourth consecutive Super Bowl; Al Gore chairs the Superhighway Summit to discuss the growing importance of the Internet; the United States host the FIFA World Cup (which is won by Brazil).

12. The Panama Canal opens; Archduke Franz Ferdinand of Austria is assassinated, leading, a month later, to the opening of hostilities of the First World War; Babe Ruth makes his debut for the Boston Red Sox; St. Petersburg changes its name to Petrograd; the first successful blood transfusion is made.

13. Richard Nixon is sworn in for a second term; Arab oil producers blockade oil supplies to the West, leading to a global energy crisis; U.S. forces complete their withdrawal from Vietnam; *The Godfather* wins the Oscar for Best Picture; Pink Floyd release *The Dark Side of the Moon*; the Miami Dolphins win Super Bowl VII to achieve a perfect season.

14. Hong Kong falls to the Japanese; Germany launches an invasion of Russia code-named Operation Barbarossa; Japanese air forces mount a surprise attack on the U.S. naval base at Pearl Harbor; the *Bismarck* is sunk by the British navy; penicillin is used for the first time; Orson Welles directs *Citizen Kane*†; work on Mount Rushmore is completed.

15. North Vietnam mounts the Tet Offensive; Martin Luther King Jr. and Robert Kennedy are assassinated; Russia sends tanks into Czechoslovakia; astronauts orbit the moon for the first time in Apollo 8‡;

---

* The book on which the film was based was *Schindler's Ark*, written by Thomas Keneally. In October 1980, while en route to the airport, Keneally visited a luggage shop in Beverly Hills to buy a new briefcase. The shop was owned by Leopold Pfefferberg, one of the 1,200 people saved by Oskar Schindler, who would tell his story to any writer, producer, or director who came into his store. Pfefferberg (who produced two filing cabinets of documents backing up his claims) was able to convince Keneally to tell his story, and it became his next book.
† The film is based on William Randolph Hearst, who was so angered that he accused Orson Welles of being a communist in an unsuccessful bid to prevent its release.
‡ Astronauts Frank Borman, Jim Lovell and William A. Anders become the first people to see the dark side of the moon.

mass student protests take place in Paris; the Gibson Flying V guitar is patented; *2001: A Space Odyssey* premieres in the U.S.

16. The Altair 8800 computer is launched, sparking the personal computing revolution; Bill Gates founds Microsoft; *One Flew Over the Cuckoo's Nest* wins five Oscars, including Best Picture, Best Actor, and Best Director; *Jaws* becomes the first ever summer blockbuster, earning a record $100 million in North America; Communist forces seize Saigon, ending the Vietnam War; Gerald Ford posthumously restores Robert E. Lee's rights of citizenship.

17. Queen Victoria dies; President William McKinley is assassinated, and Theodore Roosevelt succeeds him as president; the Boxer Rebellion ends in China; the British Royal Navy launches its first submarine; Marconi receives the first transatlantic radio communication.*

18. The Cultural Revolution begins in China; John Lennon makes the controversial comment that the Beatles are "more popular than Jesus"; the Beach Boys release *Pet Sounds*; the first ever episode of *Star Trek* airs; the Beatles play their last ever concert at Candlestick Park in San Francisco; the first ever artificial heart is implanted in a patient in Houston, Texas.

19. King George V dies; Edward VIII abdicates in order to marry American divorcée Wallis Simpson; Germany occupies the Rhineland; the Spanish Civil War begins; Mao Tse-tung begins the Long March; Hitler purges the Nazi party in "the night of the long knives."

20. Yuri Gagarin becomes the first man in space; Cuban rebels assisted by U.S. forces land at the Bay of Pigs; the Berlin Wall is raised; John F. Kennedy is inaugurated as U.S. president; UN General Secretary Dag Hammarskjöld is killed in a plane crash.

21. Alaska and Hawaii join the United States, becoming the forty-ninth and fiftieth states; Fidel Castro seizes power in Cuba; the Dalai Lama is forced to flee Tibet; the Barbie doll is launched in the U.S.; the St. Lawrence Seaway opens to shipping; *Ben-Hur*, starring Charlton Heston, is released.

22. Peace is achieved between the combatants in the Balkan War but tensions in the region continue to simmer; the first ever crossword is published in *New York World*; the Seventeenth Amendment allows American senators to be elected for the first

---

* A transmission of the letter "S" in Morse code (i.e., three dots).

time; Vincencio Peruggia tries to sell the stolen *Mona Lisa* in Florence and is arrested.

23. San Francisco is destroyed by a severe earthquake; the Simplon tunnel is opened between Italy and Switzerland to become the world's longest tunnel; "SOS" becomes an international distress signal; Rolls-Royce is founded; HMS *Dreadnought* is launched, revolutionizing battleship design and leading to a major arms race in the buildup to the First World War.

24. Ernest Rutherford proposes the theory of atomic structure; Roald Amundsen reaches the South Pole; Standard Oil is broken up under antitrust laws; the first coast-to-coast flight of the U.S. is made by Calbraith Rogers (with sixty-nine stops and sixteen crash landings); Italy declares war on Turkey in its attempt to conquer Tripolitania (Libya); Machu Picchu is discovered in the Peruvian Andes.

THE FELLOWSHIP OF THE RING Name the *nine* characters who made up the Fellowship of the Ring in the novel by J. R. R. Tolkien. Go to page 252 for the solution. [**Target: 8**]

POKER HANDS List the *nine* types of hand in poker. Find the solution on page 278. [**Target: 8**]

CHARACTERS IN LITERATURE III Identify the works of literature in which these characters appear. For advanced play, name the authors as well. The solutions are on page 297. [**Target: 12**]

1.	Phileas Fogg	2.	The Queen of Hearts
3.	T. S. Garp	4.	The Miller
5.	Bob Cratchit	6.	Captain Ahab
7.	Uriah Heep	8.	Dorian Gray
9.	Oliver Mellors	10.	Alexey Karenin
11.	Bill Sikes	12.	Catherine Earnshaw
13.	Kurtz	14.	Tonya Gromeko
15.	Patrick Bateman	16.	Pinkie Brown
17.	Annie Wilkes	18.	Rabbit Angstrom
19.	Clarissa Dalloway	20.	Alex DeLarge
21.	Aureliano Buendia	22.	Aunt Polly
23.	Blind Pew	24.	Fanny Price

STATES PREFIXED BY ADJECTIVES Name the *nine* states of the U.S. which have names that are prefixed by adjectives. Turn to page 315 for the solution. [**Target: 7**]

NIMITZ-CLASS AIRCRAFT CARRIERS Try to name the *ten* Nimitz-class aircraft carriers* of the U.S. Navy. Look for the solution on page 252. [**Target: 5**]

MOST OSCAR-NOMINATED ACTORS Name the *ten* actors who have received seven or more Oscar[†] nominations in their careers. You can find the solution on page 334. [**Target: 5**]

LINKED MISCELLANY VII In providing the correct solutions to these questions, deduce the connecting theme that links them. Go to page 210 for the solution. [**Target: 5**]

1. Which volcanic lake, in Oregon, is the deepest lake in the United States?
2. Which city is home to the Suns, the Coyotes, and the Diamondbacks?
3. With which team did Walter Payton and William "The Refrigerator" Perry win Super Bowl XX in 1986?
4. Which well-known organization only admits people with IQs in the top two percent of the population and includes Isaac Asimov, Geena Davis, Jodie Foster, and Scott Adams[‡] among its members?
5. Which Michael Crichton novel recounts the story of an outbreak of an extraterrestrial microorganism which causes in its victims sudden and deadly clotting of the blood?
6. Which river runs from the Tibetan Plateau through Kashmir and emerges in the Arabian Sea near Karachi?

---

* Nimitz-class aircraft carriers are the largest military vessels in the world, displacing 100,000 tons and powered by two A4W nuclear reactors. They have a cruising speed of 30 knots and cost $4.5 billion.

† The Oscar statuette was designed in 1927 by Cedric Gibbons, MGM Art Director, who was to win the award himself eleven times. The first Oscars were made of bronze although plaster was substituted during the war. Today they are fashioned from gold-plated Britannium (an alloy of tin, copper and antimony). The statuette is $13\frac{1}{2}$ inches tall and weighs 8 lb.

‡ The creator of *Dilbert*.

---

7. Which song, the opening song of the musical *Hair*, was a 1969 hit for *The Fifth Dimension*?

8. Oncology is the medical term for the study and treatment of which disease?

9. Who starred in the *Gangs of New York*, *The Aviator*, and *Titanic*?

10. Which Lockheed-manufactured four-engine turboprop aircraft is used as a transport aircraft by the U.S.A.F., the U.S. Marine Corps and the R.A.F.?

PLAGUES OF EGYPT Name the *ten* plagues of Egypt, as told in Exodus in the Old Testament. You will find the solution on page 230. [**Target: 5**]

TYPES OF CLOUD List the *ten* types of naturally forming* clouds. Go to page 253 for the solution. [**Target: 7**]

PHOBIAS Identify the stimuli which trigger these phobias. Turn to page 279 for the solutions. [**Target: 12**]

1. Claustrophobia	2. Technophobia
3. Arachnophobia	4. Xenophobia
5. Bacteriophobia	6. Agoraphobia
7. Aviophobia	8. Ornithophobia
9. Haemophobia	10. Acrophobia
11. Heliophobia	12. Demophobia
13. Coitophobia	14. Noctiphobia
15. Ablutophobia	16. Androphobia
17. Bathophobia	18. Brontophobia
19. Spermaphobia	20. Ophidiophobia
21. Sesquipedalophobia	22. Pentheraphobia
23. Triskaidekaphobia	24. Hexakosioihexekontahexaphobia

CHARACTERS IN *CHEERS* Name the *ten* major characters to feature in *Cheers*. Find the solution on page 297. [**Target: 7**]

---

* Additionally, the condensation trails left across the sky by airplanes (contrails) are technically classified as a type of cloud.

COUNTRIES WITH FOUR-LETTER NAMES Name the *ten*
countries which have four-letter names. The solution is on page 315.
[Target: 6]

ARTISTS Identify the artists* who created these works. You will
find the solutions on page 334. [Target: 12]

1. *Mona Lisa (La Giaconda*, 1503–6), *The Last Supper* (c.1495–98)
2. *Starry Night* (1889), *Sunflowers* (1888), *The Potato Eaters* (1885)
3. *The Haywain* (1821), *Salisbury Cathedral* (1823)
4. *The Creation of Adam*† (1508–12), *David* (1501–4)
5. *Water-Lilies* (1914), *Gare Saint-Lazare, Paris* (1877), *Impression: Sunrise* (1873)
6. *The Birth of Venus* (c.1485), *Primavera* (*c.*1482)
7. *Guernica* (1937), *Three Dancers* (1925), *Les Demoiselles d'Avignon* (1907)
8. *Campbell's Soup Can* (1964), *Marilyn* (1964)
9. *The Scream* (1893)
10. *Christ of St. John of the Cross* (1951), *The Persistence of Memory* (1931)
11. *The Fighting Temeraire* (1838), *Rain, Steam and Speed* (1844)
12. *The Milkmaid* (c. 1658–60), *Girl with a Pearl Earring* (c. 1665)
13. *A Bar at the Folies-Bergère* (1882), *Olympia* (1863)
14. *Luncheon of the Boating Party* (1881), *La Moulin de la Galette* (1876), *Umbrellas* (1883)
15. *Bacchus and Ariadne* (1520–2), *The Assumption* (1516–18)
16. *As I Opened Fire* (1964), *Whaam!* (1963)
17. *The Snail* (1953), *Blue Nude IV* (1952)
18. *The Kiss* (1908), *Danae* (1907–8)

---

* Many artists have called on a mathematical idea known as the Golden Ratio in their work. It is a number that approximates to 1.618 and is normally represented by the Greek letter phi π but has some unusual mathematical properties. In antiquity it was believed that shapes derived using the ratio were aesthetically pleasing; this is evident in many examples of ancient architecture, including occurrences in the Parthenon in Athens and the Great Pyramid at Giza. The idea resurfaced during the Renaissance after the publication in 1509 of the *Divina Proportione* by Luca Pacioli which greatly influenced contemporary artists. A golden ratio can be found in the face of the *Mona Lisa* as well as in the dimensions of the painting itself.
† Fresco in the Sistine Chapel.

19. *Dance Class* (1874), *Orchestra Musicians* (1870–1)
20. *The Arnolfini Portrait* (1434)
21. *The Night Watch* (1642), *The Feast of Belshazzar* (c. 1635)
22. *The Ambassadors* (1533), *Portrait of Sir Thomas More* (1527)
23. *Garden of Earthly Delights* (c. 1510), *The Ship of Fools* (1490–1500)
24. *The Hunters in the Snow* (1565), *Children's Games* (1560)

CHART-TOPPING SINGLES BY STEVIE WONDER Name the *ten* songs with which Stevie Wonder has had number one hits on the Billboard Hot 100. Look to page 210 for the answer. [**Target: 4**]

COMMANDMENTS Recall the *Ten* Commandments. Find the solution on page 231. [**Target: 5**]

MISCELLANY XIII Answer these questions of a miscellaneous nature. Go to page 253 for the solutions. [**Target: 8**]

1. Which word for madman is derived from a French word meaning "moonstruck"?
2. Which is the nearest planet to earth?
3. Which sculptor created *The Thinker*?
4. What links the brand names of Nike, Hermès, and Mars?
5. What was the tallest building in the world before the Empire State Building?
6. The flag of which country includes at its center a blue wheel known as Ashoka Chakra?
7. What are black-eyed peas?
8. Which spice comes from the crocus?
9. According to Greek mythology, who was the first woman?
10. In 2005, whose ashes were fired from a cannon on top of a 150-foot tower to the sound of Bob Dylan's "Mr. Tambourine Man"?
11. In humans, which sex possesses both X and Y chromosomes?
12. Which of the United States is northernmost?
13. Which two sequels have won a Best Picture Oscar?
14. Who said to whom, "You're a drunk, a tramp, and an unfit mother"?
15. Who composed *Carmen*?
16. In the context of geography, what is the opposite of oriental?

17. Which famous book, published in 1816, is subtitled *The Modern Prometheus*?
18. How is "beginner's all-purpose symbolic instruction code" better known?
19. In which city would you find an arch called "The Gateway to India"?
20. How was William H. Bonney better known?
21. Who played Tony Manero in a 1978 film?
22. During the course of a party, everybody shook hands with everybody else. There were sixty-six handshakes. How many people were there at the party?
23. What happened in Britain between September 3 and 13, 1752?
24. On Wednesday, when Sally is visiting Molly's house, she remarks that the clock is five minutes slow. Molly says that it loses five minutes every hour. The following week, Sally visits Molly and notices the clock is telling the right time. "You've fixed your clock," says Sally. "No I haven't," says Molly. What day is it?

TALLEST BUILDINGS IN THE U.S. Name the *ten* tallest buildings in the U.S.* You will find the solution on page 279. [**Target: 6**]

MEMBERS OF ASEAN List the *ten* members of the Association of Southeast Asian Nations. The solution is on page 297. [**Target: 6**]

POLITICAL QUOTATIONS Identify the authors of these quotations of a political† nature. Note that more than one of these quotations may be attributable to the same author. The solutions may be found on page 315. [**Target: 16**]

---

* The Chicago Spire is due for completion in 2010 and will stand 2,001 ft (610 m) tall, making it the tallest tower in the U.S. The Freedom Tower is expected to be complete in 2010 and at 1,776 ft (541 m) will be the tallest building in the U.S. if completed before the Chicago Spire.
† The political sound bite has gained major importance in the media age. A sound bite is a short excerpt—usually one line—from a longer delivery which very simply encapsulates the message which its author is attempting to put across. Although politicians (and their spin doctors) try to deliver sound bites in every speech they write, the ones that truly resonate can often do so inadvertently and may even have negative connotations.

1. "I am not a crook."
2. "I did not have sexual relations with that woman."
3. "Today, in the world of freedom, the proudest boast is, 'Ich bin ein Berliner.'"
4. "I have a dream that one day this nation will rise up and live out the true meaning of its creed."
5. "There can be no whitewash at the White House."
6. "Read my lips. No new taxes."
7. "Senator, you're no Jack Kennedy."
8. "Now this is not the end. It is not even the beginning of the end. But it is, perhaps, the end of the beginning."
9. "England expects every man will do his duty."
10. "Ask not what your country can do for you; ask what you can do for your country."
11. "I came, I saw, I conquered."
12. "Religion is the opium of the people."
13. ". . . government of the people, by the people, for the people."
14. "I know I have the body but of a weak and feeble woman; but I have the heart and stomach of a king."
15. "If you can't stand the heat, you better get out of the kitchen."
16. "It is true that you may fool all of the people some of the time; you can even fool some of the people all of the time; but you can't fool all of the people all of the time."
17. "Mr. Gorbachev, tear down this wall."
18. "Every nation in every region now has a decision to make. Either you are with us, or you are with the terrorists."
19. "Let me assert my firm belief that the only thing we have to fear is fear itself."
20. "The buck stops here."
21. "Power is the ultimate aphrodisiac."
22. "Speak softly and carry a big stick."
23. "We will bury you."
24. "Trust in God and keep your powder dry."

EVENTS IN THE DECATHLON Recall the *ten* events in the decathlon. Find the solution on page 335. [**Target: 8**]

OLOGIES II Describe the subjects that are studied in each of these disciplines. Look for the solutions on page 231. [**Target: 10**]

1.	Arachnology	2.	Parapsychology
3.	Seismology	4.	Gastroenterology
5.	Osteology	6.	Etymology
7.	Paleontology	8.	Hippology
9.	Ophthalmology	10.	Topology
11.	Toxicology	12.	Cryptology
13.	Lexicology	14.	Allergology
15.	Pharmacology	16.	Oncology
17.	Mycology	18.	Epistemology
19.	Pedology	20.	Dendrochronology
21.	Graphology	22.	Angiology
23.	Speleology	24.	Vexillology

ALPHA WORLD CITIES List the *ten* cities which have been classed as alpha world Cities.* Find the solution on page 279. [**Target: 6**]

LINKED MISCELLANY VIII Answer these questions and deduce the connecting theme that links them. Find the solution on page 297. [**Target: 5**]

1. Which 1979 film starring Dustin Hoffman and Meryl Streep won the Oscar for Best Picture?
2. What type of companies are DHL, FedEx, and UPS examples of?
3. What is the state capital of Texas?
4. Who wrote *Doctor Zhivago*?
5. In the original film, who is the Terminator sent to kill?
6. Aside from the moon, what is the brightest object in the night sky?
7. Which German "pocket battleship" was scuttled after the Battle of the River Plate?
8. What is the name of the residue which remains after a fire?
9. What is the name of the alien antagonists in *Star Trek: First Contact*?
10. Which was the first song from Michael Jackson's *Thriller* album to go to number one on the Billboard Hot 100?

---

* The Globalization and World Cities Study Group and Network (GaWC) categorizes world cities according to a number of criteria such as international familiarity, population size, economic importance, cultural importance, or impact on international events. The GaWC has identified ten cities in the highest band as being "full service cities" or alpha world cities.

MOST VALUABLE SPORTING EVENTS Name the *ten* sporting events identified by Forbes as being the most valuable in the world. Turn to page 316 for the solution. [**Target: 7**]

STATES NAMED AFTER PEOPLE Name the *ten* states of the U.S. which are named after people. You can find the solution on page 335. [**Target: 5**]

OLYMPIANS I Identify these U.S. Olympians* from their medal honours. The solutions are on page 210. [**Target: 8**]

1. Athlete winning gold at Los Angeles in 1984, Seoul in 1988, Barcelona in 1992, and Atlanta in 1996 in the Men's Long Jump; gold at Los Angeles and at Seoul in the Men's 100m; gold at Los Angeles in the Men's 200m; gold at Los Angeles and at Seoul in the Men's 4 × 100m Relay; silver at Seoul in the Men's 200m.

2. Athlete winning five medals at Sydney in 2000 including gold in the Women's 100m and Women's 200m but who was stripped of them in 2007 after admitting drug use.

3. Athlete winning gold at Atlanta in 1996 in the Men's 200m; gold at Atlanta and at Sidney in 2000 in the Men's 400m; gold at Barcelona in 1992 and Sydney in the Men's 4 × 400m Relay.

4. Light heavyweight boxer winning gold at Rome in 1960.

5. Speed skater winning five gold medals at Lake Placid in 1980 in the Men's 500m, 1000m, 1500m, 5000m and 10,000m events.

6. Athlete winning gold at Barcelona in 1992 and Atlanta in 1996 in the Women's 100m; gold in Atlanta in the Women's 4 × 400m Relay.

7. Athlete winning gold in Seoul in 1988 in the Women's Long Jump; gold in Seoul and in Barcelona in 1992 in the Heptathlon; silver at Los Angeles in 1984 in the Heptathlon; bronze at Barcelona and at Atlanta in 1996 in the Women's Long Jump.

8. Athlete winning gold at Los Angeles in 1984 in the Women's 200m, the Women's 400m and the Women's 4 × 400m Relay; silver at Seoul in 1988 in the Women's 4 × 400m Relay.

---

* At the inaugural modern Olympics in Paris in 1896, there were 245 competitors from fifteen different countries. This figure has grown every year since—the 2004 Athens Olympics featured 11,099 competitors from 202 countries.

9. Athlete winning gold in the Men's 400m Hurdles and the Men's 4 × 400m Relay at Sydney in 2000.

10. Athlete winning gold in the Men's 400m Hurdles at Atlanta in 1996.

11. Heavyweight boxer winning gold at Mexico in 1968.

12. Diver winning gold at Los Angeles in 1984 in the Men's 10m Platform and the Men's 3m Springboard; gold at Seoul in 1988 in the Men's 10m Platform and the Men's 3m Springboard; silver at Montreal in 1976 in the Men's 10m Platform.

13. Athlete winning gold at Athens in 2004 in the Men's 400m and gold at Athens in the Men's 4 × 400m Relay.

14. Athlete winning gold at Los Angeles in 1984 in the Women's Marathon.

15. Athlete winning gold at Melbourne in 1956, Rome in 1960, Tokyo in 1964, and Mexico City in 1968 in the Men's Discus.

16. Athlete winning gold at Atlanta in 1996 in the Men's Triple Jump.

17. Athlete winning gold at Sydney in 2000 in the Men's 100m and the Men's 4 × 100m Relay; Silver at Athens in 2004 in the Men's 4 × 100m Relay; Bronze at Athens in the Men's 100m.

18. Athlete winning gold at Barcelona in 1992 in the Men's Triple Jump and silver at Los Angeles in 1984 in the Men's Triple Jump.

19. Athlete winning gold at Los Angeles in 1984 and at Seoul in 1988 in the 110m Hurdles.

20. Athlete winning gold at Seoul in 1988 in the Men's 400m and the Men's 4 × 400m Relay; gold at Barcelona in 1992 in the Men's 4 × 400m Relay; silver at Barcelona in the Men's 400m.

21. Athlete winning gold in the Men's High Jump at Atlanta in 1996.

22. Athlete winning gold at Helsinki in 1952 and at Melbourne in 1956 in the Shot and silver at Rome in 1960 in the Shot.

23. Athlete winning gold in the Women's 100m, Women's 200m, and the Women's 4 × 100m Relay at Rome in 1960; bronze in Women's 4 × 100m Relay at Melbourne in 1956.

24. Athlete winning gold in the Men's 800m at London in 1948; gold at the Men's 4 × 400m Relay at Helsinki in 1952; silver at the Men's 4 × 400m Relay at Helsinki; bronze in the Men's 400m at London.

CHART-TOPPING SINGLES BY WHITNEY HOUSTON Name the *eleven* Whitney Houston songs to top the Billboard Hot 100. The solution is on page 231. [**Target: 5**]

TRAGEDIES BY SHAKESPEARE List the *eleven* tragedies written by Shakespeare. The solution is on page 210. [**Target: 6**]

FILMS STARRING GRACE KELLY Name the *eleven* films in which Grace Kelly* starred. Find the solution on page 253. [**Target: 3**]

CAPITAL CITIES IV Identify the countries which have these capital cities. The solutions can be found on page 279. [**Target: 10**]

1.	Vienna	2.	Kingston
3.	Teheran	4.	Beirut
5.	Kathmandu	6.	Islamabad
7.	Damascus	8.	Manila
9.	La Paz	10.	Kabul
11.	Tallinn	12.	Dar es Salaam
13.	Kampala	14.	Vilnius
15.	Asunción	16.	Bridgetown
17.	Port-of-Spain	18.	Skopje
19.	Freetown	20.	Muscat
21.	Managua	22.	Yaoundé
23.	Suva	24.	Santo Domingo

THE WALTONS Recall the *eleven* members of the Walton family (who were the main characters in the television show). Look for the solution on page 298. [**Target: 6**]

MINERALS List the *eleven* minerals that are required as part of a healthy human diet. Find the solution on page 316. [**Target: 5**]

MISCELLANY XIV Answer these questions of a miscellaneous nature. The solutions may be found on page 335. [**Target: 10**]

---

* Later Princess Grace of Monaco.

1. In electronics, what does LED stand for?
2. In which state was the 2000 presidential election finally decided by a margin of just 537 votes?
3. Who was the first person to be pictured on a postage stamp?
4. George W. Bush is the forty-third president, but how many other people have held the office before him?
5. In which sport would you go to a Basho?
6. What device, invented in 1817 by Sir David Brewster, was given a name from Greek meaning "viewer of beautiful shapes"?
7. What Japanese word means "loveable egg"?
8. Where is the Simpson Desert?
9. What character was created by Edgar Rice Burroughs?
10. Who travelled with William Dawes and Dr. Joseph Warren on the night of April 18, 1775?
11. What was celluloid first used for (in 1869)?
12. What landmark would you find in La Place de la Concorde in Paris, Central Park in New York, and Victoria Embankment in London?
13. Where in the human body would you find loops and whorls?
14. Who wrote *Under Milk Wood*?
15. What was unusual about Holly Hunter's Oscar-winning performance?
16. A drawer contains six red socks and six blue socks. Without looking, how many socks would have to be picked out of the drawer to be absolutely sure of having a pair the same color?
17. Which natural phenomenon travels at speeds of up to 60,000 meters per second and can reach temperatures of 50,000°F?
18. Which country has a flag consisting of a single color?
19. How is the B2 better known?
20. Which two words are pronounced the same but do not share any common letters? (two possibilities)
21. Which conflict between Britain and Spain in 1739 was caused by a severed body part?
22. Which musician was the first to be awarded a gold disc, for sales of over a million records?
23. What word describing a mad panic derives from the nickname of London's Hospital of Mary of Bethlehem for mentally ill people?
24. A right-handed glove is inverted and worn on the left hand. Which part of the hand (i.e. the palm or the back) is now in contact with the palm of the glove?

COUNTRIES ON THE EQUATOR Name the *eleven* countries through which the Equator passes. Look for the solution on page 279. [**Target: 5**]

CONFEDERACY Name the *eleven* Southern states which made up the Confederacy* of 1861 to 1865. The solution may be found on page 231. [**Target: 7**]

CHARACTERS IN *M*A*S*H* Recall the *eleven* main characters in *M*A*S*H*. Find the solution on page 335. [**Target:7**]

SCANDALS Identify the individuals at the center of these scandals. Turn to page 254 for the solutions. [**Target: 14**]

1. British pop star arrested for committing a "lewd act" in a public toilet in Beverly Hills.
2. White House intern whose relationship with Bill Clinton lead to his impeachment† in 1998.
3. Athlete who was stripped of his Olympic 100m gold medal after failing a drug test.
4. Pop star alleged to have engaged in sexual activities with teenage boys during sleepovers at his house, but who was acquitted of all charges at trial.
5. Lieutenant Colonel who, while working for the Reagan Administration, diverted funds from the sale of weapons to Iran to the Contra rebels in Nicaragua.
6. Film star who was arrested by Los Angeles Police for indecent conduct in a car with prostitute Divine Brown.
7. Major accounting firm which collapsed after indictment following the Enron accounting scandal.
8. Pop star who experienced a "wardrobe malfunction" during the

---

* The Confederate States of America declared their independence from the United States of America following the election of Abraham Lincoln with a policy of abolition of slavery. The CSA was never formally recognized by the Union, which held its existence as illegal, and the Confederacy collapsed following the surrender of General Robert E. Lee to Union forces in April 1865.

† Clinton's defense (against perjury) relied much upon the definition and interpretation of terms such as "sexual relations." At one point during his Grand Jury testimony Clinton said, "It depends on what the meaning of the word 'is' is."

halftime show of the Super Bowl, generating thousands of complaints from viewers.

9. Homemaking author and television personality convicted of lying to investigators about a stock sale and imprisoned for five months.

10. U.S. Senator prosecuted for leaving the scene of an accident after driving his car off a bridge between Chappaquiddick Island and Martha's Vineyard, killing passenger Mary Jo Kopechne.

11. Car manufacture at the center of a scandal involving a design fault in one of their models in which the rear fuel tank was prone to explode in a rear-end accident.

12. Film director who separated from his partner after she discovered he had taken nude photos of his adopted daughter (whom he later married).

13. U.S. Vice President who resigned in 1973 after being charged with tax evasion.

14. MLB team involved in the "Black Sox Scandal," a betting scandal in which the 1919 World Series was intentionally lost to the Cincinnati Reds.

15. New York Governor who resigned after it was revealed he had used a high-class prostitute service, spending several thousand dollars in the process.

16. U.S. Senator whose presidential ambitions were thwarted after being photographed with Donna Rice on a boat called *Monkey Business*.

17. U.S. Representative who was the subject of media attention after admitting he had had an affair with murdered intern Chandra Levy.

18. Failed real estate venture in which Bill and Hillary Clinton were partners and which led to allegations about the misuse of public funds.

19. NFL team involved in the "Love Boat Scandal," an alleged sex party which took place on two boats on Lake Minnetonka in 2005.

20. Olympic ice skater involved in a conspiracy to harm fellow competitor Nancy Kerrigan at the U.S. Figure Skating Championships in 1994, causing an injury which forced Kerrigan to withdraw.

21. Television evangelist who lost his ministry after being photographed meeting prostitutes in 1988.
22. Singer who caused controversy by ripping up a picture of the pope on *Saturday Night Live*.
23. Female athlete stripped of her record-breaking title in the 1980 Boston Marathon after it emerged that she had jumped in from the crowd and sprinted to the finish.
24. Children's television host arrested in Sarasota, Florida, in 1991 for indecent exposure.

PROLIFIC SUPER BOWL–WINNING COACHES

Name the *twelve* head coaches who have led their teams to two or more Super Bowl victories. Find the solution on page 211. [Target: 7]

WORDS CONTAINED IN "THEREIN"

Identify the *twelve* words that are contained in the word "therein" (without rearranging or separating any letters). Find the solution on page 253. [Target: 9]

SIGNS OF THE ZODIAC

Name the *twelve* signs of the zodiac (of Western astrology). Go to page 298 for the solution. [Target: 12]

NICKNAMES OF STATES I

Identify the state from its nickname. The solutions may be found on page 316. [Target: 8]

1.	The Aloha State	2.	The Sunshine State
3.	The Empire State	4.	The Prairie State
5.	The Show-me State	6.	The Green Mountain State
7.	The Evergreen State	8.	The Constitution State
9.	The Land of Enchantment	10.	The Centennial State
11.	The Pine Tree State	12.	The Sooner State
13.	The Granite State	14.	The Volunteer State
15.	The Old Dominion	16.	The Badger State
17.	The Palmetto State	18.	The Bay State
19.	The First State	20.	The Cornhusker State
21.	The Equality State	22.	The Sunflower State
23.	The North Star State	24.	The Beehive State

GREEK GODS Name the *twelve* gods of the Dodekatheon—those gods who, according to Greek mythology, resided on Mount Olympus. Find the solution on page 336. [**Target: 5**]

MEMBERS OF OPEC List the *twelve* members of the Organization of Petroleum Exporting Countries (OPEC). Turn to page 254 for the solution. [**Target: 6**]

PRESIDENTIAL INITIALS What names do these presidential initials (in bold) stand for? Find the solutions on page 231. [**Target: 10**]

1.	John **F.** Kennedy	2.	William **J.** Clinton
3.	George **W.** Bush	4.	George **H. W.** Bush
5.	William **H.** Harrison	6.	Harry **S.** Truman
7.	Franklin **D.** Roosevelt	8.	Dwight **D.** Eisenhower
9.	Lyndon **B.** Johnson	10.	Richard **M.** Nixon
11.	James **E.** Carter	12.	Ronald **W.** Reagan
13.	James **K.** Polk	14.	Rutherford **B.** Hayes
15.	Chester **A.** Arthur	16.	William **H.** Taft
17.	Warren **G.** Harding	18.	Gerald **R.** Ford, Jr.
19.	James **A.** Garfield	20.	Herbert **C.** Hoover
21.	**S.** Grover Cleveland	22.	**T.** Woodrow Wilson
23.	**J.** Calvin Coolidge	24.	Ulysses **S.** Grant

SOVIET HERO CITIES Name the *twelve* Hero Cities of the Soviet Union.* Go to page 298 for the solution. [**Target: 5**]

PEOPLE ON DOLLAR BILLS Name the *twelve* people who have appeared on the different denominations of dollar bills issued by the U.S. Federal Reserve. Turn to page 316 for the solution. [**Target: 6**]

---

* "Hero City" is an honorary title awarded by the Soviet Union in recognition of mass acts of heroism in some its cities during the Second World War (the Great Patriotic War). The Hero City is issued with the Order of Lenin and the Gold Star Medal. An obelisk is also erected in the city to mark the achievement.

MISCELLANY XV Answer these questions of a miscellaneous nature. Find the solutions on page 336. [**Target: 10**]

1.   Which American state has previously been under French, Spanish, and Mexican control?

2.   Thespis, in 535 BC, is thought to be the first member of which profession?

3.   The battle of Fort McHenry in Baltimore in 1812 inspired which famous piece of music?

4.   What is the most common street name in Britain?

5.   Which American institution has its headquarters in Langley, Virginia?

6.   Which was the first color film to win the Oscar for Best Picture?

7.   What right for baseball fans was established in 1921 when Reuben Berman won a lawsuit against the New York Giants?

8.   Of which native American tribe were Sitting Bull and Crazy Horse members?

9.   Which president saw the last U.S. troops leave Vietnam?

10. Which singer was once married to Renata Blauel?

11. Which popular expression was first used by tour manager Al Drorin at the end of a concert in Minneapolis in 1954?

12. What type of military hardware is associated with the designers Mikoyan and Gurevich?

13. What was the first major American export good?

14. Which are the only two English words containing the letter group "sthm"?

15. What does NASDAQ stand for?

16. What property was named after Grace Toof, daughter of S. E. Toof, a Memphis newspaper publisher?

17. Which two lakes are connected by the Niagara Falls?

18. A rope ladder hangs over the side of a ship with rungs that are one meter apart. The incoming tide rises at the rate of 80 cm an hour. If, at low tide, water just covers the bottom rung, how many rungs are covered three hours later?

19. Who directed *Alien*?

20. Which English letter corresponds with the letter "c" in Cyrillic?

21. From which flower are vanilla pods obtained?

22. Who is the only person to have won both an Oscar and a Nobel Prize?

23. What procedure at the Montreal Olympics was Princess Anne the only female competitor not to undergo?

24. You have a three-gallon jug, a five-gallon jug and an ample supply of water. How can you measure four gallons of water?

CREATURES IN CHINESE ASTROLOGY Name the *twelve* creatures in Chinese* astrology. Find the solution on page 211. [Target: 10]

CHRISTMAS GIFTS Name the *twelve* gifts sent by "My True Love" in "The Twelve Days of Christmas." The solution is on page 232. [Target: 10]

COOKING TERMS II Identify the cooking terms and dishes from the descriptions provided. Find the solutions on page 254. [Target: 7]

1. Small cubes of fried bread used as a garnish for soups.
2. A Mexican dip made from avocado, garlic, and lime juice.
3. Chicken stuffed with garlic, butter, and chives, covered in bread crumbs and fried.
4. Small pasta squares stuffed with meat or vegetables.
5. French sauce made from egg yolk, butter, and vinegar; served with eggs Benedict.
6. A style of Indian cooking (literally meaning "bucket") where dishes are cooked in a karahi (a small, two-handled, wok-shaped pan).
7. The French term for a clear soup.
8. The Italian term for toasted bread brushed with oil and garlic and served with a variety of toppings.
9. A spicy pork sausage from Spain or Mexico.
10. A green Italian pasta sauce made from olive oil, pine nuts, garlic, and basil.
11. A French term meaning "cooked slowly in the oven with cream and garlic."

---

* Chinese horoscopes relate to the twelve-year cycle of the Chinese calendar and the association of an animal with each year of the cycle.

12. The French term for vegetables cut into thin strips.
13. The food flavoring made from sodium salt and glutamic acid.
14. A French term meaning "between the ribs," usually applied to steak.
15. A Provençal fish stew cooked in a strongly flavored stock, usually with saffron and tomatoes.
16. Oysters wrapped in bacon.
17. The French term for a smooth and thick fruit or vegetable purée (literally, "strained").
18. The French term for custard.
19. Bow tie- or butterfly-shaped pasta.
20. Italian omelette usually made with meat, cheese, and vegetables.
21. Spiral-shaped pasta.
22. Soya-bean paste used in Japanese cooking.
23. Paste made from black olives, anchovies, and capers often served on crostini or bruschetta.
24. A French white sauce flavored with onion.

BRIDGES AND TUNNELS IN NEW YORK CITY Name the *twelve* bridges and tunnels which connect to Manhattan Island. Find the solution on page 279. [**Target: 11**]

APOSTLES Name the *twelve* Apostles. Look for the solution on page 298. [**Target: 5**]

DICTATORS Identify the dictators* of these countries from the period of their rule. The solutions are on page 317. [**Target: 10**]

---

* The first use of the term "dictator" was to describe a temporary executive of the Roman Republic, invested with absolute power as an emergency measure deployed during wartime. Probably the best known of these was Lucius Quinctius Cincinnatus, a farmer, who was called to the Senate in 460 B.C. when the Roman Army had got itself into difficulty with the neighbouring Aequi. Although invited to rule for a six-month period, Cincinnatus took just two weeks to defeat the Aequi and sixteen days after taking office was able to return to his farm. The modern use of the word describes an autocratic or tyrannical leader who usually controls a brutal or oppressive regime. Regardless of where in the world they set up their rule, dictatorships have many common characteristics: a swift and often violent rise to power, a preoccupation with remaining in power as long as naturally possible and a tendency to amass huge fortunes and/or to kill a lot of people. Some dictators fall from power as swiftly and violently as they ascended, but a surprising number manage to live out their entire lives in relative comfort.

1. Germany 1933–45
2. USSR 1924–53
3. Iraq 1979–2003
4. Cuba 1959–2008
5. Zimbabwe 1980–present
6. Uganda 1971–79
7. Italy 1922–43
8. Cambodia 1976–79
9. China 1935–76
10. Iran 1979–89
11. Spain 1939–75
12. Serbia/Yugoslavia 1989–2000
13. Chile 1973–1990
14. Panama 1983–89
15. North Korea 1994–present
16. Romania 1965–89
17. Philippines 1965–86
18. Yugoslavia 1945–80
19. Ethiopia 1930–6; 1941–74
20. Democratic Republic of Congo 1997–2001
21. Liberia 1997–2003
22. Fiji 2000
23. Malawi 1963–97
24. Nigeria 1993–98

SATURDAY NIGHT LIVE "5 TIMERS" Name the *twelve* people who have hosted *Saturday Night Live* five or more times.* Look to page 336 for the solution. [**Target: 6**]

CHART-TOPPING SINGLES BY THE SUPREMES Name the *twelve* songs by the Supremes to top the Billboard Hot 100. The solution is on page 211. [**Target: 4**]

LINKED MISCELLANY IX Answer these questions and deduce the theme that links them. Find the solutions on page 232. [**Target: 6**]

---

* Excluding appearances as musical guest.

1. Which 1992 Robert Altman film, about a film executive who believes he is being blackmailed by a scriptwriter, is famous for the large number of cameo roles by Hollywood stars?

2. Who was Sherlock Holmes's sidekick?

3. What name is given to the system of logic where truth is handled on a relative scale (a scale from completely true to completely false) rather than as absolute values (true or false)?

4. How did the summer of 1967, which saw sexual and creative freedom emerge with the Hippie movement, particularly centered on San Francisco, become known?

5. Which British admiral was killed at the Battle of Trafalgar after leading his fleet to victory?

6. Who did the Beatles sing "for the benefit of" on their album *Sgt. Pepper's Lonely Hearts Club Band*?

7. Who played Crocodile Dundee?

8. What name is given to a pair of equal and opposite forces whose lines of action do not coincide, for example the forces exerted by your hand on a screwdriver?

9. Which correctional facility is situated in Ossining, New York, about 30 miles north of New York City?

10. What name from the natural world is given to an economy that experiences rapid levels of growth?

SGT. PEPPER'S LONELY HEARTS CLUB BAND Recall the *twelve* tracks on *Sgt. Pepper's Lonely Hearts Club Band*, the acclaimed Beatles album. (Note there are thirteen actual tracks but one is repeated.) You will find the solution on page 254. [**Target:** 5]

FILMS BY STANLEY KUBRICK Name the *thirteen* feature films directed by Stanley Kubrick. Go to page 280 for the solution. [**Target:** 5]

TAGLINES OF POPULAR FILMS II Identify the films from their taglines and dates of release. The solutions are on page 298. [**Target:** 10]

1. "Houston, we have a problem." (1995)
2. "They're on a mission from God." (1980)

3. "He's having the day of his life . . . over and over again." (1993)

4. "Twelve is the new eleven." (2004)

5. "The list is life." (1993)

6. "Five criminals. One lineup. No coincidence." (1995)

7. "How far does a girl have to go to untangle her tingle?" (1972)

8. "A comedy about the greatest love story almost never told . . ." (1998)

9. "Come to laugh, come to cry, come to care, come to terms." (1983)

10. "Revenge is a dish best served cold." (2004)

11. "Collide with destiny." (1997)

12. "An undercover cop in a class by himself." (1990)

13. "A hero will rise." (2000)

14. "On the air, unaware." (1998)

15. "One dream. Four Jamaicans. Twenty below zero." (1993)

16. "Boy, have we got a vacation for you . . ." (1973)

17. "An epic of miniature proportions." (1998)

18. "With the right song and dance, you can get away with murder" (2002)

19. "They're not just getting rich . . . they're getting even." (1983)

20. "Flesh seduces. Passion kills." (1992)

21. "An assassin on the loose. A president in danger. Only one man stands between them . . ." (1993)

22. "We don't need no education" (2003)

23. "Love is in the hair." (1998)

24. "It's better to be a fake somebody than a real nobody" (1999)

DREAM TEAM Recall the *twelve* members of the Dream Team, the U.S. basketball Team at the 1992 Summer Olympics.* The solution is on page 232. [**Target: 5**]

---

* At the Barcelona Olympics, NBA players were allowed to compete in the Basketball tournament for the first time. The U.S. Basketball team contained ten players who would be named in the NBA's 50 Greatest Players of All Time and cruised to the gold medal easily; coach Chuck Daly did not use a single time-out.

CHARACTERS IN *HAPPY DAYS* Recall the *thirteen* main*
characters in *Happy Days*.† The solution is on page 317.
[**Target: 6**]

COUNTRIES WITH NAMES CONTAINING ADJECTIVES List
the *thirteen* countries with names that contain adjectives (but
excluding adjectives in the titles of countries, for example
"Democratic"). Turn to page 336 for the solution. [**Target: 7**]

NOTORIOUS SHIPS II Identify each of these ships from the clues
provided. Find the solutions on page 212. [**Target: 10**]

1. Vessel that sailed from Plymouth to Cape Cod in
    Massachusetts in 1620 carrying pilgrim fathers who founded
    the first colony in New England.
2. Soviet Typhoon-class submarine of the eponymous 1984
    thriller novel by Tom Clancy.
3. Vessel on which Columbus first sailed to the New World in
    1492.
4. Jack Sparrow's pirate ship.
5. Galley commanded by Jason in greek mythology.
6. Vessel featuring in the eponymous song on the *Revolver* album
    by the Beatles.
7. Russian attack submarine that sank in 2000 with the loss of
    her entire crew.
8. German battleship sunk in 1941 after an engagement with the
    British Navy in which HMS *Hood* was sunk.
9. Supertanker that ran aground off the coast of Alaska in 1989
    causing widespread environmental damage.
10. Cruise ship launched in 2006 and currently the largest
    passenger liner in the world.
11. Launched in 1797, one of six original ships commissioned for
    the American Navy and the oldest warship afloat.

---

* These characters all appeared in twenty-five episodes or more.
† *Happy Days* gave rise to the term "jumping the shark," used to describe the
moment a television series has passed its peak or strayed beyond the bounds of its
original quality. The term refers to a 1977 episode of *Happy Days* in which a
waterskiing Fonzie, wearing swimming trunks and his trademark leather jacket, jumps
a shark.

12. U.S. aircraft carrier on which the Japanese surrender in the Second World War was officially taken in 1945.

13. British battleship launched in 1906 that so revolutionized battleship design that existing vessels became regarded as obsolete.

14. Launched in 1968, the lead ship of the largest class of U.S. aircraft carrier.

15. The world's first nuclear-powered submarine.

16. Fictional vessel of the eponymous third book of the Chronicles of Narnia.

17. Fictional minesweeper featuring in the *Caine Mutiny*.

18. Frigate from which John Paul Jones captured HMS *Serapis* during the American Revolutionary War.

19. Italian cruise liner sunk by a collision with another liner, the *Stockholm*, in fog in the Atlantic in 1956.

20. U.S. Navy warship sunk by a Japanese submarine four days after carrying the first atomic bomb from San Francisco to Guam.

21. Captain Ahab's whaling vessel in *Moby-Dick*.

22. The first ever ironclad and turreted warship, which took part in the Battle of Hampton Roads on March 9th, 1862, during the American Civil War.

23. Mr. Burns's yacht in *The Simpsons*.

24. American battleship commissioned in 1916 and sunk during the Japanese attack on Pearl Harbor in 1941.

PUNCTUATION Identify the *thirteen* types of punctuation marks used in written English. Turn to page 232 for the solution. [Target: 10]

CANADIAN PROVINCES AND TERRITORIES Name the *thirteen* provinces and territories of Canada. Find the solution on page 255. [Target: 7]

MISCELLANY XVI Answer these questions of a miscellaneous nature. Turn to page 280 for the solutions. [Target: 8]

1. If it rains on St. Swithin's Day, for how many more days is it supposed to rain?

2. In which city would you find the Spanish Steps?

3. Where did the first subway system open in the U.S. in 1897?

4. Montezuma II was the last Emperor of which civilization?

5. What did Edwin Drake find in Titusville, Pennsylvania, in 1859?

6. What overtook ketchup as the bestselling condiment in the U.S. in 1991?

7. What common English word is derived from the phrase "God be with you"?

8. According to the song, what did Molly Malone sell on the streets of Dublin?

9. If you travelled due east from Cape Horn, where would you next hit land?

10. James Monroe in 1820 and which other U.S. president were the only two presidential candidates to run unopposed?

11. Which fabric is woven from metallic yarns and has a name deriving from the Latin "lamina" meaning a thin layer of metal?

12. Which English county gave its name to a geological era?

13. Which character is the female lead in *Chitty Chitty Bang Bang*?

14. In which organ of the body is insulin produced?

15. What is significant about the geological period called the Holocene?

16. What is the deepest lake in the U.S.?

17. The accidental ommission of which word led to a bible published in 1632 becoming known as the "wicked bible"?

18. Which TV show features a pair of cynical characters called Statler and Waldorf?

19. The assault on which D-Day beach is depicted in *Saving Private Ryan*?

20. What number is represented in the Seal of the United States?

21. A clock chimes to signal six o'clock (with six chimes) in five seconds. How long will it take for the same clock to signal twelve o'clock?

22. Which family* has produced three generations of Oscar winners?

23. The town of Ytterby, in Sweden, is unique in having given its name to four types of what?

---

* Two families have achieved this—name either.

24. When the day after tomorrow is yesterday, then today is as far away from Saturday as the day that was today when the day before yesterday was tomorrow. What day is it tomorrow?

VITAMINS Name the *thirteen* vitamins that are required as part of a healthy diet. Find the solution on page 299. [**Target: 6**]

COUNTRIES IN SOUTH AMERICA Name the *thirteen* countries in the continent of South America. Turn to page 318 for the solution. [**Target: 11**]

IMPERIAL UNITS Identify the single imperial unit* that measures each of the quantities presented. The solutions are on page 337. [**Target: 8**]

1.	12 inches	2.	3 feet
3.	16 ounces	4.	$\frac{1}{36}$ yard
5.	$\frac{1}{8}$ gallon	6.	14 pounds
7.	5,280 feet	8.	4 quarts
9.	20 hundredweight	10.	$\frac{1}{20}$ pint
11.	4,840 square yards	12.	$\frac{1}{8}$ mile
13.	16 drams	14.	4 inches
15.	2 yards	16.	112 pounds
17.	3 nautical miles	18.	$\frac{1}{10}$ furlong
19.	2 pints	20.	5 fluid ounces
21.	6,076 feet	22.	120 acres
23.	18 inches	24.	8 gallons

HIGHEST-EARNING DEAD CELEBRITIES Name the *thirteen* highest-earning dead celebrities.† Look to page 212 for the solution. [**Target: 6**]

---

* The imperial system of units originated in Britain and is so called because of its export and use in the colonies of the British Empire. The system has been largely abandoned in the UK and the Commonwealth, losing its legal status in the UK in 1995 (although the use of pints, miles, acres, and troy ounces is still permitted). Imperial units, in spite of their irregularity, are still in widespread use in the United States.

† As named by *Forbes* in 2007.

FOUNDING STATES Recall the *thirteen* founding states of the U.S. Look to page 233 for the solution. [**Target: 11**]

LAST LINES OF POPULAR FILMS I Identify each film from its concluding line of dialogue. (The date of the film is provided to assist you.) Find the solutions on page 255. [**Target: 10**]

1. "The name's Bond . . . James Bond." (2006)
2. "I'm not gonna leave here ever, ever again because I love you all! And oh, Auntie Em, there's no place like home!" (1939)
3. "I do wish we could chat longer, but I'm having an old friend for dinner." (1991)
4. "Louis, I think this is the beginning of a beautiful friendship." (1942)
5. "The greatest trick the Devil ever pulled was convincing the world he didn't exist. And like that, he's gone." (1995)
6. "I hope I can make it across the border. I hope to see my friend and shake his hand. I hope the Pacific is as blue as it has been in my dreams. I hope." (1994)
7. "It was Beauty killed the Beast." (1933)
8. "Roads? Where we're going, we don't need roads." (1985)
9. "Hey, I don't have all the answers. In life, to be honest, I failed as much as I succeeded, but I love my wife, I love my life, and I wish you my kind of success." (1996)
10. "He's my brother." (1983)
11. "Way to go, Paula! Way to go!" (1982)
12. "The horror. The horror." (1979)
13. "Mein Führer! I can walk!" (1964)
14. "Good. For a moment there, I thought we were in trouble." (1969)
15. "Alright Mr. De Mille. I'm ready for my close-up." (1950)
16. "It will be a love story . . . for she will be my heroine for all time. And her name will be . . . Viola." (1998)
17. "You be careful John Book, out among them English!" (1985)
18. "The old man was right, only the farmers won. We lost. We'll always lose." (1960)
19. "Some men get the world, others get ex-hookers and a trip to Arizona." (1997)

20. "OK folks, nothin' to worry about. Just a little illness. We'll be in Miami in just a few minutes." (1969)
21. "Oh, yes, I believe in friends, I believe we need them, but if, one day, you find you can't trust them any more, well, what then, what then?" (1994)
22. "This is Hollywood. Always time to dream, so keep on dreamin.'" (1990)
23. "This was the story of Howard Beale, the first known instance of a man who was killed because he had lousy ratings." (1976)
24. "Madness. Madness." (1957)

COUNTRIES BORDERING CHINA List the *fourteen* countries that border China. Turn to page 281 for the solution. [**Target: 9**]

AMERICAN LEAGUE OF MAJOR LEAGUE BASEBALL Recall the *fourteen* MLB teams in the American League. The solution is on page 212. [**Target:12**]

MARX BROTHERS FILMS Name the *fourteen* Marx Brothers films. You will find the solution on page 299. [**Target: 4**]

BRITISHISMS II For each of these words, supply the equivalent word or words that would be used in Britain. The solutions are on page 318. [**Target: 8**]

1.	Candy	2.	Elevator
3.	Potato chips	4.	Gas
5.	Résumé	6.	Checkers
7.	Closet	8.	Drapes
9.	Faucet	10.	Freeway
11.	Line	12.	Sidewalk
13.	Subway	14.	Tuxedo
15.	Zucchini	16.	Jelly
17.	Tic Tac Toe	18.	Yam
19.	Teller	20.	Icebox
21.	Suspenders	22.	Stroller
23.	Parakeet	24.	Mortician

BRITISH NOBILITY Identify the *fourteen* titles of the British nobility. (Note the list includes both masculine and feminine variants.) Find the solution on page 337. [**Target: 10**]

COUNTRIES BORDERING RUSSIA List the *fourteen* countries that have borders with Russia. Go to page 212 for the solution. [**Target: 9**]

STATE CAPITALS I Identify each state from its capital. The solution is on page 233. [**Target: 12**]

1.	Oklahoma City	2.	Honolulu
3.	Indianapolis	4.	Denver
5.	Austin	6.	Sacramento
7.	Salt Lake City	8.	Baton Rouge
9.	Des Moines	10.	Augusta
11.	Harrisburg	12.	Columbus
13.	Springfield	14.	Providence
15.	Montpelier	16.	Saint Paul
17.	Topeka	18.	Madison
19.	Salem	20.	Lincoln
21.	Bismarck	22.	Lansing
23.	Annapolis	24.	Olympia

VICE PRESIDENTS BECOMING PRESIDENT Name the *fourteen* people to have held the both the offices of vice president and president of the United States. Look to page 255 for the solution. [**Target: 7**]

MUSICALS BY ANDREW LLOYD WEBBER Name the *fourteen* musicals composed by Andrew Lloyd Webber. The solution is on page 281. [**Target: 5**]

"ISMS" I Identify the philosophies, beliefs, concepts, or practices from the descriptions provided. (Note that all of the solutions contain the suffix "~ism.") You will find the solutions on page 299. [**Target: 12**]

1. The practice of exclusion of meat and fish from diet.
2. An eponymous ideological theory or practice based on the works of Karl Marx and Friedrich Engels.
3. A doctrine defined separately as either the entire Christian religion or the branch of the Christian religion distinct from Protestantism and Eastern Orthodoxy.
4. The belief in the nonexistence of God.
5. A hostility or institutionalized prejudice against Jews.
6. The promotion of the rights of women and of gender equality.
7. The practice of deriving pleasure from the combination of inflicting and receiving physical or emotional abuse.
8. The economic system in which capital and the means of production are privately owned and not subject to government intervention.
9. The favoritism shown to relatives by those in positions of power.
10. A political ideology that emerged in Europe in the 1920s emphasising the power of the state, the right of a self-constituted elite to run it, the desirability of war to advance it and the ruthless exclusion of political ideologies, religions, or ethnic groups deemed not to fit with the vision of the state.
11. The doctrine founded by Prince Siddhartha Gautama, known as "The Enlightened One," in which a cycle of lives leading to nirvana is a central belief.
12. A political system in which governmental power is divided between a center and autonomous regional units.
13. The view that matter and material items are the only reality and emotions and mental experiences can be described in material terms; the desire for material or monetary items over spiritual or ethical pursuits.
14. The advocacy of the abolition of government and state apparatus and the rule of law.
15. An ambiguous term meaning either a general opposition to change or a political ideology incorporating beliefs such as advocacy of minimal government intervention, tight fiscal control, and protection of existing social conventions.
16. The oldest of the three desert monotheist religions, from which both Christianity and Islam developed.

17. An eponymous political and ethical ideology inspired by the teaching of Confucius.

18. A social system in which serfs are bound to work for landowners in return for security and justice.

19. The doctrine that all human beings are equal and the advocacy of equality through political means.

20. The moral philosophy proposed by John Stuart Mill and Jeremy Bentham that the greatest happiness of the greatest number of people is the central criterion to morality.

21. A belief, in contrast to the doctrine of free will, which asserts all actions and events are predetermined and causally linked and that only a single set of outcomes is possible in the future.

22. A philosophical movement asserting the meaning of the human state should be derived from the beliefs, experiences, and choices of the individual and in contradiction to classical philosophy, which sought to understand the meaning of the human state and derive from this how humans should behave. The movement was promoted particularly by the work of Jean-Paul Sartre, Friedrich Nietzsche, and Albert Camus.*

23. The philosophical view that the world and all human experience is without meaning.

24. The belief that statements are only meaningful so long as they are empirical (measurable) or tautological (true or false by definition); a statement such as "God exists," being neither measurable by human experience nor provable by logic, would be irrelevant in this philosophy.

PROLIFIC CHART-TOPPING FEMALE ARTISTS List the *fourteen* female artists who have topped the Billboard Hot 100 singles chart four or more times. Look to page 318 for the solution. [**Target: 9**]

CAREER GRAND SLAMS Name the *fourteen* tennis players to have accomplished a career grand slam—singles titles in each of the four major tennis tournaments. Find the solution on page 337. [Target: 6]

---

* Camus played goalie for Algeria until tuberculosis cut short his soccer career. He once said: "All I know most surely about morality and obligations, I owe to soccer."

MISCELLANY XVII Answer these questions of a miscellaneous nature. The solutions are on page 213. [**Target: 10**]

1. In geometry, what type of line bisects a circle?
2. Who wrote *The Blue Danube*?
3. In *A Christmas Carol*, what did the Cratchits have for their Christmas dinner?
4. Which year followed 1 B.C.?
5. Who wrote the novels *The Invisible Man* and *The Island of Doctor Moreau*?
6. Scenes from which film were shot in a Brooklyn night club called 2001 Odyssey?
7. In which city is the European Central Bank?
8. Which state takes its name from a phrase meaning "green mountain"?
9. What is Spider-Man's real name?
10. Which game show was originally going to be called "what's the question"?
11. The Gulf of Tonkin Resolution, passed by the U.S. Congress, authorized the use of force in which area of the world?
12. To the nearest million, what was the slave population of the U.S. at its height?
13. What scientific English word, coined in 1805 by Jean-Baptiste Lamarck, comes from a Greek word meaning "to talk about life"?
14. What is Adam's Ale?
15. What does VSOP on a brandy bottle stand for?
16. Which fabric is so named because it originally came from the French town of Nîmes?
17. It has been known as Hi-Catoctin and Shangri-La and is now called the Naval Support Facility Thurmont, but how is it popularly known?
18. Which fictional character was based on the exploits of a mutinous Scottish sailor named Alexander Selkirk?
19. Which major American city is named after a British prime minister?
20. What does a cotton gin do?
21. If you were born on the Feast of Epiphany, which star sign would you be?
22. Which five cities beginning with the letter "M" have hosted the Summer Olympic Games?

23. Whose catchphrase was "Heavens to Murgatroid"?
24. A tramp discovers that he can roll a new cigarette from the tobacco of seven discarded cigarette butts. He picks up forty-nine butts and decides to smoke all the cigarettes he can make from them. How many cigarettes did he smoke?

COMIC OPERAS BY GILBERT AND SULLIVAN Name the *fourteen* comic operas by Gilbert and Sullivan. Find the solution on page 233. [**Target:** 5]

EUROZONE List the *fifteen* member states of the Eurozone, that is, countries which have adopted the Euro* as their currency. The solution is on page 317. [**Target:** 7]

UNION OF SOVIET SOCIALIST REPUBLICS Recall the *fifteen* member nations of the USSR.† Turn to page 255 for the solution. [**Target:** 7]

---

* Slovakia is due to join on January 1, 2009. There are more than 600 billion euros in circulation.

† When the Cold War was at its height, the Soviet Union and United States employed a military defense strategy known as Mutually Assured Destruction. Under this strategy, a large nuclear capability was amassed in order to deter an opponent from launching a preemptive strike; although certain to be destructive, such a strike would effectively be suicidal as it would ensure an equally destructive retaliation. A potential flaw in the strategy was that it placed a good deal of faith in electronic detection and early warning systems and in the individuals who operated them. One such individual was a Russian colonel named Stanislav Petrov who worked in a military bunker just outside Moscow. Just past midnight on the morning of Monday November 26, 1983, Colonel Petrov was alerted by a warning of the approach of an incoming American ICBM. This was followed by further warnings consistent with a preemptive nuclear strike against the Soviet Union. The correct procedure for Petrov was to alert the Soviet high command, who may have ordered a counterstrike against NATO. Petrov's intuition was not to trust his computer system and as such he did not respond to the warnings as he should. When the expected strike failed to materialize, while Petrov's judgement was proved to be correct, his failure to follow orders resulted in his being taken for questioning and reassigned and he left the military soon after. The events of that September day came to light in 1998 after the breakup of the Soviet Union and, although his mother country never recognized the significance of his actions, Petrov received recognition of sorts from a California-based organization called the Association of World Citizens who in 2004 honored him with its World Citizen Award. He received a trophy and $1,000.

FORMER NAMES OF COUNTRIES What are these countries called today? The solutions may be found on page 281. [**Target: 8**]

1. Rhodesia
2. Persia
3. Ceylon
4. Siam
5. Kampuchea
6. Mesopotamia
7. Dutch East Indies
8. Abyssinia
9. Tripolitania
10. Transjordan
11. East Pakistan
12. Outer Mongolia
13. Formosa
14. British Honduras
15. South West Africa
16. Upper Peru
17. New France
18. Aden
19. Upper Volta
20. Gold Coast
21. Trucial States*
22. Basutoland
23. Bessarabia
24. Seven Sisters

MOST CAREER STRIKEOUTS BY A PITCHER Name the *fifteen* pitchers who have achieved 3,000 or more strikeouts in their careers.† The solution is on page 299. [**Target: 5**]

FILMS BY DAVID LEAN Recall the *sixteen* films directed by David Lean. Find the solution on page 318. [**Target: 4**]

---

* So called because of a truce Britain had with a number of Arab sheiks in the nineteenth century.
† The 3,000 Strikeout Club.

METRIC UNITS Identify the physical quantities that are measured by these SI units.* Turn to page 337 for the solutions. [Target: 8]

1.	Celsius (C)	2.	Decibel (dB)
3.	Ampere (A)	4.	Joule (J)
5.	Kelvin (K)	6.	Hertz (Hz)
7.	Watt (W)	8.	Pascal (Pa)
9.	Ohm (W)	10.	Newton (N)
11.	Volt (V)	12.	Candela (cd)
13.	Coulomb (C)	14.	Mole (mol)
15.	Radian (rad)	16.	Becquerel (Bq)
17.	Lux (lx)	18.	Steradian (sr)
19.	Tesla (T)	20.	Farad (F)
21.	Roentgen (R)	22.	Henry (H)
23.	Weber (Wb)	24.	Siemens (S)

NOVELS BY CHARLES DICKENS Name the *sixteen* novels written by Charles Dickens.† Turn to page 215 for the solution. [Target: 8]

---

* The metric system is analogous to the SI system of units which is widely adopted by the international scientific community. SI is an abbreviation of Système International d'Unités, the governing body for the system. The system defines a small number of base units; all other quantities (derived units) are derived from these units. Consequently under this system most measurable quantities that occur in nature are readily comparable and interchangeable. The base units are: metre, kilogram, second, ampere, Kelvin, mole and candela.

† Charles Dickens was born in 1812 and endured an unsettled and impoverished childhood. At the age of sixteen, having taught himself shorthand, Dickens found a job as a court reporter and later as a parliamentary reporter. It was during this period that his twin passions for writing and social reform were to develop, and he started to contribute articles urging reform to radical publications (pressure from Dickens and other campaigners helped bring about the Reform Act of 1832). Dickens also began writing fiction and in 1833 had a story published in the *Monthly Magazine* under the pen name of Boz. He continued to write stories and was commissioned to write his first novel in 1836. Dickens kept up his outspoken campaign for social change by continuing to write articles for journals, but in the end it was his fiction that was probably most effective in drawing attention to the problems of the times in which he lived. He died in 1870.

NATIONAL LEAGUE OF MAJOR LEAGUE BASEBALL Recall the *sixteen* MLB teams in the National League. The solution is on page 282. [Target:14]

PERFORMERS OF JAMES BOND THEMES Name the *seventeen* performers who have sung the theme music to James Bond films.* The solution may be found on page 233. [Target: 10]

LINKED MISCELLANY X Answer the questions below and ascertain the theme linking them. The solutions are on page 255. [Target: 5]

1. Which undefeated military commander was King of Macedon in ancient Greece from 336 until 323 B.C.?
2. How is the area covered by New York County, the most densely populated area in the United States, more commonly known?
3. In *Grease*, what was the name of the gang which Jan, Marty, Frenchy, and Betty Rizzo belong to?
4. Which 1988 film starred Mel Gibson and Michelle Pfeiffer?
5. Which Japanese word, used in a military context, translates as "divine wind"?
6. Which Scottish folk hero was made famous by Daniel Defoe in 1723 and by Sir Walter Scott in 1817?
7. Which 1971 film starring Gene Hackman won a clutch of Academy Awards including Best Picture?
8. How is a Stratofortress better known?
9. Which guitar manufacturer produced the Les Paul, the SG, the Explorer, and the Flying V?
10. Which magazine did Helen Gurley Brown, author of *Sex and the Single Girl*, famously turn around when she become editor-in-chief in 1965?

---

* The James Bond theme is one of the most recognizable pieces of music in the world, but the credit for writing it has been a subject of controversy. Monty Norman, who wrote the soundtrack for *Dr. No* in 1962, is credited with the composition, but it has often been claimed that the theme itself was written by John Barry, brought in by producers Cubby Broccoli and Harry Saltzman to work on it for a one-off fee. The matter was settled in the High Court when Norman successfully sued *The Sunday Times*, who had made such an allegation, for libel in 2001, and was awarded £30,000 in damages.

BOXING WEIGHT DIVISIONS Identify the *seventeen* weight categories* in the sport of boxing† (as defined by the World Boxing Association). Find the solution on page 281. [**Target: 6**]

BEACH BOYS HITS Recall the *seventeen* singles which have been top ten hits on the Billboard Hot 100. Look to page 234 for the solution. [**Target: 5**]

SUPER BOWL WINNERS Recall the *seventeen* teams which have won the Super Bowl. The solution is on page 300. [**Target: 14**]

LATIN PHRASES I Identify the commonly-used Latin phrase or its abbreviation from these English translations.‡ The solutions are on page 319. [**Target: 8**]

1.	Before midday	2.	The Year of Our Lord
3.	Written after	4.	Which was demonstrated
5.	The state which exists	6.	By year
7.	Interrupted intercourse	8.	That is
9.	Bountiful mother	10.	At first sight
11.	Around, approximately	12.	For a special purpose
13.	On behalf of	14.	For example
15.	Compare with	16.	Remarkable year
17.	A great work	18.	One thing for another
19.	With good faith	20.	In fact
21.	First among equals	22.	And other things
23.	In the act of a crime	24.	Said in passing

---

* There are seventeen recognized weight divisions, although only eight of these are commonly used. Olympic fights have eleven weight divisions, including super heavyweight.

† The Queensberry Rules were drafted in 1857 by a boxer called John Chambers and patronized by John Douglas, the eighth Marquis of Queensberry. Prior to this, boxing had been dangerous, brutal, and mostly illegal. The Queensberry Rules mandated the use of gloves and divided matches into three-minute rounds with one-minute intervals between them. It remains the code governing professional boxing today.

‡ In 1844, General Charles Napier, in violation of his orders, led a British force to conquer Sind (nowadays the area of southern Pakistan containing Hyderabad). It is apocryphal that, after his conquest, Napier sent a one-word communication to his superiors; "Pecavvi," meaning: "I have sinned."

NOVELS BY THOMAS HARDY Recall the titles of the *seventeen* novels by Thomas Hardy.* The solution may be found on page 338. [Target: 5]

ANIMAL CRACKERS Name the *eighteen* types of animals currently found in Barnum's Animal Crackers. Turn to page 213 for the solution. [Target: 12]

ADVERTISING SLOGANS III Identify the products that were promoted with these advertising slogans. Look to page 234 for the solutions. [Target: 14]

1. "M'm! M'm! Good!"
2. "Don't leave home without it"
3. "Where's the beef?"
4. "Think outside the bun"
5. "All the news that's fit to print"
6. "Good to the last drop"
7. "The breakfast of champions"
8. "Born to perform"
9. "It gives you wings"
10. "Like a rock"
11. "You're the boss"
12. "Do you have the bunny inside?"
13. "The ultimate driving machine"
14. "Plink plink fizz"
15. "Live in your world, play in ours"
16. "Stock market for the digital world"

---

* Thomas Hardy was born in Dorset in 1840 and wrote novels depicting the harsh lives and bleak outlook of ordinary country people during the nineteenth century. For the early part of his career Hardy lived in London, but after his books became popular he moved back down to Dorset, where he settled with his first wife, Emma Lavinia Gifford (whom he had married in 1874), at Max Gate in Dorchester, a house Hardy designed. In the latter part of his life, Hardy turned his attention to writing poetry, which had always been his great passion. After the death of Emma in 1912, he married his secretary, Florence Dugdale (who was forty years his junior), and died at the age of eighty-eight in 1928. After his death, Hardy's ashes were interred in Westminster Abbey, but his heart was buried in Stinsford in Dorset.

17. "When good is not enough"
18. "1,000 songs in your pocket"
19. "Full speed ahead"
20. "Jack's back"
21. "Wouldn't you really rather have a _____?"
22. "We answer to a higher authority"
23. "Just what the doctor ordered"
24. "The spirit of '76"

OLYMPIC HOST NATIONS Name the *eighteen* nations to have hosted the Olympic Games. Find the solution on page 256.
[Target: 10]

MISCELLANY XVIII Answer these questions of miscellaneous nature. The solutions are on page 300.
[Target: 12]

1. Which British Prime Minister won the Nobel Prize for Literature in 1953?
2. What links the characters of Banquo in *Macbeth* and Jacob Marley in *A Christmas Carol*?
3. What was Vermont the first colony to abolish in 1777?
4. What is the sum of degrees in the internal angles in a triangle?
5. Which patterned textile of tear-shaped motifs takes its name from a town in Scotland?
6. Which mountain, until 1865, was known as Peak XV?
7. Which artistic movement are Degas, Renoir, and Monet said to belong to?
8. Who lives at 123-½ Sesame Street?
9. What color is the bottom stripe of the Stars and Stripes?
10. What were the first names of Lewis and Clark?
11. How many funnels did the *Titanic* have?
12. Which organiszation has the motto: "Fidelity, Bravery, Integrity"?
13. What was first sold as the "Pluto Platter," becoming known by its more familiar name in 1958?
14. What links Caesar Cardini, Philippe de Mornay, and Anna Pavlova?

15. Which 1924 composition was billed as "An experiment in modern music"?
16. Which two countries have names beginning with the letter "A" but not ending with the letter "A"?
17. Which musical features the Cole Porter song "Who Wants to Be a Millionaire"?
18. Musky Muskrat is the sidekick of which cartoon character?
19. What is the title of the film about a Scottish village that awakens once every 100 years?
20. Who founded the Library of Congress?
21. The cost of painting lines on a road to divide it into three lanes is $100. How much would it cost to divide the road into six lanes?
22. Which two countries fought the Football War in 1969?
23. Which English word originates from the practice in the French royal court of providing tickets to visiting dignitaries with written instructions describing the expected code of behavior?
24. A bottle of wine costs $10. If the wine costs $9 more than the bottle, how much is the bottle worth?

STORIES BY ROALD DAHL Name the *eighteen* children's stories written by Roald Dahl. The solution is on page 319. [**Target:** 5]

CHART-TOPPING SINGLES BY ELVIS PRESLEY Name the *eighteen* singles by Elvis Presley* to have topped the Billboard Hot 100. Find the solution on page 338. [**Target:** 5]

FILMS AND THEIR STARS IV Identify the films from these selected cast members and the date of release. Find the solutions on page 213. [**Target:** 10]

---

* Elvis Aaron Presley was born in Tupelo, Mississippi, in 1935. By his death in 1977, he had outsold every other recording artist, then or since, with global record sales of over 1 billion copies. Over 130 of his albums and singles have achieved gold (sales of over 500,000 copies), platinum (sales of over 1 million) or multiplatinum status. He also made thirty-three films.

1. John Hurt, Ian Holm, Harry Dean Stanton, Sigourney Weaver (1979)
2. Julie Andrews, Christopher Plummer (1965)
3. Robert Shaw, Richard Dreyfuss, Roy Scheider (1975)
4. Harrison Ford, Robert Duvall, Martin Sheen, Dennis Hopper, Marlon Brando (1979)
5. Robert De Niro, Andy Garcia, Sean Connery, Kevin Costner (1987)
6. Antonio Banderas, Denzel Washington, Tom Hanks (1993)
7. Julianne Moore, Steve Buscemi, Jeff Bridges, John Goodman (1998)
8. Michelle Pfeiffer, Jeff Bridges, Beau Bridges (1989)
9. Daniela Bianchi, Robert Shaw, Sean Connery (1963)
10. Elizabeth Taylor, Rock Hudson, James Dean (1956)
11. Robert Redford, Dustin Hoffman (1976)
12. Omar Sharif, Julie Christie, Alec Guinness (1965)
13. Elizabeth Taylor, Paul Newman (1958)
14. Bill Murray, Scarlett Johansson, Giovanni Ribisi (2003)
15. Ray Winstone, Anthony Hopkins, Angelina Jolie, Crispin Glover, Robin Wright Penn, John Malkovich (2007)
16. Gene Hackman, Anjelica Huston, Gwyneth Paltrow, Ben Stiller, Luke Wilson, Owen Wilson, Danny Glover, Bill Murray (2001)
17. James Mason, Julie Christie, Warren Beatty (1978)
18. Danny Glover, Whoopi Goldberg (1985)
19. Nicolas Cage, Giovanni Ribisi, Angelina Jolie, Robert Duvall (2000)
20. Tom Berenger, Glenn Close, Jeff Goldblum, William Hurt, Kevin Kline (1983)
21. Jude Law, Nicole Kidman, Renée Zellweger (2003)
22. Adam Sandler, Kate Beckinsale, Christopher Walken, Henry Winkler, Julie Kavner, David Hasselhoff (2006)
23. Maggie Smith, Michael Gambon, Kristin Scott Thomas, Charles Dance, Kelly MacDonald, Clive Owen, Richard E. Grant, Helen Mirren, Eileen Atkins, Emily Watson, Derek Jacobi (2001)
24. Charlize Theron, Christina Ricci, Bruce Dern (2003)

WORLD HERITAGE SITES IN THE UNITED STATES Recall the *nineteen* World Heritage Sites* in the U.S.† You can find the solution on page 235. [**Target: 7**]

BEATRIX POTTER TALES Identify the *nineteen* Beatrix Potter tales.‡ The solution§ can be found on page 256. [**Target: 5**]

NICKNAMES OF MONARCHS Identify each of these British monarchs from their nicknames. You will find the solutions on page 282. [**Target: 10**]

1.	The Lionheart	2.	The Virgin Queen
3.	The Confessor	4.	The Great
5.	Bloody Mary	6.	Longshanks
7.	The Unready	8.	Bluff King Hal
9.	Crookback	10.	The Nine-day Queen
11.	The Bastard	12.	The Merry Monarch
13.	The Widow of Windsor	14.	Lackland
15.	Farmer George	16.	Rufus
17.	Brandy Nan	18.	Ironside
19.	Curtmantle	20.	Beauclerc

---

* The World Heritage List was established by UNESCO (United Nations Educational, Scientific and Cultural Organization) in 1972 to define and help protect cultural or natural sites of "outstanding universal value." In June, 2007, there were 830 Heritage Sites listed in 138 countries; higher-profile sites include the Grand Canyon National Park, the Great Wall of China, Machu Picchu, the Acropolis, the Pyramids at Giza, and the Great Barrier Reef.

† The list excludes La Fortaleza and the San Juan National Historic Site in Puerto Rico.

‡ Beatrix Potter was born in 1866 in Kensington, London. As a child she spent her summers in the Lake District where her love of nature developed and she would while away her time drawing and sketching the many animals that she brought back to the house. The sketches would eventually accompany the stories that she wrote in adulthood. In 1905 she bought Hill Top Farm, which has become the most visited house in the Lake District, and devoted the latter part of her life to farming and particularly to breeding Herdwick sheep. She died in 1943, aged seventy-seven, leaving £200,000 and more than 4,000 acres of land to the National Trust.

§ Specifically titles beginning "*The Tale of . . .*"; Beatrix Potter also penned *The Story of a Fierce Bad Rabbit, The Story of Miss Moppet, Appley Dapply's Nursery Rhymes,* and *Cecil Parsley's Nursery Rhymes.*

21.	Builder	22.	Denmark
23.	Empress Maud	24.	The Sailor King

LARGE BODIES OF WATER List the *twenty* largest bodies of water* (for example oceans, seas, gulfs, and bays) in the world. The solution can be found on page 301. [**Target: 10**]

POPULAR LANGUAGES Name the *twenty* most widely spoken languages in the world (including native speakers and second-language speakers). Turn to page 320 for the solution. [**Target: 10**]

FIRST LINES OF POP SONGS IV Identify the titles of these songs from the first lines below. (The year each song was a hit is supplied to assist you.) For advanced play, name the performers as well. Turn to page 339 for the solutions. [**Target: 10**]

1. "There is a house in New Orleans." (1964)
2. "Get up, get on up." (1970)
3. "Oh baby baby, how was I supposed to know?" (1999)
4. "Goodbye Norma Jean." (1974)
5. "If you see a faded sign by the side of the road." (1989)
6. "On a dark desert highway." (1977)
7. "I wanna kiss you in Paris" (1991)
8. "My baby don't mess around because she loves me so." (2004)
9. "Hey there, here I am, I'm the man on the scene." (1968)
10. "Get your motor running." (1969)
11. "You could have a steam train if you'd just lay down your tracks." (1986)
12. "Nobody on the road, nobody on the beach." (1985)
13. "Though I've tried before to tell her of the feelings I have for her in my heart." (1981)

---

* Two-thirds of the surface of the earth are covered by water but very little is actually known about the ocean floors (around 90% is unexplored). The deepest point in the world is the Challenger Deep of the Marianas Trench, at 10,924 metres (just shy of seven miles) below the surface of the Pacific Ocean off the Philippines. It has been visited only once by man: in 1960 by Jacques Piccard and Don Walsh in their bathyscaphe, *Trieste*. In spite of the staggering pressures, Walsh and Piccard were surprised to witness a strange flatfish swimming on the ocean floor but were unable to take pictures, and the creature was lost to posterity. The cost and high risks of such dives has meant that the pair remain the only men to have been so deep.

14. "I need love, love to ease my mind" (1966)
15. "My tea's gone cold, I'm wondering why I got out of bed at all." (2001/2000)
16. "Girl you know we belong together." (1991)
17. "Well east coast girls are hip I really dig those styles they wear." (1965)
18. "You've been around all night and that's a little long." (1982)
19. "There's no point in asking, you'll get no reply." (1977)
20. "I want to run, I want to hide." (1987)
21. "California . . . knows how to party." (1995)
22. "Time goes by so slowly." (2005)
23. "Come gather round people wherever you roam." (1965)
24. "Here comes Johnny Yen again." (1996)

PROLIFIC CHART-TOPPING ARTISTS Name the *twenty* most prolific chart-topping artists—artists who have had six or more number one singles on the Billboard Hot 100. Find the solution on page 214. [**Target: 10**]

BRITISH PRIME MINISTERS List the *twenty* British Prime Ministers* of the twentieth century. The solution is on page 235. [**Target: 5**]

---

* The term "Prime Minister" was first documented during the premiership of Benjamin Disraeli but not used as an official title until 1905. Robert Walpole (whose tenure endured from 1721 to 1742) is generally regarded to have been the first Prime Minister, although at no point was the position formally created; it came into being mainly because of the way that Walpole dominated politics at the time. Walpole, a Whig, used his influence on the dying Queen Anne to name the Hanoverian George as her successor (rather than the Catholic James Stewart, son of James II). When George arrived from Germany he had no experience of politics or of British life, and relied heavily on the Whigs who had arranged for his succession. He made Walpole his Chancellor of the Exchequer in 1715, and although Walpole briefly fell out of favor, he rose back to prominence as the only member of the government not to be tarnished by the scandal of the South Sea Bubble financial disaster. He subsequently became known as the King's "First Minister." It was widely expected that the succession of George II (in 1727) would be the end of Walpole's tenure, but Walpole had been courting the Waleses by becoming advisor to the Princess of Wales (the future Queen Caroline) and it was even rumored that Mrs. Walpole had become the Prince of Wales's mistress. Such political maneuverings ensured that after the succession of George II, Walpole remained as Prime Minister, a post he kept until 1742. Not only did he define the role of Prime Minister, he is remembered as one of the most skilful political operators ever to rise to high office.

BATTLES II

Name the wars in which these battles were fought. (Note that the same answer may occur more than once.) Look for the solutions on page 257. [**Target: 10**]

1.	Fredericksburg	2.	Saratoga
3.	Britain	4.	Hampton Roads
5.	Dong Xoai	6.	Waterloo
7.	El Alamein	8.	Cowpens
9.	Trafalgar	10.	Arnhem
11.	Ypres	12.	River Plate
13.	Rorke's Drift	14.	Kursk
15.	Sevastopol	16.	Marathon
17.	Ardennes	18.	Arbela
19.	Monte Cassino	20.	Antioch
21.	Austerlitz	22.	Thermopylae
23.	Naseby	24.	Bannockburn

BESTSELLING ALBUMS

Identify the *twenty* best selling albums of all time in the U.S.* Find the solutions on page 282. [**Target: 6**]

LARGE ISLANDS

Name the *twenty* largest islands in the world (not including continental landmasses). The solution can be found on page 301. [**Target: 8**]

PSEUDONYMS II

Identify the pseudonyms by which these people are famously known. You will find the solutions on page 320. [**Target: 12**]

1.	Cherilyn Sarkisian La Pierre	2.	Gerry Dorsey
3.	Theodore Suess Geisel	4.	Eric Blair
5.	Jennifer Anastassakis	6.	Vladimir Ilyich Ulyanov
7.	Cassius Clay	8.	Richard Starkey
9.	Edda Hepburn van Heemstra	10.	Richard Melville Hall
11.	Demetria Gene Guynes	12.	Reginald Dwight
13.	Mary Ann Evans	14.	Greta Gustaffson
15.	Prince Nelson	16.	Sophia Scicolini

---

* As measured by the RIAA.

17.	Robert Van Winkle	18.	Walter Matuschanskayasky
19.	Harry Crosby	20.	Lee Yuen Kam
21.	Martha Jane Burke	22.	Carlos Estevez
23.	Paul Hewson	24.	Calvin Broadus

FREQUENTLY OCCURRING WORDS List the *twenty* most frequently occurring words in written English. Turn to page 339 for the solution. [**Target: 10**]

LARGE LAKES Name the *twenty* largest lakes* in the world. The solution may be found on page 214. [**Target: 6**]

MISCELLANY XIX Answer these questions of a miscellaneous nature. Go to page 236 for the solutions. [**Target: 8**]

1. What links Vienna, Budapest, and *2001: A Space Odyssey*?
2. Which well-known film is an anagram of "Long Fridge"?
3. In what type of auction does the price of an item reduce until a bid is received?
4. What was the Warren Commission established in 1963 to investigate?
5. What did the Thirteenth Amendment to the U.S. Constitution of 1865 prohibit?
6. Who wrote, "You're a better man than I am, Gunga Din!"?
7. How many sides does a STOP sign have?
8. Which two cities are referred to in Charles Dickens's *A Tale of Two Cities*?
9. Which country's presidency was offered to but declined by Albert Einstein?
10. Which sport was established at the Hurlingham Club in London in 1874?
11. Whose birth followed the Immaculate Conception?
12. How many holes are major golf tournaments played over?
13. What was the name of Rosco P. Coltrane's dog in *The Dukes of Hazzard*?

---

* The word lake is a generic term and refers to an area of water surrounded by land, usually of considerable size. See the footnote of the solution (page 214) for a discussion of some candidates that have not been included in the list.

14. The 1905 mutiny on which Russian battleship was the subject of an eponymous, ground-breaking, and highly influential silent film of 1925?

15. Who was the last British monarch to lead an army into battle?

16. Where would you find the Islands of Langerhans?

17. A man dies, leaving $10,000 to be shared between his widow, five sons, and four daughters. According to his will, each daughter should receive an equal amount, each son should receive twice as much as each daughter, and his widow should receive three times as much as each son. How much did the widow receive?

18. Which U.S. state has the motto "Eureka"?

19. What were Eugene Cernan and Harrison Schmitt the last men to do?

20. Which two football teams compete annually in a game known as "The Game"?

21. Which character did Quentin Tarantino play in *Reservoir Dogs*?

22. Who wrote *The Railway Children*?

23. What is the medical name for the collarbone?

24. How many times do the hour and minute hands of an ordinary clock cross in any twelve-hour period of time?

METRIC PREFIXES Name the *twenty* metric prefixes. (Metric prefixes are words which are put before quantities such as scientific units or units of computing capacity to indicate their scale.) The solution is on page 257. [**Target: 10**]

WEALTHY COUNTRIES Identify the *twenty* wealthiest countries in the world, based on per capita Gross Domestic Product. Turn to page 320 for the solution. [**Target: 12**]

ETYMOLOGY OF ROCK AND POP NAMES I Identify the name of the groups or artists from the etymology of their names. The solutions can be found on page 302. [**Target: 10**]

1. After a character in the film *Barbarella* (and also the name of the club in Birmingham where the band first performed).

2. From "Boys Entering Anarchistic States Towards Inner Excellence."

3. A shock name referring to the assassination of two prominent U.S. politicians.
4. From "Ladies Love Cool James."
5. After a medieval torture instrument.
6. Renamed from their original name "The Bangs."
7. From the name of a famous agriculturalist and author of *Horse-Hoeing Husbandry*.
8. From school nicknames of two of the band members, referring to owl-like eyes and puffed-up cheeks.
9. Taken from a French magazine title and meaning "fast fashion."
10. After a German art movement of the 1920s and 1930s.
11. After a pair of characters in the Tintin cartoons by Hergé.
12. Inspired by the band's cramped living conditions while working on their debut album.
13. After a friend's dog who walked with a limp.
14. After a term for obsessive computer enthusiasts.
15. From a Muddy Waters song.
16. Inspired by the Velvet Underground and their song "Venus in Furs."
17. From the title of a "video nasty" featuring a large number of enraged antagonists.
18. From a book by J. R. R. Tolkien.
19. Originally as a parody of Fats Domino's name.
20. After the silver ball in the Woody Allen film, *Sleeper*, which had a drug-like effect when touched.
21. Taken from the title of a Steely Dan song.
22. After the high priestess of Vulcan in *Star Trek*.
23. After the German word for "power plant."
24. From the names of the two founding members added to that of a trucking magazine.

LARGE COUNTRIES List the *twenty* largest countries in the world (by area). Turn to page 283 for the solution. [**Target: 10**]

100 CAREER TOUCHDOWNS Try to name the *twenty* players to have scored one hundred or more touchdowns in the NFL. The solution is on page 321. [**Target: 5**]

WIT AND WISDOM II The following quotations are attributed to either Dorothy Parker, Mae West,* or Joan Rivers. Identify the correct author of each quotation. The solutions are on page 215. [Target: 18]

1. "When I'm good, I'm very good, but when I'm bad, I'm even better."
2. "I told my mother-in-law that my house was her house, and she said, 'Get the hell off my property.'"
3. "One more drink and I'll be under the host."
4. "I used to be Snow White, but I drifted."
5. "My best birth control now is just to leave the lights on."
6. "It's not the men in my life; it's the life in my men."
7. "You can lead a horticulture, but you can't make her think."
8. "The first time I see a jogger smiling, I'll consider it."
9. "All I need is room enough to lay a hat and a few friends."
10. "Keep a diary, and someday it'll keep you."
11. "She runs the gamut of emotions from A to B."
12. "I hate housework. You make the beds, you wash the dishes and six months later you have to start all over again."
13. "It's so long since I've had sex I've forgotten who ties up who."
14. "It is better to be looked over than overlooked."
15. "If all the girls at the Yale Prom were laid end to end, I wouldn't be at all surprised."
16. "The one thing women don't want to find in their stockings on Christmas morning is their husband."
17. "I've never been a millionaire but I just know I'd be darling at it."

---

* Mae West is best known as a screen star but she was also a writer and penned the screenplays of many of the films she appeared in. Having experienced limited success writing a series of risqué Broadway plays (leading to an eight-day prison sentence on public obscenity charges) her breakthrough came in the 1932 film *Night after Night*. Although West only had a small role, she persuaded the producers to allow her to rewrite her lines and gave herself these classic words:

Cloakroom Girl: Goodness, what lovely diamonds!

Mae West: Goodness has nothing to do with it, dearie.

West's next roles would be starring ones and by 1935 she was the highest-earning woman in America. During the war, Allied soldiers gave her name to their inflatable lifejackets, inspired by her well-proportioned figure.

18. "When women go wrong, men go right after them."
19. "This is not a novel to be tossed aside lightly. It should be thrown with great force."
20. "When choosing between two evils I always like to take the one I've never tried before."
21. "Take care of the luxuries and the necessities will take care of themselves."
22. "If God wanted us to bend over he'd put diamonds on the floor."
23. "If you want to know what God thinks of money, just look at the people he gave it to."
24. "That woman speaks eight languages and can't say 'no' in any of them."

CHART-TOPPING SINGLES BY THE BEATLES Try to recall the *twenty* singles by the Beatles* which topped the Billboard Hot 100. Find the solution on page 236. [**Target:10**]

CHARACTERS IN *DALLAS* Recall the *twenty* major† characters in *Dallas*. You can find the solution on page 339. [**Target: 12**]

MEDITERRANEAN COUNTRIES Name the *twenty-one* countries that have coastlines on the Mediterranean Sea (excluding overseas territories). Turn to page 258 for the solution. [**Target: 16**]

---

* Shortly after the Beatles signed to EMI in 1962, their producer, George Martin, was keen for them to release material written by other songwriters, as was the norm for commercial recording artists of the day. The song picked by Martin for the Beatles' first A-side was "How Do You Do It" by Mitch Murray. Although they recorded the Murray song, the group resisted the pressure put on them by the record company to release it. Martin eventually gave in to John and Paul's wish to release their own material, and in September, 1962, "Love Me Do," a credited Lennon/McCartney composition, hit the record stores and, soon after, the charts. The Beatles had created a sound that was fresh and stood out from the beat combo acts that filled the charts at the time. The success of the song assured the future of the Lennon/McCartney writing partnership and the release of many more songs of extraordinary originality and appeal. More significantly, the song broke the mold of the music industry and paved the way for thousands of talented artists to be able to record and release original work from which the world of music has greatly benefited.
† Characters who appeared in any of the opening credits in the show's run of thirteen seasons from 1978 to 1991.

LINKED MISCELLANY XI Answer these questions and determine the theme that links the solutions. Turn to page 283 for the solution. [**Target: 5**]

1. Which 1991 film won Oscars in each of the five major categories (Best Picture, Director, Screenplay, Actor, and Actress), including an award for Jodie Foster?
2. Which Bob Dylan song has been covered by Eric Clapton, Bob Marley, Mark Knopfler, and Guns N' Roses?
3. What is the common name given to any species of insect of the order Diptera, a species which begins life as a maggot?
4. What is the name of the park at the southern tip of Manhattan Island, overlooking New York Harbor?
5. What term was coined by journalist and social commentator H. L. Mencken, in the early 1920s, to describe the geographical area of the U.S. where evangelical Protestantism is a dominant part of the culture?
6. Which 1971 blaxploitation movie starred Richard Roundtree in the title role?
7. What term describes a small camera connected to a PC used to send images over the Internet?
8. What name is given to the marketing of a product for free in the media?
9. How is an intrauterine device better known?
10. Which former member of the Jeff Beck Group and the Faces was once married to Britt Ekland?

JAMES BOND FILMS Name the *twenty-two* (official*) James Bond films. The solution is on page 302. [**Target: 17**]

WORLD SERIES WINNERS Recall the *twenty-two* MLB teams to have won the World Series. Look to page 321 for the solution. [**Target: 10**]

INNOVATIONS II Identify the innovations which were created by these individuals or organizations. The solutions may be found on page 340. [**Target: 12**]

---

* Unofficial films include *Never Say Never Again* (1983) *and Casino Royale* (1965).

1. John Logie Baird (1926)
2. Graf Ferdinand von Zeppelin (1900)
3. Igor Sikorsky (1939)
4. Boeing (1970)
5. Louis Pasteur (1867)
6. Mesopotamians (c. 3500 B.C.)
7. Alexander Fleming (1928)
8. Samuel Colt (1835)
9. Elisha Otis (1851)
10. Anders Celsius (1742)
11. Gottlieb Daimler (1884)
12. Jacques Cousteau (1943)
13. Tim Berners-Lee (1991)
14. Charles Babbage (1835)
15. Thomas Edison (1877)
16. Edward Jenner (1770)
17. Kenneth Wood (1947)
18. Percy Shaw (1934)
19. George Eastman (1889)
20. Tsai Lun (105)
21. Kirkpatrick Macmillan (1839)
22. David Bushnell (1776)
23. Hurley Machine Company (1907)
24. Dan Bricklin and Bob Frankston (1979)

SUPER BOWL LOSERS Recall the *twenty-two* NFL teams to have lost in the Super Bowl. Find the solutions on page 216. [**Target: 16**]

OLYMPIC HOST CITIES Recall the *twenty-two* cities to have hosted the Summer Olympic Games* in the modern era. The solution is on page 237. [**Target: 12**]

---

* The Olympic Games were originally held every four years at Olympia in ancient Greece in honor of the god Zeus, and included competitions in literature, drama, and music as well as sports. These events took place, with intervals, from 776 B.C. until A.D. 394. The modern Olympics began in 1896, appropriately enough, in Greece (the winter games were introduced in 1924). The founder of the modern games, Pierre de Coubertin, had a vision of amateur international athletes competing against each other for the love of sport, once famously saying: "The most important thing in the Olympic Games is not to win but to take part."

TAGLINES OF POPULAR FILMS III

Name the films from the clues provided. The solutions are on page 258. [**Target: 10**]

1. "Just when you thought it was safe to go back into the water . . ." (1978)
2. "Check in. Relax. Take a shower." (1960)
3. "To enter the mind of a killer she must challenge the mind of a madman." (1991)
4. "The toys are back in town." (1995)
5. "Getting back was only the beginning." (1989)
6. "His whole life was a million-to-one shot" (1976)
7. "Five good reasons to stay single." (1994)
8. "The classic story of power and the press." (1941)
9. "With great power comes great responsibility." (2002)
10. "Protecting the earth from the scum of the universe." (1997)
11. "December 7, 1941—a day that shall live in infamy." (2001)
12. "For anyone who's ever been set up, stood up or felt up." (2001)
13. "This is Benjamin . . . he's a little worried about his future." (1967)
14. "They're mean, green and on the screen." (1990)
15. "The year's most revealing comedy." (1997)
16. "Lust. Seduction. Revenge. See the game played as you've never seen it before." (1988)
17. "For God's sake, get out of that house!" (1979)
18. "Same Make. Same Model. New Mission." (1991)
19. "They're young . . . they're in love . . . and they kill people." (1967)
20. "The first casualty of war is innocence" (1986)
21. "Everything you've heard is true." (1999)
22. "His story will touch you, even though he can't." (1990)
23. "In the middle of nowhere there is nowhere to hide." (1989)
24. "Some lines shouldn't be crossed." (1990)

THE CANTERBURY TALES

Name the *twenty-two* pilgrims' tales which make up *The Canterbury Tales.* * Find the solution on page 283. [**Target: 4**]

---

* *The Canterbury Tales,* written by Geoffrey Chaucer, is a collection of stories told by pilgrims on their way to Thomas Becket's shrine in Canterbury. The pilgrims meet at the Tabard Inn, Southwark, where the tavern host, Harry Bailly, proposes they each tell stories on the road, the best of which will receive a free supper. The book was begun around 1387 and remains the most significant literary work of the fourteenth century.

MISCELLANY XX Answer these questions of a miscellaneous nature. The solutions are on page 322. [**Target: 12**]

1. Which is the most westerly country in Europe?
2. What mineral were the Seven Dwarfs mining for?
3. What links the words "racecar" and "kayak"?
4. Which well-known song has these six sections: intro, ballad, guitar solo, opera, heavy metal, outro?
5. With an exhibition of paintings of which consumer product did Andy Warhol first achieve success in 1962?
6. What links the plays *Who's Afraid of Virginia Woolf?* and *Waiting for Godot*?
7. Every Seinfeld episode contained a reference to which super hero?
8. What was the first word spoken from the moon?
9. In Henry Wadsworth Longfellow's famous poem, "Hiawatha," what was the name of Hiawatha's wife?
10. Which English word originally used to describe a medieval mercenary is now applied to any professional hired for a specific piece of work without a long-term commitment to the employer?
11. Which American state is last alphabetically?
12. Which of the Dirty Dozen was also one of the Magnificent Seven?
13. Measured from base to summit, which U.S. mountain is the tallest in the world?
14. In the nursery rhyme, how was Jack's head treated after he had fallen down the hill?
15. Where is the hypo-center of an earthquake in relation to its epicenter?
16. There are a certain number of children in a family. Each boy has the same number of brothers as he has sisters. Each girl has twice as many brothers as she has sisters. How many boys are there and how many girls?
17. Which two countries are connected by the Simplon Pass?
18. For the capture of which English king did Parliament offer a reward of £1,000?
19. What is the nickname of the Nevada State Route 375?
20. How is computerized axial tomography better known?

21. What was first installed in the White House, during the term of Benjamin Harrison in 1889?

22. What does the NFL require teams to provide twenty-four of for each home game?

23. Which blood vessel carries deoxygenated blood from the heart to the lungs?

24. Which number is equal to five times the sum of its digits?

TAROT CARDS List the *twenty-two* cards which make up the Major Arcana (or picture cards) of a deck of Tarot cards.* Find the solution on page 340. [**Target: 8**]

BESTSELLING ARTISTS Recall the *twenty-two* bestselling recording artists—artists who have sold over 50 million records† in the U.S. The solution is on page 216. [**Target: 12**]

EVENTS IN HISTORY III Identify the century in which each of these historical events took place (be even more precise and name the year if you wish). Find the solutions on page 237. [**Target: 12**]

1. Christopher Columbus reaches America.
2. Charles Darwin publishes *On the Origin of Species*.
3. Jesus of Nazareth is crucified in Jerusalem.
4. The Spanish Armada is defeated.
5. English prisoners die in the "Black Hole of Calcutta."
6. The Suez Canal opens.

---

* A traditional Tarot deck consists of seventy-eight cards. There are fourteen cards in each of the four suits (Rods or Wands, Cups, Swords, and Coins or Pentacles) and fifty-six cards which make up the Minor Arcana (Arcana derives from the Latin "arcanum" meaning "hidden things"). In addition, there are twenty-two picture cards which are illustrated with specific symbols and these are known as the Major Arcana. The precise origin of the Tarot deck is not well understood, but is often linked with ancient Egypt or India—although the earliest decks that we know about appeared in Italy in the fifteenth century. It is thought that the Tarot predates the standard fifty-two-card deck and not vice versa, with Clubs corresponding to Rods, Hearts to Cups, Spades to Swords, and Coins to Diamonds. Tarot has a fourth court card, the Knight, which has been dropped in the modern playing deck.

† According to the RIAA.

7. Martin Luther nails his protest to a church door at Wittenberg.
8. Richard III is defeated by Henry Tudor at Bosworth.
9. The Gregorian calendar is adopted in Britain.
10. Marlborough defeats the French at Blenheim.
11. The American Civil War begins.
12. The formulation of the rules of cricket.
13. The Wars of the Roses begin.
14. *On the Revolutions of Heavenly Bodies* is published by Copernicus.
15. The *Daily Courant* becomes the first English newspaper.
16. Lloyds Coffee House becomes an insurance trading center.
17. Michelangelo completes the painting of the Sistine Chapel.
18. Vasco da Gama reaches India.
19. Accession of James VI of Scotland as James I of England.
20. Marco Polo first visits China.
21. Duncan, King of Scotland, is killed by Macbeth.
22. The Great Schism separates Christendom into Eastern Orthodox and Western Roman Catholic churches.
23. St. Bartholomew's Day massacre takes place in Paris.
24. The Archbishopric of Canterbury is founded.

500 HOME RUN CLUB Try to name the *twenty-two* MLB batters who have scored five hundred or more home runs in their careers. The solution may be found on page 322. [**Target: 7**]

ARAB LEAGUE Identify the *twenty-two* members of the Arab League. You will find the solution on page 284. [**Target: 12**]

NICKNAMES OF STATES II Identify each state from its nickname. The solutions are on page 303. [**Target: 12**]

1.	The Golden State	2.	The Grand Canyon State
3.	The Lone Star State	4.	The Bluegrass State
5.	The Last Frontier	6.	The Yellowhammer State
7.	The Keystone State	8.	The Mount Rushmore State
9.	The Buckeye State	10.	The Wolverine State
11.	The Ocean State	12.	The Treasure State
13.	The Tar Heel State	14.	The Peace Garden State

15.	The Mountain State	16.	The Magnolia State
17.	The Peach State	18.	The Hawkeye State
19.	The Hoosier State	20.	The Pelican State
21.	The Silver State	22.	The Old Line State
23.	The Beaver State	24.	The Garden State

COASTAL STATES Name the *twenty-three* states of the U.S. which have coastlines. The solution is on page 258. [**Target: 20**]

LANGUAGES OF THE EUROPEAN UNION Name the *twenty-three* official languages of the European Union. The solution is on page 340. [**Target: 14**]

GOVERNMENTS Identify these types of government by the descriptions provided (the solutions are words ending in "~cracy" or "~archy"). Turn to page 217 for the solutions. [**Target: 8**]

1. Government by a single individual such as a king or queen, perpetuated through the right of inheritance
2. Government by officials or civil servants; implied inefficiency
3. Government by the people, via elections
4. Government by nobility or upper classes; a general term for the upper classes
5. Government by a single individual wielding unlimited power; a dictatorship
6. Government by men or fathers; any social system where men have authority
7. Government by those most deserving; any social system where rewards are earned
8. Government by the Pope
9. Government according to a structured series of ranks or tiers; any organization with a series of tiers
10. Government by the wealthy
11. Government by a few
12. Government by women or mothers; any social system where women have authority
13. Government by foreigners
14. Government by thieves
15. Government by technical experts

16. Government on the basis of religious law or by priests
17. Government by two people
18. Government by simple majority
19. Government by women
20. Government by men
21. Government by elders or the elderly
22. Government by children
23. Government by many people
24. Government by prostitutes

RYDER CUP CAPTAINS Name the *twenty-three* golfers to have captained the U.S. or European Ryder Cup teams since 1979.* Find the solution on page 237. [Target: 5]

ROLLING STONES HITS Recall the *twenty-three* singles by the Rolling Stones† which have reached number ten or higher in the Billboard Hot 100. Look to page 259 for the solution. [Target: 7]

OFFICER RANKS IN THE U.S. MILITARY Recall the *twenty-three* officer ranks in the U.S. armed forces. Look to page 340 for the solution. [Target: 14]

---

* The Ryder Cup was first contested between the U.S. and Europe in 1979. Originally it was contested between the U.S. and Great Britain; however, U.S. dominance of the event led to Great Britain enlisting the help of Ireland in 1971 before enlarging the team to represent the whole of Europe.

† While the group enjoyed sustained commercial success throughout the 1960s their fortunes took a turn for the worse in 1969. With possible prison sentences already looming over the band members for drugs convictions, Brian Jones, became resentful of the Jagger/Richards writing partnership and his loss of creative control of the band. He descended into a cycle of drink, drugs, and ill-health, which was only compounded by Anita Pallenberg, Jones's girlfriend, starting an affair with Richards (she would have two children by him). On June 8, Jagger, Richards, and Watts drove to Jones's Sussex mansion and sacked him from the band. On July 3, Brian Jones was found dead in his swimming pool. In December of the same year at a concert in San Francisco, Meredith Hunter, the victim of a racially motivated attack, was hacked and stomped to death by members of the Hell's Angels who the band had invited to provide security at the gig.

NICKNAMES OF PEOPLE II
Identify the people famously associated with these nicknames. The solutions can be found on page 284. [**Target: 16**]

1. J.Lo
2. Ol' Blue Eyes
3. The Hoff
4. The Boss
5. Stormin' Norman
6. The Muscles from Brussels
7. Joe Cool
8. The Great One
9. Mimi
10. Sweetness
11. The Great White Shark
12. Bonecrusher
13. Da Whoop
14. The Georgia Peach
15. The Rock Iguana
16. Her Madgesty
17. Lawrence of Arabia
18. The Liberator
19. The Golden Bear
20. Million Dollar Legs
21. The Human Riff
22. America's Sweetheart
23. The Lone Eagle
24. The Jewish Elvis

RUSHES OVER 10,000 YARDS
Try to name the *twenty-three* NFL players who have rushed for 10,000 yards or more in their careers. Look to page 303 for the solution. [**Target: 7**]

GREEK ALPHABET
Identify the *twenty-four* characters in the Greek alphabet. The solution may be found on page 323. [**Target: 10**]

UNTIMELY DEATHS Identify these well-known people whose untimely deaths are described as follows. Find the solutions on page 341. [Target: 10]

1. Rock and pop icon; heart failure caused by drugs use and overeating, 1977.
2. Punk guitarist; drug overdose after murdering his girlfriend in New York in 1978.
3. Rock star; shot by a delusional fan in New York in 1980.
4. Iconic movie actress; suicide by a drug overdose, 1962.
5. Big Band leader; died in a plane crash in 1944.
6. Australian rock star; suicide or death by possible sexual misadventure in 1997.
7. Princess and former actress; killed in a car crash in Monaco in 1982.
8. Iconic movie actor; died in a car crash in 1955.
9. Mentally ill Dutch artist; suicide by shooting himself in the chest, 1890.
10. Legendary rock guitarist; choked on vomit, 1970.
11. American grunge rock star; suicide by shotgun to the head in 1994.
12. West Coast gangsta rapper; killed in a drive-by shooting in Las Vegas in 1996.
13. Iconic singer and movie actress, died from an overdose of barbiturates in 1969 at the age of forty-seven after a long battle with addiction.
14. Singer, songwriter, and drummer; died from anorexia nervosa in 1983.
15. Soul singer; shot by his father during an argument in 1984.
16. Female singer and songwriter; hit by speedboat while swimming off the coast of Mexico in 2000.
17. American poet; suicide by gassing herself in 1963.
18. Fashion mogul; shot by a serial killer in 1997.
19. American record producer, singer, and politician; died in a skiing accident in 1998.
20. East Coast gangsta rapper; killed in a drive-by shooting in L.A. in 1997.
21. Author and feminist; drowned herself in the river Ouse, 1941.

22. Actor, died of an overdose of heroin and cocaine at the age of twenty-three outside a Hollywood nightclub in 1993.
23. Actor, died from an overdose of prescribed medicines in his New York apartment in January 2008 at the age of twenty-eight.
24. Female American blues and folk singer; died following a drug overdose in 1970.

HIGHEST CAREER BATTING AVERAGES
Name the batters with the *twenty-five* highest career batting averages in MLB. Turn to page 217 for the solution. [**Target: 7**]

PROLIFIC BASKETBALL SCORERS
Name the *twenty-five* NBA players to have scored the highest average points per game. The solution may be found on page 238. [**Target: 7**]

MISCELLANY XXI
Respond to these questions of a miscellaneous nature. Find the solutions on page 259. [**Target: 14**]

1. Which religion has Five Pillars?
2. What is located on Bullion Boulevard?
3. Which U.S. state has the lowest population?
4. Who played Hans Grüber in *Die Hard*?
5. Which English word comes from a Greek phrase meaning "wandering star"?
6. Which is the oldest university in the U.S.?
7. Which TV character had a poster in his office of a UFO with the caption "I want to believe"?
8. Who was managed by Colonel Tom Parker?
9. Who wrote *The Old Man and the Sea*?
10. Which is the most southern U.S. state?
11. How many curves are there on a standard paper clip?
12. What links Anne Boleyn, Lady Jane Grey, Robert Devereux Earl of Essex, and the German spy Josef Jakobs?
13. Where in the UK does the law forbid the Queen from entering?
14. Who wrote *Heart of Midlothian*, *Ivanhoe*, and *Rob Roy*?
15. Which country takes its name from the Latin word for "southern"?
16. What is the chemical symbol for ozone?

17. What did John Sutter start in California in 1848?
18. Which city has the most hotel rooms in the world?
19. Which disease caused the worst epidemic in U.S. history?
20. How many people have walked on the moon?
21. In medicine, what is a lancet?
22. What is the largest number you can write in roman numerals using each character only once?
23. What was first marketed in the 1880s in the U.S. by the Scott Paper Company and in Britain by the British Perforated Paper Company?
24. Which is the lowest number that, when written out, has its letters in alphabetical order?

POPULAR GIRLS' NAMES Name the *twenty-five* most popular girls' names in the U.S.* Find the solution on page 284. [**Target: 7**]

BUSIEST AIRPORTS Identify the *twenty-five* busiest airports† in the world (according to the number of passengers carried in 2007).‡ Turn to page 303 for the solution. [**Target: 10**]

RECENT HISTORY III Identify the year from the descriptions provided. The solutions may be found on page 323. [**Target: 10**]

1. 200,000 people are killed in Asia by tsunamis caused by a massive undersea earthquake; Athens hosts the Olympic Games; the New England Patriots beat the Carolina Panthers to win the Super Bowl, Adam Vinatieri kicks the winning points with four seconds remaining; Howard Dean quits the race for the Democratic nomination after "the Dean Scream"

---

* According to figures from the U.S. Census Bureau for 2006.
† Data for airports including domestic flights is dominated by the U.S. due to the size of the domestic air transport industry. Atlanta is also the busiest airport in terms of traffic movements (takeoffs and landings). The world's busiest airport for international passengers is London's Heathrow airport. Memphis is the world's busiest airport for freight traffic. During the British Grand Prix, Silverstone race circuit temporarily becomes the world's busiest airport with helicopter flights departing and arriving every few seconds.
‡ According to Airports Council International figures for January–December 2007.

generates intense press coverage; John Kerry secures the Democratic nomination but loses the election to George W. Bush; Yasser Arafat dies; *The Return of the King* wins eleven Oscars.

2. Pope John Paul II dies and is succeeded by Benedict XVI; Lance Armstrong wins a seventh successive Tour de France; Angela Merkel becomes Germany's first female Chancellor; New Orleans is devastated by Hurricane Katrina; a Pennsylvania judge rules that the teaching in schools of Intelligent Design is unconstitutional; William Mark Felt, a former FBI agent reveals himself to be Deep Throat, the Watergate informer; Elton John marries David Furnish.

3. The Winter Olympics are held in Salt Lake City; the Queen confers an honorary knighthood on Rudolph Giuliani for his leadership in the aftermath of 9/11; traditional coins and notes cease to be legal tender in Eurozone member states and are replaced with the Euro; Worldcom files for Chapter 11 bankruptcy after a massive accounting fraud; George W. Bush establishes the Department of Homeland Security.

4. George H. W. Bush is elected U.S. president, defeating Michael Dukakis; Ben Johnson is stripped of his 100m gold medal for failing a drug test at the Seoul Olympics; two years after the *Challenger* disaster, NASA resumes Space Shuttle flights with *Discovery*; Michael Jackson moves into his Neverland ranch; *Rain Man*, starring Dustin Hoffman and Tom Cruise, is the top grossing film of the year.

5. Race riots sparked in Los Angeles after not-guilty verdicts are pronounced on Rodney King's attackers; Dan Quayle incorrectly spells the word "potato"*; Bill Clinton is elected

---

* While electioneering on a visit to a school in Trenton, New Jersey in 1992, vice president Dan Quayle corrected a schoolboy's spelling in front of the assembled media placing an "e" on the end of "potato." The error led to Quayle suffering widespread ridicule and greatly contributed to media portrayal of the vice president as an intellectual lightweight. Quayle ran as a Republican presidential candidate in 1999, but in the first contest finished in eighth (and last) place and withdrew from the race.

U.S. president for the first time; fire breaks out in Windsor Castle, leading the Queen to describe the year as her "annus horribilis"; Boutros Boutros-Ghali becomes UN Secretary General; Barcelona hosts the Summer Olympics; Sinéad O'Connor causes controversy by ripping up a picture of the pope on *Saturday Night Live*.

6. German reunification takes place; Nelson Mandela is released from prison; Iraq invades Kuwait, sparking the First Gulf War; Lithuania announces independence from the Soviet Union, the first Soviet Republic to do so; F. W. de Klerk begins to dismantle apartheid in South Africa, McDonald's opens its first fast-food outlet in Moscow; the Hubble telescope is launched aboard the space shuttle *Discovery*; Milli Vanilli have their Grammy for Best New Artist revoked after it is revealed that they did not sing on their record.*

7. Jimmy Carter is sworn in as U.S. president; EMI fires the Sex Pistols; *Star Wars* is released and quickly becomes the highest-grossing film to date; New York City experiences a blackout for twenty-five hours; Elvis Presley dies; *Roots* airs on ABC; Steven Biko dies from a head injury he sustained in police custody in South Africa.

8. Solidarity win the Polish elections; Communist governments collapse in Eastern Europe; the Berlin Wall is torn down; General Noriega is deposed by U.S. troops in Panama; protests in Tiananmen Square in Beijing are crushed by the Chinese military, many demonstrators lose their lives; the Ayatollah Khomeini dies; the *Exxon Valdez*

---

* West German record producer Frank Farian created Milli Vanilli using Fab Morvan and Rob Pilatus as the "face" of the band, while having competent, but "unmarketable" singers supply the vocals on their recordings. By the time of their second album, *Girl You Know It's True* Milli Vanilli had become enormously popular and they were awarded the Grammy for Best New Artist in 1990. Rumours about the contribution of Morvan and Pilatus began to circulate and led to Farian admitting the truth in November of 1990. The band were stripped of their Grammy award (the only group to ever suffer this indignity) and dropped by their record company. A court ruling was even passed in the U.S. entitling disgruntled fans a full refund from any Milli Vanilli records they had purchased. After a disastrous attempt to resurrect the act, Pilatus descended into a drug addiction and petty crime. He died of a drug overdose in 1998.

runs aground off Alaska causing widespread environmental damage; *The Simpsons* airs in its own right for the first time.

9. Winston Churchill replaces Neville Chamberlain as British Prime Minister; Germany invades the Low Countries with rapid assaults which become known as "Blitzkrieg"; the British expeditionary force is evacuated from Dunkirk; France surrenders to Germany and Vichy France is established; the Battle of Britain takes place in the skies over southeast England; Leon Trotsky is assassinated in Mexico; Franklin D. Roosevelt is elected for a third term.

10. The American embassy in Tehran is seized by Islamic extremists and its occupants held hostage; Margaret Thatcher is elected British Prime Minister for the first time; Soviet troops invade Afghanistan; a radiation leak occurs at the Three Mile Island nuclear plant; Idi Amin is overthrown in Uganda but escapes into exile; the World Health Organization certifies the eradication of smallpox; The Knack reach number one with "My Sharona."

11. Iraqi forces attack Iran leading to ten years of war; Zimbabwe gains independence from Britain and Robert Mugabe becomes president; Mount St. Helens erupts spectacularly, killing fifty-seven people and causing widespread devastation; the Sony Walkman is introduced; John Lennon is shot dead in New York by a deranged fan; the U.S. boycotts the Moscow Olympics to protest the Soviet invasion of Afghanistan; millions watch *Dallas* to find out who shot J.R.

12. Hillary and Tensing reach the summit of Mount Everest, the first men to do so; Stalin dies and is replaced by Nikita Khrushchev as Soviet leader; the Korean War ends in stalemate; Elizabeth II is crowned in Westminster Abbey; Watson and Crick reveal the structure of DNA; the first James Bond novel, *Casino Royale*, is published in the UK; the Korean War ends.

13. Ronald Reagan is sworn in as president; Iran releases the hostages taken in the American embassy in Tehran; Pope John Paul II survives an assassination attempt by a Turkish gunman; the space shuttle *Columbia* completes the first successful shuttle

mission; Prince Charles marries Lady Diana Spencer; Simon and Garfunkel reunite to perform a free concert in New York's Central Park.

14. German forces surrender at Stalingrad; the Warsaw ghetto is attacked by German soldiers and the survivors are deported to concentration camps; the largest tank battle in history, the Battle of Kursk, takes place between Germany and Russia; Italy surrenders to Allied forces, *Casablanca* wins the Academy Award for best picture; LSD is synthesised by Swiss chemist Albert Hofmann.

15. The final episode of *M*A*S*H* airs in the U.S.; Ronald Reagan announces the Strategic Defense Initiative, dubbed "Star Wars"; *Gandhi* wins eight Oscars; *Stern* magazine publishes fabricated diaries of Adolf Hitler; Korean Air Lines Flight 007 is shot down by Soviet fighters, the Soviet Union claims it had violated Soviet airspace and was on a spying misson*; Michael Jackson's "Thriller" video is broadcast for the first time.

16. Compact discs are first introduced; Argentina occupies the Falkland Islands; Leonid Brezhnev dies and is succeeded by Yuri Andropov; Wayne Gretzky scores ninety-two goals for the Edmonton Oilers, the most ever achieved in a single season; emoticons are used for the first time by computer scientist Scott Fahlman; "The Computer" wins *Time* magazine's Man of the Year; Stevie Wonder and Paul McCartney reach number one with "Ebony and Ivory."

17. The first Balkan War begins; the *Titanic* sinks on its maiden voyage after hitting an iceberg; the Chinese republic is founded under Sun Yat-Sen; Arizona becomes the forty-eighth state of the U.S.; Fenway Park, home of the Red Sox, opens in Boston, the Red Sox win the World Series later the same year; Woodrow Wilson is elected president.

18. Mata Hari is executed as a spy; Britain issues the Balfour Declaration for a Jewish homeland in Palestine; the Russian Revolution takes place; Tsar Nicholas II abdicates and Lenin

---

* The incident brought fierce condemnation from the United States. As a result of the shooting down, Ronald Reagan authorized the Global Positioning System (GPS), then a purely military system, to be made available free for civilian use.

assumes power; the U.S. enters the First World War*; conscription is introduced; the first Pulitzer prizes are awarded.

19. The Vatican City is established as an independent state; rivals of Al Capone are killed in the St. Valentine's Day Massacre in Chicago; the Wall Street Crash takes place followed by a period of economic depression; Douglas Fairbanks and William C. DeMille host the first Academy Awards at the Hotel Roosevelt in Hollywood; *Wings* wins Best Picture.

20. Mohandas Gandhi is assassinated; the state of Israel is created; the Berlin airlift takes place in response to a Soviet blockade; apartheid laws are passed in South Africa; the National Health Service is created in Britain; the World Health Organization is established and the Universal Declaration of Human Rights is adopted by the United Nations; the Hells Angels are formed in California; Harry S. Truman is elected president.

21. Winston Churchill coins the term "Iron Curtain" in a speech; the first meeting of the UN General Assembly takes place;

---

* The entry of the United States into the First World War was primarily brought about by the frequent German attacks on American shipping (including the sinking of the *Lusitania*) but was hastened by the interception of a communication known as the Zimmermann Telegram. The telegram was a coded message sent by Arthur Zimmermann, the foreign secretary of the German Empire, to the German ambassador in Mexico, Heinrich von Eckardt. The message contained instructions for von Eckardt to approach the Mexican government, which at the time was involved in border conflicts with the U.S., to propose a military alliance with Germany. The message was sent from Berlin, first to the German embassy in Washington via the submarine transatlantic cable (which the U.S. had allowed Germany to use for encoded diplomatic communications), before being forwarded to the German embassy in Mexico City. It was intercepted by British Naval Intelligence, who were monitoring transmissions along the cable, and decrypted using a code book acquired from a German agent captured in the Middle East. This posed a dilemma for the British: while it was important for British interests that the contents of the telegram were made known to the Americans, this would reveal to Germany the British capability in code-breaking, and reveal to the U.S. that Britain had been monitoring its diplomatic communications. The solution presented itself when the British government guessed that the telegram most probably reached Mexico City from Washington via the public telegraph system. An agent was dispatched to the telegraph office in Mexico City and, in bribing a local official, was able to retrieve a copy of the telegram. The telegram was presented to the U.S. ambassador in London as the work of British intelligence in Mexico. Six weeks later, the U.S. declared war on Germany.

UNICEF is founded; the first programmable electronic computer becomes operational; Juan Perón becomes president of Argentina; the Fourth Republic begins in France; war crimes trials begin in Tokyo; *It's a Wonderful Life* is released.

22. The contraceptive pill is introduced; the first transatlantic telephone cable is laid; Elvis Presley has his first hit in the U.S. with "Heartbreak Hotel"; Grace Kelly marries Prince Rainier III of Monaco; Norma Jeane Mortenson changes her name to Marilyn Monroe; Dwight D. Eisenhower creates the interstate highway system; Cecil B. DeMille's epic *The Ten Commandments* is the top-grossing film of the year.

23. President William G. Harding introduces radio to the White House; Howard Carter opens Tutankhamen's tomb; the USSR is established; Mussolini seizes power in Italy; *Ulysses,* by James Joyce, is published; construction begins on Yankee Stadium in the Bronx; the Lincoln Memorial is dedicated; insulin is extracted and successfully used to treat diabetes.

24. The first round-the-world flight takes 175 days (by the Army Air Service, precursor of the United States Air Force); Lenin dies and is buried in Red Square; Stalin begins purges against his rivals; the first Winter Olympic Games take place in Chamonix in France; Gershwin's *Rhapsody in Blue* is performed for the first time in New York City.

POPULOUS COUNTRIES Name the *twenty-five* most populous countries* in the world. Turn to page 341 for the solution.
[**Target: 14**]

---

* The population of the world is growing at an enormous rate. The world's population first reached 1 billion in 1804 and took 123 years to add a second billion. It reached 3 billion thirty-three years later in 1960, 4 billion just fourteen years later in 1974, and 5 billion in 1987. In 1999 the 6 billionth person was born somewhere in the world. Encouragingly, the rate of population growth seems to have slowed from a peak of an annual addition of 87 million people in the late 1980s to 81 million a year by the 1990s, and this is projected to fall to 50 million people a year in the 2040s. By that time, however, it is predicted that the world population will have risen by 3 billion people over today's number, and nobody is sure quite how many people the earth is capable of supporting.

POPULAR BOYS' NAMES Name the *twenty-five* most popular boys' names in the U.S.* Find the solution on page 218. [**Target: 7**]

SINGERS AND BACKERS II Complete the names of these groups by identifying the singer most closely associated with the backing band. The solutions may be found on page 239. [**Target: 12**]

1. _____ and the Family Stone
2. _____ and the Comets
3. _____ and the Dominos
4. _____ and the Bunnymen
5. _____ and the MGs
6. _____ and the Supremes
7. _____ and the Heartbreakers
8. _____ and the Commotions
9. _____ and the New Power Generation
10. _____ and the Plastic Population
11. _____ and the Blowfish
12. _____ and the Mechanics
13. _____ and the Modern Lovers
14. _____ and the Shondells
15. _____ and the Soul City Symphony
16. _____ and the Stooges
17. _____ and the Tijuana Brass
18. _____ and the Impressions
19. _____ and the Magic Band
20. _____ and the Egyptians
21. _____ and the Tabulations
22. _____ and the Famous Flames
23. _____ and the Mysterians
24. _____ and the Mindbenders

SLUGGERS Identify the *twenty-six* MLB batters who have hit fifty or more home runs in a single season. Find the solution on page 260. [**Target: 7**]

---

* According to figures from the U.S. Census Bureau for 2006.

NATO ALPHABET Recall the *twenty-six* words representing letters in the NATO phonetic alphabet.* The solution is on page 284. [Target: 22]

LINKED MISCELLANY XII Respond to the questions and work out the theme that links them. The solutions may be found on page 304. [Target: 6]

1. In which state would you find Glacier National Park, the site of the Battle of Little Bighorn, and Yellowstone National Park?
2. Which object in the solar system is 2,160 miles in diameter and is located anywhere between 225,000 and 250,000 miles from earth?
3. Which classical city was subject to a lengthy siege depicted in *The Iliad*?
4. What colloquial name is given to a person born during the population spike which occurred immediately after World War II?
5. What is the name of the Milwaukee family around which *Happy Days* is based?
6. Which 1974 horror spoof starred Gene Wilder and was directed by Mel Brooks?
7. Who wrote the songs "Needles and Pins" and "I Got You Babe"?
8. Which character in *Friends* was played by Matthew Perry?
9. In computing, what was the predecessor of the Dual In-Line Memory Modules (or DIMMs) expansion memory for PCs?
10. Which ABC television sitcom famously opened with the faces of the cast appearing in a three-by-three grid with all of the cast members appearing to look around at each other?

---

* The development of radio communication gave rise to the need to be able to unambiguously convey letter sounds and as a result the British Army introduced the first phonetic alphabet in 1904. The original alphabet consisted of only six phonetic letter sounds but was expanded to a full alphabet in 1927. The entry of the United States into the Second World War led to the standardization of the phonetic alphabet across all the Allied services, and, with the creation of NATO in 1953, the alphabet was changed into its current form.

COUNTRIES WITH FIVE-LETTER NAMES
Recall the *twenty-six* countries that have five-letter names. Go to page 323 for the solution. [Target: 18]

TRACK-AND-FIELD EVENTS
Name the *twenty-six* Olympic* track-and-field events. Find the solution on page 342. [Target: 20]

ADVERTISING SLOGANS IV
Name the products or companies that were being advertised with these slogans. Look to page 218 for the solutions. [Target: 12]

1. "See what brown can do for you"
2. "Snap, crackle and pop"
3. "You'll love the way we fly"
4. "When it absolutely, positively has to be there overnight"
5. "The champagne of beers"
6. "We bring good things to life"
7. "Unleash the power of the sun"
8. "You've got questions, we've got answers"
9. "The world puts its stock in us"
10. "Once you pop the fun don't stop"
11. "Delightfully tacky, yet unrefined"
12. "Rip. Mix. Burn"
13. "The uncola"
14. "Grab life by the horns"
15. "The miracles of science"
16. "We keep your promises"

---

* The 1908 London Olympics was the first (and not the last) games to be mired in controversy. Rome was originally due to host the 1908 Games, but was forced to withdraw when Mount Vesuvius erupted, throwing Italy into chaos. Animosity began at the opening ceremony when the American flag-bearer, Ralph Rose, refused to dip his flag to the royal box, greatly offending the British organizers. The rest of the games was characterised by a string of controversial judging decisions in which American athletes often came off second best. The final of the 400m was contested by four athletes, three Americans and a British runner Wyndham Halswelle. The race was ordered to be run again after J. C. Carpenter, the American "winner," was judged to have interfered with the British athlete. The three Americans refused, and Halswelle competed on his own in the rerun, winning the event.

17. "Cross into the blue"
18. "One in a billion"
19. "The one and only"
20. "The best built cars in the world"
21. "Ugly is only skin-deep"
22. "Look your best while you wear your least"
23. "Lifts and separates"
24. "The beer that made Milwaukee famous"

MEMBERS OF NATO Name the *twenty-six* members of NATO.*
The solution is on page 239. [**Target: 14**]

BOOKS OF THE NEW TESTAMENT Name the *twenty-seven*
books of the New Testament.† Turn to page 260 for the solution.
[**Target: 6**]

QUOTATIONS FROM POPULAR FILMS II Identify the films
from which these quotations‡ are taken. (The date each film was released
is given to assist you.) Look for the solutions on page 284. [**Target: 14**]

1. "I know what you're thinking. Did he fire six shots or only
   five?" (1971)
2. "The point is, ladies and gentlemen, that greed, for lack of a
   better word, is good. Greed is right. Greed works." (1987)
3. "I'll have what she's having." (1989)

---

* The North Atlantic Treaty Organization is a military alliance of twenty-six nations
which have made a commitment to their mutual defense. The commitment appears
in article 5 of the North Atlantic Treaty, which states that an attack on a single
alliance country is regarded as an attack against all the signatories. The treaty was
signed in Washington in 1949 by the twelve founding nations and other nations
have since joined the alliance. The breakup of the Soviet Union and Warsaw Pact
led to groups of Eastern Bloc countries joining in 1999 and 2004.
† The New Testament is made up of four books describing the ministry of Jesus
Christ (the Gospels, a narrative of the ministry of the Apostles), twenty-one letters
(the Epistles), and an apocalyptic prophecy.
‡ In spite of being one of the most quoted movie lines, it is apocryphal that
Humphrey Bogart delivered the line, "Play it again, Sam" in *Casablanca.* In fact he
never said it; Ingrid Bergman's Ilsa says the line: "Play it, Sam. Play 'As Time Goes
By.'" Other common movie misquotes include James Cagney's "You dirty rat," and
Mae West's "Is that a gun in your pocket, or are you just glad to see me?"

4. "You had me at 'hello.' " (1996)
5. "But, I'm funny how? Funny like a clown? I amuse you? I make you laugh?" (1990)
6. "No, Mr. Bond. I expect you to die!" (1963)
7. "Are you suggesting coconuts migrate?" (1975)
8. "Meet you in Malkovich in one hour." (1999)
9. "Ten oughta do it, don't you think? Do you think we need one more? You think we need one more? All right, we'll get one more." (2001)
10. "Don't be stupid, be a smarty, come and join the Nazi Party!" (1968)
11. "Who needs reasons when you've got heroin?" (1996)
12. "Hello, my name is Inigo Montoya. You killed my father. Prepare to die." (1987)
13. "You either surf or you fight." (1979)
14. "I hate Illinois Nazis." (1980)
15. "Are you gonna bark all day, little doggy, or are you gonna bite?" (1992)
16. "O pointy birds, O pointy pointy, anoint my head, anointy-nointy." (1983)
17. "I was a better man with you as a woman than I ever was with a woman as a man." (1982)
18. "They're coming outta the walls. They're coming outta the goddamn walls!" (1986)
19. "Love is a many-splendored thing, love is what makes the world go round, all you need is love." (2001)
20. "Fasten your seatbelts, it's going to be a bumpy night." (1950)
21. "One man's life touches so many others, when he's not there it leaves an awfully big hole." (1946)
22. "In Italy, for thirty years under the Borgias, they had warfare, terror, murder and bloodshed, but they produced Michelangelo, Leonardo da Vinci, and the Renaissance. In Switzerland, they had brotherly love; they had five hundred years of democracy and peace—and what did that produce? The cuckoo clock." (1949)
23. "I'm on this new diet for Paris. I don't eat anything until I feel like I'm about to faint, then I eat a cube of cheese. I'm one stomach flu away from reaching my goal weight." (2006)
24. "I don't train girls." (2004)

3,000 HIT CLUB Try to name the *twenty-seven* MLB batters who have scored over 3,000 hits in their careers. The solution may be found on page 304. [**Target:** 7]

COURSES HOSTING THE U.S. OPEN Try to list the *twenty-seven* golf clubs that have hosted the U.S. Open since 1945. Look to page 323 for the solution. [**Target:** 6]

MISCELLANY XXII Answer these questions of a miscellaneous nature. Turn to page 342 for the solutions. [**Target:** 14]

1. From which military conflict do we get the balaclava and the cardigan?
2. 20500 is the ZIP code for where?
3. Who left the Faces to join the Rolling Stones?
4. The first rule of Fight Club is: "You do not talk about Fight Club." What is the second rule of Fight Club?
5. What is a Bolshoi Mac?
6. Which 1962 novel featured a character called Alex and his gang of Droogs?
7. Who is Yogi Bear's girlfriend?
8. What links Jamrud in Pakistan with Torkham in Afghanistan?
9. Which type of character are *Julius Caesar*, *Richard III*, *Hamlet*, and *Macbeth* the only of Shakespeare's plays to feature?
10. Who was the first man to exceed the speed of sound?
11. Which Olympic sport requires a planting box?
12. What was first televised on September 26th, 1960?
13. Use of what costs $54,000 on average but has cost as much as $249,165 and as little as 36 cents?
14. A water lily growing in a circular pond doubles in size every day. If it takes ten days to cover the whole pond, how long does it take to cover half the pond?
15. Which is the only U.S. state to have a border with only one other U.S. state?
16. The first interracial kiss on American television took place in which series?
17. Who orchestrated the St. Valentine's Day Massacre in 1929?

18. Which artistic term can be used to describe the painters Rembrandt, Caravaggio, and Rubens and the composers Vivaldi, Handel, and J. S. Bach?

19. Which is the only sea that has no contact with land?

20. How many pairs of ribs do humans have?

21. What makes a pink gin pink?

22. Which two chemical products result from burning pure methane?

23. Which ministry did Winston Smith work for in *Nineteen Eighty-four*?

24. Martin has a clock that chimes every hour and every half hour. The clock chimes once at one o'clock, twice at two o'clock, three times at three o'clock, and so on. The clock also chimes once on the half hour. One day, Martin arrives home and hears the clock chime once. Half an hour later he hears it chime once again. Half an hour later it chimes once and another half an hour later it chimes once again. Given that the clock is functioning correctly, what time did Martin arrive home?

MONARCHIES Name the *twenty-seven* countries of the world that are governed by monarchs* (excluding Commonwealth Realms where the monarch is represented by a governor general). Find the solution on page 218. [**Target: 7**]

MICHAEL JACKSON HITS Recall the *twenty-eight* singles by Michael Jackson† which have reached number ten or higher in the Billboard Hot 100. Look to page 239 for the solution. [**Target: 7**]

---

* A monarchy may be defined as an autocracy governed by a monarch who has usually inherited the title. In a monarchy, the monarch demands the service of the people, in contrast to a republic, where the role of the leader is to serve the people. Examples of titles of monarchs are King, Emperor, Emir, Sultan, Sheik, and Tsar. (Tsar is derived from Julius Caesar, and was the title first chosen by Ivan IV in 1547 to convey to his subjects a sense that he was a person with dictatorial powers. The German word Kaiser has the same derivation.)

† Michael Jackson first started performing at the age of four and by the time he was ten, the Jackson 5 signed their first record deal with Motown Records in 1968. When MGM launched the solo career of Donny Osmond from rival band the Osmonds, Motown responded by launching Michael as a solo act. Hits followed, but his collaboration with producer Quincy Jones on the *Off the Wall* album and then *Thriller* led to Jackson attaining superstardom.

FILMS AND THEIR STARS V Name the films from these selected acting appearances and dates of release. The solutions are on page 260. [**Target: 8**]

1. Tom Hanks, Robin Wright, Gary Sinise (1994)
2. Kevin Spacey, Annette Bening, Mena Suvari (1999)
3. Bruce Willis, Toni Collette, Hayley Joel Osment (1999)
4. Kevin Costner, Morgan Freeman, Christian Slater (1991)
5. Clint Eastwood, Gene Hackman, Morgan Freeman, Richard Harris (1992)
6. Burt Reynolds, Roger Moore, Peter Fonda, Farrah Fawcett, Jackie Chan, Dean Martin, Sammy Davis Jr. (1981)
7. Sally Field, Dolly Parton, Daryl Hannah, Julia Roberts, Shirley MacLaine (1989)
8. Chow Yun-Fat, Michelle Yeoh, Zhang Ziyi (1999)
9. Rex Harrison, Richard Burton, Elizabeth Taylor (1963)
10. Linda Blair, Max von Sydow (1973)
11. Johnny Depp, Winona Ryder, Vincent Price (1990)
12. Julia Roberts, Denzel Washington (1993)
13. Tom Berenger, Willem Dafoe, Charlie Sheen, Forest Whitaker (1986)
14. Juliette Binoche, Carrie-Anne Moss, Judi Dench (2000)
15. Michael Douglas, Demi Moore, Donald Sutherland (1994)
16. Jon Voight, Bert Reynolds, Ned Beatty (1972)
17. Dustin Hoffman, Jessica Lange, Bill Murray (1982)
18. Owen Wilson, Matt Dillon, Kate Hudson, Michael Douglas (2006)
19. Christopher Walken, Andy Garcia, Christopher Lloyd, Steve Buscemi (1995)
20. Tom Cruise, Rebecca De Mornay (1983)
21. Denzel Washington, Kevin Kline (1987)
22. Meryl Streep, Shirley MacLaine, Dennis Quaid, Gene Hackman (1990)
23. Gwyneth Paltrow, Blythe Danner, Daniel Craig (2003)
24. Frank Sinatra, Laurence Harvey, Janet Leigh, Angela Lansbury (1962)

RED, WHITE, AND BLUE FLAGS Name the *twenty-nine* countries that have red, white, and blue* flags (that is, in which the predominant colors are red, white, and blue). Turn to page 285 for the solution. [**Target: 7**]

200 CAREER TOUCHDOWN PASSES Name the *twenty-nine* NFL quarterbacks to have thrown 200 or more touchdown passes in their careers. The solution is on page 305. [**Target: 7**]

CATCHPHRASES II Identify the authors of these catchphrases (real or fictional). Turn to page 324 for the solutions. [**Target: 12**]

1. "That's another nice mess you've got me into."
2. "You're fired!"
3. "You cannot be serious!"
4. "The truth is out there."
5. "Zoinks!"
6. "Go ahead, make my day."
7. "We were on a break!'
8. "Schwing!"
9. "Can we talk?"
10. "Good night, John Boy."
11. "And that's the way it is."
12. "Good grief."
13. "Let's get ready to rumble!"
14. "Danger, Will Robinson."

---

* Colors have strong associations with psychology and emotion. These emotional characteristics are deliberately exploited in flag design, with colors chosen to represent qualities that the flag bearer wishes to endorse. Red is associated with passion, courage, and energy as well as with ambition, anger, and aggression. It has been used on the flags of the Russian Revolution, by the Nazis, and by many communist dictatorships. White has associations with peace, purity, protection, and healing. It is used as a symbolic color by medical and peacekeeping organizations and the white flag is the recognized international symbol for calling a truce. Blue is the color of harmony, reflection, truth, and cooperation and has been adopted by the United Nations and European Union in their flags. Red, white, and blue is a combination of colors that seemingly makes for an appealing package, being the most common color combination appearing on national flags.

15. "Makin' whoopie."
16. "Release the hounds, Smithers."
17. "No soup for you."
18. "Nudge nudge, wink wink."
19. "Jane, you ignorant slut."
20. "Bite my shiny metal ass!"
21. "Whatchoo talkin' 'bout, Willis?"
22. "We've got a really big show!"
23. "De plane! De plane!"
24. "Baby, you're the greatest."

NHL TEAMS Recall the *thirty* teams in the National Hockey League. You can find the solution on page 343. [**Target: 27**]

CHRISTIAN FEASTS Name the *thirty* feast days (or festivals) in the Christian calendar.* The solution is on page 218. [**Target: 6**]

---

* Throughout history and across many societies religious practice and the calendar are interconnected. The link between gods and the names for the days of the week first appeared in about 300 B.C. ("Before Christ") and the division of a week into seven days has its origins in Genesis. The modern calendar comes from the Romans, and particularly the Julian calendar adopted in 45 B.C. Julius Caesar arranged the days in months, every odd month having thirty-one days, even months having thirty and February having twenty-nine days or thirty in a leap year. The emperor Augustus insisted a day were taken from February and added to the month of August (which had taken his name) so it didn't have fewer days than any of the other months. The problem with the Julian calendar was that it erred from the solar calendar by about 11½ minutes every year. By the sixteenth century this had created an error of ten days between the Julian and the solar calendars; the spring equinox had crept forward to March 10. This was increasingly a problem for the Catholic Church as Easter, the most important day in the Christian calendar, was calculated according to the spring equinox. If the date of the equinox was wrong, Easter was being celebrated on the wrong day and, furthermore, most of the other movable feasts were calculated according to when Easter fell. Pope Gregory XIII fixed the problem in 1582 by moving the calendar forward by ten days, and removing leap years from century years that were not divisible by 400 (e.g., 1800, 1900, but not 2000). The Protestant countries of northern Europe took longer to switch to the Gregorian calendar, with Britain changing in 1752. Under the Julian calendar, New Year was celebrated on April 1 but was moved to January 1 with the introduction of the Gregorian calendar. People who continued to celebrate the New Year on April 1, ignorant of the change, gave rise to the tradition of April Fools.

NICKNAMES OF PLACES
Identify these places from the nicknames that are presented. The solutions are on page 240. [Target: 10]

1.	The Big Apple	2.	The Big Smoke
3.	Tinseltown	4.	The Pond
5.	The Emerald Isle	6.	The Windy City
7.	The Roof of the World	8.	The Garden of England
9.	Motown	10.	City of Dreaming Spires
11.	Sin City	12.	The Big Easy
13.	The Granite City	14.	City of David
15.	The Gateway of India	16.	City of Light
17.	The Eternal City	18.	Mile High City
19.	City of Brotherly Love	20.	Bride of the Sea
21.	The Pink City	22.	The Mistake on the Lake
23.	The White City	24.	Pearl of the Orient

MAJOR LEAGUE BASEBALL STADIUMS
Try to name the *thirty* MLB stadiums. Look to page 261 for the solution. [Target: 15]

LONGEST AMERICAN RIVERS
Name the *thirty-one* rivers in the U.S. that are over 600 miles in length. Find the solution on page 324. [Target: 7]

NBA TEAMS
Name the *thirty-two* teams in the National Basketball Association. Find the solution on page 285. [Target: 28]

STATE CAPITALS II
Recall the states which have these capitals. The solution is on page 305. [Target: 14]

1.	Nashville	2.	Atlanta
3.	Boston	4.	Little Rock
5.	Charleston	6.	Albany
7.	Hartford	8.	Phoenix
9.	Boise	10.	Jackson
11.	Dover	12.	Santa Fe
13.	Trenton	14.	Tallahassee
15.	Richmond	16.	Concord

17.	Jefferson City	18.	Cheyenne
19.	Montgomery	20.	Columbia
21.	Helena	22.	Carson City
23.	Juneau	24.	Pierre

NFL TEAMS Name the *thirty-two* teams in the National Football League. Look for the solution on page 343. [**Target: 30**]

ENTREPRENEURS II Identify the industry sectors most closely associated with these entrepreneurs. Turn to page 219 for the solutions. [**Target: 10**]

1.	Charles Merrill	2.	Milton Hershey
3.	Aristotle Onassis	4.	Hugh Hefner
5.	John Pierpont Morgan	6.	Donald Trump
7.	Martha Stewart	8.	Martha Lane Fox
9.	Michael Bloomberg	10.	John Rockefeller
11.	Howard Hughes	12.	Warren Buffet
13.	Paul Warburg	14.	Ted Turner
15.	George Soros	16.	Jean Paul Getty
17.	Cornelius Vanderbilt	18.	Andrew Carnegie
19.	Debbie Fields	20.	David Geffen
21.	Mark McCormack	22.	James Jerome Hill
23.	Theodore Vail	24.	Frederick W. Smith

FILMS STARRING MARILYN MONROE Recall the *thirty-two* films in which Marilyn Monroe starred. Find the solution on page 240. [**Target: 5**]

NFL STADIUMS Name the *thirty-two* stadiums of the NFL. You can find the solution on page 343. [**Target: 22**]

MISCELLANY XXIII Respond to these questions of a miscellaneous nature. Look for the solutions on page 285. [**Target: 10**]

1. How was a construction known in the Soviet Union as the "Anti-Fascist Protective Rampart" better known in the West?

2. *My Fair Lady* was based on which play by George Bernard Shaw?

3. In which general direction is the River Niagara flowing as it passes over the Niagara Falls?

4. In which country would you find Sheriff's Courts?

5. What scientific discovery was made by Francis Crick and James Watson in 1953?

6. What is the key characteristic of a ship that is described as "Post-Panamax"?

7. How was Samuel Clemens better known?

8. What links Charles Dickens, Laurence Olivier, Isaac Newton, and Edward the Confessor?

9. What was developed by the Manhattan Project?

10. How many gold medals did Mark Spitz win at the 1972 Munich Olympics?

11. Specifically, what did Nelson lose on Tenerife in 1797?

12. What is known as The Main Street of America and the Mother Road?

13. How many semitones are there in an octave?

14. Which TV family lives at 742 Evergreen Terrace?

15. Where did William Travis and Davy Crockett meet their ends?

16. Which trophy was held by the U.S.A. for 132* years until won by Australia in 1983?

17. Which two books of the bible are named after women?

18. Which slang word for a socially inept person first appeared in a Dr. Seuss book?

19. In 1999, which two actresses received Oscar nominations for playing the same role, but in different films?

20. "Yellow Submarine" was released as a double A-side with which other Beatles song?

21. Mr. Smith weighs 40lb. more than Mrs. Smith. Together they weigh 130lb. How much do they each weigh?

22. What do Scots describe as Grahams, Corbetts, and Munros?

23. In which sport are the team members known as lead, second, third, and skip?

24. A bookworm encounters a ten-volume set of books on a shelf and starts eating them. Each book, pages and covers together,

---

* The longest winning run in sport.

is 5 cm thick. Each cover is $\frac{1}{2}$ cm thick. If the bookworm eats at a rate of 1cm every hour, how long will it take the bookworm to eat its way from page one of the first volume to the last page of the last volume?

AMERICAN GLADIATORS Recall the *thirty-two* American Gladiators from the original* television series. Find the solution on page 306. [**Target: 7**]

FIRST LINES OF POP SONGS V Recall the titles of these songs from the first lines provided. (The year each song was a hit is supplied to assist you.) If you wish, name the performers as well. Turn to page 344 for the solutions. [**Target: 14**]

1. "Billy-ray was a preacher's son and when his daddy would visit he'd come along." (1969)
2. "Sittin' in the mornin' sun I'll be sittin' when the evenin' come." (1968)
3. "I said a hip hop the hippie the hippie to the hip hip hop a you don't stop the rock it to the bang bang boogie say up jumped the boogie to the rhythm of the boogie the beat." (1979)
4. "I met her in a club down in north Soho." (1970)
5. "I thought I saw a man brought to life." (1997)
6. "Sometimes I feel I've got to run away." (1981)
7. "Ooh it's so good, it's so good, it's so good, it's so good, it's so good." (1977)
8. "Ooh, baby, baby, baby, baby, ooh, baby, baby, baby, baby." (1987)
9. "The lights are on, but you're not home." (1986)
10. "I made it through the wilderness." (1984)
11. "Look at the stars, look how they shine for you." (2000)
12. "Once I had a love and it was a gas." (1979)
13. "So if you're lonely you know I'm here waiting for you." (2004)
14. "I need a lover to give me the kind of love that would last always." (1993)

---

* Gladiators from the revival show are Blast, Crush, Fury, Hammer, Hellga, Justice, Mayhem, Militia, Siren, Stealth, Titan, Toa, Venom, and Wolf.

15. "May I have your attention please?" (2000)
16. "You know that it would be untrue." (1967)
17. "When the moon is in the seventh house and Jupiter aligns with Mars." (1969)
18. "Well I guess it would be nice if I could touch your body." (1987)
19. "In the day we sweat it out in the streets of a runaway American dream." (1975)
20. "I've known a few guys who thought they were pretty smart." (1999)
21. "Oh, yeah, I'll tell you something." (1963)
22. "People say I'm the life of the party because I tell a joke or two." (1965)
23. "Get up in the morning, slaving for bread, sir." (1969)
24. "One, two, three and to the fo' Snoop Doggy Dogg and Dr. Dre are at the do.'" (1993)

SQUARES ON THE MONOPOLY BOARD Recall the *thirty-six** unique squares on the original Atlantic City Monopoly† board on which players may land. The solution is on page 220. [**Target: 18**]

MADONNA HITS Recall the *thirty-six* singles by Madonna which have reached number ten or higher in the Billboard Hot 100. Look to page 241 for the solution. [**Target: 7**]

CHARACTERS IN LITERATURE IV Identify the works of literature in which each of these characters appears. Turn to page 261 for the solutions. [**Target: 10**]

1. Major Major Major Major
2. Aunt Spiker and Aunt Sponge
3. The Wife of Bath
4. Winston Smith

---

* There are actually forty squares on the board (ten along each side of the board) but some squares are duplicated.

† Charles Darrow conceived the game of Monopoly in 1934 based on properties in Atlantic City and by the time of his death in 1967 was the world's first game-designer millionaire. Over the years, Monopoly has been released in different versions all over the world, and it is estimated that 200 million games have been sold to date (which equates to an estimated 5 billion little green houses).

5.	Injun Joe	6.	Mr. Tumnus
7.	Tweedledum and Tweedledee	8.	Abraham Van Helsing
9.	Rikki Tikki Tavi	10.	Holden Caulfield
11.	Mrs. Malaprop	12.	Leopold Bloom
13.	Miss Havisham	14.	Maxim de Winter
15.	Mr. Knightley	16.	Raskolnikov
17.	Pelagia Iannis	18.	Piggy
19.	Guy Montag	20.	Aunt Pittypat
21.	George Milton	22.	Anne Shirley
23.	Jack Torrance	24.	Bathsheba Everdene

PLAYS BY WILLIAM SHAKESPEARE Name the *thirty-seven* plays by William Shakespeare.* You can find the solution on page 286. [**Target:** 12]

SUPER BOWL MVPS Recall the *thirty-eight* players who have been named Most Valuable Player† in a Super Bowl. The solution is on page 306. [**Target:** 7]

---

* William Shakespeare was born in Stratford-upon-Avon in 1564 (the same year as his rival, Christopher Marlowe) but given his status today, surprisingly little is known about his life. He married Anne Hathaway, eight years his senior, when he was only eighteen, with Anne giving birth to their first child, Susanna, six months later (which may provide the reason for their union). Their twins Hamnet and Judith arrived two years later, in 1585. Shakespeare is thought to have left Anne about this time to move to London to pursue a career as an actor and playwright, and probably began writing around 1588. Shakespeare acted with the Lord Chamberlain's Men (renamed the King's Men in 1603) along with Richard Burbage (the top celebrity actor of his day); their company had stakes in two London theatres, Blackfriars and the Globe. The first written reference to Shakespeare appears in a highly critical review by the playwright Robert Greene in 1592 which may coincide, ironically, with Shakespeare's first taste of commercial success. In 1596 Shakespeare's father, John, applied for a coat of arms, perhaps as a result of his son's accomplishments. Shakespeare died in 1616 after retiring to Stratford-upon-Avon but most of his plays were published posthumously in a volume called the First Folio in 1634, making it difficult to know the exact dates that the plays were written.

† Since 1989 the winner of the Super Bowl MVP has been presented with the Pete Rozelle Trophy and a Cadillac model of the winner's choice.

LINKED MISCELLANY XIII Respond to these miscellaneous questions and deduce the connecting theme linking them. The solution is on page 325. [**Target: 7**]

1. Which country is the fifth largest in size in both area and population?
2. How is the constellation of Orion otherwise known?
3. Which New York borough, located on the mainland, is separated from Manhattan by the Harlem River?
4. Which character, taken from the name of his 1972 album, was David Bowie's alter ego between 1972 and 1973?
5. Who was the American First Lady from 1961 until 1963?
6. Which Ian Fleming novel, published in 1956, was the first in a series?
7. Which scientific quantity, by convention symbolized by Q, can be defined as "energy in transit"?
8. Which famous city is overlooked by Table Mountain?
9. In golf, how is a Number 1 Wood more commonly known?
10. What term is given to the market conditions where investors have confident expectations of capital gains?

FIRST SPOUSES Name the *thirty-nine* first spouses*—women who have been married to a U.S. president while he has been in office. Turn to page 344 for the solution. [**Target: 7**]

BOOKS OF THE OLD TESTAMENT Name the *thirty-nine* books of the Old Testament.† Find the solution on page 220. [**Target: 7**]

FOREIGN WORDS AND PHRASES II Identify the foreign word or phrase from the description provided. Each word or phrase is in common use in English but has been loaned from another language. Look for the answers on page 242. [**Target: 14**]

1. Outdoors (Italian)
2. Military takeover or a success (French)

---

* Under the First Spouse Program, the spouses of each of the presidents are being honored with the issuing of a half-ounce $10 golf coin featuring their images. The term "spouse" is being used because while to date all first spouses have been women, that could change by the end of the program.

† The Bible is one of the oldest texts in existence and is also the world's best-selling book. The Old Testament is a collection of books believed to be written by around forty different authors between 1500 B.C. AND 400 B.C.

3. Reason for being (French)
4. A zigzag course through obstacles (Norwegian)
5. The area adjacent to and behind the coast (German)
6. Ground floor balcony (Sanskrit)
7. Spirit of the times (German)
8. An incorrigible child (French)
9. A child prodigy (German)
10. Bugbear or pet fear (French)
11. A vast selection (Swedish)
12. Complete freedom to act, literally "white card" (French)
13. An expert, especially one who gives a critical opinion (Hindi)
14. The lowest point (Arabic)
15. Appetite for travel (German)
16. Temporary lodging or small flat, literally "a foothold" (French)
17. Pursuit of political interests ahead of ethical concerns (German)
18. Easy, without hard work (Hindi)
19. Out of control (Malay)
20. Type of mathematical notation, literally "reunion of broken parts" (Arabic)
21. Taking pleasure in the misfortune of others (German)
22. Eager, zealous (Mandarin Chinese)
23. Strong criticism (German)
24. Government official responsible for investigating complaints (Swedish)

NHL 500 CLUB Try to name the *forty* NHL players to have scored 500 or more regular season goals. Find the solution on page 262. [**Target: 7**]

LONGEST RIVERS Name the *forty* longest rivers* in the world. You can find the solution on page 287. [**Target: 7**]

---

* Estimates for river lengths vary enormously for the following reasons: (i) seasonal fluctuations in precipitation; (ii) alternative interpretations of routes and particularly in the definition of tributaries; (iii) accuracy of measurement of length (for example, as measurement becomes more accurate river length will tend to increase as more directional fluctuations are included); (iv) definition of the river source may be arbitrary (for example, where many tributaries exist); (v) definition of the river mouth may be arbitrary (for example, where there is a large estuary which gradually opens into the sea). Figures tend to be inconsistent between different sources and must be treated as indicative.

WIT AND WISDOM III The following quotations are attributed to either Groucho Marx or Woody Allen or Homer Simpson. Identify the correct author of each quotation. Look for the solutions on page 307. [**Target: 20**]

1. "I don't care to belong to a club that accepts people like me as members."
2. "If you don't like your job you don't strike. You just go in there every day and do it really half-assed. That's the American way."
3. "I was raised in the Jewish tradition, taught never to marry a Gentile woman, shave on a Saturday night and, most especially, never to shave a Gentile woman on a Saturday night."
4. "Weaselling out of things is important to learn. It's what separates us from the animals . . . except the weasel."
5. "Outside of a dog, a book is man's best friend. Inside of a dog, it's too dark to read."
6. "It's not easy to juggle a pregnant wife and a troubled child, but somehow I managed to fit in eight hours of TV a day."
7. "I failed to make the chess team because of my height."
8. "What's the point of going out? We're just going to wind up back here anyway."
9. "He may look like an idiot and talk like an idiot but don't let that fool you. He really is an idiot."
10. "Getting out of jury duty is easy. The trick is to say you're prejudiced against all races."
11. "I have had a perfectly wonderful evening, but this wasn't it."
12. "Money is better than poverty, if only for financial reasons."
13. "Either he's dead or my watch has stopped."
14. "I like my beer cold, my TV loud, and my homosexuals flaming."
15. "I think crime pays. The hours are good, you travel a lot."
16. "A child of five would understand this. Get me a child of five!"
17. "I took a speed-reading course and read *War and Peace* in twenty minutes. It involves Russia."
18. "I never forget a face, but in your case I'll make an exception."
19. "No one asked me to volunteer."
20. "How can I believe in God when just last week I got my tongue caught in the roller of an electric typewriter?"

21. "Those are my principles. If you don't like them I have others."
22. "Why was I with her? She reminds me of you. In fact, she reminds me more of you than you do!"
23. "I don't want to achieve immortality through my work. I want to achieve it through not dying."
24. "What if we chose the wrong religion? Each week we just make God madder and madder."

AMERICAN PRESIDENTS Recall the *forty-two* presidents of the United States of America.* The solution is on page 325. [**Target: 15**]

MISCELLANY XXIV Respond to these questions of a miscellaneous nature. Go to page 221 for the solutions. [**Target: 12**]

1. A person experiencing a photic sneeze reflex sneezes in response to what external stimulus?
2. What does the flag of Belize have more of than any other national flag?
3. Which term for a period of isolation is derived from the biblical period of forty days?
4. In which month is the vernal equinox?
5. Who composed *Aida*?
6. From which television series was *Mork and Mindy* a spin-off?
7. Which singer has the middle name "Hercules"?
8. In which town did the gunfight at the OK Corral take place?
9. A ship traveling along the Panama Canal from the Pacific Ocean to the Atlantic Ocean would be sailing in which general direction?
10. Which is the only U.S. state with a one-syllable name?
11. If the president and vice president both die at the same time, who takes over?
12. In which human organ would you find aqueous humor and vitreous humor?
13. The name of which common cooking ingredient comes from

---

* Although George W. Bush is the forty-third president, to date, a total of forty-two people have held the office. American presidents swear an oath on entering office, as specified in Article II, Section 1, of the Constitution: "I do solemnly swear (or affirm) that I will faithfully execute the office of President of the United States, and will to the best of my ability, preserve, protect, and defend the Constitution of the United States."

the French meaning "sour wine"?

14. In chess, what is the minimum number of moves a pawn must make to become a queen?

15. Which American university is located at New Haven, Connecticut?

16. What was the name of the blind Benedictine monk who, it is claimed, first produced champagne?

17. If it takes Belinda six hours to paint a fence and Janice three hours to paint the same fence, how long would it take to paint if they both worked at the same time?

18. What TV icon has a diameter of eight and a half feet?

19. In *Alice's Adventures in Wonderland*, what did Alice use as a croquet mallet?

20. What was the first major construction project in which workers were required to wear hard hats?

21. What Shakespeare play was the inspiration for the film *Forbidden Planet*?

22. Africa was the Roman name for which modern-day country?

23. What was known as the "noble experiment"?

24. Two trains are heading directly towards each other. One is moving at 70 mph, the other at 50 mph. How far apart will they be one minute before they meet?

ENGLISH MONARCHS Recall the *forty-three* sovereign rulers of England or Britain since 1066.* Go to page 263 for the solution. [Target: 32]

QUOTATIONS FROM POPULAR FILMS III Identify the films from which these quotations have been taken. (The date of the film is provided to assist you.) Look for the solutions on page 288. [Target: 12]

1. "Of all the gin joints in all the towns in all the world, she walks into mine." (1942)

---

* Although England had kings prior to 1066, the Norman invasion defined and strengthened the institution of the monarchy. The succession of 1603 united the monarchies of England and Scotland, and all monarchs since have ruled the kingdom of Britain.

2. "This is an occasion for genuinely tiny knickers." (2001)
3. "Everybody listen! We have to put a barrier between us and the snakes!" (2006)
4. "Go back to the shadow. You shall not pass!" (2001)
5. "Fräulein, were you this much trouble at the Abbey?" (1965)
6. "Cancel the kitchen scraps for lepers and orphans, no more merciful beheadings, and call off Christmas." (1991)
7. "They only see what they want to see. They don't know they're dead." (1999)
8. "A boy's best friend is his mother." (1960)
9. "With fronds like these, who needs anemones?" (2003)
10. "You know I'm retired from hero work." (2004)
11. "Have you ever danced with the devil in the pale moonlight?" (1989)
12. "I know you and Frank were planning to disconnect me, and I'm afraid that's something I cannot allow to happen." (1968)
13. "If your family circle joins my family circle, they'll form a chain. I can't have a chink in my chain." (2004)
14. "I got a feeling that behind those jeans is something wonderful just waiting to get out." (1997)
15. "Oh, I'm sorry. Did I break your concentration?" (1994)
16. "Hope can drive a man insane." (1994)
17. "Joey, have you ever been to a Turkish prison?" (1980)
18. "Keep your friends close, but your enemies closer." (1974)
19. "Would you like me to seduce you?" (1967)
20. "If he invites us to stay, then we'll go . . . He's got to invite us to stick around." (1969)
21. "She cooks as good as she looks, Ted." (1975)
22. "The trick . . . is not minding that it hurts." (1962)
23. "If I'm not back in five minutes . . . just wait longer!" (1996)
24. "It's awfully easy to lie when you know that you're trusted implicitly. So very easy, and so very degrading." (1945)

LANDLOCKED COUNTRIES Name the *forty-three* landlocked countries* in the world; that is, countries which neither have direct

---

* Landlocked countries are disadvantaged because of their reliance on the cooperation of neighboring states for economic and military activity.

access to an ocean nor to a sea that is accessible to an ocean. Look for the solution on page 307. [Target: 12]

MASTERS CHAMPIONS Name the *forty-four* players to have won the Masters.* The solution is on page 345. [Target: 7]

LATIN PHRASES II Identify each of these commonly used Latin† phrases or their abbreviations from their English translations. The solutions are on page 346. [Target: 8]

1.	After midday	2.	And so on
3.	After death	4.	Unwelcome person
5.	With the order reversed	6.	By each head of population
7.	Way of operating	8.	Note well
9.	Other self	10.	Of sound mind
11.	Other things being equal	12.	Against
13.	For the time being	14.	Course of life
15.	In place of parents	16.	You must have the body
17.	My fault	18.	Under penalty
19.	From cause to effect	20.	It does not follow
21.	A god from a machine	22.	By fact itself
23.	Beneath one's dignity	24.	Among other things

EUROPEAN CAPITAL CITIES Name the *forty-four* capital cities in the continent of Europe. The solution is on page 288. [Target: 10]

TAGLINES OF POPULAR FILMS IV Name the films from their taglines below. The solutions are on page 265. [Target: 10]

---

* The Masters is held every year at Augusta National Golf Club.
† Latin has existed for around 2,500 years and although no longer spoken has provided the basis for the Romance languages of Italian, French, Spanish, Portuguese, and Romanian. It has influenced English both directly and through words that have been incorporated from French. From the later Middle Ages until the nineteenth century, Latin was the language of religious, legal, administrative, scientific, and academic texts, areas in which many Latin phrases are still in common use today.

1. "In space no one can hear you scream." (1979)
2. "He is afraid. He is alone. He is three million light years from home." (1982)
3. "Poultry in Motion." (2000)
4. "Seek the truth, seek the codes." (2006)
5. "What a feeling." (1983)
6. "A little pig goes a long way." (1995)
7. "And you thought your parents were embarrassing." (2004)
8. "Deadly. Silent. Stolen." (1990)
9. "A family comedy without the family." (1990)
10. "Sit back. Relax. Enjoy the fright." (2006)
11. "The future of law enforcement." (1987)
12. "Magic will happen." (2001)
13. "Marilyn Monroe and her bosom companions." (1959)
14. "His passion captivated a woman. His courage inspired a nation. His heart defied a king." (1995)
15. "3.14159265358979." (1998)
16. "Cute. Clever. Mischievous. Intelligent. Dangerous." (1984)
17. "A perfect assassin. An innocent girl. They have nothing left to lose except each other." (1994)
18. "Fridays will never be the same again." (1980)
19. "When he said I do, he didn't say what he did." (1994)
20. "The music is on his side." (1984)
21. "Does for rock 'n' roll what *The Sound of Music* did for hills." (1984)
22. "Nice planet. We'll take it!" (1996)
23. "Fifty million people watched, but no one saw a thing." (1994)
24. "The story that won't go away." (1991)

COUNTRIES IN EUROPE List the *forty-four* countries in the continent of Europe.* Go to page 288 for the solution. [**Target: 34**]

REFEREE SIGNALS IN THE NFL List the *forty-five* signals that may be given by a referee in an NFL football game. Look to page 242 for the solution. [**Target: 15**]

---

* Europe has an area of 3.8 million square miles and a population of 567 million people, about 9% of the world's population.

SINGERS AND BACKERS III Complete the names of these groups by naming the singer most closely associated with these particular backing bands. Find the solutions on page 326. [**Target: 14**]

1. _____ and the Ants
2. _____ and the Sunshine Band
3. _____ and Miami Sound Machine
4. _____ and the Pips
5. _____ and the Plastic Ono Band
6. _____ and the Wailers
7. _____ and the Gang
8. _____ and the News
9. _____ and the E Street Band
10. _____ and the Coconuts
11. _____ and the Dreamers
12. _____ and the Bad Seeds
13. _____ and the Crickets
14. _____ and Tubeway Army
15. _____ and the Starliters
16. _____ and the Mothers of Invention
17. _____ and the E-Train
18. _____ and the Miracles
19. _____ and the Rebelettes
20. _____ and the Fireballs
21. _____ and the Dakotas
22. _____ and the Tremeloes
23. _____ and the Blue Flames
24. _____ and the Tuxedos

U.S.A. FOR AFRICA Recall the *forty-six* artists who as members of U.S.A. for Africa performed on the single "We Are the World." Turn to page 347 for the solution. [**Target: 12**]

FIRST LADIES Name the *forty-nine* First Ladies.* The solution is on page 345. [**Target: 7**]

---

* First Lady is an unofficial title for the hostess at the White House. The role has existed since the inception of the presidency, however the term First *cont'd over*

ASIAN CAPITAL CITIES Name the *fifty* capital cities in the continent of Asia. The solution is on page 221. [**Target: 13**]

MUSICAL TERMS Describe the meaning of each of these musical terms.[†] Find the solution on page 244. [**Target: 7**]

1.	Piano	2.	Crescendo
3.	Staccato	4.	Forte
5.	Allegro	6.	Accelerando
7.	Diminuendo	8.	Adagio
9.	A cappella	10.	Lento

---

cont'd   Lady was first used in 1849 by Zachary Taylor. Usually the first lady is the wife of the president (the first spouse) but several women have taken on the position first lady when the president was a bachelor or a widower. In these cases the role has been taken on by a close friend or female relative of the president.

† Musical notation originates with a Roman philosopher called Boethius (c. 475–525 A.D.) who first used letters to represent notes. The system was expanded in the twelfth century by Guido d'Arrezo, a Benedictine monk who came up with the idea of a staff on to which notes could be placed to indicate their pitch. Guido was also an inspirational teacher and, to help his students, devised a system using syllables to represent notes. He took these syllables from "Ut queant laxis," a popular hymn of the time:

"UT queant laxis REsonare fibri
MIra gestorum FAmuli tuorum
SOLve polluti LAbii reatum
Sancte Ioannes"

The piece was notable because the first note of each musical phrase begins with a successively higher note, coinciding with the first six notes of the scale of C major, which Guido called "UT," "RE," "ME," "FA," "SOL" and "LA." Since Guido's time, "UT" has been replaced with the more sing-able "DOH" and a seventh note, "TE" has been added to complete the scale, leading to the familiar "DOH-RE-ME" octave. (Guido represented the lowest line on his staff with the Greek letter gamma. Under his notation, the lowest note, "UT"—which would now be called Middle C—became known as "gamma ut" or "gamut." The word gamut later took on the connotation of describing the whole of the scale, from where it took on its current meaning of an entire range of anything.) During the Renaissance, devotional choral music gave way to new forms of music (such as opera) and composers started to write polyphonic arrangements for musical instruments as well as human voices. The use of Italian in musical notation is a legacy of the dominance of Italian composers and musicians in Western music during the seventeenth century.

11.	Vibrato	12.	Ritardando
13.	Largo	14.	Grave
15.	Legato	16.	Vivace
17.	Soave	18.	Con brio
19.	Al fine	20.	Presto
21.	Da capo	22.	Ma non troppo
23.	Tremolo	24.	Pizzicato

VALUABLE GLOBAL BRANDS Name the *fifty* most valuable brand* names in the world. Turn to page 222 for the solution. [**Target: 15**]

AMERICAN STATES Recall the *fifty* states making up the United States of America.† Go to page 289 for the solution. [**Target: 40**]

MISCELLANY XXV Respond to these questions of a miscellaneous nature. The solutions may be found on page 308. [**Target: 8**]

1. What was banned in the U.S. by the Eighteenth Amendment to the Constitution?
2. What do the stripes represent on the stars and stripes?
3. Which harmful bacterium was first identified by Daniel Elmer Salmon?
4. Who played the Riddler in the 1995 film *Batman Forever*?
5. Which opera features Lieutenant Pinkerton?
6. Where is the only palace which is used as an official royal residence in the U.S.?

---

* The advertiser David Ogilvy once defined brand as "the intangible sum of a product's attributes: its name, packaging, and price, its history, its reputation, and the way it's advertised."

† With a population of 280 million people and a GDP of $10 trillion, the United States is currently the world's only true superpower. The U.S. spends more money on arms ($277 billion) than the next twelve largest military spenders combined and consumes more energy than India, the Middle East, South America, Africa, Southeast Asia, and Australasia combined. America became independent from Britain in 1776 and was recognized internationally as the United States of America by the Treaty of Paris in 1783. The original thirteen states were joined by thirty-seven others over the next two centuries as the settlers spread west.

7. In *Star Trek*, what color blood do Vulcans have?

8. Which is the only U.S. state which produces coffee?

9. Which two common fruits have names that are anagrams of each other?

10. Which is the only one of New York's five boroughs located on the mainland?

11. What was the name of Long John Silver's parrot in *Treasure Island*?

12. From which language does the word "safari" originate?

13. In a town, 60% of the population speak English and 70% of the population speak French. Assuming these are the only languages spoken in the town, what proportion of the town is bilingual?

14. Whose body was exhumed from Westminster Abbey and subject to a posthumous execution?

15. What links the Vatican, Palestine, and Taiwan?

16. How many possible opening moves are there in a game of checkers?

17. Which piece of sporting equipment measures 9' long by 5' wide and is 30' tall?

18. What are sodium thiopental, pancuronium bromide, and potassium chloride, when administered in that order, used for?

19. Which is the only U.S. state from which rivers flow into three different oceans?

20. What is the maximum number of match points that can be held at one time in a tennis* match at Wimbledon?

21. What is the collective name for the "Nine Handmaidens of Odin"?

22. According to Genesis, on which day of creation did God make the sun, the moon, and the stars?

---

* The scoring system of tennis is somewhat arcane and the origins are not well understood. It is likely tennis derives from a game played in medieval France in which a clock face was used to keep the score. Points in the games were incremented in multiples of fifteen (the "forty" call is thought simply to be short for "forty-five," and sixty, the top score, was never called as the game ended when this score was reached). Other peculiarities of tennis scoring include the term "deuce," possibly a corruption of the French phrase "a deux du jeu" meaning "two points away from the (end of the) game." The origins of the term "love" are less clear. It may derive from "l'oeuf" meaning "egg" (which is the same shape as a zero), or from the idea that the player with zero points must be playing for love rather than money.

23. In *The Simpsons*, what is the name of Springfield's founder?
24. If it were two hours later, it would be half as long to midnight as if it were an hour later. What time is it now?

ASSASSINATIONS Identify the victims of these assassinations* from the clues. Find the solutions on page 226. [**Target: 10**]

1. Shot by Lee Harvey Oswald in Dallas in 1963.
2. Stabbed by Brutus and others in the Senate in 44 B.C.
3. Shot by actor John Wilkes Booth in Ford's Theatre, Washington, in 1865.
4. Shot by Mark Chapman outside his New York apartment in 1980.
5. Shot by Gavrilo Princip in Sarajevo; the assassination precipitated the First World War.
6. International guerrilla leader captured and executed in Bolivia in 1967.
7. Shot and killed by Jack Ruby on live television in 1963.
8. Murdered with an ice pick while in exile in Mexico in 1940.
9. Shot by James Earl Ray in Memphis, Tennessee, in 1968.
10. Shot by a Hindu fanatic in New Delhi in 1948.
11. Shot in the Hotel Ambassador, Los Angeles, in 1968.
12. Pakistan opposition leader and former prime minister murdered by a suicide bomber in 2007.
13. Murdered by members of her Sikh bodyguard in New Delhi in 1984.
14. King of Scotland, murdered by Malcolm III in 1057.
15. American Muslim leader, shot during a political rally in 1965.
16. Sinn Fein leader, killed in an ambush in the Irish Republic in 1922.

---

* The word "assassin" is derived from a word translating as "hashish-eater," the name given to certain members of the Nizari Ismaili, a tribe originating in twelfth-century Syria. According to legend, the assassins carried out killings on behalf of the Nizari leader, who controlled them through the use of hashish. The word was brought into English by returning crusaders, where it entered common use as a noun meaning "murderer." Assassination has since come to its current meaning as the killing of a prominent person usually for a politically motivated reason.

17. Swedish Prime Minister, shot walking home from the cinema by an unknown assassin in 1986.
18. Israeli Prime Minister, murdered by a Jewish extremist in 1995.
19. Roman Emperor, poisoned by his wife in A.D. 54.
20. Egyptian president murdered in Cairo in 1981 by soldiers in a military parade.
21. Founder of the American Nazi Party, shot in 1967 by John Patler.
22. Japanese Fleet Admiral killed when his transport plane was ambushed by U.S. fighters over the Solomon Islands in 1943 after U.S. military intelligence intercepted and decoded Japanese communications revealing details of his movements.
23. Roman Emperor, murdered by members of the Praetorian Guard in A.D. 41.
24. U.S. president, shot in a railway station by Charles Guiteau in 1881.

COUNTRIES IN ASIA Name the *fifty* countries in the continent of Asia.* Go to page 221 for the solution. [**Target: 25**]

POPULOUS AMERICAN CITIES Try to list the *fifty* most populous cities in the United States.† Find the solution on page 347. [**Target: 20**]

"ISMS" II Identify the philosophies, beliefs, concepts, or practices from the descriptions provided. (Note that all of the solutions contain the suffix "-ism.") You will find the solutions on page 223. [**Target: 10**]

---

* Asia is the largest continent in the world, covering approximately 17 million square miles, a third of the world's total land area, and also the most populous; it is home to over 60 percent of the world's population. Asia is notable for its ethnic diversity: the sub-regions of Central Asia, Southeast Asia, the Middle East, and India (particularly) are sometimes regarded as continents in their own right. The western boundaries of Asia are not well defined; Asia meets Africa somewhere near the Suez Canal. The European border could be said to include the Sea of Marmara, the Black Sea, the Caucasus, the Caspian Sea, the Ural River, and the Ural Mountains.
† According to U.S. Census Bureau figures from 2006

1. The belief that a particular race is inherently superior or inferior to others; the discrimination against individuals based on their race.
2. The use of unlawful and often horrific violence against civilians in order to coerce or intimidate societies or governments for political or ideological purposes.
3. A term describing an extreme and excessive devotion to a cause or group but now more commonly applied to sexist males.
4. A general belief that things are bad and tend to become worse.
5. A political system in which all property belongs to the community and where all individuals have equal social and economic status.
6. The pursuit of pleasure as an end in itself.
7. A vague term for a cultural, artistic, or philosophical movement that has moved beyond modernism.
8. An ancient polytheistic religion dating from 2,000 B.C. and the majority religion in India.
9. The practice of worship of the earth and nature, particularly by ancient European religions*; the term is often used to imply a backward or culturally unsophisticated set of beliefs.
10. The practice of expansion by a nation through the annexation of foreign territories to create an empire.
11. The branch of communism in China, associated with Mao Tse-tung, which focused on the peasantry as the revolutionary force.
12. The religious movement founded by John Wesley in 1738.
13. A form of imperialism in which the mother country allows semiautonomous legal and social institutions in the dependent states.
14. A political system in which capital and the means of production are owned either collectively or by a central government that controls the economy.
15. A term describing adherence in religious groups to strict or literal interpretations of religious texts or ideas and often associated with belligerent and violent activities.
16. A religion meaning literally "divine path," based on the worship of "kami"—gods, ancestors, and natural forces; the native religion of Japan.
17. The belief in more than one god.
18. The belief and proclamation of the Christian gospel with particular emphasis on rebirth or conversion.

---

* For example Wicca, Druidism, Asatru, and Shamanism.

19. An extreme form of dictatorship under which all individuals are completely subject to the wishes of the state.
20. A term describing a belligerent or hawkish stance towards opposition supposed to be technically or culturally inferior.
21. The psychological method of studying the behaviour of individuals and how it changes in response to different stimuli.
22. A philosophy derived from Hegel's dialectics and Marx's materialism in which successive contradictory statements (thesis, antithesis, synthesis) are used to explain the evolution of human society.
23. A branch of Protestantism with the central tenet that people are predestined for either salvation or eternal damnation regardless of wealth or piety.
24. A philosophy that opposes the separation of Church and State, first recorded in 1858, but perhaps better known for being one of the longest English words.

COMMONWEALTH COUNTRIES Name the *fifty-three* members of the Commonwealth.* Find the solution on page 244. [**Target:** 7]

ALFRED HITCHCOCK FILMS List the *fifty-four* films directed by Alfred Hitchcock.† The solution is on page 265. [**Target:** 7]

---

* The Commonwealth is a loose political union of former colonies of the British Empire. The term was coined by Lord Rosebery in 1884, referring to a "commonwealth of nations" as the status of the British colonies evolved into self-governing dominions (Canada in 1867, Australia 1900, New Zealand 1907, South Africa 1910, Irish Free State 1921). After the independence of India and Pakistan, in 1949 the Commonwealth took on its present form, with the word "British" being dropped from the title.
† The "Master of Suspense" was born in Leytonstone, London in 1899 and, in a career that lasted over fifty years, almost single-handedly defined the movie-thriller genre. As a young film enthusiast, Hitchcock got a job as a title designer at the new Paramount studios in London and worked his way up to the position of director, completing his first film in 1925. His films began to win international acclaim and Hitchcock himself was gaining notoriety for his trademark cameo appearances. In 1940 and with the outbreak of war, Hitchcock moved to the U.S. and started working in Hollywood, and in the 1950s produced what many critics regard as his best work. Although recognized by the American Film Institute and receiving a knighthood in Britain, Hitchcock was largely ignored by the Oscars, never winning the award for Best Director. Hitchcock's work and his unique understanding of his audience was perhaps best summed up when he once said: "There is no terror in the bang, only in the anticipation of it." Alfred Hitchcock died in 1980.

SCENTS Identify the producers of each of these scents.* (Note that the same producer may be the solution to more than one of these.) Go to page 290 for the solutions. [**Target: 7**]

1.	No. 5	2.	Polo
3.	CK One	4.	Coco
5.	Dune	6.	Opium
7.	Obsession	8.	Anaïs Anaïs
9.	Poison	10.	Chloé
11.	Jazz	12.	Eternity
13.	Fahrenheit	14.	Fifth Avenue
15.	Poême	16.	So Pretty
17.	Passion	18.	Intuition
19.	Organza	20.	All About Eve
21.	La Nuit	22.	Xeryus
23.	Accenti	24.	Clandestine

COUNTRIES IN AFRICA List the *fifty-four* countries that make up the continent of Africa.† You can find the solution on page 308. [**Target: 20**]

OLYMPIC DISCIPLINES Name the *fifty-six* Olympic disciplines (in both the summer and winter games). Note that "disciplines" are not necessarily synonymous with "sports" or "events"; for example,

---

* Modern perfume is made up of a mixture of essential oils, fixative, and alcohol. The essential oils provide the scent, the fixative is used to bind the oils together, and alcohol evaporates on contact with the skin, leaving the fragrance behind to evaporate over a period of hours. Perfume consists mostly of alcohol (about 78% to 95%); the strength (and therefore cost) of a perfume is defined by the concentration of the essential oils in the alcohol. Concentrations of over 22% essential oils are called perfume, 15–22% eau de perfume, 8–15% eau de toilette and those under 8% are known as eau de cologne. Really subtle scents of 3% or less are called eau fraiche. Essential oils are produced through the distillation of plants and flowers or sometimes through a process called "enfleurage" where they are absorbed into wax. Common organic products used include anise, bay leaf, bergamot, cardamom, cedar wood, eucalyptus, frankincense, gardenia, geranium, iris, jasmine, lavender, lemon, lilac, lily, lily of the valley, magnolia, moss, neroli, orange, orris, patchouli, pine, raspberry, rose, sage, sandalwood, tuberose, vanilla, violet, and ylang-ylang.
† Africa is the second largest of the world's continents, with an area of 11.69 million square miles.

the sport of cycling has four associated disciplines for which eighteen medals are contested.* The solution is on page 326. [**Target: 40**]

LINKED MISCELLANY XIV
In responding to these miscellaneous questions, deduce the connecting theme linking the solutions. The solution is on page 348. [**Target: 6**]

1. Which actress appeared in *Grease 2*, *The Witches of Eastwick*, and *Batman Returns*?
2. Which nocturnal and omnivorous mammal of the genus Procyon is naturally found throughout the Americas and is noted for its manual dexterity, for example an ability to open rubbish bins?
3. What nationality were the explorers Thor Heyerdahl and Roald Amundsen?
4. What common name is applied to the edible plants of the Capsicum genus?
5. Which aircraft holds the record for flying from New York to London in the shortest time[†]?
6. Which singer has been romantically linked with John F. Kennedy Jr., Warren Beatty, Vanilla Ice, and Sandra Bernhard?
7. Which global federation was formed in 1922 and dissolved in 1991?
8. What is 2^6?
9. The title of which James Bond film is based on an advertising slogan?
10. Which poem by Lewis Carroll tells the story of its two eponymous characters taking a walk on a beach with some friendly oysters?

SIGNATORIES OF THE DECLARATION OF INDEPENDENCE
Try to name the *fifty-six* signatories of the Declaration of Independence.[‡] The solution is on page 223. [**Target: 5**]

---

* The current Olympic program consists of thirty-five sports and just shy of 400 events (for which each medal is awarded).

† Set with a time of 1 hour and 54 minutes in 1974.

‡ The full title of the declaration was "The unanimous Declaration of the thirteen united States of America" and it was signed on July 4, 1776. The Declaration consists of five parts: the Introduction, the Preamble, the Indictment of George III, the Denunciation of the British people, and the Conclusion.

NATIONAL PARKS List the *fifty-six* national parks in the United States. Turn to page 244 for the solution. [**Target: 12**]

ETYMOLOGY OF ROCK AND POP NAMES II Identify the names of the groups or artists from these brief descriptions of their etymology. The solutions can be found on page 267. [**Target: 10**]

1. After the lead singer's bleached hair.
2. From an electrical acronym describing different types of current.
3. Changed their name from the "Chicago Transit Authority" after legal action by the City of Chicago.
4. Prompted by a newspaper headline reporting Frank Sinatra's move to California.
5. Inspired by the term "rhythmic gymnastics," a method of teaching music.
6. From the desperate financial situation the band members once found themselves in.
7. After the Buddhist term for enlightenment.
8. After a shop selling garden water features on Route 46 in Wayne, New Jersey.
9. From a road sign warning of construction activity.
10. As a parody of many groups whose names start with "the."
11. Named after the river in Greek mythology that separates the earth from the underworld.
12. From a slang term for lesbian.
13. Inspired by an aboriginal practice of cuddling a dog to keep warm at night and an expression for a particularly cold night.
14. After a slang term for spending a day smoking cannabis.
15. From a joke once made about the band's future prospects "going down like a lead balloon."
16. Based on the Italian phrase for "political writings."
17. Named after a character in the *Back to the Future* series of films.
18. The nickname for the bouffant hairstyle sported by its female members.
19. Originally named after a children's book called *Mr. Crowe's Garden.*
20. Spanish for "the Wolves."

21. After a book written by Herman Melville, this artist's great-uncle.
22. From the nicknames of the two lead singers, Joseph Simmons and Darryl McDaniels.
23. After Marlon Brando's motorcycle gang in the "The Wild One."
24. From a term for the detached gaze of a battle-weary or shell-shocked soldier.

COCKTAILS Try to name the *sixty-five* "official" cocktails of the International Bartender Association. Look to page 290 for the solution. [Target: 15]

NOVELS BY AGATHA CHRISTIE Name the *sixty-six* mystery novels written by Agatha Christie.* Look to page 267 for the solution. [Target: 7]

OLYMPIANS II Identify these U.S. Olympians from their medal honors. Look to page 327 for the solutions. [Target: 10]

1. Athlete winning gold at Berlin in 1936 in the Men's 100m, Men's 200m, Men's Long Jump and the Men's 4 × 100m Relay.
2. Swimmer winning gold at Mexico City in 1968 in the Men's 4x100m Freestyle Relay and the Men's 4 × 200m Freestyle Relay; gold at Munich in 1972 in the Men's 100m Butterfly, the Men's 100m Freestyle, the Men's 200m Butterfly, the Men's 200m Freestyle, the Men's 4 × 100m Freestyle Relay, the Men's 4 × 100m Medley Relay, and the Men's 4 × 200m Freestyle Relay; silver at Mexico City in the Men's 100m Butterfly; bronze at Mexico City in the Men's 100m Freestyle.
3. Athlete winning gold at Mexico City in the Men's Long Jump.
4. Athlete winning gold at Montreal in 1976 in the Men's 400m Hurdles; gold at Los Angeles in 1984 in the Men's 400m Hurdles; bronze at Seoul in 1988 in the Men's 400m Hurdles.

---

* Dame Agatha Christie was born in Torquay in 1890. By her death in 1976, she had written a total of sixty-six novels and several short-story collections. She also wrote more than a dozen plays one of which, *The Mousetrap*, is the longest-running play in theatrical history, opening in London on November 25, 1952.

5. Athlete winning gold at Seoul in 1988 in the Women's 100m, the Women's 200m, and the Women's 4 × 100m Relay; silver at Los Angeles in 1984 in the Women's 200m; silver at Seoul in the Women's 4 × 400m Relay.

6. Athlete winning gold at Barcelona in 1992 in the Women's 200m and the Women's 4 × 100m Relay; gold at Atlanta in 1996 in the Women's 4 × 100m Relay; silver at Barcelona in the Women's 4 × 400m Relay; bronze at Atlanta in the Women's 100m.

7. Athlete winning gold at Athens in 2004 in the Men's 100m; silver at Athens in the Men's 4 × 100m Relay; bronze at Athens in the Men's 200m.

8. Athlete winning gold at Los Angeles in 1984 in the Men's 400m and the Men's 4 × 400m Relay.

9. Athlete winning gold at Atlanta in 1996 in the Decathlon.

10. Athlete winning gold at Mexico City in 1968 in the Men's High Jump.

11. Athlete winning gold at Los Angeles in 1984 in the Women's 100m and the Women's 4 × 100m Relay; gold at Seoul in 1988 in the Women's 4 × 100m Relay; gold at Barcelona in 1992 in the Women's 4 × 100m Relay; silver at Seoul in the Women's 100m.

12. Athlete winning gold at Mexico City in 1968 in the Men's 100m and the Men's 4 × 100m Relay.

13. Heavyweight boxer winning gold at Tokyo in 1964.

14. Athlete winning gold at Athens in 2004 in the Women's 100m Hurdles.

15. Swimmer winning gold at Paris in 1924 in the Men's 100m Freestyle, the Men's 400m Freestyle, and the Men's 800m Freestyle Relay; gold at Amsterdam in 1928 in the Men's 100m Freestyle and the Men's 800m Freestyle Relay; bronze at Paris in the Water Polo.

16. Ice skater winning gold at Albertville in 1992 in the Ladies' Singles Figure Skating.

17. Swimmer winning gold at Los Angeles in 1984 in the Men's 4 × 100m Freestyle; gold at Seoul in 1988 in the Men's 50m Freestyle, the Men's 100m Freestyle, the Men's 4 × 100m Freestyle Relay, the Men's 4 × 200m Freestyle Relay, and the Men's 4 × 100 m Medley Relay; gold at Barcelona in 1992 in

the Men's 4×100m Freestyle Relay and the Men's 4×100m Medley Relay; silver at Seoul in the Men's 100m Butterfly; silver at Barcelona in the Men's 50m Freestyle; bronze at Seoul in the Men's 200m Freestyle.

18. Swimmer winning gold at Athens in 2004 in the Men's 100m Butterfly, the Men's 200m Butterfly, the Men's 200m Individual Medley, the Men's 400m Individual Medley, the Men's 4×200m Freestyle Relay, and the Men's 4×100m Medley Relay; bronze at Athens in the Men's 200m Freestyle and the Men's 4×100m Freestyle Relay.

19. Athlete winning gold at Barcelona in 1992 in the Men's 400m and the Men's 4×400m Relay.

20. Athlete winning gold at Athens in 2004 in the Men's 200m and silver at Athens in the Men's 4×100m Relay.

21. Athlete winning gold at Los Angeles in the Men's Triple Jump.

22. Ice skater winning silver at Lillehammer in 1994 in the Ladies' Singles Figure Skating and bronze at Albertville in 1992 in the Ladies' Singles Figure Skating.

23. Ice skater winning gold at Sarajevo in 1984 in the Men's Singles Figure Skating.

24. Athlete winning gold at Tokyo in 1964 at the Women's 100m; gold at Mexico in 1968 at the Women's 100m and the Women's 4×100m Relay; silver at Tokyo in 1964 in the Women's 4×100m Relay.

SEAS Name the *seventy-one* seas of the world; that is, those bodies of water having the word "Sea" as part of their name.* Go to page 349 for the solution. [**Target: 25**]

CONSTELLATIONS List the *eighty-eight* modern constellations.[†] The solution is on page 224. [**Target: 16**]

---

* As defined by the International Hydrographical Association (IHO).
† The eighty-eight constellations align to distinct areas of the sky with precise boundaries defined by the International Astronomical Union. Every place in the sky belongs within one of these constellations. Stars which make up constellations may appear to be close together when viewed from Earth but in three-dimensional space have no relationship to one another and may be vast distances apart.

MISCELLANY XXVI Respond to these questions of a miscellaneous nature. The solution is on page 246. [**Target: 14**]

1. Who was the centerfold in the first edition of *Playboy*?
2. Which planet was reclassified as a Dwarf Planet on August 24, 2006?
3. Which artist is famous for painting a portrait of his mother?
4. What was the name of the legislation passed in Britain in 1715 giving local authorities the power to declare any crowd of over twelve people an unlawful assembly and to disperse it accordingly?
5. What is the defining characteristic of an endorheic basin, such as Lake Chad, the Great Salt Lake, the Caspian Sea, or Lake Eyre?
6. In medicine, how is Methicillin Resistant Staphylococcus Aureus more commonly known?
7. Who won the tennis "Golden Slam" in 1988 by winning the Grand Slam of singles titles and winning a gold medal at the Olympic Games?
8. What links Edward III, Japan, and the Animals?
9. What is the last word in the Bible?
10. Which cocktail was invented by New York socialite Jenny Jerome, the mother of Winston Chruchill?
11. In the human body, what is the function of the endocrine system?
12. Which word, meaning an odd or whimsical person, is derived from the Greek, meaning literally "out of center"?
13. What percentage of the world's population is under the age of twenty-five?
14. Which cartoon character was uncle to Knothead and Splinter?
15. What is measured in Floating Point Operations Per Second or FLOPS?
16. What is the official language of Pakistan?
17. In the U.S., what is celebrated on February 2 and is also the title of a popular film?
18. What does QANTAS stand for?
19. In a knockout tennis tournament with 256 entrants, how many matches must be played to produce a winner?
20. Historically, for what is St. Augustine, Florida, famous?

21. Where would you find an American flag that has never been lowered?
22. What is the middle day in a (non-leap) year?
23. How many stars are there on the flag of the European Union?
24. A brick weighs 1lb and half a brick. How heavy is the brick?

CHEMICAL ELEMENTS List the *one hundred and eighteen* elements of the periodic table. Find the solution on page 269. [**Target: 25**]

GREATEST FILMS Try to name the *hundred* best films of all time as judged by the 2007 poll conducted by the American Film Institute. The solution is on page 290. [**Target: 25**]

LAST LINES OF POPULAR FILMS II Identify the films from the closing lines. Find the solutions on page 349. [**Target: 12**]

1. "Cargo and ship destroyed. I should reach the frontier in about six weeks. With a little luck, the network will pick me up. This is Ripley, last survivor of the *Nostromo*, signing off." (1979)
2. "After all, tomorrow is another day." (1939)
3. "Don Corleone." (1972)
4. "I do." (1994)
5. "I look up at the moon, and wonder: when will we be going back? And who will that be?" (1995)
6. "Oh, now I suppose you're gonna say it's not enough. Well tough, Erin. Too goddamn bad. 'Cause this is absolutely, positively, where I draw the line." (2000)
7. "Th-th-th-that's all, Folks!" (1988)
8. "I'm an average nobody. I get to live the rest of my life like a schnook." (1980)
9. "Sam . . . I'm glad you're with me." (2001)
10. "Gaff had been there, and let her live. Four years, he figured. He was wrong. Tyrell had told me Rachael was special: no termination date. I didn't know how long we had together. Who does?" (1982)
11. "Asshole!" (1988)
12. "That's right, that's right. Attaboy, Clarence." (1946)

13. "I'm the boss, I'm the boss, I'm the boss, I'm the boss, I'm the boss . . . boss, boss, boss, boss, boss, boss." (1980)

14. "Eliza? Where the devil are my slippers?" (1964)

15. "Hey! What's this I see? I thought this was a party. Let's dance!" (1984)

16. "It's Mrs. Danvers. She's gone mad. She said she'd rather destroy Manderley than see us happy here." (1940)

17. "When I despair, I remember that all through history the way of truth and love has always won. There have been tyrants and murderers and for a time they can seem invincible, but in the end they always fall. Think of it. Always." (1980)

18. "Merry Christmas!" (1954)

19. "Love means never having to say you're sorry." (1970)

20. "Well, nobody's perfect." (1959)

21. "Little girls, I am in the business of putting old heads on young shoulders, and all my pupils are the crème de la crème. Give me a girl at an impressionable age and she is mine for life." (1969)

22. "Say, friend—you got any more of that good sarsaparilla?" (1998)

23. "Man, if this is their idea of Christmas, I gotta be here for New Year's." (1988)

24. "Now, where was I?" (2000)

SOLUTIONS

"Knowledge is the food of the soul."

Plato

BRONTË SISTERS (from page 4)

Anne Brontë / Charlotte Brontë / Emily Brontë

TEAMS WINNING FIVE SUPER BOWLS (from page 7)

Dallas Cowboys .... played 8
Pittsburgh Steelers .... played 6
San Francisco '49ers .... played 5

WIT AND WISDOM I (from page 9)

1. "I have nothing to declare but my genius." .... Wilde
2. ". . . and you, madam, are ugly . . ." .... Churchill
3. "I can resist anything but temptation." .... Wilde
4. "The report of my death was an exaggeration." .... Twain
5. "It is better to keep your mouth closed . . ." .... Twain
6. "There is only one thing in the world worse than . . ." .... Wilde
7. "I have taken more out of alcohol . . ." .... Churchill
8. "A classic is something that . . ." .... Twain
9. "This is the sort of English up with which . . ." .... Churchill
10. "Work is the curse of the drinking classes." .... Wilde
11. "He hadn't a single redeeming vice." .... Wilde
12. "I am ready to meet my Maker . . ." .... Churchill
13. "Truth is more of a stranger than fiction." .... Twain
14. "He has all the virtues I dislike . . ." .... Churchill
15. "I must decline your invitation . . ." .... Wilde
16. "Man is the only animal that blushes. Or needs to." .... Twain
17. "A modest man, who has much . . ." .... Churchill*
18. "If you tell the truth . . ." .... Twain
19. "I am not young enough to know everything." .... Wilde
20. "I am always ready to learn . . ." .... Churchill
21. "Familiarity breeds contempt—and children" .... Twain
22. "It has been said that democracy . . ." .... Churchill
23. "America is the only country to go from barbarism . . ." .... Wilde
24. "Men stumble over the truth from time to time . . ." .... Churchill

OFFICIAL RESIDENCES (from page 12)

The White House / Camp David†
Number One Observatory Circle / Blair House

---

* In reference to Clement Attlee.

† Officially known as the Naval Support Facility Thurmont, Camp David was built in 1935 for Federal employees and their families before being converted to a presidential retreat for Franklin D. Roosevelt. Dwight Eisenhower named it Camp David after his grandson.

MONOPOLY STATIONS (from page 15)
Baltimore and Ohio Railroad / Pennsylvania Railroad
Reading Railroad / Short Line*

MISCELLANY II (from page 21)
1. 273°; 2. Alabama; 3. General Issue; 4. Cymbal; 5. The statement is false; 6. "(Sittin' on) The Dock of the Bay"; 7. Nevada; 8. "In the beginning . . ."; 9. Sapphire; 10. Lee Harvey Oswald (in 1963); 11. Nicole Kidman; 12. Q and Z (worth ten points each); 13. Twenty-three; 14. Christopher Marlowe; 15. The USS *Enterprise*; 16. The tongue; 17. (*The*) *Kama Sutra*; 18. Gerald Ford; 19. They are anagrams of months (march, may); 20. Alaska; 21. Oedipus†; 22. They have no singular form; 23. The Belmont; 24. Sergei Rachmaninov (*Piano Concerto Number 2*).

TELETUBBIES (from page 23)
Tinky Winky / Dipsy / Laa-Laa / Po

BONES OF THE LEG (from page 24)
Femur / Tibia / Fibula / Patella

EVENTS IN HISTORY I (from page 26)
1. 1666; 2. 1860; 3. 1086; 4. 1775; 5. 1815; 6. 1848; 7. 1876; 8. 1347; 9. 1642; 10. 1534; 11. 1415; 12. 1870; 13. 1688; 14. 1215; 15. 1620; 16. 1314; 17. 1066; 18. 1707; 19. 1453; 20. 597; 21. 1202; 22. 1206; 23. 625; 14. 1337.

CHARACTERISTICS OF DIAMONDS (from page 31)
Carat / Clarity / Color / Cut

EVANGELISTS (from page 33)
Matthew / Mark / Luke / John

FILMS AND THEIR STARS II (from page 35)
1. *Pulp Fiction*; 2. *Kramer vs Kramer*; 3. *The Da Vinci Code*; 4. *Wall Street*; 5. *Blade Runner*; 6. *Apollo 13*; 7. *Good Will Hunting*; 8. *The Bourne Identity*; 9. *Rebel without a Cause*; 10. *Fight Club*; 11. *Nine to Five*; 12. *Footloose*; 13. *Chinatown*; 14. *A Bridge Too Far*; 15. *The Hours*; 16. *Logan's Run*; 17. *The Golden Compass*; 18. *National Velvet*; 19. *The African Queen*; 20. *It's a Wonderful Life*; 21. *Klute*; 22. *The Ice Storm*; 23. *North Country*; 24. *Eternal Sunshine of the Spotless Mind*.

---

* Probably named after the Shore Fast Line, a trolley car service which ran along the shore connecting Atlantic City, Ocean City and New Jersey.
† The riddle was: "What walks on four legs in the morning, two legs in the afternoon, and three legs in the evening?" The answer is man; the riddle is referring to a baby crawling, an adult walking, and an old man bent over a stick.

JACKSON 5 (from page 38)
Jackie / Jermaine / Marlon / Michael / Tito

RAT PACK (from page 40)
Frank Sinatra / Dean Martin / Sammy Davis Jr.
Peter Lawford / Joey Bishop

CAPITAL CITIES II (from page 42)
1. Stockholm; 2. New Delhi; 3. Brasília; 4. Khartoum; 5. Phnom Penh; 6. Hanoi; 7. Reykjavik; 8. Caracas; 9. Algiers; 10. Riyadh; 11. Bucharest; 12. Lima; 13. Ottawa; 14. Tashkent; 15. Abuja; 16. Kuala Lumpur; 17. Minsk; 18. Nicosia; 19. Jakarta; 20. Monrovia; 21. Amman; 22. Ashgabat; 23. Lilongwe; 24. Maseru.

BOOKS OF MOSES (from page 44)
Genesis / Exodus / Leviticus / Numbers / Deuteronomy

BIG GAME (from 47)
African elephant / Buffalo / Leopard / Lion / Rhinoceros

SINGERS AND BACKERS I (from page 49)
1. Gerry; 2. Cliff Richard; 3. Ian Dury; 4. Siouxsie; 5. Paul McCartney; 6. Bruce Hornsby; 7. Doctor; 8. Steve Harley; 9. Martha Reeves; 10. Elvis Costello; 11. Joan Jett; 12. Prince; 13. Katrina; 14. Frankie Valli; 15. Neil Young; 16. Archie Bell; 17. Bo Donaldson; 18. Maurice Williams; 19. Elvis Presley; 20. Harold Melvin; 21. Dr. Hook; 22. Johnny; 23. Terry Dactyl; 24. Eddie.

NEW ENGLAND STATES (from page 53)
Connecticut / Maine / Massachusetts
New Hampshire / Rhode Island / Vermont

ENGLISH ROMANTIC POETS (from page 56)
William Blake / Samuel Taylor Coleridge / George Gordon, Lord Byron
John Keats / Percy Bysshe Shelley* / William Wordsworth

COOKING TERMS I (from page 59)
1. Chili con carne; 2. Lasagne; 3. Moussaka; 4. Paella; 5. Salsa; 6. Blini; 7. Gnocchi; 8. Couscous; 9. Calzone; 10. Escalope; 11. Jus; 12. Antipasto; 13. Bombay Duck; 14. Poussin; 15. Penne; 16. Prosciutto; 17. Tagine; 18. Devils on Horseback; 19. Compote; 20. En croute; 21. Roux; 22. Marinière (à la); 23. Panna cotta; 24. Aioli.

---

* Husband of Mary Shelley, author of Frankenstein and also influential in the Romantic movement.

WEAPONS IN CLUE (from page 63)

Candlestick / Dagger / Lead Pipe
Rope / Pistol / Wrench

SYMBOLS IN ROMAN NUMERALS (from page 65)

I V X L C D M

MISCELLANY IX (from page 68)

1. Morphine (Morpheus); 2. Russia and France*; 3. lb[†]; 4. Roald Amundsen; 5. O; 6. Goat (cashmere goat); 7. *The Silence of the Lambs*; 8. Chihuahua; 9. Montreal; 10. *All's Well that Ends Well*; 11. Kidney; 12. Salvador Dalí (at the International Surrealist Exhibition); 13. Danny and Sandy; 14. Touché; 15. Teaching evolution in a Tenessee school; 16. Angela Lansbury (*Murder, She Wrote*); 17. Indonesia; 18. 24; 19. Xylophone; 20. Barbie; 21. Hindu[‡]; 22. Herbert Hoover; 23. London; 24. 54.

DEADLY SINS (from page 71)　　　　　　VIRTUES[§] (from page 73)

Deadly Sins	Virtues
Lust	Chastity
Gluttony	Temperance
Envy	Charity
Sloth	Diligence
Wrath	Forgiveness
Avarice	Generosity
Pride	Humility

AIRPORT CODES II (from page 77)

1. London (Heathrow); 2. Miami; 3. Atlanta (Hartsfield-Jackson); 4. Sydney (Kingsford-Smith); 5. Newark (Liberty); 6. Madrid (Barajas); 7. Zurich; 8. Washington (Dulles); 9. Frankfurt; 10. Beijing (formerly Peking); 11. Singapore (Changi); 12. Minneapolis Saint Paul; 13. Copenhagen; 14. Dublin; 15. Denver; 16. Havana (José Martí); 17. Phoenix (Sky Harbor); 18. Fort Lauderdale; 19. Rio de Janeiro (Galeão); 20. Houston (George Bush); 21. Orlando; 22. Rome (Leonardo da Vinci); 23. Charlotte-Douglas; 24. Toronto (Pearson).

CLASSICAL PLANETS (from page 79)

Sun / Moon / Mercury / Venus / Mars / Jupiter / Saturn

---

* "La Marseillaise" and "God Save the Tsar!"
† Derived from Libra, the scales.
‡ Kumbh Mela is a Hindu pilgrimage that gathers in India four times every twelve years. It rotates between four locations and each cycle contains a Great Kumbh Mela at Prayag, which is attended by huge numbers. In 2001, this was attended by some 70 million people, a number greater than the population of the UK.
§ An alternative list of the Seven Virtues is derived from a combination of the four Cardinal Virtues from Plato (Prudence, Justice, Temperance, and Fortitude) and the three Theological Virtues (Faith, Hope and Love) from 1 Corinthians.

FIRST LINES OF POP SONGS III (from page 83)

1. "Rockafeller Skank" (Fatboy Slim); 2. "The Greatest Love of All" (Whitney Houston); 3. "(They Long to Be) Close to You" (The Carpenters); 4. "Killing Me Softly" (Roberta Flack); 5. "Money for Nothing" (Dire Straits); 6. "Let's Go Crazy" (Prince and the Revolution); 7. "Respect" (Aretha Franklin); 8. "Mambo No. 5" (Lou Bega); 9. "One Day I'll Fly Away" (Randy Crawford); 10. "Come on Eileen" (Dexy's Midnight Runners); 11. "The Boxer" (Simon and Garfunkel); 12. "Blue (Da Ba De)" (Eiffel 65); 13. "Superstition" (Stevie Wonder); 14. "True Faith" (New Order); 15. "All Along the Watchtower" (Jimi Hendrix); 16. "Walk on the Wild Side" (Lou Reed); 17. "50 Ways to Leave Your Lover" (Paul Simon); 18. "Centerfold" (J. Geils Band); 19. "Owner of a Lonely Heart (Yes); 20. "Up Where We Belong"*(Joe Cocker & Jennifer Warnes); 21. "You've Lost That Loving Feeling" (Righteous Brothers); 22. "Jump" (Van Halen); 23. "Getting Jiggy With It" (Will Smith); 24. "Sweet Child of Mine" (Guns 'N' Roses).

NEW WONDERS OF THE WORLD (from page 81)

Great Wall of China	China
Petra	Jordan
Statue of Christ the Redeemer	Brazil
Machu Picchu	Peru
Chichen Itza	Mexico
Colosseum	Italy
Taj Mahal	India

PLANETS† (from page 87)

Mercury / Venus / Earth / Mars
Jupiter / Saturn / Uranus / Neptune

BOOKS BY GEORGE ORWELL (from page 89)

Down and Out in Paris and London	1933
Burmese Days	1934
A Clergyman's Daughter	1935
Keep the Aspidistra Flying	1936
The Road to Wigan Pier	1937
Homage to Catalonia	1938
Coming Up for Air	1939
Animal Farm	1945
Nineteen Eighty-four	1949

---

* The song was the theme to *An Officer and a Gentleman*, starring Richard Gere and Debra Winger.

† In 2006, Pluto lost its planet status and was reclassified as a Dwarf Planet. At the time of writing, the International Astronomical Union, which adjudicates on astronomical nomenclature, has identified the Dwarf Planets of Ceres, Pluto, and Eris in the solar system although more are likely to be discovered.

LINKED MISCELLANY VII (from page 95)

1. Crater Lake*; 2. Pheonix; 3. The Chicago Bears; 4. Mensa; 5. *The Andromeda Strain*; 6. River Indus; 7. Aquarius; 8. Cancer; 9. Leonardo DiCaprio; 10. C-130 Hercules

The link is constellations.†

CHART-TOPPING SINGLES BY STEVIE WONDER (from page 98; at the time of publishing)

"Fingertips - Part 2"	1963
"Superstition"	1972
"You Are the Sunshine of My Life"	1973
"You Haven't Done Nothin"‡	1974
"I Wish"	1977
"Sir Duke"	1977
"Ebony and Ivory"§	1982
"I Just Called to Say I Love You"	1984
"Part-Time Lover"	1985
"That's What Friends Are For"¶	1985

TRAGEDIES BY SHAKESPEARE (from page 104)

Antony and Cleopatra / Coriolanus / Hamlet / Julius Caesar
King Lear / Macbeth / Othello / Romeo and Juliet
Timon of Athens / Titus Andronicus / Troilus and Cressida

OLYMPIANS I (from page 102)

1. Carl Lewis**; 2. Marion Jones; 3. Michael Johnson††; 4. Cassius Clay‡‡; 5. Eric

---

* Crater Lake is 594m deep and is only fed by falling rain and snow. The water in the lake is extremely clear as a result.

† Crater, Phoenix, the Great Bear (Ursa Major), Mensa, Andromeda, Indus, Aquarius, Cancer, Leo and Hercules.

‡ With The Jackson 5.

§ With Paul McCartney.

¶ with Dionne Warwick, Elton John, and Gladys Knight

** One of the greatest Olympians of all time, his fourth Long Jump gold at Atlanta was achieved in exceptional circumstances. Past his best, he only just made it into the U.S. Olympic team and was lying in fifteenth place in the competition with only one qualifying jump remaining. He then produced a leap of 8.50 m to win gold.

†† Johnson's 200m record at Atlanta of 19.32s was one of the greatest Olympic performances of all time. Johnson's average time for each 100 m was 9.66 seconds, and twelve years later nobody has come close to beating it. Johnson said of his performance that it was like "going downhill in a go kart."

‡‡ Mohammad Ali (as he became) threw his gold medal into the Ohio River in disgust after being refused at a whites-only restaurant. He was presented with a replacement at the opening ceremony of the 1996 Atlanta games.

Heiden; 6. Gail Devers; 7. Jackie Joyner-Kersee*; 8.Valerie Brisco-Hooks; 9. Angelo Taylor; 10. Derrick Adkins; 11. George Foreman; 12. Greg Louganis; 13. Jeremy Wariner; 14. Joan Benoit; 15. Al Oerter; 16. Kenny Harrison; 17. Maurice Greene; 18. Mike Conley; 19. Roger Kingdom; 20. Steve Lewis; 21. Charles Austin; 22. Parry O'Brien; 23. Wilma Rudolph; 24. Mal Whitfield.[†]

PROLIFIC SUPER BOWL-WINNING COACHES (from page 106, as at time of publishing)

Chuck Noll (4 wins) Pittsburgh Steelers (IX, X, XIII, XIV)

Bill Walsh (3) San Francisco 49ers (XVI, XIX, XXIII)

Joe Gibbs (3) Washington Redskins (XVII, XXII, XXVI)

Bill Belichick (3) New England Patriots (XXXVI, XXXVIII, XXXIX)

Vince Lombardi (2) Green Bay Packers (I, II)

Don Shula (2) Miami Dolphins (VII, VIII)

Tom Landry (2) Dallas Cowboys (VI, XII)

Tom Flores (2) Oakland/Los Angeles Raiders (XV, XVIII)

Bill Parcells (2) New York Giants (XXI, XXV)

Jimmy Johnson (2) Dallas Cowboys (XXVII, XXVIII)

George Seifert (2) San Francisco 49ers (XXIV, XXIX)

Mike Shanahan (2) Denver Broncos (XXXII, XXXIII)

CREATURES IN CHINESE ASTROLOGY (from page 111)

Rat[‡] / Ox / Tiger / Rabbit / Dragon / Snake

Horse / Sheep (or Goat) / Monkey / Rooster / Dog / Pig

CHART-TOPPING SINGLES BY THE SUPREMES (from page 113, as at time of publishing)

"Where Did Our Love Go"	1964
"Baby Love"	1964
"Come See About Me"	1964
"Stop! In the Name of Love"	1965
"Back in My Arms Again"	1965
"I Hear a Symphony"	1965

* One of the greatest female all-round female athletes of all time, she was named Jacqueline after the wife of President Kennedy because, according to her grandmother: "someday this girl will be the first lady of something."

† In the four-year period between each of his gold medals, Mal Whitfield flew twenty-seven bomber missions as a tailgunner in the Korean War.

‡ In Chinese legend, the rat was given the task of assembling all the animals to be selected as zodiac signs by the Jade Emperor, the ruler of Heaven. The rat forgot to invite his friend the cat, and cats have hated rats ever since. Another legend relates how the order of the zodiac was determined by a race between the animals. The rat cheated by standing on the ox's head, jumping off at the last minute to win the race.

NOTORIOUS SHIPS II (from page 116)

1. *Mayflower*; 2. *Red October*; 3. *Santa Maria*; 4. *The Black Pearl*; 5. *The Argo*; 6. *Yellow Submarine*; 7. *Kursk*; 8. *Bismarck*; 9. *Exxon Valdez*; 10. *Freedom of the Seas**; 11. U.S.S. *Constitution*; 12. U.S.S. *Missouri*; 13. HMS *Dreadnought*; 14. U.S.S. *Nimitz*; 15. U.S.S. *Nautilus*; 16. *The Dawn Treader*; 17. U.S.S. *Caine*; 18. U.S.S. *Bonhomme Richard*; 19. *Andrea Doria*; 20. U.S.S. *Indianapolis*†; 21. *Pequod*; 22. U.S.S. *Monitor*; 23. *Gone Fission*; 24. U.S.S. *Arizona*.

HIGHEST-EARNING DEAD CELEBRITIES (from page 119)

Elvis Presley / John Lennon / Charles Schulz / George Harrison
Albert Einstein / Andy Warhol / Dr. Seuss / Tupac Shakur
Marilyn Monroe / Steve McQueen / James Brown / Bob Marley
James Dean

AMERICAN LEAGUE OF MAJOR LEAGUE BASEBALL (from page 121)

Baltimore Orioles[E] / Boston Red Sox[E] / Chicago White Sox[C]
Cleveland Indians[C] / Detroit Tigers[C] / Kansas City Royals[C]
Los Angeles Angels of Anaheim[W] / Minnesota Twins[C]
New York Yankees[E] / Oakland Athletics[W] / Seattle Mariners[W]
Tampa Bay Rays[E] / Texas Rangers[W] / Toronto Blue Jays[E]
[E] East Division [C] Central Division [W] West Division

COUNTRIES BORDERING RUSSIA (from page 122)

Azerbaijan / Belarus / China / Estonia / Finland / Georgia
Kazakhstan / Latvia / Lithuania[K] / Mongolia

---

* *Freedom of the Seas* has two sister ships, *Liberty of the Seas* (launched in 2007) and *Independece of the Seas* (2008). The *Freedom Class* will be superceded by the *Genesis Class* as the largest passenger vessel in 2009.

† While most of the crew of 1,196 survived the sinking, only 321 men were rescued when help arrived four days later. Rescue attempts were greatly delayed by the secrecy which had surrounded the final voyage of the Indianapolis. Most of the victims succumbed to exposure; the stories of shark attacks which are associated with the tragedy are probably exaggerated—not least by a monologue by Richard Shaw in *Jaws*. The U.S.S. *Indianapolis* was the last major surface vessel lost by the U.S. Navy in World War II. Her sinking on the July 30, 1945 occurred only a month before the end of World War II (on September 2), an event which her final payload had hastened.

North Korea / Norway / Poland[K] / Ukraine
[K] indicates a border with Kaliningrad, a Russian enclave in Eastern Europe.

MISCELLANY XVII (from page 125)

1. The diameter; 2. Johann Strauss II; 3. Goose; 4. AD1 5. H. G. Wells; 6. *Saturday Night Fever*; 7. Frankfurt; 8. Vermont; 9. Peter Parker; 10. *Jeopardy*; 11. Southeast Asia; 12. 4 million*; 13. Biology; 14. Water; 15. Very Special Old Pale; 16. Denim; 17. Camp David; 18. Robinson Crusoe; 19. Pittsburgh; 20. Removes seeds from cotton without damaging the fiber; 21. Capricorn (6 January); 22. Melbourne, Mexico City, Munich, Montreal and Moscow; 23. Snagglepuss; 24. Eight.†

NOVELS BY CHARLES DICKENS (from page 128)

The Pickwick Papers	1836–37
Oliver Twist	1837–39
Nicholas Nickleby	1838–39
The Old Curiosity Shop	1840–41
Barnaby Rudge	1841
A Christmas Carol	1843
Martin Chuzzlewit	1843–44
Dombey and Son	1846–48
David Copperfield	1849–50
Bleak House	1852–53
Hard Times	1854
Little Dorrit	1855–57
A Tale of Two Cities	1859
Great Expectations	1860–61
Our Mutual Friend	1864–65
The Mystery of Edwin Drood‡	1870

ANIMAL CRACKERS (from page 000)

Bear / Bison / Camel / Cougar / Elephant / Giraffe / Gorilla
Hippopotamus / Hyena / Kangaroo / Koala§/ Lion / Monkey
Rhinoceros / Seal / Sheep / Tiger / Zebra

FILMS AND THEIR STARS IV (from page 133)

1. *Alien*; 2. *The Sound of Music*; 3. *Jaws*; 4. *Apocalypse Now*; 5. *The Untouchables*; 6. *Philadelphia*; 7. *The Big Lebowski*; 8. *The Fabulous Baker Boys*; 9. *From Russia with Love*; 10. *Giant*; 11. *All the President's Men*; 12. *Doctor Zhivago*; 13. *Cat on a Hot*

---

* In 1860 on the eve of the Civil War.
† He makes seven cigarettes from those he picks up, and he makes another one from the butts of these
‡ Unfinished.
§ The Koala was added to celebrate the centenary of the brand in 2002. It won a consumer vote, beating a penguin, a cobra, and a walrus.

PROLIFIC CHART-TOPPING ARTISTS (from page 137; as at time of publishing)

The Beatles	20 *number ones*
Elvis Presley	18
Mariah Carey	17
Michael Jackson	13
Madonna	12
The Supremes	12
Whitney Houston	11
Janet Jackson	10
Stevie Wonder	10
Bee Gees	9
Elton John	9
George Michael	8
The Rolling Stones	8
Phil Collins	7
Usher	7
Paula Abdul	6
Pat Boone	6
Daryl Hall and John Oates	6
Diana Ross	6
Wings	6

LARGE LAKES* (from page 139)

Caspian Sea	Asia	143,250
Lake Superior	N. America	31,700
Lake Victoria	Africa	26,560
Lake Huron	N. America	23,010
Lake Michigan	N. America	22,320

---

* Other notable lakes include: Lake Maracaibo in Venezuela, a body of salt water connected to the Gulf of Venezuela by a narrow strait, is 5,100 square miles in size. Tonle Sap, a lake and river system in Cambodia, is subject to seasonal monsoon flooding which can cover an area of 11,000 square miles. Lake Vostok, a giant lake trapped under about 3 km of ice has recently been discovered in Antarctica. It is thought to be about 4,000 square miles in size and 500 meters deep but further surveys are required to confirm this. Lake Chad (in North Africa) used to be about the same size as Lake Victoria in the 1960s, but reduced rainfall and increased irrigation have seen it shrink to a fraction of that size. Lake Michigan and Lake Huron are sometimes considered as a single lake as they are connected by a channel five miles wide.

Lake Tanganyika [Africa]	12,700
Great Bear Lake [N. America]	12,100
Lake Baikal* [Asia]	11,780
Lake Nyasa† [Africa]	11,600
Great Slave Lake [N. America]	11,030
Lake Erie [N. America]	9,920
Lake Winnipeg [N. America]	9,420
Lake Ontario [N. America]	7,320
Lake Ladoga [Europe]	7,100
Lake Balkhash [Asia]	6,720
Aral Sea‡ [Asia]	6,620
Lake Onega [Europe]	3,710
Lake Nicaragua [N. America]	3,330
Lake Titicaca [S. America]	3,220
Lake Athabaska [N. America]	3,060

All figures are in square miles and are approximate

WIT AND WISDOM II (from page 142)

1. "When I'm good . . ."	West
2. "I told my mother-in-law . . ."	Rivers
3. "One more drink . . ."	Parker
4. "I used to be Snow White . . ."	West
5. "My best birth control now . . ."	Rivers
6. "It's not the men in my life . . ."	West
7. "You can lead a horticulture . . ."	Parker§
8. "The first time I see a jogger smiling . . ."	Rivers
9. "All I need is room enough to lay a hat . . ."	Parker
10. "Keep a diary . . ."	West
11. "She runs the gamut of emotions . . ."	Parker
12. "I hate housework . . ."	Rivers
13. "It's so long since I've had sex . . ."	Rivers
14. "It is better to be looked over . . ."	West
15. "If all the girls at the Yale Prom . . ."	Parker

* With a depth of 1,740 m, Lake Baikal in Siberia is the deepest lake in the world. It contains more water than all of the North American Great Lakes combined and is estimated to contain 20% of the earth's fresh water.

† Also known as Lake Malawi.

‡ The Aral Sea, in Central Asia, was the fourth largest lake in the world in 1960. It has since lost 80% of its volume of water due to the diversion of rivers for irrigation projects in the area (before 1960, 55 million cubic metrers of water flowed into the Aral Sea; nowadays the annual flow is between 1 and 5 million cubic meters). It is expected to have dried up by 2015.

§ While playing a word game, Dorothy Parker was asked to create a sentence which included the word "horticulture."

16. "The one thing women don't want to find . . ." .... Rivers
17. "I've never been a millionaire . . ." .... Parker
18. "When women go wrong . . ." .... West
19. "This is not a novel to be tossed aside lightly . . ." .... Parker
20. "When choosing between two evils . . ." .... West
21. "Take care of the luxuries . . ." .... Parker
22. "If God wanted us to bend over . . ." .... Rivers
23. "If you want to know what God thinks of money . . ." .... Parker
24. "That woman speaks eight languages . . ." .... Parker

SUPER BOWL LOSERS (from page 145; as at time of publishing)

Buffalo Bills (4)	XXV, XXVI, XXVII, XXVIII
Denver Broncos (4)	XII, XXI, XXII, XXIV
Minnesota Vikings (4)	IV, VIII, IX, XI
Dallas Cowboys (3)	V, XIII, X
Miami Dolphins (3)	VI, XVII, XIX
New England Patriots (3)	XX, XXXI, XLII
Cincinnati Bengals (2)	XVI, XXIII
Los Angeles Rams (2)	XIV, XXXIV
Oakland Raiders (2)	II, XXXVII
Philadelphia Eagles (2)	XV, XXXIX
Washington Redskins (2)	VII, XVIII
Atlanta Falcons	XXXIII
Baltimore Colts	III
Carolina Panthers	XXXVIII
Chicago Bears	XLI
Green Bay Packers	XXXII
Kansas City Chiefs	I
New York Giants	XXXV
Pittsburgh Steelers	XXX
San Diego Chargers	XXIX
Seattle Seahawks	XL
Tennessee Titans	XXXIV

BESTSELLING ARTISTS (from page 148; as at time of publishing)

The Beatles	170
Garth Brooks	128
Elvis Presley	118.5
Led Zeppelin	109.5
Eagles	98
Billy Joel	79.5
Pink Floyd	74.5
Barbra Streisand	71
Elton John	69.5
AC/DC	69

George Strait 67
Aerosmith 66.5
The Rolling Stones 66
Bruce Springsteen 63.5
Madonna 63
Mariah Carey 61.5
Michael Jackson 60.5
Metallica 57
Van Halen 56.5
Whitney Houston 54
Kenny Rogers 51
U2 .... 50.5

Figures are millions of units.

GOVERNMENTS (from page 150)

1. Monarchy; 2. Bureaucracy; 3. Democracy*; 4. Aristocracy; 5. Autocracy; 6.
Patriarchy; 7. Meritocracy; 8. Paparchy; 9. Hierarchy; 10. Plutocracy; 11. Oligarchy;
12. Matriarchy; 13. Xenocracy; 14. Kleptocracy; 15. Technocracy; 16. Theocracy;
17. Biarchy; 18. Arithmocracy; 19. Gynocracy; 20. Androcracy; 21. Gerontocracy;
22. Paedarchy; 23. Polyarchy; 14. Pornocracy.

HIGHEST CAREER BATTING AVERAGES (from page 154; as at time of publishing)

Ty Cobb[L] .... .3664
Rogers Hornsby[R] .... .3585
"Shoeless" Joe Jackson[L] .... .3558
Lefty O'Doul[L] .... .3493
Ed Delahanty[R] .... .3459
Tris Speaker[L] .... .3447
Ted Williams[L] .... .3444
Billy Hamilton[L] .... .3443
Dan Brouthers[L] .... .3421
Babe Ruth[L] .... .3421
Dave Orr[R] .... .3420
Harry Heilmann[R] .... .3416
Pete Browning[R] .... .3415
Willie Keeler[L] .... .3413
Bill Terry[L] .... .3412
George Sisler[L] .... .3402
Lou Gehrig[L] .... .3401
Jake Stenzel[R] .... .3386
Jesse Burkett[L] .... .3384

* The word "democracy" comes from the Greek words demos, meaning "common people," and kratos, meaning "rule" or "strength."

Tony Gwynn[L] .... .3382
Nap Lajoie[R] .... .3381
Riggs Stephenson[R] .... .3361
Al Simmons[R] .... .3342
John McGraw[L] .... .3336
Ichiro Suzuki[LA] .... .3335

[L] left-handed batter [R] right-handed batter [A] currently active player

POPULAR BOYS' NAMES* (from page 162)

Jacob [(1)] / Michael / Joshua / Ethan / Matthew / Daniel
Christopher / Andrew / Anthony / William / Joseph / Alexander
David / Ryan / Noah / James / Nicholas / Tyler / Logan / John
Christian / Jonathan / Nathan / Benjamin / Samuel [(25)]

ADVERTISING SLOGANS IV (from page 164)

1.UPS; 2. Kellogg's Rice Krispies; 3. Delta Airlines; 4. FedEx; 5. Miller High Life; 6.
GE; 7. Sunny Delight; 8. Radio Shack; 9. NYSE; 10. Pringles; 11. Hooters; 12.
Apple Computer; 13. 7-Up; 14. Dodge; 15. DuPont; 16. DHL; 17. U.S. Air Force;
18. MacDonald's; 19. Cheerios; 20. Toyota; 21. Volkswagen; 22. Jockey Shorts; 23.
Playtex Cross-Your-Heart Bra; 24. Schlitz.

MONARCHIES† (from page 168; as at the time of publishing)

Bahrain / Belgium / Bhutan / Brunei / Cambodia / Denmark
Japan / Jordan / Kuwait / Lesotho / Liechtenstein
Luxembourg / Malaysia / Monaco / Morocco /
Netherlands / Norway / Oman / Qatar / Saudi Arabia
Spain / Swaziland / Sweden / Thailand
Tonga / United Arab Emirates / United Kingdom

CHRISTIAN FEASTS (from page 173)

Solemnity of Mary, Mother of God .... January 1
Epiphany .... January 6
Baptism of Jesus .... January 11
Conversion of Paul the Apostle .... January 25
Candlemas Day .... February 2
Ash Wednesday[M] .... February 4–March 10
Chair of Peter the Apostle .... February 22
Palm Sunday[M] .... Sunday before Easter
Good Friday[M] .... Friday before Easter

---

* In order of popularity (i.e., Jacob is the most popular, Samuel twenty-fifth most
popular).

† Note the Vatican is a theocracy in which the Supreme Pontiff is elected by a
conclave of cardinals.

Holy Saturday^M .... Saturday before Easter
Easter^M* .... March 22–April 25
Annunciation of the Virgin Mary .... March 25
Ascension^M .... April 30–June 3
Whit Sunday^M .... May 10–June 13
Trinity Sunday^M .... May 17–June 20
Corpus Christi^M .... May 21–June 24
Birth of John the Baptist .... June 24
Transfiguration .... August 6
Assumption of the Virgin Mary .... August 15
Queenship of Mary .... August 22
Birthday of the Virgin Mary .... September 8
Exaltation of the Holy Cross .... September 14
Guardian Angels .... October 2
All Saints .... November 1
All Souls .... November 2
Presentation of the Virgin Mary .... November 21
First Sunday in Advent^M .... Sunday nearest November 30
Immaculate Conception .... December 8
Christmas Day† .... December 25
Holy Innocents .... December 28

^M indicates a movable feast falling on or between the dates indicated

ENTREPRENEURS II (from page 173)

1. Banking; 2. Food (chocolate); 3. Shipping; 4. Media (*Playboy* magazine); 5.
Banking; 6. Property; 7. Broadcasting; 8. E-commerce (Lastminute.com); 9. Financial
information; 10. Oil; 11. Oil, cinema, property; 12. Finance and investment‡; 13.
Banking; 14. Media (CNN); 15. Finance and investment§; 16. Oil and property;

---

* Easter was originally a pagan festival which was adopted by Christianity as it spread
through northern Europe. Bede, in his *Ecclesiastical History of the English People* (A.D.
731), refers to a Saxon goddess called Eostre who was related to the dawn, to spring,
and fertility. The festival of Eostre was celebrated on the spring equinox, and the
words "Easter" and "East" (the direction in which the sun rises) seem to derive from
this. It became appropriate for the Christian Easter, which is about rebirth and
renewal, to be celebrated on this day.
† Christmas derives from a pagan festival called Yule which celebrated the shortest
day of the year. Many Christmas traditions date back to this pre-Christian festival
such as holly, mistletoe, the Yule log, and the twelve days.
‡ Buffet has been nicknamed the "Oracle of Omaha" and has amassed an enormous
fortune, making him the world's second-richest man (after Bill Gates).
§ Soros is best known for profiting to the tune of over $1 billion at the expense of the
Bank of England on Black Wednesday. He later admitted, ". . . when Norman
Lamont said just before the devaluation he would borrow nearly $15 billion to defend
sterling, we were amused because that was about how much we wanted to sell."

17. Railways*; 18. Steel and railways[†]; 19. Food (Mrs. Fields Cookies); 20. Recording (Geffen Records); 21. Sports representation; 22. Railways; 23. Telecoms (AT&T); 24. Logistics (FedEx).

SQUARES ON THE MONOPOLY BOARD (from page 176)

Go / Mediterranean Avenue [Pu] / Community Chest / Baltic Avenue [Pu]
Income Tax / Reading Railroad / Oriental Avenue [LB] / Chance
Vermont Avenue [LB] / Connecticut Avenue [LB] / Jail
St. Charles Place [Pi] / Electric Company / States Avenue [Pi]
Virginia Avenue [Pi] / Pennsylvania Railroad / St. James Place [O]
Tennessee Avenue [O] / New York Avenue[‡] [O] / Free Parking
Kentucky Avenue [R] / Indiana Avenue [R] / Illinois Avenue [R]
B&O Railroad / Atlantic Avenue [Y] / Ventnor Avenue [Y]
Water Works / Marvin Gardens [Y] / Go To Jail / Pacific Avenue [G]
North Carolina Avenue [G] / Pennsylvania Avenue [G] / Short Line
Park Place [DB] / Luxury Tax / Boardwalk [DB]
[Pu] Purple [LB] Light Blue [Pi] Pink [O] Orange
[R] Red [Y] Yellow [G] Green [DB] Dark Blue

BOOKS OF THE OLD TESTAMENT (from page 178)

Law:
Genesis[§] / Exodus / Leviticus / Numbers / Deuteronomy

---

* Vanderbilt made his fortune as a steamship operator before moving into railways relatively late in his life. A ruthless man, he once said to a competitor: "You have undertaken to cheat me. I won't sue you, for the law is too slow. I'll ruin you."

† The son of a Scottish weaver, Carnegie was born in 1835 and moved in 1948 to America, where he made his fortune with a series of companies including the Carnegie Steel Company (which launched the steel industry in Pittsburgh and was sold to J.P. Morgan for $480 million). Carnegie believed that the rich had an obligation to redistribute their wealth and formed the Carnegie Corporation which, among other things, created 2,509 new libraries around the world.

‡ The probability of landing on each property on the board is not equal. Given that Chance and Community Chest cards and the Go to Jail square can send players to other locations, some properties will on average be visited more often than others. Combining this with the cost of development, which also varies around the board, an expected return on investment may be calculated for each property. The top ten properties on the board in terms of expected return are: 1. New York Avenue; 2. Connecticut Avenue; 3. St. James Place; 4. Tennessee Avenue; 5. Boardwalk; 6. Oriental Avenue; 7. Vermont Avenue; 8. Illinois Avenue; 9. Virginia Avenue; 10. Marvin Gardens (this assumes the properties are developed with a hotel).

§ "Genesis" is a Greek word meaning "origin" or "creation." The name comes from the translation of the Hebrew "bereshith," meaning "in the beginning," which are the first words of the text. The oldest character in the Bible is Methuselah, described in Genesis 5:27, who lived to the age of 969.

History:

Joshua / Judges / Ruth / 1 Samuel / 2 Samuel / 1 Kings / 2 Kings
1 Chronicles / 2 Chronicles / Ezra / Nehemiah / Esther*

Poetry:

Job[†] / Psalms / Proverbs / Ecclesiastes / Song of Solomon

Major Prophets:

Isaiah / Jeremiah / Lamentations / Ezekiel / Daniel

Minor Prophets:

Hosea / Joel / Amos / Obadiah / Jonah / Micah / Nahum
Habakkuk / Zephaniah / Haggai / Zechariah / Malachi[‡]

MISCELLANY XXIV (from page 181)

1. Sunlight; 2. Colors; 3. Quarantine; 4. March; 5. Giuseppe Verdi; 6. *Happy Days*; 7. Elton John (Reginald Hercules Dwight); 8. Tombstone, Arizona; 9. Northwest; 10. Maine; 11. The Speaker of the House; 12. The eyes; 13. Vinegar[§]; 14. Five; 15. Yale; 16. Dom Perignon; 17. Two hours[¶]; 18. The Wheel of Fortune; 19. A flamingo; 20. Golden Gate Bridge; 21. The Tempest; 22. Tunisia; 23. Prohibition; 24. Two miles.**

COUNTRIES IN ASIA[†]   ASIAN CAPITAL CITIES

(from page 191)	(from page 187)
Afghanistan	Kabul
Armenia	Yerevan
Azerbaijan	Baku
Bahrain	Manama
Bangladesh	Dhaka
Bhutan	Thimphu
Brunei	Bandar Seri Begawan
Cambodia	Phnom Penh
China	Beijing
Cyprus	Nicosia
East Timor	Dili
Georgia	Tbilisi

---

* The Book of Esther does not include the word "God."

† Job is believed to be the oldest book, dating from around 1500 B.C.

‡ Malachi is the most recently written book of the Old Testament, believed to date from around 400 B.C.

§ Vin aigre.

¶ In one hour Belinda can paint one sixth of the fence and Janice one third, one half of the whole fence in total. Therefore it will take two hours to paint the whole fence.

** The trains are travelling towards one another at a velocity of 120mph (their combined velocities). An object travelling at this velocity in one minute would travel a distance of two miles. The trains are therefore two miles apart one minute before they meet.

†† Note that parts of Russia and Turkey are in both Asia and Europe.

Country	Capital
India	New Delhi
Indonesia	Jakarta
Iran	Tehran
Iraq	Baghdad
Israel	Jerusalem
Japan	Tokyo
Jordan	Amman
Kazakhstan	Astana
Kuwait	Kuwait City
Kyrgyzstan	Bishkek
Laos	Vientiane
Lebanon	Beirut
Malaysia	Kuala Lumpur
Maldives	Malé
Mongolia	Ulaanbaatar
Burma	Rangoon
Nepal	Kathmandu
North Korea	Pyongyang
Oman	Muscat
Pakistan	Islamabad
Philippines	Manila
Qatar	Doha
Russia	Moscow
Saudi Arabia	Riyadh
Singapore	Singapore City
South Korea	Seoul
Sri Lanka	Colombo
Syria	Damascus
Taiwan	Taipei
Tajikistan	Dushanbe
Thailand	Bangkok
Turkey	Ankara
Turkmenistan	Ashkhabad
United Arab Emirates	Abu Dhabi
Uzbekistan	Tashkent
Vietnam	Hanoi
West Bank	Ramallah
Yemen	Sana

VALUABLE GLOBAL BRANDS* (from page 188, as at date of publishing)
Accenture / American Express / Apple / BMW

---

* The list is according to data from Interbrand and *Business Week* magazine. The list is limited to those organizations for which financial data is publicly available and does not include airlines.

Budweiser / Canon / Cisco / Citi / Coca-Cola
Dell / Disney / eBay / Ford / GE / Gillette
Goldman Sachs / Google / Gucci / Harley-Davidson
Hewlett-Packard / Honda / HSBC / IBM / Ikea
Intel / JPMorgan / Kellogg's / Louis Vuitton
Marlboro / McDonald's / Mercedes-Benz
Merrill Lynch / Microsoft / Morgan Stanley
MTV / Nescafé / Nike / Nokia / Novartis / Oracle
Pepsi / Pfizer / Philips / Samsung / SAP
Siemens / Sony / Toyota / UBS / UPS

"ISMS" II (from page 191)

1. Racism; 2. Terrorism; 3. Chauvinism*; 4. Pessimism; 5. Communism†; 6. Hedonism; 7. Postmodernism; 8. Hinduism; 9. Paganism; 10. Imperialism; 11. Maoism; 12. Methodism; 13. Colonialism; 14. Socialism; 15. Fundamentalism; 16. Shintoism; 17. Polytheism; 18. Evangelism; 19. Totalitarianism; 20. Jingoism‡; 21. Behaviorism; 22. Dialectical materialism; 23. Calvinism; 24. Antidisestablishmentarianism.

SIGNATORIES OF THE DECLARATION OF INDEPENDENCE (from page 195)

Samuel Adams	Massachusetts
John Adams	Massachusetts
Josiah Bartlett	New Hampshire
Carter Braxton	Virginia
Charles Carroll of Carrollton	Maryland
Samuel Chase	Maryland
Abraham Clark	New Jersey
George Clymer	Pennsylvania
William Ellery	Rhode Island
William Floyd	New York
Benjamin Franklin	Pennsylvania
Elbridge Gerry	Massachusetts
Button Gwinnett	Georgia
Lyman Hall	Georgia
John Hancock	Massachusetts

* The term is from Nicholas Chauvin, a French officer whose support for Napoleon Bonaparte was so enthusiastic as to be deemed embarrassing by his peers.

† Frank Zappa once said, "Communism doesn't work because people like to own stuff."

‡ During the 1870s, at the peak of the British Empire, Russia was in military conflict with the Ottoman Empire. Although Prime Minister Disraeli opposed British intervention, the mood in the country was more belligerent. A popular chorus at the time gave rise to the term: *"We don't want to fight / But, by Jingo, if we do / We've got the ships / We've got the men / We've got the money, too."*

Benjamin Harrison .... Virginia
John Hart .... New Jersey
Richard Henry Lee .... Virginia
Joseph Hewes .... North Carolina
Thomas Heyward Jr. .... South Carolina
William Hooper .... North Carolina
Stephen Hopkins .... Rhode Island
Francis Hopkinson .... New Jersey
Samuel Huntington .... Connecticut
Thomas Jefferson .... Virginia
Francis Lewis .... New York
Francis Lightfoot Lee .... Virginia
Philip Livingston .... New York
Thomas Lynch Jr. .... South Carolina
Thomas McKean .... Delaware
Arthur Middleton .... South Carolina
Lewis Morris .... New York
Robert Morris .... Pennsylvania
John Morton .... Pennsylvania
Thomas Nelson Jr. .... Virginia
William Paca .... Maryland
John Penn .... North Carolina
George Read .... Delaware
Caesar Rodney .... Delaware
George Ross .... Pennsylvania
Benjamin Rush .... Pennsylvania
Edward Rutledge .... South Carolina
Roger Sherman .... Connecticut
James Smith .... Pennsylvania
Richard Stockton .... New Jersey
Thomas Stone .... Maryland
George Taylor .... Pennsylvania
Matthew Thornton .... New Hampshire
Robert Treat Paine .... Massachusetts
George Walton .... Georgia
William Whipple .... New Hampshire
William Williams .... Connecticut
James Wilson .... Pennsylvania
John Witherspoon .... New Jersey
Oliver Wolcott .... Connecticut
George Wythe .... Virginia

CONSTELLATIONS (from page 199)

Andromeda / Antlia / Apus / Aquarius / Aquila / Ara
Aries / Auriga / Boötes / Caelum / Camelopardalis

Cancer / Canes Venatici / Canis Major / Canis Minor
Capricornus / Carina / Cassiopeia / Centaurus / Cepheus
Cetus / Chamaeleon / Circinus / Columba / Coma Berenices
Corona Austrina / Corona Borealis / Corvus / Crater
Crux* / Cygnus / Delphinus / Dorado / Draco / Equuleus
Eridanus / Fornax / Gemini / Grus / Hercules / Horologium
Hydra / Hydrus / Indus / Lacerta / Leo / Leo Minor
Lepus / Libra / Lupus / Lynx / Lyra / Mensa
Microscopium / Monoceros / Musca / Norma / Octans
Ophiuchus / Orion / Pavo / Pegasus / Perseus
Phoenix / Pictor / Pisces / Piscis Austrinus / Puppis
Pyxis / Reticulum / Sagitta / Sagittarius / Scorpius
Sculptor / Scutum / Serpens / Sextans / Taurus
Telescopium / Triangulum / Triangulum Australe
Tucana / Ursa Major[†] / Ursa Minor[‡] / Vela
Virgo / Volans / Vulpecula

TRIPLE CROWN (from page 4)

The Kentucky Derby / The Preakness Stakes / The Belmont Stakes

LINKED MISCELLANY I (from page 7)

1. Mike Myers; 2. Charlie Brown; 3. Victor Hugo; 4. November; 5. Sierra Nevada;
6. India; 7. 1 kilogram; 8. Alpha; 9. Grand Hotel 10. X-Rays.
The link is the NATO phonetic alphabet.[§]

COMPONENTS OF THE MIND (from page 10)

Id[¶] / Ego[**] / Super-ego[††]

THE MONKEES (from page 12)

Davy Jones / Micky Dolenz
Michael Nesmith / Peter Tork

ADVERTISING SLOGANS I (from page 15)

1. L'Oréal; 2. Kellogg's Frosted Flakes; 3. Exxon; 4. M 5. Subway; 6. KFC; 7. Visa;

---

* Commonly known as the Southern Cross.
† Or the Great Bear; colloquially known as the Plow or the Big Dipper.
‡ Or the Lesser Bear; colloquially known as the Little Plow or the Little Dipper.
§ Mike, Charlie, Victor, November, Sierra, India, Kilo, Alpha, Hotel, and X-Ray.
¶ In Freud's model, the id represents the desire for impulsive and instinctive behavior and is strongly present in young children.
** The ego is the part of the human mind that mediates between the desires of the id and the superego.
†† The superego sustains an individual's conscience and sense of morality. It stands in opposition to the desires of the id.

8. Greyhound Lines; 9. United Airlines; 10. GE; 11. Sara Lee Foods; 12. Disneyland; 13. Diet Coke; 14. Meowmix Cat Food; 15. Bank of America; 16. Nintendo 64; 17. Twix; 18. Nokia; 19. Pedigree Chum; 20. Cisco Systems; 21. American Airlines; 22. Wall Street Journal; 23. Quaker Oats; 24. Amtrak.

ASSASSINATED U.S. PRESIDENTS (from page 21)
Abraham Lincoln (1860) / James A. Garfield (1881)
William McKinley (1901) / John F. Kennedy (1963)

AMERICAN STATES BEGINNING WITH "I" (from page 23)
Idaho / Illinois / Indiana / Iowa

ASSASSINATIONS (from page 190)
1. John F. Kennedy; 2. Julius Caesar; 3. Abraham Lincoln*; 4. John Lennon[†]; 5. Archduke Franz Ferdinand; 6. Che Guevara; 7. Lee Harvey Oswald; 8. Leon Trotsky; 9. Martin Luther King Jr.; 10. Mohandas Gandhi; 11. Robert F. Kennedy; 12. Benazir Bhutto ; 13. Indira Gandhi; 14. Macbeth; 15. Malcolm X; 16. Michael Collins; 17. Olaf Palme; 18. Yitzhak Rabin; 19. Claudius; 20. Anwar Sadat; 21. George Lincoln Rockwell; 22. Isoroku Yamamoto[‡]; 23. Caligula; 24. James A. Garfield.

COMMONWEALTH STATES (from page 27)
Kentucky / Massachusetts / Pennsylvania / Virginia

HORSEMEN OF THE APOCALYPSE[§] (from page 31)
Pestilence / War / Famine / Death

MISCELLANY IV (from page 33)
1. The Fosbury Flop; 2. Robert Louis Stevenson; 3. France and Mexico; 4. Pixel; 5. Spandex; 6. (Chiricahua) Apache; 7. four; 8. i and j; 9. 1; 10. Liberace; 11. Hydrogen; 12. Peanuts; 13. Colorado; 14. Geoffrey Chaucer; 15. 28; 16. Charles de Gaulle; 17. Franklin D. Roosevelt; 18. 4077; 19. Red and yellow cards; 20. J. R. R. Tolkien; 21. 85 degrees; 22. The Black Sea; 23. *Treasure Island*; 24. Fourteen horses, eight men.

---

* Wilkes Booth broke his leg as he leapt to the stage; it has been suggested that the theatrical expression "break a leg" derives from this.
† Lennon's killer, Mark Chapman, was carrying a copy of *Catcher in the Rye* when he was arrested.
‡ Yamamoto had masterminded the attack on Pearl Harbor and Franklin D. Roosevelt personally ordered the mission to shoot down Yamamoto's plane. His death was a major blow to Japanese morale in World War II.
§ The Four Horsemen of the Apocalypse are described in Chapter 6 of the Book of Revelation in the Bible.

UNITED NATIONS SECURITY COUNCIL (from page 36)

China / France / Russia / United Kingdom / United States

HOUSE OF TUDOR* (from page 38)

Henry VII / Henry VIII / Edward VI / Mary I / Elizabeth I

CATCHPHRASES I (from page 40)

1. Homer Simpson (*The Simpsons*); 2. Mr. Spock (*Star Trek*); 3. Arnold Schwarzenegger (*The Terminator*); 4. Bugs Bunny; 5. Ed McMahon (*The Tonight Show*); 6. Hannibal Smith (*The A-Team*); 7. Kojak; 8. Joey Tribbiani (*Friends*); 9. Johnny Olson (*The Price is Right*); 10. *Columbo*; 11. *Beavis and Butthead*; 12. The Fonz (*Happy Days*); 13. J. J. (*Good Times*); 14. *Seinfeld*; 15. Ned Flanders (*The Simpsons*); 16. *Cheers*; 17. Dr. McNamara and Dr. Troy (*Nip/Tuck*); 18. David Banner (*The Incredible Hulk*); 19. Steve McGarrett (*Hawaii Five-O*); 20. Sgt. Esterhaus (*Hill Street Blues*); 21. Cartman (*South Park*); 22. Lurch (*The Addams Family*); 23. Sgt. Joe Friday (*Dragnet*); 24. *Rowan & Martin's Laugh-In*.

PRESIDENTS WITH BEARDS (from page 43)

Abraham Lincoln / Ulysses S. Grant / Rutherford B. Hayes
James Garfield / Benjamin Harrison

HALOGENS (from page 45)

Fluorine F
Chlorine Cl
Bromine Br
Iodine I
Astatine At[†]

FILMS AND THEIR STARS III (from page 47)

1. *The Godfather*; 2. *The Lord of the Rings: The Fellowship of the Ring*; 3. *Schindler's List*; 4. *Trading Places*[‡]; 5. *Casablanca*; 6. *L.A. Confidential*; 7. *Driving Miss Daisy*; 8. *The Accused*; 9. *King Kong*; 10. *Lawrence of Arabia*; 11. *The Name of the Rose*; 12. *Erin Brockovich*; 13. *The Talented Mr. Ripley*; 14. *Million Dollar Baby*; 15. *The Thomas Crown Affair*; 16. *Mystic River*; 17. *1984*; 18. *The People vs. Larry Flynt*; 19. *Sense and Sensibility*; 20. *Rear Window*; 21. *Walk the Line*; 22. *Fried Green Tomatoes*; 23. *Brazil*; 24. *Hotel Rwanda*.

---

* Lady Jane Grey reigned in England for nine days during the Tudor period but was never crowned. She was executed in the Tower of London in 1554.

† Astatine is a naturally occurring radioactive element.

‡ The theme music is from Mozart's *The Marriage of Figaro*, a story in which a servant turns the tables on his master. The climax of the film may have been inspired by the Hunt brothers of Texas who lost $100 million trying to corner the silver market during the "Silver Thursday" crash on March 27, 1980.

ORIGINAL SIX (from page 50)

Montreal Canadiens / Toronto Maple Leafs
Boston Bruins / Detroit Red Wings
Chicago Black Hawks / New York Rangers

NUTRIENTS (from page 53)

Carbohydrate / Fat / Protein / Vitamins / Minerals / Fiber

DANCES (from page 56)

1. Limbo; 2. Twist; 3. Belly dance; 4. Flamenco; 5. Cancan; 6. Lap dance; 7. Conga; 8. Foxtrot; 9. Tango; 10. Paso doble; 11. Salsa; 12. Bolero; 13. Samba; 14. Bossa nova; 15. Jig; 16. Mexican hat dance; 17. Charleston; 18. Hula; 19. Waltz; 20. Bhangra; 21. Merengue*; 22. Rumba; 23. Lambada; 24. Polka.

TEXAN GOVERNMENTS (from page 60)

Spain / France / Mexico / Republic of Texas
Confederate States of America / United States of America

WIVES OF HENRY VIII (from page 63)

Catherine of Aragon / Anne Boleyn / Jane Seymour
Anne of Cleves / Catherine Howard / Catherine Parr

FRUIT AND VEGETABLES (from page 66)

1. Potato†; 2. Orange; 3. Apple; 4. Grape; 5. Chilli; 6. Mushroom; 7. Tomato; 8. Broccoli; 9. Lettuce; 10. Plum; 11. Cabbage; 12. Aubergine; 13. Beetroot;

---

* According to a story, during the civil war in the Dominican Republic a hero was wounded in the leg but escaped and arrived at a friendly village. A victory celebration was held, and so as not to offend the injured soldier, everybody danced with a limp. The dance became known as the merengue.

† The potato was imported from South America in the sixteenth century. It was first grown by tribes in the foothills of the Andes in what today would be Peru and Bolivia and quickly became a staple food in Europe, so much so that failures the potato crop soon would have devastating results. In 1845, 1846, and 1848, the Irish potato crop was devastated by the fungus phytophthora infestans, commonly known as "potato blight." In the ensuing famine, an estimated 1 million people died and between 1 and 2 million emigrated, mainly to Britain and the United States. Ireland's population would never recover from the famine. Nowadays, each person in the U.S. consumes around 126lbs of potatoes per year (of which over one third is fries). The largest world producer is now China, which grows 47 million tons of potatoes annually. The many hundreds of potato varieties that are available fall into two categories. Waxy potatoes (such as Charlotte or Pink Fir Apple) have a low starch and high moisture content. They hold their shape after cooking and are good for boiling or potato salads. Floury potatoes (such as Maris Piper or Golden Wonder) have a high starch and low moisture content making them better for mashing, roasting or frying.

14. Cucumber; 15. Onion; 16. Pea; 17. Carrot; 18. Brussels spouts; 19. Cherry; 20. Parsnip; 21. Lemon; 22. Banana; 23. Grapefruit; 24. Pear.

SOVIET COMMUNIST PARTY LEADERS (from page 69)

Vladimir Lenin	1917–22
Joseph Stalin	1922–53
Nikita Khrushchev	1953–64
Leonid Brezhnev	1964–82
Yuri Andropov	1982–84
Konstantin Chernenko	1984-8-5
Mikhail Gorbachev	1985–91

MOST OSCAR-NOMINATED ACTRESSES (from page 71; as at the time of publishing)

Meryl Streep	13 nominations (2 wins)
Katharine Hepburn	12 (4)
Bette Davis	11 (2)
Geraldine Page	8 (1)
Ingrid Bergman	7 (3)
Jane Fonda	7 (2)
Greer Garson	7 (1)

FIRST LINES OF POPULAR NOVELS III (from page 73)

1. *Peter Pan* (J. M. Barrie); 2. *The Wonderful Wizard of Oz* (Frank Baum); 3. *The World According to Garp* (John Irving); 4. *Around the World in 80 Days* (Jules Verne); 5. *The Tale of Peter Rabbit* (Beatrix Potter); 6. *Brave New World* (Aldous Huxley); 7. *The Odyssey* (Homer); 8. *The Hunchback of Notre Dame* (Victor Hugo); 9. *Middlemarch* (George Eliot); 10. *Great Expectations* (Charles Dickens); 11. *Jaws* (Peter Benchley); 12. *Crash* (J. G. Ballard); 13. *Charlie and the Chocolate Factory* (Roald Dahl); 14. *Stuart Little* (E. B. White); 15. *The Metamorphosis* (Franz Kafka); 16. *The Golden Compass* (Philip Pullman); 17. *The Godfather* (Mario Puzo); 18. *Passage to India* (E.M. Forster); 19. *The Jungle Book* (Rudyard Kipling); 20. *The Color Purple* (Alice Walker); 21. *The Last of the Mohicans* (James Fenimore Cooper); 22. *To Kill a Mockingbird* (Harper Lee); 23. *Airport* (Arthur Hailey); 24. *Heart of Darkness* (Joseph Conrad).

CHARACTERISTICS OF LIVING THINGS (from page 77)

Movement / Respiration / Sensitivity / Growth
Reproduction / Excretion / Nutrition

THE MAGNIFICENT SEVEN (from page 79)

Yul Brynner	Chris Adams
Steve McQueen	Vin
Charles Bronson	Bernardo O'Reilly
James Coburn	Britt

Horst Buchholz .... Chico
Brad Dexter .... Harry Luck
Robert Vaughn .... Lee

MISCELLANY XI (from page 81)

1. Johnny Carson; 2. Oman; 3. World Cup mascots; 4. Julius Caesar and Mark Antony; 5. Ten; 6. Conversation; 7. Golf; 8. Eight; 9. The lungs; 10. Upstream; 11. Orville Wright; 12. Rhode Island; 13. St. Paul's; 14. Franklin D. Roosevelt; 15. Slip of the tongue; 16. Spelling and grammar check; 17. The Southern Lights; 18. Trombone; 19. James Stewart—Brigadier General; 20. *The French Connection*; 21. Seven pigs and eight geese; 22. Elvis Presley 23. Paul Bunyan; 24. Today is January 1 and my birthday is on December 31.

WARSAW PACT* (from 84)

Albania[†] / Bulgaria / Czechoslovakia / East Germany
Hungary / Poland / Romania / Soviet Union

REINDEER (from page 87)

Dasher / Dancer / Prancer / Vixen / Comet
Cupid / Donner / Blitzen / Rudolph

RECENT HISTORY II (from page 89)

1. 2000; 2. 2001; 3. 1998; 4. 1995; 5. 1996; 6. 1978; 7. 1969; 8. 1972; 9. 1944; 10. 1987; 11. 1994; 12. 1914; 13. 1973; 14. 1941; 15. 1968; 16. 1975; 17. 1901; 18. 1966; 19. 1936; 20. 1961; 21. 1959; 22. 1913; 23. 1906; 24. 1911.

PLAGUES OF EGYPT (from page 96)

Rivers turn to blood / Frogs / Lice / Flies / Pestilence
Boils / Hail and fire / Locusts / Darkness / Death of the firstborn[‡]

---

* Despite being part of Eastern Europe, Yugoslavia was never a member of the Warsaw Pact.

† Withdrew in 1968.

‡ There is evidence to suggest a series of calamitous events did affect Egypt at around this time (thought to be about 1300 BC) and are recorded independently in Egyptian and Hebrew texts. Attempts have been made to scientifically explain the ten plagues. It has been suggested that a bloom of a toxic algae in the Nile (such as physteria) would have the effect of turning the water red and killing all the fish. This would bring about many of the other plagues, for example, frogs would leave the poisonous river, and a lack of predators would increase insect populations, in turn spreading disease to people and animals. Some historians have noted the events described in Exodus could have coincided with the eruption of Thera, the largest volcanic eruption in civilized history, and could also explain many of the phenomena in the recorded accounts, for example fire and hail, darkness and poisoned rivers.

COMMANDMENTS (from page 98)

First .... Thou shalt have no other gods before me
Second .... Thou shalt not make unto thee any graven image
Third .... Thou shalt not take the name of the Lord thy God in vain
Fourth .... Remember the Sabbath day, to keep it holy
Fifth .... Honor thy father and thy mother
Sixth .... Thou shalt not kill
Seventh .... Thou shalt not commit adultery
Eighth .... Thou shalt not steal
Ninth .... Thou shalt not bear false witness against thy neighbor
Tenth .... Thou shalt not covet thy neighbor's house, wife, ox, etc.

OLOGIES II (from page 100)

1. Spiders; 2. Mental phenomena; 3. Earthquakes; 4. Diseases of the stomach and intestine; 5. Bones; 6. The origin of words; 7. Life in the geological past; 8. Horses; 9. The eyes; 10. Mathematical connectedness; 11. Poisons; 12. Codes and ciphers; 13. Words; 14. Allergies; 15. The action of drugs on the body; 16. Cancers; 17. Fungi; 18. Knowledge; 19. Soil; 20. Age of trees by rings; 21. Handwriting; 22. The anatomy of blood and lymphatic systems; 23. Caves; 24. Flags.

CHART-TOPPING SINGLES BY WHITNEY HOUSTON (from page 104, as at time of publishing)

"How Will I Know" 1985
"Saving All My Love for You" 1985
"Greatest Love of All" 1986
"Didn't We Almost Have It All" 1987
"I Wanna Dance With Somebody (Who Loves Me)" 1987
"So Emotional" 1987
"Where Do Broken Hearts Go" 1988
"All the Man That I Need" 1990
"I'm Your Baby Tonight" 1990
"I Will Always Love You" 1992
"Exhale Shoop, Shoop" 1995

CONFEDERACY* (from page 106)

South Carolina / Mississippi / Florida / Alabama
Georgia / Louisiana / Texas / Virginia
Arkansas / Tennessee / North Carolina

PRESIDENTIAL INITIALS (from page 109)

1. Fitzgerald; 2. Jefferson; 3. Walker; 4. Herbert Walker; 5. Henry;

---

* Slavery was also permitted in the border states of Missouri and Kentucky, although these states also had Union ties and were never under the control of the Confederacy.

6. Nothing*; 7. Delano; 8. David; 9. Baines; 10. Milhous; 11.Earl; 12. Wilson; 13. Knox; 14. Birchard; 15. Alan; 16. Howard; 17. Gamaliel; 18. Rudolph; 19. Abram; 20. Clark; 21. Stephen; 22. Thomas; 23. John; 24. Nothing.[†]

CHRISTMAS GIFTS (from page 111)

Twelve drummers drumming / Eleven pipers piping
Ten lords a-leaping / Nine ladies dancing
Eight maids a-milking / Seven swans a-swimming
Six geese a-laying / Five golden rings
Four calling birds / Three French hens
Two turtle doves / A partridge in a pear tree

LINKED MISCELLANY IX (from page 113)

1. *The Player*; 2. Dr. Watson; 3. Fuzzy logic; 4.The Summer of Love; 5. Horatio Nelson; 6. Mr. Kite; 7. Paul Hogan; 8. Couple; 9. Sing Sing; 10. Tiger
The link is golfers[‡]

DREAM TEAM (from page 115)

Charles Barkley	Phoenix Suns
Larry Bird	Boston Celtics
Clyde Drexler	Portland Trail Blazers
Patrick Ewing	New York Knicks
Earvin "Magic" Johnson	Los Angeles Lakers
Michael Jordan	Chicago Bulls
Christian Laettner	Duke University
Karl Malone	Utah Jazz
Chris Mullin	Golden State Warriors
Scottie Pippen	Chicago Bulls
David Robinson	San Antonio Spurs
John Stockton	Utah Jazz

PUNCTUATION (from page 117)

Period	ends a sentence
Comma	to give additional information
Colon	before a list, summary or quotation
Semicolon	to link two sentences that are related

---

* Truman was given only a middle initial as his parents felt unable to choose a name in favor of either of his grandfathers—Anderson Shippe Truman and Solomon Young.
† When Grant was nominated for West Point at the age of seventeen, his name was incorrectly entered in the form as Ulysses S. Grant (Grant's mother's maiden name was Simpson). The school refused to accept any other name than that written on the nomination form and so the name stuck.
‡ Gary Player, Tom Watson, Fuzzy Zoeller, David Love III, Larry Nelson, Tom Kite, Ben Hogan, Fred Couples, Vijay Singh, and Tiger Woods.

Dash	for emphasis or parenthesis
Hyphen	to form compound words
Apostrophe	to indicate possession or missing letters
Question mark	to indicate that a response is expected
Exclamation mark	to add emphasis
Quotation marks	for direct speech, quotations, titles of short texts
Round brackets	for parenthetical elements
Square brackets	for editorial comments
Ellipsis (three dots)	to replace missing words

FOUNDING STATES (from page 120)

Connecticut / Delaware / Georgia / Maryland
Massachusetts / New Hampshire / New Jersey
New York / North Carolina / Pennsylvania
Rhode Island / South Carolina / Virginia

STATE CAPITALS I (from page 122)

1. Oklahoma; 2. Hawaii; 3. Indiana; 4. Colorado; 5. Texas; 6. California; 7. Utah;
8. Louisiana; 9. Iowa; 10. Maine; 11. Pennsylvania; 12. Ohio; 13. Illinois; 14.
Rhode Island; 15. Vermont; 16. Minnesota; 17. Kansas; 18. Wisconsin; 19. Oregon;
20. Nebraska; 21. North Dakota; 22. Michigan; 23. Maryland; 24. Washington.

COMIC OPERAS BY GILBERT AND SULLIVAN (from page 126)

Thespis	1871
Trial by Jury	1875
The Sorcerer	1877
HMS Pinafore	1878
The Pirates of Penzance	1879
Patience	1881
Iolanthe	1882
Princess Ida	1884
The Mikado	1885
Ruddigore	1887
The Yeomen of the Guard	1888
The Gondoliers	1889
Utopia, Limited	1893
The Grand Duke	1896

PERFORMERS OF JAMES BOND THEMES* (from page 129; as at the time of publishing)

A-ha	*The Living Daylights*

* The themes to *Dr. No* and *On Her Majesty's Secret Service* were instrumentals composed by Monty Norman and John Barry respectively. Although not an official Bond film, the theme to *Never Say Never Again* was sung by Lani Hall.

Carly Simon	*The Spy Who Loved Me*
Chris Cornell	*Casino Royale*
Duran Duran	*A View to a Kill*
Garbage	*The World Is Not Enough*
Gladys Knight	*License to Kill*
Lulu	*The Man with the Golden Gun*
Madonna	*Die Another Day*
Matt Monro	*From Russia with Love*
Nancy Sinatra	*You Only Live Twice*
Paul McCartney and Wings	*Live and Let Die*
Rita Coolidge	*Octopussy*
Sheena Easton	*For Your Eyes Only*
Sheryl Crow	*Tomorrow Never Dies*
Shirley Bassey	*Goldfinger, Diamonds Are Forever, Moonraker*
Tina Turner	*Goldeneye*
Tom Jones	*Thunderball*

BEACH BOYS HITS (from page 130; as at time of publishing)

"Barbara Ann"	1966 reaching number 2
"Be True To Your School"	1963, 6
"California Girls"	1965, 3
"Dance, Dance, Dance"	1964, 8
"Fun, Fun, Fun"	1964, 5
"Good Vibrations"	1966, 1
"Help Me, Rhonda"	1965, 1
"I Get Around"	1964, 1
"Little Saint Nick"	1963, 3
"Rock And Roll Music"	1976, 5
"Sloop John B"	1966, 3
"Surfer Girl"	1963, 7
"Surfin' U.S.A."	1963, 3
"When I Grow Up (To Be A Man)"	1964, 9
"Wouldn't It Be Nice"	1966, 8
"The Man With All The Toys"	1964, 3
"Kokomo"	1988, 1

ADVERTISING SLOGANS III (from page 131)

1. Campbell's Soup; 2. American Express; 3. Wendy's Restaurants; 4. Taco Bell; 5. *New York Times*; 6. Maxwell House; 7. Wheaties; 8. Jaguar; 9. Red Bull; 10. Chevrolet Trucks; 11. Burger King; 12. Energizer Max; 13. BMW; 14. Alka Seltzer; 15. Sony Playstation and PS2; 16. NASDAQ; 17. Chevrolet Aveo; 18. iPod Nano; 19. U.S. Navy; 20. Jack in the Box; 21. Buick; 22. Hebrew National*; 23. L&M Cigarettes[†]; 24. Unocal.

---

* Kosher hot dogs and sausages.
† From the 1953 commercial.

WORLD HERITAGE SITES IN THE UNITED STATES (from page 135; as at time of publishing)

Wrangell-St. Elias and Glacier Bay National Parks[N] (Alaska)

Grand Canyon National Park[N] (Arizona)

Redwood National and State Parks[N] (California)

Yosemite National Park[N] (California)

Mesa Verde National Park[C] (Colarado)

Everglades National Park[N] (Florida)

Hawaii Volcanoes National Park[N] (Hawaii)

Cahokia Mounds State Historic Site[C] (Illinois)

Mammoth Cave National Park[N] (Kentucky)

Waterton-Glacier International Peace Park[N] (Montana)

Statue of Liberty National Monument[C] (New York / New Jersey)

Carlsbad Caverns National Park[N] (New Mexico)

Chaco Culture National Historical Park[C] (New Mexico)

Pueblo de Taos[C] (New Mexico)

Great Smoky Mountains National Park[N] (North Carolina / Tennessee)

Independence Hall National Historic Park[C] (Pennsylvania)

Monticello and the University of Virginia[C] (Virginia)

Olympic National Park[N] (Washington)

Yellowstone National Park[N] (Wyoming / Montana)

Sites indicated as [N] Natural [C] Cultural

BRITISH PRIME MINISTERS (from page 137)

The Marquess of Salisbury[Con]*	1895–1902
Arthur Balfour[Con]	1902–5
Sir Henry Campbell-Bannerman[Lib]	1905–8
Herbert Henry Asquith[Lib]	1908–16
David Lloyd George[Lib]	1916–22
Andrew Bonar Law[Con]	1922–23
Stanley Baldwin[Con]	1923, 1924–29, 1935–27
James Ramsay MacDonald[Lab]	1924, 1929–35
Neville Chamberlain[Con]	1937–40
Sir Winston Churchil[Con]	1940–45, 1951–55
Clement Richard Attlee[Lab]	1945–51
Sir Anthony Eden[Con]	1955–57
Harold Macmillan[Con]	1957–63
Sir Alec Douglas-Home[Con]	1963–64
Harold Wilson[Lab]	1964–70, 1974–76
Edward Heath[Con]	1970–47
James Callaghan[Lab]	1976–79
Margaret Thatcher[Con]	1979–90
John Major[Con]	1990–97

* Also in office from 1885–86 and 1886–92.

Tony Blair[Lab] .... elected 1997

MISCELLANY XIX (from page 139)

1. The Danube*; 2. *Goldfinger*; 3. A Dutch auction; 4. The assassination of John F. Kennedy; 5. Slavery[†]; 6. Rudyard Kipling; 7. Eight; 8. London and Paris; 9. Israel; 10. Polo; 11. The Virgin Mary[‡]; 12. Seventy-two; 13. Flash; 14. *Potemkin*[§]; 15. George II[¶]; 16. In the human body - they are in the pancreas; 17. $3,000; 18. California; 19. Walk on the moon; 20. Harvard and Yale**; 21. Mr. Brown; 22. Edith Nesbit; 23. Clavicle; 24. Eleven.

CHART-TOPPING SINGLES BY THE BEATLES (from page 000; as at time of publishing)

"I Want to Hold Your Hand" 1964
"She Loves You" 1964
"Can't Buy Me Love" 1964
"Love Me Do" 1964
"A Hard Day's Night" 1964
"I Feel Fine" 1964
"Eight Days a Week" 1965
"Ticket to Ride" 1965
"Help!" 1965
"Yesterday" 1965
"We Can Work It Out" 1965
"Paperback Writer" 1966
"Penny Lane" 1967
"All You Need Is Love" 1967
"Hello, Goodbye" 1967
"Hey Jude" 1968
"Get Back" 1969

---

* *The Blue Danube* by Johann Strauss was famously used in the soundtrack to *2001: A Space Odyssey*.

† The Amendment was ratified in 1865 by the required three-quarters of states to allow it to pass into law, although some states opposed it. It was ratified by Kentucky in 1976 and by the state of Mississippi as recently as 1995.

‡ The Immaculate Conception is not to be confused with the Virgin Birth. In order to give birth to Jesus Christ, Catholic theologians believe that from the very first moment of her existence, Mary was free from sin, and therefore her conception was "immaculate."

§ The film was *The Battleship Potemkin*.

¶ Battle of Dettingen, 1743

** "The Game" of 1968 is generally considered to be the best; Harvard pulled back a 16-point deficit in the dying seconds including a touchdown pass with the final play to tie the match 29–29. The Harvard student newspaper later crowed: "Harvard beats Yale 29–29."

"Something" / "Come Together" 1969
"Let It Be" 1970
"The Long and Winding Road" 1970

OLYMPIC HOST CITIES (from page 150)

Amsterdam 1928
Antwerp 1920
Athens 1896, 2004
Atlanta 1996
Barcelona 1992
Beijing 2008
Berlin 1936
Helsinki 1952
London 1908, 1948
Los Angeles 1932, 1984
Melbourne 1956
Mexico City 1968
Montreal 1976
Moscow 1980
Munich 1972
Paris 1900, 1924
Rome 1960
Seoul 1988
St. Louis 1904
Stockholm 1912
Sydney 2000
Tokyo 1964

EVENTS IN HISTORY III (from page 148)
1. 1492; 2. 1859; 3. c.A.D.30; 4. 1588; 5. 1756; 6. 1869; 7. 1517; 8. 1485; 9.
1752; 10. 1704; 11. 1861; 12. 1774; 13. 1455; 14. 1543; 15. 1702; 16. 1688*; 17.
1512; 18. 1498; 19. 1603; 20. 1271; 21. 1040; 22. 1054; 23. 1572; 24. 602.

RYDER CUP CAPTAINS (from page 151; as at time of publishing)
Tony Jacklin[E] .... 1983, 1985[W], 1987[W], 1989[W]

---

* Many of London's institutions began in coffee houses. The Stock Exchange
operated from coffee houses, most notably Jonathan's and Garraway's, until 1773.
Maritime traders frequented the house of Edward Lloyd, at 16 Lombard Street, and
the business of underwriting ships began there in 1727 (where it remained until the
foundation of Lloyds of London in 1771). Coffee houses in Westminster catered for
the political classes; the Tories would meet at the Cocoa Tree, the Whigs at the St.
James. Covent Garden coffee houses became popular with the literati (John Dryden
would frequent Will's House on Russell Street) and the men of the Royal Society
(such as Isaac Newton and Edmund Halley) preferred the Graecian on the Strand.

Bernard Gallacher[E] .... 1991, 1993, 1995[W]
John Jacobs[E] 1979, 1981
Jack Nicklaus[U.S.] 1983, 1987
Paul Azinger[U.S.] 2008
Seve Ballesteros[E] .... 1997[W]
Billy Casper[U.S.] .... 1979[W]
Ben Crenshaw[U.S.] .... 1999[W]
Nick Faldo[E] 2008
Ray Floyd[U.S.] 1989
Mark James[E] 1999
Tom Kite[U.S.] 1997
Bernhard Langer[E] .... 2004[W]
Tom Lehman[U.S.] 2006
Dave Marr[U.S.] .... 1981[W]
Dave Stockton[U.S.] .... 1991[W]
Curtis Strange[U.S.] 2002
Hal Sutton[U.S.] 2004
Sam Torrance[E] .... 2002[W]
Lee Trevino[U.S.] 1985
Lanny Wadkins[U.S.] 1995
Tom Watson[U.S.] .... 1993[W]
Ian Woosnam[E] .... 2006[W]

[U.S.] U.S. captain [E] European captain [W] Winning captaincy

PROLIFIC BASKETBALL SCORERS (from page 154; as at time of publishing)

Michael Jordan 30.12
Wilt Chamberlain 30.07
Allen Iverson[A] 27.83
Elgin Baylor 27.36
Jerry West 27.03
Bob Pettit 26.36
George Gervin 26.18
Oscar Robertson 25.68
Shaquille O'Neal[A] 25.61
Karl Malone[A] 25.02
Dominique Wilkins 24.83
Kobe Bryant[A] 24.75
Kareem Abdul-Jabbar 24.61
Larry Bird 24.29
Adrian Dantley 24.27
Pete Maravich 24.24
Vince Carter[A] 23.96
Paul Pierce[A] 23.42
Rick Barry 23.17

George Mikan 23.13
Paul Arizin 22.81
Bernard King 22.49
Tracy McGrady[A] 22.44
Dirk Nowitzki[A] 22.27
Charles Barkley 22.14

[A] denotes currently active player

SINGERS AND BACKERS II (from page 162)

1. Sly; 2. Bill Haley; 3. Derek; 4. Echo; 5. Booker T; 6. Diana Ross; 7. Tom Petty;
8. Lloyd Cole; 9. Prince; 10. Yazz; 11. Hootie; 12. Mike; 13. Jonathan Richman;
14. Tommy James; 15. Van McCoy; 16. Iggy Pop; 17. Herb Alpert; 18. Curtis
Mayfield; 19. Captain Beefheart; 20. Robyn Hitchcock; 21. Brenda; 22. James
Brown; 23. Question Mark; 24. Wayne Fontana.

MEMBERS OF NATO (from page 165; as at the time of publishing)

Belgium / Bulgaria / Canada / Czech Republic / Denmark
Estonia / France / Germany / Greece / Hungary / Iceland
Italy / Latvia / Lithuania / Luxembourg / Netherlands
Norway / Poland / Portugal / Romania / Slovakia / Slovenia
Spain / Turkey / United Kingdom / United States

MICHAEL JACKSON HITS (from page 168; as at time of publishing)

"Got To Be There" .... reaching number 4 in 1971
"Ben" 1, 1972
"Rockin' Robin" 2, 1972
"Don't Stop 'Til You Get Enough" 1, 1979
"Rock With You" 1, 1980
"Off The Wall" 10, 1980
"She's Out Of My Life" 10, 1980
"Beat It" 1, 1983
"Billie Jean" 1, 1983
"Say Say Say"[PMc] 1, 1983
"Human Nature" 7, 1983
"P.Y.T. (Pretty Young Thing)" 10, 1983
"Wanna Be Startin' Somethin" 5, 1983
"The Girl Is Mine"[PMc] 2, 1983
"Thriller" 4, 1984
"Bad" 1, 1987
"I Just Can't Stop Loving You" 1, 1987
"The Way You Make Me Feel" 1, 1987
"Dirty Diana" 1, 1988
"Man in the Mirror" 1, 1988
"Smooth Criminal" 7, 1988

"Black or White"	1, 1991
"In the Closet"	6, 1992
"Remember the Time"	3, 1992
"Will You Be There"	7, 1993
"You Are Not Alone"	1, 1995
"Scream"	5, 1995
"You Rock My World"	10, 2001

[PMc] denotes collaboration with Paul McCartney

NICKNAMES OF PLACES (from page 172)

1. New York*; 2. London; 3. Hollywood[†]; 4. Atlantic Ocean; 5. Ireland; 6. Chicago; 7. Tibet; 8. Kent; 9. Detroit; 10. Oxford[‡]; 11. Las Vegas; 12. New Orleans; 13. Aberdeen; 14. Jerusalem; 15. Mumbai; 16. Paris; 17. Rome; 18. Denver; 19. Philadelphia; 20. Venice; 21. Jaipur; 22. Cleveland; 23. Belgrade; 24. Manila.

FILMS STARRING MARILYN MONROE (from page 173)

Dangerous Years	1947
Scudda Hoo! Scudda Hay!	1948
Ladies of the Chorus	1948
Green Grass of Wyoming	1948
You Were Meant for Me	1948
Love Happy	1949
A Ticket to Tomahawk	1950
The Asphalt Jungle	1950
The Fireball	1950
All About Eve	1950
Right Cross	1950
Home Town Story	1951
As Young as You Feel	1951
Love Nest	1951
Let's Make It Legal	1951
We're Not Married	1952
O. Henry's Full House	1952
Clash by Night	1952
Monkey Business	1952

---

* The term probably stems from "apple," musician's slang for a performing engagement. A date in New York was the "big apple"; New York is also known as the Empire City.

† The name may stem from Oscar Levant's 1930s quote: "Strip the phoney tinsel off Hollywood and you'll find real tinsel underneath."

‡ An ironic term, implying its inhabitants were not concerned with real issues, coined by the poet Matthew Arnold (1822–88) in the poem "Thyrsis," calling Oxford the "sweet city with her dreaming spires."

MADONNA HITS (from page 176; as at time of publishing)

FOREIGN WORDS AND PHRASES II (from page 178)

1. Al fresco; 2. Coup d'état; 3. Raison d'être; 4. Slalom; 5. Hinterland; 6. Verandah; 7. Zeitgeist; 8. Enfant terrible; 9. Wunderkind; 10. Bête noir; 11. Smorgasbord; 12. Carte blanche; 13. Pundit*; 14. Nadir; 15. Wanderlust; 16. Pied-à-terre; 17. Realpolitik; 18. Cushy; 19. Amok; 20. Algebra; 21. Schadenfreude; 22. Gung-ho; 23. Flak; 24. Ombudsman.

REFEREE SIGNALS IN THE NFL (from page 186)

Call	Referee's Signal
Touchdown[†]	both arms extended above head
Safety	palms together above head
First down	arm pointed toward defensive team's goal
Crowd noise[‡]	one arm above head with an open hand
Fourth down	one arm above head with fist closed
Ball illegally touched	fingertips tap both shoulders
Time out	arms criss-crossed above head
Referee's time	out arms crossed above head then placing one hand on top of cap

---

* During the nineteenth century the empires of the two largest world powers, Russia and Great Britain, converged on the territories of central Asia. The struggle for political influence over this region lasted for most of the nineteenth century and became known as the Great Game. It became a strategic concern of the British that the lands to the north of India, such as Tibet, which were largely inaccessible to Westerners, were surveyed and mapped. These surveys were largely carried out by Indians recruited from the border provinces whose appearance would not automatically arouse suspicion beyond the Himalayas. They were trained as surveyors, disguised as lamas (Buddhist holy men) and in order to maintain their cover, used surveying tools that were disguised as objects that a lama would carry. The surveyors learned to make exactly 2,000 paces to a mile and in order to count these distances, their prayer beads were adapted from the usual 108 to a set of 100, with every tenth bead being slightly larger. Buddhist prayer wheels were also converted so that they could contain paper for making notes and drawing maps. Although it was dangerous work from which many failed to return, the surveys were completed with incredible accuracy. A measure of the high regard in which the surveyors were held is that they became known as pundits, from a Sanskrit word meaning an expert or a respected person.

† or field goal or successful try

‡ or dead ball or neutral zone established

Touchback .... arms criss-crossed above head followed by arm swung at side
No time out* .... arm circled to simulate moving clock
Delay of game† .... folded arms
False start‡ .... forearms rotated over and over in front of body
Personal foul .... one wrist striking the other above head
Roughing the kicker .... one wrist striking the other above head then swinging leg
Roughing the passer ... one wrist striking the other above head then raised arm forward
Major facemask .... one wrist striking the other above head then grasping facemask
Holding .... grasping one wrist, the fist clenched, in front of chest
Illegal use of hands§ .... grasping one wrist, hand open and forward, in front of chest
Penalty refused¶ .... hands shifted in horizontal plane
Pass juggled inbounds .... hands up and down in front of chest
Illegal forward pass .... one hand waved behind back
Intentional grounding .... parallel arms waved in a diagonal plane across body
Interference with forward pass** ... hands open, arms straight forward and horizontal
Invalid fair catch .... one hand waved above head
Ineligible receiver .... right hand touching top of cap
Illegal contact .... one open hand extended forward
Offside encroachment†† .... hands on hips
Illegal motion .... horizontal arc with one hand
Loss of down .... both hands held behind head
Interference‡‡ .... pushing movement of hands to front with arms downward
Touching a forward pass§§ .... diagonal motion of one hand across another
Unsportsmanlike conduct .... arms outstretched, palms down
Illegal cut .... hand striking front of thigh
Illegal block ... below waist one hand striking front of thigh after personal-foul signal
Chop block .... both hands striking side of thighs after personal-foul signal
Clipping .... one hand striking back of calf after personal-foul signal
Illegal crackback ... open right hand hits the right mid-thigh after personal foul signal
Player disqualified .... ejection signal
Tripping .... repeated action of right foot in back of left heel
Uncatchable forward pass ... palm of right hand moved back and forth above head
Too many men on the field¶¶ .... both hands on top of head

---

* or time in full
† or excess time out
‡ or illegal formation or kickoff or safety kick out of bounds or kicking team player
voluntarily out of bounds during a punt
§ or illegal use of arms or body
¶ or incomplete pass or play over or missed field goal or extra point
** or fair catch
†† or neutral zone infraction
‡‡ or pushing or helping runner
§§ or scrimmage kick
¶¶ or twelve men in offensive huddle

Facemask	grasping facemask with one hand
Illegal shift	horizontal arcs with two hands
Reset play clock – 25 seconds	pump one arm vertically
Reset play clock – 40 seconds	pump two arms vertically

MUSICAL TERMS (from page 187)

1. Softly; 2. Becoming louder; 3. Short and detached; 4. Loudly; 5. Fast or lively; 6. Getting gradually faster; 7. Becoming quieter; 8. Slowly; 9. Without instrumental accompaniment; 10. Very slowly; 11. Rapid fluctuation of the pitch of a note (vibrating); 12. Gradually slower; 13. Slowly and broadly; 14. Slowly and solemnly; 15. Smoothly; 16. Lively or uptempo; 17. Gently; 18. With vigor or spirit; 19. To the end; 20. Very quickly; 21. From the beginning; 22. Not too much; 23. Rapid repetition of one note (trembling); 24. Plucked (referring to a bowed instrument).

COMMONWEALTH COUNTRIES (from page 193; as at the time of publishing)

Antigua and Barbuda / Australia / Bahamas / Bangladesh
Barbados / Belize / Botswana / Brunei Darussalam
Cameroon / Canada / Cyprus / Dominica / Fiji Islands*
Gambia / Ghana / Grenada / Guyana / India
Jamaica / Kenya / Kiribati / Lesotho / Malawi / Malaysia
Maldives / Malta / Mauritius / Mozambique / Namibia
Nauru / New Zealand / Nigeria / Pakistan / Papua New Guinea
St. Kitts and Nevis / St. Lucia / St. Vincent and the Grenadines
Samoa / Seychelles / Sierra Leone / Singapore / Solomon Islands
South Africa / Sri Lanka / Swaziland / Tonga
Trinidad and Tobago / Tuvalu / Uganda
United Kingdom / Tanzania / Vanuatu / Zambia

NATIONAL PARKS (from page 196; as at time of publishing)

Acadia National Park	Maine
Arches National Park	Utah
Badlands National Park	South Dakota
Big Bend National Park	Texas
Biscayne National Park	Florida
Black Canyon of the Gunnison National Park	Colorado
Bryce Canyon National Park	Utah
Canyonlands National Park	Utah
Capitol Reef National Park	Utah
Carlsbad Caverns National Park	New Mexico
Channel Islands National Park	California
Congaree National Park	South Carolina
Crater Lake National Park	Oregon

---

* Membership suspended following a coup in December 2006.

Cuyahoga Valley National Park .... Ohio
Death Valley National Park .... California, Nevada
Denali National Park and Preserve .... Alaska
Dry Tortugas National Park .... Florida
Everglades National Park .... Florida
Gates of the Arctic National Park and Preserve .... Alaska
Glacier National Park .... Montana
Glacier Bay National Park and Preserve .... Alaska
Grand Canyon National Park .... Arizona
Grand Teton National Park .... Wyoming
Great Basin National Park .... Nevada
Great Sand Dunes National Park and Preserve .... Colorado
Great Smoky Mountains National Park .... North Carolina, Tennessee
Guadalupe Mountains National Park .... Texas
Haleakala National Park .... Hawaii
Hawaii Volcanoes National Park .... Hawaii
Hot Springs National Park .... Arkansas
Isle Royale National Park .... Michigan
Joshua Tree National Park .... California
Katmai National Park and Preserve .... Alaska
Kenai Fjords National Park .... Alaska
Kings Canyon National Park .... California
Kobuk Valley National Park .... Alaska
Lake Clark National Park and Preserve .... Alaska
Lassen Volcanic National Park .... California
Mammoth Cave National Park .... Kentucky
Mesa Verde National Park .... Colorado
Mount Rainier National Park .... Washington
North Cascades National Park .... Washington
Olympic National Park .... Washington
Petrified Forest National Park .... Arizona
Redwood National and State Parks .... California
Rocky Mountain National Park .... Colorado
Saguaro National Park .... Arizona
Sequoia National Park .... California
Shenandoah National Park .... Virginia
Theodore Roosevelt National Park .... North Dakota
Voyageurs National Park .... Minnesota
Wind Cave National Park .... South Dakota
Wrangell-St. Elias National Park and Preserve .... Alaska
Yellowstone National Park .... Idaho, Montana, Wyoming
Yosemite National Park .... California
Zion National Park .... Utah

MISCELLANY XXVI (from page 200)

1. Marilyn Monroe; 2. Pluto; 3. James Whistler; 4. The Riot Act*; 5. They do not drain into an ocean; 6. MRSA; 7. Steffi Graf; 8. The Rising Sun†; 9. Amen; 10. The Manhattan; 11. Production of hormones; 12. Eccentric; 13. 50%; 14. Woody Woodpecker; 15. Computer processing speed; 16. Urdu; 17. Groundhog Day; 18. Queensland and Northern Territory Aerial Services; 19. 255; 20. The first settlement in the U.S. by Europeans in 1565; 21. On the moon; 22. 2 July; 23. Twelve; 24. 2 lb.

CELEBRITY BABY NAMES (from page 12)

1. David & Victoria Beckham; 2. Courtney Cox & David Arquette; 3. David & Angela Bowie; 4. Jermaine Jackson & Alejandra Genevieve Oaziaza; 5. Michael Jackson & Debbie Rowe; 6. Madonna & Carlos Leon; 7. Gwyneth Paltrow & Chris Martin; 8. Frank and Gail Zappa; 9. Penn Jillette and Emily Zolten; 10. Madonna & Guy Ritchie; 11. Britney Spears & Kevin Federline; 12. Uma Thurman & Ethan Hawke; 13. Sean Penn & Robin Wright; 14. Angelina Jolie & Brad Pitt; 15. Debra Messing & Daniel Zelm; 16. Frank & Gail Zappa; 17. Woody Allen & Mia Farrow; 18. Simon & Yasmine Le Bon; 19. Bruce Willis & Demi Moore; 20. Jason Lee & Beth Riesgraf; 21. Sharleen Spiteri & Ashley Heath; 22. Bono & Alison Stewart; 23. Sylvester Stallone & Sasha Czack; 24. John Mellencamp & Elaine Irwin.

CREW OF APOLLO 11 (from page 8)

Neil Armstrong .... Commander
Michael Collins .... Command Module Pilot
Edwin "Buzz" Aldrin .... Lunar Module Pilot

BONES OF THE EAR‡ (from page 10)

Malleus (hammer) / Incus (anvil) / Stapes (stirrup)

FIRST LINES OF POP SONGS I (from page 13)

1. "Stand By Your Man" (Tammy Wynette); 2. "My Way" (Frank Sinatra); 3. "You're So Vain, Carly Simon; 4. "All You Need Is Love" (The Beatles); 5. "Seasons in the Sun," Terry Jacks; 6. "I Heard It Through the Grapevine" (Marvin Gaye); 7. "Lose Yourself" (Eminem); 8. "Wonderwall" (Oasis); 9. "A Groovy Kind of Love" (Phil Collins); 10. "Eye of the Tiger" (Survivor); 11. "Danger High

---

* "Our sovereign Lord the King chargeth and commandeth all persons, being assembled, immediately to disperse themselves, and peaceably to depart to their habitations, or to their lawful business, upon the pains contained in the act made in the first year of King George, for preventing tumults and riotous assemblies. God save the King."

† Heraldic symbol of Edward III, Japanese flag and "The House of the Rising Sun."

‡ The ossicles amplify sounds received by the ear drum and transmit them to the cochlea, a coiled chamber filled with fluid (named from the Latin word for "snail"). Tiny hairs inside this detect vibrations in the fluid and transmit them as nerve signals to the brain.

Voltage" (Electric Six); 12. "Kiss" (Prince and the Revolution); 13. "Take Me Home, Country Roads" (John Denver); 14. "These Boots Are Made for Walking" (Nancy Sinatra); 15. "Born in the U.S.A" (Bruce Springsteen); 16. "Somethin' Stupid" (Frank & Nancy Sinatra); 17. "Walk Like an Egyptian" (The Bangles); 18. "Gypsies, Tramps and Thieves," (Cher); 19. Fight for Your Right (The Beastie Boys); 20. "Graceland" (Paul Simon); 21. "West End Girls" (Pet Shop Boys); 22. "Everything I Do (I Do It For You)" (Bryan Adams); 23. "The Logical Song" (Supertramp); 24. "Sympathy for the Devil" (The Rolling Stones).

BLOOD GROUPS* (from page 16)

A / B / O / AB

SEVEN SUMMITS (from page 64)

Kilimanjaro	Africa/Tanzania
Vinson Massif	Antarctica
Puncak Jaya†	Australasia/Indonesia
Everest	Asia/Nepal
Elbrus	Europe/Russia
Mount McKinley	North America/U.S.A
Aconcagua	South America/Argentina

LINKED MISCELLANY II (from page 23)

1. Mack the Knife; 2. Daryl Hall and John Oates; 3. Lead; 4. The Green Berets; 5. Egg white; 6. Library of Congress; 7. Candlestick Park; 8. Mustard gas; 9. Pistol Pete; 10. Scarlett Johansson

The link is Clue.‡

---

* This is known as the AOB system which is determined by red blood-cell type. Each blood group may also be termed positive or negative depending on the existence or absence of the Rhesus D antigen. While it is always preferable to donate or receive blood from a member of the same blood group, compatibility is defined as follows: blood group O can donate blood to any other group but can only receive blood from other members of O; blood group A can donate to A and AB but can only receive blood from A or O; blood group B can donate to B and AB but can only receive blood from B and O; blood group AB can receive blood from any other group but can only donate blood to AB.

† An original list, postulated and first climbed by Richard Bass, included Mount Kosciuszko (2,228 m) on mainland Australia. Most mountaineers prefer the Messner list as Puncak Jaya in New Guinea, at 4,884 meters, is technically the highest mountain in Australasia. It is also a much more difficult climb; until recently the summit of Mount Kosciuszko was accessible by car. It has been observed that as a mountaineering challenge, climbing the second highest summit on each continent presents a much greater challenge as in almost every case the second highest peak is a technically harder climb and without a significant reduction in height.

‡ Knife, Hall, Lead Pipe, Reverend Green, Mrs. White, Library, Candlestick, Colonel Mustard, Pistol, Miss Scarlet.

INFORMATION SUPPLIED BY PRISONERS OF WAR (from page 25)

Name / Date of Birth / Rank / Service Number

LITTLE WOMEN (from page 27)

Amy / Beth / Jo / Meg

ADVERTISING SLOGANS II (from page 31)

1. Taco Bell; 2. Gillette; 3. U.S. Army; 4. Budweiser; 5. McDonald's; 6. Coca Cola; 7. Calvin Klein Jeans; 8. Ford; 9. Avis Rent-a-Car*; 10. Sprite; 11. MetLife; 12. Pepsi; 13. eBay; 14. Burger King; 15. Lexus; 16. Chevron; 17. IBM; 18. EA Games; 19. DHL; 20. Yellow Pages; 21. Adidas; 22. GlaxoSmithKline; 23. Maidenform[†] (bra); 24. American Coach Lines.

BATMEN (from page 34; as at the time of publishing)

Adam West	*Batman* (1966)
Michael Keaton . . . . *Batman* (1989), *Batman Returns* (1992)
Val Kilmer . . . . *Batman Forever* (1995)
George Clooney . . . . *Batman & Robin* (1997)
Christian Bale . . . . *Batman Begins* (2005), *The Dark Knight* (2008)

EVENTS OF THE MODERN PENTATHLON (from page 36)

Fencing / Running / Riding / Shooting / Swimming

AIRPORT CODES I (from page 38)

1. London (Gatwick); 2. New York (John F. Kennedy); 3. Los Angeles; 4. Hong Kong; 5. Mexico City (Juarez); 6. Boston (Logan); 7. Dallas Fort Worth; 8. Philadelphia; 9. Paris (Charles De Gaulle); 10. Bangkok (Don Muang); 11. Detriot (Metropolitan Wayne County); 12. Amsterdam (Schipol); 13. Honolulu; 14. Mumbai (formerly Bombay); 15. San Francisco; 16. Auckland; 17. Las Vegas; 18. Seattle (Tacoma); 19. Chicago (O'Hare) 20. Johannesburg (Jan Smuts); 21. Moscow (Sheremetyevo); 22. Berlin (Schonefeld); 23. Dubai; 24. Tokyo (Narita).

BONES OF THE SHOULDER AND ARM (from page 41)

Clavicle / Scapula / Humerus / Radius / Ulna

HOLLYWOOD FILM STUDIOS (from page 43)

20th Century Fox / Metro-Goldwyn-Mayer / Paramount Pictures
RKO Radio Pictures / Warner Brothers

---

* The slogan cleverly made a positive emphasis on the status of the company at the expense of the much larger Hertz.

† From a campaign of the 1950s and 1960s featuring women in public situations looking happy and confident wearing only their underwear. The slogan was always a variation of "I dreamed I . . . in my Maidenform bra."

MISCELLANY VI (from page 45)

1. Rio de Janeiro; 2. Adjacent to the kidneys; 3. The Eiffel Tower; 4. San Francisco (Oakland Athletics and the San Francisco Giants); 5. Earth; 6. Meg Ryan; 7. (A pink) Rolls Royce*; 8. Kenya; 9. Twelve; 10. Beagle; 11. Can opener; 12. SARS; 13. 30 minutes; 14. Al Gore; 15. The House of Commons; 16. The height of the Brooklyn Bridge and the width of the Panama Canal; 17. Fyodor Dostoevsky; 18. Brazil, Colombia, Ecuador; 19. Pompeii and Herculaneum; 20. Middle Earth†; 21. Toyota Corolla; 22. They both killed presidential assassins‡; 23. 14; 24. Twenty-four days.

NOVELS BY GEORGE ELIOT (from page 65)

Adam Bede	1859
The Mill on the Floss	1860
Silas Marner	1861
Romola	1863
Felix Holt, the Radical	1866
Middlemarch	1872
Daniel Deronda	1876

FIRST LINES OF POPULAR NOVELS II (from page 53)

1. *Bridget Jones's Diary* (Helen Fielding); 2. *Moby-Dick* (Herman Melville); 3. *Gone with the Wind* (Margaret Mitchell); 4. *Harry Potter and the Philosopher's Stone* (J. K. Rowling); 5. *The Hound of the Baskervilles* (Sir Arthur Conan Doyle); 6. *A Christmas Carol* (Charles Dickens); 7. *Don Quixote* (Miguel de Cervantes); 8. *Anna Karenina* (Leo Tolstoy); 9. *Goldfinger* (Ian Fleming); 10. *Rosemary's Baby* (Ira Levin); 11. *The War of the Worlds* (H. G. Wells); 12. *Slaughterhouse-Five* (Kurt Vonnegut); 13. *Jane Eyre* (Charlotte Brontë); 14. *Tom Sawyer* (Mark Twain); 15. *Frankenstein* (Mary Shelley); 16. *The Go-Between* (L. P. Hartley); 17. *Bridge to Terabithia* (Katherine Paterson); 18. *Dracula* (Bram Stoker); 19. *Fahrenheit 451* (Ray Bradbury); 20. *Of Mice and Men* (John Steinbeck); 21. *The Great Gatsby* (F. Scott Fitzgerald); 22. *The Old Man and the Sea* (Ernest Hemingway); 23. *Alphabetical Africa*§ (Walter Abish); 24. *Catch-22* (Joseph Heller).

---

* Lady Creighton Ward is also known as Lady Penelope from *Thunderbirds*.

† The Mediterranean is named from the Latin, "medius" meaning middle and "terra" meaning earth. Middle Earth is the fantasy setting for *The Hobbit* and *Lord of the Rings*.

‡ Boston Corbett shot John Wilkes Booth and Jack Ruby shot Lee Harvey Oswald. The shooting of Lee Harvey Oswald occurred live on American television.

§ *Alphabetical Africa* is an experimental work of constrained writing in the form of a novel. In the first chapter Abish only used words beginning with the letter "a." In the second chapter only words beginning with the letter "a" or "b" are used and each subsequent chapter adds words beginning with the next letter of the alphabet. Chapter 26 is written without constraint, all words being permissible. In the second half of the book, chapters 27–52, permissible words are dropped by a letter a time in reverse alphabetical order. Thus no words beginning with "z" appear in chapter 27, no words beginning "z" and "y" in chapter 28 and so on. The book is written in the first person but this does not become apparent until chapter 9.

QUARTERBACK CLASS OF '83 (from page 58)

QB	Draft #
John Elway ^HoF SB	1
Todd Blackledge	7
Jim Kelly ^HoF SB	14
Tony Eason ^SB	15
Ken O'Brien	24
Dan Marino ^HoF SB	27

HoF Hall of Fame   SB Appearance in Super Bowl

WOODWIND INSTRUMENTS (from page 60)

Piccolo / Flute / Oboe / Cor Anglais / Clarinet / Bassoon

TAGLINES OF POPULAR FILMS I (from page 63)

1. *Star Wars*; 2. *Forrest Gump*; 3. *Se7en*; 4. *Austin Powers: International Man of Mystery*; 5. *Dirty Dancing*; 6. *Erin Brockovich*; 7. *The Wizard of Oz**; 8. *The Magnificent Seven*; 9. *Mission: Impossible*; 10. *Jurassic Park*; 11. *Three Men and a Baby*; 12. *The Perfect Storm*; 13. *Meet the Parents*; 14. *The Sixth Sense*; 15. *Saving Private Ryan*†; 16. *Scream*; 17. *The Shawshank Redemption*; 18. *Misery*; 19. *The Pianist*; 20. *The Matrix*; 21. *Speed*; 22. *Mrs. Doubtfire*; 23. *Brokeback Mountain*; 24. *Saturday Night Fever*.

SPACE SHUTTLES (from page 67)

Columbia‡	destroyed 2003
Challenger	destroyed 1986
Discovery§	active
Atlantis	active
Endeavor	active
Enterprise	atmospheric test flights
Pathfinder	ground test simulator

CITIES OF HAMPTON ROADS (from page 70)

Chesapeake / Hampton / Newport News / Norfolk
Portsmouth / Suffolk / Virginia Beach

---

* Production of the film had to be stopped and the set repainted when the yellow brick road appeared green in the first color prints. *The Wizard of Oz* pioneered the use of Technicolor film.

† To enhance the look and feel of the film, Steven Spielberg reduced the color saturation of the print in the laboratory by 60% to mirror the color film reels produced during the war. When the film was later aired on cable channels in the U.S., the broadcasters were forced to increase the colour saturation after they were inundated with complaints from subscribers about their picture quality.

‡ *Columbia* was the first shuttle to enter space on April 12, 1981.

§ *Discovery* has flown the most missions of any shuttle, and flew both of the "return to flight" missions following the *Challenger* and *Columbia* disasters. *Discovery* was the shuttle which launched the Hubble telescope.

EPONYMOUS AIRPORTS (from page 71)

1. New York; 2. Paris; 3. Rome; 4. Liverpool; 5. Tehran; 6. Delhi; 7. New Orleans; 8. Venice; 9. Istanbul; 10. Tel Aviv; 11. Pisa; 12. Salzburg; 13. Chicago; 14. Montreal; 15. Washington, DC; 16. Houston; 17. Mexico City; 18. Springfield, Illinois; 19. Burbank, California; 20. Boston; 21. Warsaw; 22. Nairobi; 23. Tirana; 24. Rafah (Gaza Strip).

LIBERAL ARTS (from page 75)

Grammar / Logic / Rhetoric*
Arithmetic / Geometry / Music / Astronomy[†]

FRAT PACK (from page 76)

Jack Black / Will Ferrell / Ben Stiller / Vince Vaughn
Owen Wilson / Luke Wilson / Steve Carell

ROAD PICTURES (from page 77)

Road to Singapore	1940
Road to Zanzibar	1941
Road to Morocco	1942
Road to Utopia	1946
Road to Rio	1947
Road to Bali	1952
The Road to Hong Kong	1962

NICKNAMES OF PRESIDENTS (from page 79)

1. Richard Nixon; 2. Dwight D. Eisenhower; 3. William Clinton; 4. Jimmy Carter; 5. George H. W. Bush; 6. Ronald Reagan; 7. Lyndon Johnson; 8. Harry S. Truman; 9. John F. Kennedy; 10. Abraham Lincoln; 11. George Washington; 12. Herbert Hoover; 13. Thomas Jefferson; 14. Theodore Roosevelt; 15. Gerald Ford; 16. Zachary Taylor; 17. George W. Bush;[‡]18. Franklin D. Roosevelt; 19. Calvin Coolidge; 20. Woodrow Wilson; 21. James Madison; 22. Ulysses S. Grant; 23. James Abram Garfield; 24. Grover Cleveland.[§]

BASEBALL TEAMS YET TO WIN THE WORLD SERIES (from page 82; at the time of publishing)

San Diego Padres / Houston Astros / Milwaukee Brewers
Seattle Mariners / Texas Rangers / Washington Nationals
Colorado Rockies / Tampa Bay Devil Rays

---

* Grammar, logic, and rhetoric were collectively known as the Trivium.

[†] Arithmetic, geometry, music, and astronomy were collectively known as the Quadrivium.

[‡] The nickname has derived from an observation that unlike some of his predecessors, with their "teflon" tags, most scandals have tended to stick to George W. Bush.

[§] Before becoming president, in his role as Sheriff of Erie County, New York, Cleveland hanged two men.

GOLF SCORES (from page 84)

Condor (or Vulture)* .... -4
Albatross† .... -3
Eagle .... -2
Birdie .... -1
Par 0
Bogey .... +1
Double bogey .... +2
Triple bogey .... +3

FOOTBALL OFFICIALS (from page 85)

Referee / Umpire / Head Linesman / Line Judge
Field Judge / Side Judge / Back Judge / Replay Official

QUOTATIONS FROM SHAKESPEARE II (from page 87)

1. *Julius Caesar* (Caesar); 2. *Henry V* (King Harry); 3. *Richard III* (King Richard); 4. *Julius Caesar* (Antony); 5. *Romeo and Juliet* (Chorus); 6. *The Taming of the Shrew* (Petruchio); 7. *Othello* (Iago); 8. *The Winter's Tale* (Mamillius); 9. *Romeo and Juliet* (Mercutio); 10. *Henry V* (King Harry); 11. *Romeo and Juliet* (Romeo); 12. *The Taming of the Shrew* (Katherine); 13. *Macbeth*‡ (Lady Macbeth); 14. Hamlet (Ghost); 15. *Macbeth* (Second Witch); 16. *The Merchant of Venice* (Shylock); 17. *A Midsummer Night's Dream* (Lysander); 18. *Hamlet* (Queen Gertrude); 19. *The Merchant of Venice* (Prince of Morocco); 20. *A Midsummer Night's Dream* (Oberon); 21. *Othello* (Iago); 22. *Romeo and Juliet* (Juliet); 23. *A Midsummer Night's Dream* (Lysander); 24. *Richard II* (John of Gaunt).

THE FELLOWSHIP OF THE RING (from page 94)

Frodo / Sam / Merry / Pippin
Gandalf / Aragorn / Legolas / Gimli / Boromir

NIMITZ-CLASS AIRCRAFT CARRIERS (from page 95)

U.S.S. *Nimitz*§ / U.S.S. *Dwight D. Eisenhower* / U.S.S. *Carl Vinson*
U.S.S. *Theodore Roosevelt* / U.S.S. *Abraham Lincoln*

---

* or triple eagle

† or double eagle

‡ The play has gained a reputation in the theatre for being unlucky, although no one seems to know why—members of the acting profession often refer to it only as "The Scottish Play." The link with witchcraft is an obvious answer. It is equally possible that the numerous fight scenes in the play have led to injuries to cast members over the years which have caused shows to be postponed or cancelled. It has also been suggested that being a popular play, *Macbeth* was often staged as a replacement for failing plays, giving it the association with bad luck.

§ The lead ship of the class was named after Fleet Admiral Chester W. Nimitz, who commanded the Pacific Fleet in World War II. It was commissioned in 1975.

U.S.S. *George Washington* / U.S.S. *John C. Stennis*
U.S.S. *Harry S. Truman* / U.S.S. *Ronald Reagan*
U.S.S. *George H. W. Bush* (fitting out)

TYPES OF CLOUD (from page 96)

Cirrus	high level
Cirrocumulus	high level
Cirrostratus	high level
Altostratus	medium level
Altocumulus	medium level
Nimbostratus	medium level
Stratocumulus	low level
Stratus	low level
Cumulus	low level
Cumulonimbus	vertically developed

MISCELLANY XIII (from page 98)

1. Lunatic; 2. Venus; 3. Auguste Rodin; 4. All named after gods; 5. The Chrysler Building; 6. India*; 7. Beans; 8. Saffron; 9. Pandora; 10. Hunter S. Thompson; 11. Male; 12. Alaska; 13. *The Godfather, Part II* and *Lord of the Rings: The Return of the King*; 14. J. R. Ewing to Sue Ellen; 15. Georges Bizet; 16. Occidental; 17. *Frankenstein*; 18. BASIC; 19. Mumbai (formerly Bombay); 20. Billy the Kid; 21. John Travolta (*Saturday Night Fever*); 22. Twelve; 23. Nothing†; 24. Tuesday.

WORDS CONTAINED IN "THEREIN" (from page 108)

The / There / He / I / In / Rein / Her / Here / Er / Ere / Herein / Therein

FILMS STARRING GRACE KELLY (from page 104)

Fourteen Hours	1951
High Noon	1952
Mogambo	1953
Dial M for Murder	1954
Green Fire	1954
Rear Window	1954
The Country Girl	1954
The Bridges at Toko-Ri	1954
To Catch a Thief	1955
The Swan	1956
High Society	1956

---

* The Wheel of Law. Ashoka the Great ruled India in the second century BC.
† After September 2, the next day was September 14, due to the change from the Julian to the Gregorian calendar.

SCANDALS (from page 106)

1. George Michael; 2. Monica Lewinsky; 3. Ben Johnson; 4. Michael Jackson; 5. Oliver North; 6. Hugh Grant; 7. Arthur Andersen*; 8. Janet Jackson; 9. Martha Stewart; 10. Edward Kennedy; 11. Ford[†]; 12. Woody Allen; 13. Spiro Agnew; 14. The Chicago White Sox; 15. Eliot Spitzer; 16. Gary Hart; 17. Gary Condit; 18. Whitewater; 19. The Minnesota Vikings; 20. Tonya Harding; 21. Jimmy Swaggart; 22. Sinéad O'Connor; 23. Rosie Ruiz[‡]; 24. Paul Reubens.[§]

MEMBERS OF OPEC (from page 109; as at the time of publishing)

Algeria / Angola / Ecuador / Iran

Iraq / Kuwait / Libya / Nigeria / Qatar

Saudi Arabia / United Arab Emirates / Venezuela

COOKING TERMS II (from page 111)

1. Croutons; 2. Guacamole; 3. Chicken Kiev; 4. Ravioli; 5. Hollandaise; 6. Balti; 7. Consommé; 8. Bruschetta; 9. Chorizo; 10. Pesto; 11. Dauphinoise (à la); 12. Julienne; 13. Monosodium glutamate (MSG); 14. Entrecôte; 15. Bouillabaisse; 16. Angels on Horseback; 17. Coulis; 18. Crème anglaise; 19. Farfalle; 20. Frittata; 21. Fusilli; 22. Miso; 23. Tapenade; 24. Béchamel.

SGT. PEPPER'S LONELY HEARTS CLUB BAND (from page 114)

"Sgt. Pepper's Lonely Hearts Club Band" .... McCartney

"With a Little Help from My Friends" .... Lennon and McCartney

"Lucy in the Sky with Diamonds" .... Lennon

"Getting Better" .... McCartney

"Fixing a Hole" .... McCartney

"She's Leaving Home" .... Lennon and McCartney

"Being for the Benefit of Mr. Kite!" .... Lennon

"Within You Without You" .... Harrison

"When I'm Sixty-Four" .... McCartney

"Lovely Rita" .... McCartney

"Good Morning Good Morning" .... Lennon

"Sgt. Pepper's Lonely Hearts Club Band" (Reprise) .... McCartney

"A Day in the Life" .... Lennon and McCartney

---

* At their height, Arthur Andersen employed 28,000 people in the U.S. and 85,000 worldwide. They currently employ around two hundred people, most of whom are engaged in handling law suits.

† The model in question was the Ford Pinto. Ford took no action because a cost benefit analysis they carried out had found that it would be cheaper to pay the lawsuits from the resulting deaths and injuries than the $11 per car to correct the problem. While Ford was acquitted of any criminal wrongdoing, its reputation suffered considerable damage as a result.

‡ When questioned in an interview as to why she didn't look particularly tired, Ruiz said "I got up with a lot of energy this morning."

§ Better known as Pee-wee Herman.

CANADIAN PROVINCES AND TERRITORIES (from page 117)

Alberta / British Columbia / Manitoba / New Brunswick
Newfoundland and Labrador / Northwest Territories[T]
Nova Scotia / Nunavut[T] / Ontario / Prince Edward Island
Quebec / Saskatchewan / Yukon[T]

[T] indicates a territory

LAST LINES OF POPULAR FILMS I (from page 120)

1. *Casino Royale*; 2. *The Wizard of Oz*; 3. *The Silence of the Lambs*; 4. *Casablanca*[*];
5. *The Usual Suspects*; 6. *The Shawshank Redemption*; 7. *King Kong*; 8. *Back to the Future*; 9. *Jerry Maguire*; 10. *Return of the Jedi*; 11. *An Officer and a Gentleman*; 12. *Apocalypse Now*; 13. *Dr. Strangelove*; 14. *Butch Cassidy and the Sundance Kid*; 15. *Sunset Boulevard*; 16. *Shakespeare in Love*; 17. *Witness*; 18. *The Magnificent Seven*; 19. *L.A. Confidential*; 20. *Midnight Cowboy*; 21. *Shallow Grave*; 22. *Pretty Woman*; 23. *Network*; 24. *The Bridge on the River Kwai*.

VICE PRESIDENTS BECOMING PRESIDENT (from page 122)

John Adams / Thomas Jefferson / Martin Van Buren / John Tyler
Millard Fillmore / Andrew Johnson / Chester A. Arthur
Theodore Roosevelt / Calvin Coolidge / Harry S. Truman
Richard Nixon / Lyndon B. Johnson / Gerald Ford / George H. W. Bush

UNION OF SOVIET SOCIALIST REPUBLICS (from page 126)

Armenia / Azerbaijan / Belarus / Estonia / Georgia / Kazakhstan
Kyrgyzstan / Latvia / Lithuania / Moldova / Russia
Tajikistan / Turkmenistan / Ukraine / Uzbekistan

LINKED MISCELLANY X (from page 129)

1. Alexander the Great; 2. Manhattan Island; 3.The Pink Ladies; 4. *Tequila Sunrise*;
5. Kamikaze[†]; 6. Rob Roy; 7. *The French Connection*; 8. B-52; 9. Gibson Guitar Corporation[‡]; 10. *Cosmopolitan*.

The link is cocktails[§]

---

[*] The budget for *Casablanca* was so small that in the airport scene at the end of the film, a cardboard cutout of the plane was used with midgets playing the ground crew, to give the illusion it was a full-sized aircraft.

[†] The phrase originated from the major typhoons in 1274 and 1281, which twice destroyed massive fleets of Mongolian ships under Kublai Khan, thwarting his plans to invade Japan. The word was rarely spoken by Japanese in the context of suicide attacks, but came into widespread use in the west because of an erroneous translation during World War II.

[‡] of Nashville, Tennessee

[§] Brandy Alexander, Manhattan, Pink Lady, Tequila Sunrise, Kamikaze, Rob Roy, French Connection, B52, Gibson, and Cosmopolitan

OLYMPIC HOST NATIONS (from page 132)

Australia 1956, 2000
Belgium 1920
Canada 1976
China 2008
Finland 1952
France 1900, 1924
Germany 1936, 1972
Greece 1896, 1906, 2004
Italy 1960
Japan 1964
Mexico 1968
Netherlands 1928
South Korea 1988
Spain 1992
Sweden 1912
UK 1908, 1948
U.S.A. 1904, 1932, 1984, 1996
USSR 1980

BEATRIX POTTER TALES (from page 135)

*The Tale of Peter Rabbit**
The Tale of Squirrel Nutkin
The Tale of Tailor of Gloucester
The Tale of Benjamin Bunny
The Tale of Two Bad Mice
The Tale of Mrs. Tiggy-Winkle†
The Tale of Mr. Jeremy Fisher
The Tale of Tom Kitten
The Tale of Jemima Puddle-Duck
The Tale of the Flopsy Bunnies
The Tale of Mrs. Tittlemouse
The Tale of Timmy Tiptoes
The Tale of Johnny Town-Mouse
The Tale of Mr. Tod
The Tale of Pigling Bland
The Tale of Samuel Whiskers
The Tale of the Pie and the Patty Pan
The Tale of Ginger and Pickles
The Tale of Little Pig Robinson

---

* Having been rejected by several publishers, Beatrix Potter published her first book, *The Tale of Peter Rabbit*, herself in 1901.
† Inspired by her childhood pet hedgehog.

BATTLES II (from page 138)

1. American Civil War; 2. American War of Independence (1777); 3. Second World War (1940); 4. American Civil War (1862)*; 5. Vietnam War (1965); 6. Napoleonic Wars (1815); 7. Second World War (1942); 8. American War of Independence (1781); 9. Napoleonic Wars (1805); 10. Second World War (1944); 11. First World War (1914 and 1915)[†]; 12. Second World War (1939); 13. Zulu War (1879)[†]; 14. Second World War (1943)[‡]; 15. Crimean War (1854–55); 16. Greco-Persian Wars (490BC); 17. Second World War (1945)[§]; 18. Wars of Alexander the Great (331BC); 19. Second World War (1944); 20. First Crusade (1098); 21. Napoleonic Wars (1805); 22. Greco-Persian Wars (480BC)[¶]; 23. English Civil War (1645); 24. War of Scottish Independence (1314).

METRIC PREFIXES (from page 140)

Yetta- (Y)	....	1,000,000,000,000,000,000,000,000
Zetta- (Z)	....	1,000,000,000,000,000,000,000
Exa- (E)	....	1,000,000,000,000,000,000
Peta- (P)	....	1,000,000,000,000,000
Tera- (T)	....	1,000,000,000,000
Giga- (G)	....	1,000,000,000
Mega- (M)	....	1,000,000
Kilo- (K)	....	1,000
Hecto- (H)	....	100
Deca- (da)	....	10
Deci- (d)	....	0.1
Centi- (c)	....	0.001
Milli- (m)	....	0.0001
Micro- (l)	....	0.000001
Nano- (n)	....	0.000000001
Pico- (p)	....	0.000000000001

---

* Fought between the U.S.S. *Monitor* and the C.S.S. *Virginia*, the first battle between ironclad warships.

† At Rorke's Drift, a small number of British troops repelled a numerically superior force of Zulus. Eleven Victoria Crosses were awarded after the battle.

‡The Battles of Kursk was the largest tank battle in history, with German forces comprising some 2,700 tanks, 1,800 aircraft, and 900,000 personnel, and Russian forces estimated at 3,600 tanks 2,400 aircraft, and 1.3 million men.

§ Also known as the Battle of Bulge as it was nicknamed by Churchill.

¶ At Thermopylae a small force of around 1,000 Greeks (Spartans and Thespians) led by King Leonidas of Sparta held a pass through which the Persian army under Xerxes I and numbering hundreds of thousands of men, needed to travel. In one of the most infamous last stands in history, the Persians sustained heavy and disporporianate losses before overcoming the defenders, while Leonidas, in the certain knowledge that he and his force would all be killed, bought enough time for the retreating Greek armies to recover and regroup for the next battle.

Femto~ (f)	0.000000000000001
Atto~ (a)	0.000000000000000001
Zepto~ (z)	0.000000000000000000001
Yocto~ (y)	0.000000000000000000000001

MEDITERRANEAN COUNTRIES (from page 143)

Spain / France / Monaco / Italy / Malta / Slovenia / Croatia
Bosnia and Herzegovina / Montenegro / Albania / Greece
Turkey / Cyprus / Syria / Lebanon / Israel / Egypt / Libya
Tunisia / Algeria / Morocco

TAGLINES OF POPULAR FILMS III (from page 146)

1. *Jaws 2*; 2. *Psycho**; 3. *The Silence of the Lambs*; 4. *Toy Story 2*; 5. *Back to the Future II*; 6. *Rocky*; 7. *Four Weddings and a Funeral*; 8. *Citizen Kane*; 9. *Spider-Man*; 10. *Men in Black*; 11. *Pearl Harbor*; 12. *Bridget Jones's Diary*; 13. *The Graduate*; 14. *Teenage Mutant Ninja Turtles*; 15. *The Full Monty*; 16. *Dangerous Liaisons*; 17. *The Amityville Horror*; 18. *Terminator 2: Judgment Day*†; 19. *Bonnie and Clyde*; 20. *Platoon*; 21. *The Blair Witch Project*; 22. *Edward Scissorhands*; 23. *Dead Calm*; 24. *Flatliners*.

COASTAL STATES (from page 149)

Alaska	6,640 miles of coastline
Florida	1,350
California	840
Hawaii	750
Louisiana	397
Texas	367
North Carolina	301
Oregon	296
Maine	228
Massachusetts	192
South Carolina	187
Washington	157
New Jersey	130
New York	127
Virginia	112
Georgia	100

---

* The film is famous for its shower scene and particularly the sinister music that accompanies it. Originally Hitchcock wished the shower scene to play silently. In spite of this the composer Bernard Hermann went ahead and scored it; on hearing the soundtrack Hitchcock immediately changed his mind. The "blood" used in the scene was chocolate sauce.

† Arnold Schwarzenegger delivered 700 words of dialogue and earned $15 million for the film or $21,429 per word.

ROLLING STONES HITS (from page 151; as at date of publishing)

"Time Is On My Side" .... reaching number 6 in 1964
"(I Can't Get No) Satisfaction" 1, 1965
"Get Off Of My Cloud" 1, 1965
"The Last Time" 9, 1965
"19th Nervous Breakdown" 2, 1966
"As Tears Go By" 6, 1966
"Have You Seen Your Mother, Baby, Standing In The Shadow?" 9, 1966
"Mothers Little Helper" 8, 1966
"Paint It, Black" 1, 1966
"Ruby Tuesday" 1, 1967
"Jumpin' Jack Flash" 3, 1968
"Honky Tonk Women" 1, 1969
"Brown Sugar" 1, 1971
"Tumbling Dice" 7, 1972
"Angie" 1, 1973
"Fool To Cry" 10, 1976
"Beast Of Burden" 8, 1978
"Miss You" 1, 1978
"Emotional Rescue" 3, 1980
"Start Me Up" 2, 1981
"Undercover Of The Night" 9, 1983
"Harlem Shuffle" 5, 1986
"Mixed Emotions" 5, 1989

MISCELLANY XXI (from page 154)

1. Islam; 2. United States Bullion Depository, Fort Knox; 3. Wyoming; 4. Alan Rickman; 5. Planet*; 6. Harvard; 7. Fox Mulder; 8. Elvis Presley; 9. Ernest Hemingway; 10. Hawaii; 11. Three; 12. They have all been executed in the Tower of London; 13. House of Commons; 14. Sir Walter Scott; 15. Australia; 16. O_3; 17. The Gold Rush; 18. Las Vegas; 19. Influenza[†]; 20. Twelve; 21. Scalpel; 22. (1,666) MDCLXVI; 23. Toilet paper; 24. Forty.

---

* Asteres planetai
† The disease killed 500,000 Americans in 1918, part of a pandemic that killed more than 20 million people worldwide. The disease led to more deaths than World War I.

SLUGGERS (from page 000; as at time of publishing)

Mark McGwire	(4)	70, 65, 58, 52
Sammy Sosa[A]	(4)	66, 64, 63, 50
Babe Ruth	(4)	60, 59, 54, 54
Alex Rodriguez[A]	(3)	57, 54, 52
Jimmie Foxx	(2)	58, 50
Ken GriffeyA	(2)	56, 56
Mickey Mantle	(2)	54, 52
Ralph Kiner	(2)	54, 51
Willie Mays	(2)	52, 51
Barry Bonds[A]		73
Roger Maris		61
Hank Greenberg		58
Ryan Howard[A]		58
Luis Gonzalez[A]		57
Hack Wilson		56
David Ortiz[A]		54
Ralph Kiner		54
George Foster		52
Jim Thome[A]		52
Andruw Jones[A]		51
Cecil Fielder		51
Johnny Mize		51
Albert Belle		50
Brady Anderson		50
Greg Vaughn		50
Prince Fielder[A]		50

[A] denotes a currently active player

BOOKS OF THE NEW TESTAMENT (from page 165)

Matthew / Mark / Luke / John / Acts / Romans / 1 Corinthians
2 Corinthians / Galatians / Ephesians / Philippians / Colossians
1 Thessalonians / 2 Thessalonians / 1 Timothy / 2 Timothy
Titus / Philemon / Hebrews / James / 1 Peter / 2 Peter
1 John / 2 John / 3 John / Jude / Revelation

FILMS AND THEIR STARS V (from page 169)

1. *Forrest Gump*; 2. *American Beauty*; 3. *The Sixth Sense*; 4. *Robin Hood: Prince of Thieves*; 5. *Unforgiven*; 6. *The Cannonball Run*; 7. *Steel Magnolias*; 8. *Crouching Tiger, Hidden Dragon*; 9. *Cleopatra*; 10. *The Exorcist*; 11. *Edward Scissorhands*; 12. *The Pelican Brief*; 13. *Platoon*; 14. *Chocolat*; 15. *Disclosure*; 16. *Deliverance*; 17. *Tootsie*; 18. *You, Me and Dupree*; 19. *Things to Do in Denver When You're Dead*; 20. *Risky Business*; 21. *Cry Freedom*; 22. *Postcards from the Edge*; 23. *Sylvia*; 24. *The Manchurian Candidate*.

MAJOR LEAGUE BASEBALL STADIUMS (from page 172; as at time of publishing)

Angel Stadium of Anaheim .... Los Angeles Angels of Anaheim
AT&T Park .... San Francisco Giants
Busch Stadium .... St. Louis Cardinals
Chase Field .... Arizona Diamondbacks
Citizens Bank Park .... Philadelphia Phillies
Comerica Park .... Detroit Tigers
Coors Field .... Colorado Rockies
Dodger Stadium .... Los Angeles Dodgers
Dolphin Stadium* .... Florida Marlins
Fenway Park .... Boston Red Sox
Great American Ball Park .... Cincinnati Reds
Kauffman Stadium .... Kansas City Royals
McAfee Coliseum† .... Oakland Athletics
Hubert H. Humphrey Metrodome‡ .... Minnesota Twins
Miller Park .... Milwaukee Brewers
Minute Maid Park .... Houston Astros
Nationals Park .... Washington Nationals
Oriole Park at Camden Yard .... Baltimore Orioles
PETCO Park .... San Diego Padres
PNC Park .... Pittsburgh Pirates
Progressive Field .... Cleveland Indians
Rangers Ballpark in Arlington .... Texas Rangers
Rogers Centre .... Toronto Blue Jays
Safeco Field .... Seattle Mariners
Shea Stadium§ .... New York Mets
Tropicana Field¶ .... Tampa Bay Rays
Turner Field .... Atlanta Braves
U.S. Cellular Field .... Chicago White Sox
Wrigley Field .... Chicago Cubs
Yankee Stadium** .... New York Yankees

CHARACTERS IN LITERATURE IV (from page 176)

1. *Catch-22* (Joseph Heller)††; 2. *James and the Giant Peach* (Roald Dahl); 3. *The*

---

* Due to be replaced by the New Marlins Stadium in 2011; the team will become the Miami Marlins.

† Due to be replaced by Cisco Field in 2011.

‡ Due to be replaced by the Twins Ballpark in 2010.

§ Due to be replaced by Citi Field in 2009.

¶ Possibly to be replaced by Rays Ballpark in or around 2012.

** Due to be replaced by New Yankee Stadium in 2009.

†† In the story, the character received the name Major as both of his given names by his father as a cruel joke. A computer error then resulted in Major being promoted to Major.

Canterbury Tales (Geoffrey Chaucer); 4. *Nineteen Eighty-four* (George Orwell); 5. *Tom Sawyer* (Mark Twain); 6. *The Lion, the Witch and the Wardrobe* (C. S. Lewis); 7. *Through the Looking-glass and What Alice Found There* (Lewis Carroll); 8. *Dracula* (Bram Stoker); 9. *The Jungle Book* (Rudyard Kipling); 10. *The Catcher in the Rye* (J. D. Salinger); 11. *The Rivals* (Richard Brinsley Sheridan)* 12. *Ulysses* (James Joyce); 13. *Great Expectations* (Charles Dickens); 14. *Rebecca* (Daphne du Maurier); 15. *Emma* (Jane Austen); 16. *Crime and Punishment* (Fyodor Dostoyevsky); 17. *Captain Corelli's Mandolin* (Louis de Bernières); 18. *Lord of the Flies* (William Golding); 19. *Fahrenheit 451* (Ray Bradbury); 20. *Gone With the Wind* (Margaret Mitchell); 21. *Of Mice and Men* (John Steinbeck); 22. *Anne of Green Gables* (Lucy M. Montgomery); 23. *The Shining* (Stephen King); 24. *Far from the Madding Crowd* (Thomas Hardy).

NHL 500 CLUB (from page 179; as at time of publishing)

Wayne Gretzky	894
Gordie Howe	801
Brett Hull	741
Marcel Dionne	731
Phil Esposito	717
Mike Gartner	708
Mark Messier	694
Steve Yzerman	692
Mario Lemieux	690
Luc Robitaille	668
Brendan Shanahan ^A	649
Dave Andreychuk	640
Jaromir Jagr ^A	640
Joe Sakic ^A	621
Bobby Hull	610
Dino Ciccarelli	608
Jari Kurri	601
Mike Bossy	573
Guy Lafleur	560
Joe Nieuwendyk	559
Johnny Bucyk	556
Mats Sundin ^A	555
Teemu Selänne ^A	550
Ron Francis	549
Michel Goulet	548
Maurice Richard	544
Stan Mikita	541
Frank Mahovlich	533

---

* The character was continually mixing up her words, for example: "He is the very pineapple of politeness" (instead of pinnacle). She gave her name to malapropism— the jumbling of words in a comic fashion.

[A] denotes currently active player

ENGLISH MONARCHS (from page 182)

---

* Charles II ascended to the throne following the Restoration of the Monarchy. From 1649 until 1659, England was a republic governed by Oliver Cromwell, Lord Protector (1653–58) and Richard Cromwell, Lord Protector (1658–59).

† The name of the House of Windsor was adopted by the monarchy in 1917 in preference to Saxe-Coburg due to public anti-German sentiment.

---

* Jane was never crowned and the circumstances of her accession and reign have meant her qualification as a legitimate monarch is disputed. Jane's predecessor, Edward VI, died of tuberculosis on July 6, 1553, at the age of fifteen. Edward had received a staunch Protestant upbringing and, encouraged by his adviser the Duke of Northumberland, had no desire for his Catholic half-sister Mary to succeed him. Edward first fell ill in January 1553 but when, by May of that year, it had become clear that the King would not recover, Northumberland had Edward sign a redrafted will naming Jane Grey, great-granddaughter of Henry VII (and Northumberland's own daughter-in-law) as his heir. Jane was proclaimed queen on July 10; although much of the English establishment backed the accession (concerned at the prospect of a Roman Catholic sovereign), the public supported Mary, the natural heir according to the Act of Succession of 1544. Mary rallied her supporters and on July 19 rode into London to be proclaimed Queen. Jane is known as the Nine-day Queen (or the Thirteen-day Queen if her reign was assumed to begin at the death of her predecessor). Jane Grey was executed a year later, in 1554, at the age of only sixteen.

† Mary ruled jointly with William III until her death in 1694.

‡ A maritime accident in 1120 had ramifications that would impact the course of English history for centuries to come. *The White Ship*, sailing overnight from Barfleur in France, bound for England, hit rocks and capsized, drowning all crew and passengers bar one, but including seventeen-year-old William Adelin, the only legitimate son of King Henry I. As a result, Henry named his daughter Matilda as his heir, with the consequence that, for the first time in its history, England would have a queen. When Henry I died in 1135, his nephew Stephen of Blois acted quickly in claiming the throne. In spite of Henry's barons swearing allegiance to Matilda, their doubts about the suitability of a female sovereign helped Stephen to become accepted as successor. Matilda, however, was incensed and raised an army to enforce her claim, plunging England into a period of bitter civil war which became known as the Anarchy. Matilda eventually defeated Stephen in February 1141 at the Battle of Lincoln, proclaiming herself Queen, with Stephen captured and imprisoned. Matilda struggled to win public acceptance and only a few months later their fortunes were reversed when Stephen escaped and she herself was imprisoned. A deal was eventually struck allowing Stephen to rule as King, but for Matilda's son Henry to succeed him as Henry II. The succession crisis of 1135 increased baronial power, ultimately leading to the creation of the Magna Carta, and greatly influenced future monarchs, most notably Henry VIII four centuries later, in the lengths they would go to secure a male succession. Matilda's qualification as a legitimate English monarch is disputed.

Richard I[P]	1189–99
Richard II[P][Dep]	1377–99
Richard III[Y]	1483–85
Stephen[N]	1135–54
Victoria[H]	1837–1901
William I[N]	1066–87
William II[N]	1087–1100
William III[S]*	1688–1702
William IV[H]	1830–87

Monarchs indicated as: [N]Norman; [P]Plantagenet; [L]Lancaster; [Y]York; [T]Tudor; [S]Stuart; [H]Hanover; [SC]Saxe-Coburg; [W]Windsor; [Disp]Disputed; [Dep]Deposed; [Abd]Abidicated

TAGLINES OF POPULAR FILMS IV (from page 185)

1. *Alien*; 2. *E.T. the ExtraTerrestrial*; 3. *Chicken Run*; 4. *The Da Vinci Code*; 5. *Flashdance*; 6. *Babe*; 7. *Meet the Fockers*; 8. *The Hunt for Red October*; 9. *Home Alone*; 10. *Snakes on a Plane*; 11. *Robocop*; 12. *Harry Potter and the Philosopher's Stone*; 13. *Some Like It Hot*; 14. *Braveheart*; 15. *Pi*; 16. *Gremlins*; 17. *Léon*; 18. *Friday the 13th*; 19. *True Lies*; 20. *Footloose*; 21. *This Is Spinal Tap*; 22. *Mars Attacks!*; 23. *Quiz Show*; 24. *JFK*.

ALFRED HITCHCOCK FILMS (from page 193)

The Pleasure Garden	1925
The Mountain Eagle	1927
The Lodger	1927
Downhill	1927
Easy Virtue	1927
The Ring	1927
Champagne	1928
The Farmer's Wife	1928
The Manxman	1929
Blackmail	1929
Juno and the Paycock	1930
Murder!	1930
Mary	1931
The Skin Game	1931
Number Seventeen	1932
Rich and Strange	1932
The Man Who Knew Too Much	1934
Waltzes from Vienna	1934
The Thirty-Nine Steps	1935
Sabotage	1936
Secret Agent	1936
Young and Innocent	1937

---

* William ruled jointly with Mary II following the Glorious Revolution of 1688.

---

* Hitchcock's first film after moving to Hollywood. It won the Oscar for Best Picture.

† Hitchcock appears in the "before" and "after" pictures in the newspaper ad for a weight-loss product.

‡ Hitchcock is seen disembarking from a train at Cumberland Station, carrying a cello.

§ Hitchcock appears on the left side of a class reunion photo.

¶ Hitchcock is seen winding a clock in the songwriter's apartment.

** Remake of the 1934 film.

†† Hitchcock is seen missing a bus during the opening credits.

‡‡ *Psycho* was unusual in that Hitchcock killed off his major star (Janet Leigh in the famous shower scene) a third of the way into the film—immensely shocking to audiences at the time. In 1960s America, cinema-goers were sometimes prone to drifting into showings some time after the start of the film, but Hitchcock insisted that audiences could only watch his film from the start so as not to ruin this surprise. Hitchcock appears in the film wearing a ten-gallon hat outside Janet Leigh's office.

§§ Hitchcock is seen leaving a pet shop with two white terriers.

ETYMOLOGY OF ROCK AND POP NAMES II (from page 196)

1. Blondie; 2. AC/DC; 3. Chicago; 4. Frankie Goes to Hollywood; 5. Eurythmics; 6. Dire Straits; 7. Nirvana; 8. Fountains of Wayne; 9. Men at Work; 10. The The; 11. Styx; 12. Scissor Sisters; 13. Three Dog Night; 14. Green Day; 15. Led Zeppelin; 16. Scritti Politti; 17. McFly; 18. The B52s; 19. The Black Crowes; 20. Los Lobos; 21. Moby; 22. Run DMC; 23. Black Rebel Motorcycle Club; 24. Thousand Yard Stare.

NOVELS BY AGATHA CHRISTIE (from page 197)

---

* Hitchcock is seen rising from a wheelchair, shaking hands with a man and walking off.
† Hitchcock appears in the middle of a crowd, the only one not applauding the speaker.

[P]Hercule Poirot; [M]Miss Marple; [TT]Tommy Beresford and Tuppence Cowley

---

* Written four decades earlier and stored securely, the book describes Piorot's lat case. Agatha Christie authorized the novel for pulication when she knew she would write no more novels.
† Published posthumously. The novel had been written four decades earlier and stored securely. Christie left instructions for the novel to be published in the event of her death. It relates Miss Marple's last case.

CHEMICAL ELEMENTS* (from page 201; as at the time of publishing)

Element	Symbol, Atomic Number
Actinium	Ac, 89
Aluminium	Al, 13
Americium	Am, 95
Antimony	Sb, 51
Argon	Ar, 18
Arsenic	As, 33
Astatine	At, 85
Barium	Ba, 56
Berkelium	Bk, 97
Beryllium	Be, 4

---

* Note that elements with atomic numbers 43, 61, and 95–118 can only be synthesised and do not exist naturally. Elements with atomic numbers 112–18 are placeholder names only. Chemistry as a distinct science is often said to date from 1661 and the publication by Robert Boyle of *The Sceptical Chymist*, a book which brought the subject into the open for the first time. Until that time chemical experiments were largely conducted in secrecy by alchemists. Boyle's main achievement was to define an element, being a substance that cannot be broken down into anything simpler, a discovery which represented a major breakthrough in the understanding of chemistry. The subject was further advanced by a French aristocrat named Antoine-Laurent Lavoisier who, along with his wife, discovered that a rusting object gains weight as it rusts (and not loses it as everyone had assumed) and led for the first time to an understanding about the way matter behaves in chemical reactions. Throughout the late eighteenth and early nineteenth centuries there was a huge increase in the number of known elements with chemists in open competition to make new discoveries. Humphry Davy was more prolific than most, claiming potassium, sodium, magnesium, calcium, strontium, and aluminium. When a Swedish chemist, J. J. Berzelius, suggested the use of abbreviations of Latin or Greek names to create chemical symbols, the notation of the science was born. Hence lead (plumbum) is Pb, tin (stannum) is Sn, and mercury (hydrargyrum) is Hg. The biggest breakthrough was achieved in 1869 by a young professor from St. Petersburg, Dmitri Mendeleev, who was interested in the problem of how to correctly arrange the elements. At the time, elements were grouped either according to atomic weight or according to similar chemical properties, but Mendeleev realized that these could be represented in a single arrangement. When elements were ordered by weight, certain physical and chemical properties appeared to repeat every eighth place. Mendeleev arranged these elements of similar properties in vertical rows, which he called Groups, and horizontal rows, of ascending atomic weight, called Periods, showing one set of relationships when read across and another when read down. Mendeleev's real genius was in the blank spaces he left in the table. At the time, only sixty-three elements were known to exist, but Mendeleev's periodic table predicted the elements that were still waiting to be found—predictions that turned out to be accurate as the missing elements were subsequently discovered.

* Named after Dmitri Mendeleev.

[Y] indicates an element named after the village of Ytterby, near Stockholm

PRIMARY COLORS* (from page 6)

Red / Yellow / Blue

TRIANGLES† (from page 8)

Equilateral / Isosceles / Scalene

MISCELLANY I (from page 10)

1. Kitty Hawk 2. Yom Kippur; 3. Nine ("Peter Piper picked a peck of pickled peppers"); 4. Water; 5. El Salvador; 6. Six; 7. Bromine and mercury; 8. The Fifth Amendment; 9. Puccini; 10. Counterclockwise; 11. They both died at the same address (12 Curzon Place, Mayfair, London); 12. Ash Wednesday; 13.

---

* Traditionally primary colors refer to the colored pigments used by artists to produce all other colors. In the modern context, primary colors are used in subtractive color mixing (where the color source relies on reflected light; for example, in print) and additive color mixing (where the color source uses emitted light; for example, in television). The subtractive primary colors are cyan, magenta, yellow, and black (known as the CMYK color space). The additive colors are red, green, and blue (known as the RGB color space).

† All of the sides of an equilateral triangle are of equal length and all its internal angles are 60°; an isosceles triangle has two sides of equal length and two equal internal angles; a scalene triangles sides all have different lengths and its three internal angles are different.

Breakfast at Tiffany's; 14. Richard Strauss; 15. Tug of war; 16. Yellowstone; 17. 10 Downing Street (it is a title held by the British Prime Minister); 18. Gracelands; 19. Eight; 20. *Nineteen Eighty-four*; 21. 5,280; 22. A; 23. 100 mph; 14. 1 km per hour.*

TEA PARTY IN WONDERLAND (from page 14)
Alice / The Dormouse / The Hatter[†] / The March Hare

STATES AT FOUR CORNERS MONUMENT (from page 16)
Arizona / Colorado / New Mexico / Utah

BOY BANDS (from page 22)
1. The Jackson 5; 2. Boyz II Men; 3. The Monkees; 4. The Osmonds; 5. The Bee Gees; 6. N Sync; 7. New Kids on the Block; 8. Backstreet Boys; 9. New Edition; 10. B2K; 11. Wham!; 12. The Temptations; 13. Color Me Badd; 14. The Bay City Rollers; 15. Duran Duran; 16. Westlife; 17. Take That; 18. Boyzone; 19. Village People; 20. Soul for Real; 21. Jagged Edge; 22. Hanson; 23. All-4-One; 24. 112.[‡]

PAC-MAN GHOSTS (from page 24)
Inky / Pinky / Blinky / Clyde

HOUSES AT HOGWARTS (from page 24)
Gryffindor[§] .... courage
Ravenclaw .... intellect
Hufflepuff .... hard work and fair play
Slytherin .... cunning

---

* This problem is simpler than it first seems. The current in the stream acts on the bottle and the man in the same way. Therefore if the man swims away from the bottle for half an hour, it will take half an hour for the man to swim back to the bottle. (The problem would be the same if the bottle and the water were stationary; assuming the swimmer has a constant speed, having swum away from the bottle for a fixed amount of time, it would take the same amount of time to swim back.) Given the bottle and the man reach the bridge at the same time, the bottle has travelled 1 kilometer in one hour. The speed of the current is therefore 1 km per hour.
† The Hatter is reportedly based on Theophilus Carter, an eccentric inventor, top hat wearer and proprietor of an Oxford furniture shop who was known locally as "The Mad Hatter." Sir John Tenniel, who illustrated the story, used Carter for his sketches. The association of madness with hatters came from the practice of using mercury in the process of curing felt. Mercury is a toxic substance which causes neurological damage, although this was unknown for a long time.
‡ Pronounced "One-twelve."
§ Harry and his friends Ron and Hermione are sorted into Gryffindor.

ASTRONOMERS, MATHEMATICIANS AND PHYSICISTS (from page 27)

1. Albert Einstein; 2. Isaac Newton*; 3. Archimedes; 4. Nicolaus Copernicus; 5. Galileo Galilei†; 6. Edwin Hubble; 7. Edmond Halley; 8. Pythagoras; 9. Christian Doppler; 10. René Descartes; 11. Alan Turing‡; 12. Erwin Schrödinger; 13. Florence Nightingale; 14. Michael Faraday; 15. Euclid; 16. Max Planck; 17. Charles Babbage; 18. Werner Heisenberg; 19. Blaise Pascal; 20. Wilhelm Herschel; 21. Ptolemy; 22. Ernest Rutherford; 23. Niels Bohr§; 24. Robert Hooke.¶

WILL & GRACE (from page 32)

Eric McCormack .... Will Truman
Debra Messing .... Grace Adler
Sean Hayes .... Jack McFarland
Megan Mullally .... Karen Walker

NORDIC COUNCIL (from page 34)

Denmark / Finland / Iceland / Norway / Sweden

---

* Newton's *Principia* is a candidate for the greatest scientific work of all time, but without the actions of Edmond Halley would quite possibly never have been published at all. In 1683, planets were known to have elliptical orbits but no one was able to say why. Sir Christopher Wren offered a wager to Halley and Robert Hooke, another prominent scientist of the day, to come up with a solution. The following year Halley paid a visit to the Lucasian Professor in Cambridge and was surprised to learn that Newton had solved the problem himself five years earlier. Halley insisted that Newton publish his theories and after two years of frenetic work, *Principia* was produced. Newton had absolutely no interest in contributing financially to its publication; Halley, although by no means wealthy, somehow found the money to fund it.

† Galileo was one of the first astronomers to benefit from the invention of the telescope. As well as the rings of Saturn, he discovered the four largest moons of Jupiter, the phases of Venus, sunspots, and mountains and craters on the moon. He discovered that the Milky Way was composed of stars, contrary to the thinking of the time that it was a cloud of gas. There is evidence that he also observed the planet Neptune, although he believed it to be a star. While away from stargazing, Galileo found time to note that the velocity of a falling body was independent of its mass and that a pendulum swing would always take the same time regardless of the amplitude of the swing—a discovery that paved the way for accurate timekeeping.

‡ Turing predicted that artificial intelligence would one day be possible and devised a test which could define a computer as being "sentient." In the Turing Test, a computer and a human provide text-based answers to questions asked by a human judge. If the judge cannot tell them apart, the machine is said to have passed the test. So far, no computer has passed the test.

§ Commenting on the puzzling nature of quantum theory, Bohr once said: "Anyone who is not shocked by quantum theory has not understood it."

¶ Possibly better known for his contribution to biological science, Hooke was the first person to describe a cell.

LINKED MISCELLANY III (from page 37)

1. *Raiders of the Lost Ark*; 2. Cowboy; 3. The Patriot Act; 4. James Brown; 5. Steel; 6. Giant; 7. Lionheart (or Coeur de Lion); 8. Cardinals*; 9. The 49th Parallel; 10. Dolphins.

The link is NFL teams[†]

MARX BROTHERS (from page 39)

Chico / Groucho / Gummo / Harpo / Zeppo

PLATONIC SOLIDS (from page 41)

Tetrahedron / Hexahedron (Cube) / Octahedron
Dodecahedron / Icosahedron

OLOGIES I (from page 43)

1. Birds; 2. Ancestry; 3. Weather; 4. The nervous system; 5. Bees; 6. Skin and related diseases; 7. The universe; 8. Bells and bell ringing; 9. Old age; 10. Sounds in language; 11. The nose; 12. Dates; 13. Disease; 14. The heart and related diseases; 15. Blood; 16. Characteristics of rocks; 17. Insects; 18. Plant and animal cells; 19. Trees; 20. Aquatic mammals, especially whales; 21. Eggs; 22. Ants; 23. Fingerprints; 24. Life in outer space.

TASTES (from page 46)

Bitter / Salt / Sour / Sweet / Umami[‡]

ELEMENTS WITH FOUR-LETTER NAMES (from page 48)

Gold / Iron / Lead / Neon / Zinc

MENTAL DISORDERS (from page 50)

1. Insomnia; 2. Kleptomania; 3. Anorexia nervosa; 4. Amnesia; 5. Bulimia nervosa; 6. Clinical depression; 7. Exhibitionism; 8. Nymphomania; 9. Post-traumatic stress disorder; 10. Pyromania; 11. Schizophrenia[§]; 12. Dementia; 13. Tourette's syndrome; 14. Phobia; 15. Hypochondria; 16. Megalomania; 17. Narcolepsy; 18. Stockholm syndrome[¶]; 19. Passive-aggressive disorder; 20. Obsessive-compulsive disorder; 21.

---

* The College of Cardinals.

† Oakland Raiders, Dallas Cowboys, New England Patriots, Cleveland Browns, Pittsburgh Steelers, New York Giants, Detroit Lions, Arizona Cardinals, San Francisco 49ers, and the Miami Dolphins.

‡ Umami (a Japanese word) is triggered by monosodium glutamate in the same way that a sweet taste is triggered by sugar. This fact is well known to Chinese and Japanese chefs who use it extensively in their cooking.

§ The term comes from the Greek "schizo" (split or divide) and "phrenos" (mind) and is often translated as "shattered mind."

¶ Named after a bank robbery in Stockholm in August 1973 in which bank employees were held hostage for five days. Sometimes this is referred to erroneously in the popular media as "Helsinki Syndrome," notably in the film *Die Hard*. The syndrome may stem from the instinct of newborn babies to form an emotional attachment to the nearest powerful adult.

Delusional disorder (or paranoia); 22. Bipolar disorder (or mania); 23. Munchausen's syndrome; 24. Munchausen's syndrome by proxy.

FRIENDS (from page 55)

Jennifer Aniston . . . . Rachel Green
Courteney Cox Arquette . . . . Monica Geller
Lisa Kudrow . . . . Phoebe Buffay
Matt LeBlanc . . . . Joey Tribbiani
Matthew Perry . . . . Chandler Bing
David Schwimmer . . . . Ross Geller

NOBEL PRIZES (from page 58)

Physics / Chemistry / Medicine / Literature / Peace / Economics

MISCELLANY VIII (from page 60)

1. Narcissus; 2. California; 3. *The Hitchhiker's Guide to the Galaxy*; 4. Henry VIII; 5. Jim Rockford; 6. Rocky's opponents; 7. The presidential helicopter; 8. Corduroy; 9. Badminton; 10. Blood vessels; 11. 144; 12. Iwo Jima; 13. Montague and Capulet; 14. "Mamma Mia"*; 15. The *Mona Lisa*; 16. Queen; 17. Machu Picchu; 18. Seattle; 19. *King Kong*; 20. Campbells; 21. The Battle of Bunker Hill; 22. Richard Nixon; 23. Miami†; 24. The letters are in reverse alphabetical order.

BEACH BOYS (from page 64)

Brian Wilson / Carl Wilson / Dennis Wilson / Mike Love
Al Jardine / David Marks / Bruce Johnston

FIFA WORLD CUP WINNERS‡ (from page 67; as at the time of publishing)

Uruguay / Italy / Brazil / Germany
England / Argentina / France

ANIMAL ADJECTIVES (from page 70)

1. Horse; 2. Lion; 3. Bird; 4. Zebra; 5. Ape or monkey; 6. Cow§ or ox; 7. Fish; 8. Pig; 9. Bull; 10. Dolphin; 11. Ostrich; 12. Bear; 13. Bee; 14. Goat; 15. Deer; 16.

---

* "Mamma Mia" reached number one for Abba in February 1976.
† 59% of Miami residents were born outside the United States.
‡ The World Cup trophy that Jules Rimet gave his name to weighed 3.8 kg, stood 35 cm tall and was made out of pure gold. After surviving some scrapes (it spent the Second World War hidden in a shoebox under the bed of a worried Italian football official, Ottorino Barassi; it was stolen from an exhibition in England in 1966 but recovered from a dustbin by a dog called Pickles) it was given permanently to the victorious Brazilian team of 1970, who had won the tournament for the third time. The trophy was stolen from the Brazilian FA in 1983 and has never been recovered.
§ "The cow is of the bovine ilk; one end is moo, the other, milk." —Ogden Nash.

Goat; 17. Wolf; 18. Mouse; 19. Sheep; 20. Wasp; 21. Hare; 22. Fox; 23. Goose; 24. Dove.

EVENTS IN THE HEPTATHLON (from page 72)
100 m hurdles / Long jump / High jump
200 m / Shot put / Javelin / 800 m

SEVEN SEAS (from page 75)
North Pacific / South Pacific
North Atlantic / South Atlantic
Arctic / Southern (Antarctic) / Indian

BRITISHISMS I (from page 77)
1. Flat; 2. Trousers; 3. Chips; 4. Autumn; 5. Nappy; 6. Solicitor*; 7. Postcode; 8. Biscuit; 9. Aubergine; 10. Torch; 11. Jelly; 12. Handbag; 13. Estate; 14. Boot; 15. Spanner; 16. Chemist's; 17. Dressing gown; 18. Windscreen; 19. Saloon; 20. Estate Agent; 21. Love bite; 22. Suitcase; 23. Music-hall; 24. Paraffin

COUNTRIES ENDING WITH " ~ STAN" (from page 80)
Afghanistan / Kazakhstan / Kyrgyzstan / Pakistan
Tajikistan / Turkmenistan / Uzbekistan

BRAT PACK† (from page 82)
Emilio Estevez / Anthony Michael Hall / Rob Lowe
Andrew McCarthy / Demi Moore / Judd Nelson
Molly Ringwald / Ally Sheedy

INNOVATIONS I (from page 84)
1. Telephone‡; 2. Aeroplane; 3. Printing press; 4. Waterproof material; 5. Radio; 6. Walkman; 7. Pneumatic tire; 8. Cylinder lock; 9. Personal computer; 10.

---

* In England, the word "attorney" once referred to a qualified legal agent in the courts of Common Law who prepared cases for barristers to plead. An attorney was the Common Law equivalent of a "solicitor" in the Chancery (the Chancery was a High Court under the jurisdiction of the Lord Chancellor; the Common Law courts relied on legal precedent). When the Judicature Act of 1873 merged the two courts, solicitor was assumed and attorney was dropped. In the United States, the term remained.

† These eight actors are most commonly included in the Brat Pack. Other actors often associated with the Brat Pack are Kevin Bacon, Matthew Broderick, Phoebe Cates, Tom Cruise, Charlie Sheen, and Kiefer Sutherland.

‡ The first speech to be transmitted by telephone was made by Bell on July 1, 1875. The first two-way speech (telephone conversation) was made by Bell and his assistant Watson, on March 10, 1876: "Mr. Watson, come here, I want to see you."

Steam engine; 11. Electric generator; 12. Dynamite; 13. Internal combustion engine (four-stroke cycle)*; 14. Newsreel; 15. Instant coffee; 16. Hot-air balloon; 17. Heart transplant[†]; 18. Electric battery; 19. Antiseptic surgery; 20. Atomic bomb; 21. Jet engine; 22. Hovercraft; 23. Genetic clone (Dolly the sheep); 24. Condom.

STATES CROSSED BY ROUTE 66 (from page 82)

Illinois / Missouri / Kansas / Oklahoma
Texas / New Mexico / Arizona / California

POKER HANDS (from page 94)

High card / Pair / Two pair / Three of a kind / Straight
Flush / Full house / Four of a kind / Straight flush[‡]

---

* The first automobile appeared in 1886 but the idea was not a new one. An Italian inventor, Guido da Vigevano, produced a design for a wind-powered vehicle in 1335 and Leonardo da Vinci also proposed a clockwork-driven tricycle two centuries later. The eighteenth and nineteenth centuries saw many engineers experimenting with steam, electricity, and even explosives to power an automobile engine but these attempts were largely unsuccessful. The invention of the internal combustion engine and the modern automobile was the result of the work of several men in the late nineteenth century. Jean Lenoir, a Belgian, patented a two-stroke gas-powered engine in 1860. In 1862, a Frenchman, Alphonse Bear de Rochas, worked out how to include a compression stroke into the cycle and the four-stroke cycle (intake–compression–power–exhaust) was born. De Rochas neglected to patent his invention, but a German engineer named Nikolaus Otto did not. Otto had successfully developed a four-stroke engine which he patented in 1876 and as a result the four-stroke cycle is often known as the Otto Cycle. The invention of the automobile is credited to two German engineers, Gottlieb Daimler and Carl Benz, who independently produced gas-driven cars in 1885 based on Otto's engine, which they were able to improve on. Benz was able to patent his "Motorwagen" in 1886, and his invention was given much publicity when his wife Bertha drove it sixty-two miles from Mannheim to Pforzheim to visit her mother (without her husband's prior knowledge). Although Benz and Daimler never met, the companies they founded merged in 1926 to form Daimler-Benz or Mercedes-Benz as it is now known. The basic design of the internal combustion engine has remained the same ever since.

† Barnard performed the nine-hour operation on Louis Washkansky, fifty-five, who lived for eighteen days before dying of pneumonia.

‡ A straight flush is a straight with all cards the same suit, for example 7♣ 6♣ 5♣ 4♣ 3♣, and is the highest hand in poker. A high straight flush, e.g. A♣ K♣ Q♣ J♣ 10♣, is called a royal flush; a low straight flush, e.g. 5♣ 4♣ 3♣ 2♣ A♣, is called a steel wheel.

PHOBIAS (from page 96)

1. Confined spaces; 2. Technology or computers; 3. Spiders; 4. Strangers or foreigners; 5. Bacteria; 6. Open spaces; 7. Flying; 8. Birds; 9. Blood or bleeding; 10. Heights; 11. Sunlight; 12. Crowds; 13. Sex; 14. Nighttime; 15. Washing or bathing; 16. Men; 17. Depth; 18. Thunder and lightning; 19. Germs; 20. Snakes*; 21. Long words; 22. One's mother-in-law; 23. Friday the 13th or the number 13; 24. The number 666.

TALLEST BUILDINGS IN THE U.S. (from page 99; at the time of publishing)

Sears Tower (Chicago)	1,451 ft / 442 m
Empire State Building (New York)	1,250 / 381
Bank of America Tower (New York)	1,200 / 366
Aon Center (Chicago)	1,136 / 346
John Hancock Center (Chicago)	1,127 / 344
Chrysler Building (New York)	1,046 / 319
New York Times Building (New York)	1,046 / 319
Bank of America Plaza (Atlanta)	1,023 / 312
U.S. Bank Tower (Los Angeles)	1,018 / 310
AT&T Corporate Center (Chicago)	1,007 / 307

ALPHA WORLD CITIES (from page 101)

London / New York City / Paris / Tokyo / Chicago
Frankfurt / Hong Kong / Los Angeles / Milan / Singapore

CAPITAL CITIES IV (from page 104)

1. Austria; 2. Jamaica; 3. Iran; 4. Lebanon; 5. Nepal; 6. Pakistan; 7. Syria; 8. Philippines; 9. Bolivia; 10. Afghanistan; 11. Estonia; 12. Tanzania; 13. Uganda; 14. Lithuania; 15. Paraguay; 16. Barbados; 17. Trinidad and Tobago; 18. Macedonia; 19. Sierra Leone; 20. Oman; 21. Nicaragua; 22. Cameroon; 23. Fiji; 24. Dominican Republic.

COUNTRIES ON THE EQUATOR† (from page 108)

Ecuador / Colombia / Brazil / Sâo Tomé and Príncipe / Gabon
Republic of the Congo / Democratic Republic of Congo
Uganda / Kenya / Somalia / Indonesia

BRIDGES AND TUNNELS IN NEW YORK CITY (from page 112)

George Washington Bridge / Third Avenue Bridge
Willis Avenue Bridge / Triborough Bridge

---

* Indiana Jones was a sufferer of Ophidiophobia.

† The equator passes through the Maldives and the Gilbert Islands and part of Kiribati but does not make contact with land. Surprisingly, the equator does not pass through Equatorial Guinea.

Queensborough Bridge (59th Street Bridge)
Queens Midtown Tunnel / Lincoln Tunnel
Williamsburgh Bridge / Holland Tunnel
Manhattan Bridge / Brooklyn Bridge / Brooklyn Battery Tunnel

FILMS BY STANLEY KUBRICK (from page 114)

Fear and Desire	1953
Killer's Kiss	1955
The Killing	1956
Paths of Glory	1957
Spartacus	1960
Lolita	1962
*Dr. Strangelove**	1964
2001: A Space Odyssey	1968
A Clockwork Orange	1971
Barry Lyndon	1975
The Shining	1980
Full Metal Jacket	1987
Eyes Wide Shut	1999

MISCELLANY XVI (from page 117)

1. Forty; 2. Rome; 3. Boston; 4. Aztec; 5. Oil; 6. Salsa; 7. Good-bye; 8. Cockles and mussels (alive alive-o); 9. Cape Horn; 10. George Washington; 11. Lamé; 12. Devon (Devonian); 13. Truly Scrumptious; 14. Pancreas; 15. It is now; 16. Crater Lake; 17. Not (seventh commandment: though shalt commit adultery); 18. The Muppet Show; 19. Omaha; 20. 13[†]; 21. Eleven seconds; 22. Huston or Coppola[‡]; 23. Elements (Yttrium [Y], Ytterbium [Yb], Terbium [Tb] and Erbium [Er]); 24. Sunday.

---

* Subtitled: *Or: How I Learned to Stop Worrying and Love the Bomb.*

† The number thirteen is thematic in the seal to represent the original thirteen states of the Union. On the front there are thirteen stars, thirteen stripes, thirteen arrows, thirteen olive leaves, thirteen olives, and thirteen letters in the motto (E Pluribus Unum). On the reverse there are thirteen levels of bricks in the pyramid, thirteen faces of the ribbon showing, and thirteen letters in the motto (annuit coeptis).

‡ Walter Huston (Best Supporting Actor, *The Treasure of the Sierra Madre*, 1948), John Huston (Best Director, *The Treasure of the Sierra Madre*, 1948), and Anjelica Huston (Best Supporting Actress, *Prizzi's Honor*, 1985); Carmine Coppola (Best Original Dramatic Score, *The Godfather, Part II*, 1974), Francis Ford Coppola (Best Original Screenplay, *Patton*, 1970; Best Adapted Screenplay, *The Godfather*, 1972; Best Picture, Best Director, Best Original Screenplay, *The Godfather, Part II*, 1974), Nicolas Cage (Francis Ford Coppola's nephew) (Best Actor, *Leaving Las Vegas*, 1995), Sophia Coppola (Best Original Screenplay, *Lost in Translation*, 2003)

COUNTRIES BORDERING CHINA (from page 121)

Afghanistan / Bhutan / Myanmar (Burma) / India / Kazakhstan
North Korea / Kyrgyzstan / Laos / Mongolia / Nepal
Pakistan / Russia / Tajikistan / Vietnam

MUSICALS BY ANDREW LLOYD WEBBER (from page 122)

The Likes of Us lyrics by .... Tim Rice
Joseph and the Amazing Technicolor Dreamcoat .... Tim Rice
Jesus Christ Superstar .... Tim Rice
Evita .... Tim Rice
Tell Me on a Sunday* .... Don Black
Cats .... T. S. Eliot
Starlight Express .... Richard Stilgoe
The Phantom of the Opera .... Richard Stilgoe and Charles Hart
Aspects of Love .... Don Black and Charles Hart
Sunset Boulevard .... Don Black and Christopher Hampton
By Jeeves .... Alan Ayckbourn
Whistle Down the Wind .... Jim Steinman
The Beautiful Game .... Ben Elton
The Woman in White .... David Zippel

FORMER NAMES OF COUNTRIES (from page 127)

1. Zimbabwe; 2. Iran; 3. Sri Lanka; 4. Thailand; 5. Cambodia; 6. Iraq; 7.
Indonesia; 8. Ethiopia; 9. Libya; 10. Jordan; 11. Bangladesh; 12. Mongolia; 13.
Taiwan; 14. Belize; 15. Namibia; 16. Bolivia; 17. Canada; 18. Yemen; 19. Burkina
Faso; 20. Ghana; 21. United Arab Emirates; 22. Lesotho; 23. Moldova; 24.
Seychelles.

BOXING WEIGHT DIVISIONS[†] (from page 130)

Heavyweight .... 201 lb.
Cruiserweight .... 176–200 lb.
Light Heavyweight .... 169–75 lb.
Super Middleweight .... 161–8 lb.
Middleweight .... 155–60 lb.
Super Welterweight .... 148–54 lb.
Welterweight .... 141–47 lb.
Super Lightweight .... 136–40 lb.

---

* Written for Marti Webb and first performed in 1979, *Tell Me on a Sunday*
became the first act of a show called *Song and Dance*, produced in the West
End in 1982 (the second act was a ballet choreographed to music by Lloyd
Webber). *Tell Me on a Sunday* was updated and rewritten for a 2003 production
starring Denise Van Outen. It features the song "Take That Look Off Your
Face."

† Variations of these divisions are used by the WBO, WBC and the IBF.

Lightweight	131–35 lb.
Super Featherweight	127–30 lb.
Featherweight	123–26 lb.
Super Bantamweight	119–22 lb.
Bantamweight	116–18 lb.
Super Flyweight	113–15 lb.
Flyweight	109–12 lb.
Light Flyweight	106–8 lb.
Strawweight	<105 lb.

NATIONAL LEAGUE OF MAJOR LEAGUE BASEBALL (from page 129)

Arizona Diamondbacks[W] / Atlanta Braves[E] / Chicago Cubs[C]
Cincinnati Reds[C] / Colorado Rockies[W] / Florida Marlins[E]
Houston Astros[C] / Los Angeles Dodgers[W] / Milwaukee Brewers[C]
New York Mets[E] / Philadelphia Phillies[E] / Pittsburgh Pirates[C]
San Diego Padres[W] / San Francisco Giants[W]
St. Louis Cardinals[C] / Washington Nationals[E]
[E] East Division [C] Central Division [W] West Division

NICKNAMES OF MONARCHS (from page 135)

1. Richard I (1189–99); 2. Elizabeth I (1558–1603); 3. Edward (1042–66); 4. Alfred (871–99); 5. Mary I (1553–8); 6. Edward I (1272–1307); 7. Ethelred (978–1016); 8. Henry VIII (1509–47); 9. Richard III (1483–85); 10. Lady Jane Grey (1553); 11. William I (1066–87); 12. Charles II (1660–85); 13. Victoria (1837–1901); 14. John (1199–1216); 15. George III (1760–1820); 16. William II (1087–1100); 17. Anne (1702–14); 18. Edmund II (1016); 19. Henry II (1154–89); 20. Henry I (1100–35); 21. Henry III (1216–72); 22. Edward VII (1901–10); 23. Matilda (1141); 24. William IV (1830–37).

BESTSELLING ALBUMS (from page 138; as at time of publishing)

Their Greatest Hits 1971-1975 [29P]	Eagles
Thriller [27P]	Michael Jackson
The Wall [23P]	Pink Floyd
Led Zeppelin IV [23P]	Led Zeppelin
Back in Black [22P]	AC/DC
Greatest Hits Volume I & II [21P]	Billy Joel
Double Live [21P]	Garth Brooks
Come on Over [20P]	Shania Twain
Rumours [19P]	Fleetwood Mac
The Beatles*[19P]	The Beatles
Boston [17P]	Boston
The Bodyguard (Soundtrack) [17P]	Whitney Houston
No Fences [17P]	Garth Brooks

* Sometimes called the *White Album*.

Physical Graffiti [16P] .... Led Zeppelin
Greatest Hits [16P] .... Elton John
Hotel California [16P] .... Eagles
The Beatles 1967–1970 [6P] .... The Beatles
Jagged Little Pill [16P] .... Alanis Morissette
Cracked Rear View [16P] .... Hootie & the Blowfish
Supernatural [15P] .... Santana

Figures indicate platinum sales (or millions of copies)

LARGE COUNTRIES (from page 141)

Russia	6,592,800
Canada	3,855,100
United States	3,794,100
China	3,700,600
Brazil	3,287,600
Australia	2,969,900
India	1,183,400
Argentina	1,068,300
Kazakhstan	1,049,200
Sudan	967,500
Algeria	919,600
Democratic Republic of Congo	905,600
Saudi Arabia	849,400
Mexico	761,600
Indonesia	741,100
Libya	679,400
Iran	636,300
Mongolia	604,200
Peru	496,200
Chad	495,800

Figures are in square miles and are approximate

LINKED MISCELLANY XI (from page 144)

1. *The Silence of the Lambs*; 2. "Knockin' on Heaven's Door"; 3. Fly; 4. 4. Battery Park; 5. The Bible Belt; 6. *Shaft*; 7. Webcam; 8. Plug; 9. Coil; 10. Rod Stewart. The link is the internal combustion engine.*

THE CANTERBURY TALES† (from page 146)

The Knight's Tale / The Miller's Tale

---

* Silencer, knocking, flywheel, battery, timing belt or fan belt, crankshaft, cam or cam shaft, spark plug, coil, piston rod.

† The group also included a guidesman, ploughman, carpenter, haberdasher, arrowmaker, dyer, weaver and Chaucer himself. There are two tales told by Chaucer, The Tale of Sir Thopas and The Tale of Melibee.

The Reeve's Tale / The Cook's Tale
The Man of Law's Tale / The Wife of Bath's Tale
The Friar's Tale / The Summoner's Tale
The Clerk's Tale / The Merchant's Tale
The Squire's Tale / The Franklin's Tale
The Physician's Tale / The Pardoner's Tale
The Shipman's Tale / The Prioress's Tale
The Monk's Tale / The Nun's Priest's Tale
The Second Nun's Tale / The Canon's Yeoman's Tale
The Manciple's Tale / The Parson's Tale

ARAB LEAGUE (from page 149; as at the time of publishing)

Algeria / Bahrain / Comoros / Djibouti / Egypt [F] / Iraq [F] / Jordan [F] / Kuwait / Lebanon [F] / Libya [F] / Mauritania / Morocco / Oman / Palestine / Qatar / Saudi Arabia [F] / Somalia / Sudan / Syria [F] / Tunisia / United Arab Emirates / Yemen [F]

[F] indicates founder member

NICKNAMES OF PEOPLE II (from page 152)

1. Jennifer Lopez; 2. Frank Sinatra; 3. David Hasselhoff; 4. Bruce Springsteen; 5. Norman Schwarzkopf; 6. Jean-Claude Van Damme; 7. Joe Montana; 8. Wayne Gretzky; 9. Mariah Carey; 10. Walter Payton; 11. Greg Norman; 12. James Smith; 13. Whoopi Goldberg; 14. Ty Cobb; 15. Iggy Pop; 16. Madonna; 17. T. E. Lawrence; 18. Simon Bolivar; 19. Jack Nicklaus; 20. Betty Grable; 21. Keith Richards; 22. Mary Pickford; 23. Charles Lindbergh; 24. Neil Diamond.

POPULAR GIRLS' NAMES* (from page 155)

Emily[1] / Emma / Madison / Isabella / Ava / Abigail / Olivia / Hannah
Sophia / Samantha / Elizabeth / Ashley / Mia / Alexis / Sarah / Natalie
Grace / Chloe / Alyssa / Brianna / Ella / Taylor / Anna / Lauren / Hailey [25]

NATO ALPHABET (from page 163)

Alpha / Bravo / Charlie / Delta / Echo / Foxtrot / Golf / Hotel / India / Juliet
Kilo / Lima / Mike / November / Oscar / Papa / Quebec / Romeo / Sierra
Tango / Uniform / Victor / Whiskey / X-Ray / Yankee / Zulu[†]

QUOTATIONS FROM POPULAR FILMS II (from page 167)

1. *Dirty Harry*; 2. *Wall Street*; 3. *When Harry Met Sally*; 4. *Jerry Maguire*; 5. *Goodfellas*; 6. *Goldfinger*; 7. *Monty Python and the Holy Grail*; 8. *Being John Malkovich*; 9. *Ocean's Eleven*; 10. *The Producers*; 11. *Trainspotting*; 12. *The Princess*

---

* Names in order of popularity, Emily most popular, Hailey twenty-fifth most popular.
† Also used by NATO armed forces to indicate Greenwich Mean Time.

Bride; 13. *Apocalypse Now*; 14. *The Blues Brothers*; 15. *Reservoir Dogs*; 16. *The Man with Two Brains*; 17. *Tootsie*; 18. *Aliens*; 19. *Moulin Rouge*; 20. *All About Eve*; 21. *It's a Wonderful Life*; 22. *The Third Man*; 23. *The Devil Wears Prada*; 24. *Million Dollar Baby*.

RED, WHITE, AND BLUE FLAGS (from page 170; as at the time of publishing)

Australia* / Cambodia / Chile / Costa Rica / Croatia / Cuba
Czech Republic / Dominican Republic / France / Iceland / Laos
Liberia / Luxembourg / Myanmar / Nepal / Netherlands
New Zealand / North Korea / Norway / Panama / Paraguay
Russia / Slovakia / Slovenia / Taiwan / Thailand
United Kingdom[†] / United States / Yugoslavia

NBA TEAMS (from page 172)

Eastern Conference:
Boston Celtics[A] / New Jersey Nets[A] / New York Knicks[A]
Philadelphia 76ers[A] / Toronto Raptors[A] / Chicago Bulls[C]
Cleveland Cavaliers[C] / Detroit Pistons[C] / Indiana Pacers[C]
Milwaukee Bucks[C] / Atlanta Hawks[SE] / Charlotte Bobcats[SE]
Miami Heat[SE] / Orlando Magic[SE] / Washington Wizards[SE]
Western Conference:
San Antonio Spurs[SW] / Houston Rockets[SW] / Memphis Grizzlies[SW]
New Orleans Hornets[SW] / Dallas Mavericks[SW] / Denver Nuggets[SW]
Minnesota Timberwolves[NW] / Portland Trail Blazers[NW]
Seattle SuperSonics[NW] / Utah Jazz[NW] / Golden State Warriors[P]
Los Angeles Clippers[P] / Los Angeles Lakers[P] / Phoenix Suns[P]
Sacramento Kings[P]
[A] Atlantic [C] Central [SE] Southeast [SW] Southwest [NW] Northwest [P] Pacific

MISCELLANY XXIII (from page 173)

1. The Berlin Wall; 2. *Pygmalion*; 3. West; 4. Scotland; 5. The molecular structure of DNA; 6. It is too big to be able to fit through the Panama Canal; 7. Mark Twain; 8. They are all buried in Westminster Abbey; 9. The atom bomb; 10. 7; 11. His right arm; 12. Route 66; 13. Twelve; 14. *The Simpsons*; 15. Battle of the Alamo; 16. The Americas Cup; 17. Ruth and Esther; 18. Nerd; 19. Cate Blanchett (*Elizabeth*) and Judi Dench (*Shakespeare in Love*);

---

* The flag features the constellation of the Southern Cross in the right-hand half; the larger star in the bottom left quadrant is known as the Commonwealth Star.

† The Union Jack features the heraldic symbols of St. George, St. Andrew, and St. Patrick and was introduced in 1606 with the union of England, Scotland, and Ireland. The Welsh dragon is not featured as at the time of the union the Welsh Principality was considered part of England.

20. "Eleanor Rigby"; 21. Mr. Smith weighs 85 lb and Mrs. Smith weighs 45 lb;
22. Mountains*; 23. Curling; 24. Forty-one hours.†

PLAYS BY WILLIAM SHAKESPEARE (from page 177)

---

* They describe mountain heights. Munros are mountains over 3,000 ft, Corbetts are between 2,500 and 3,000 ft, Grahams are between 2,000 and 2,500 ft.

† When looking at a book on a shelf with the spine facing outwards, the first page is actually to the right and the last page is to the left. Therefore, if the bookworm eats from the first page of the first book to the last page of the last book, it actually eats a single cover of the first book, then eats completely through the next eight books and then eats through a single cover of the last book. The "length of book" eaten is 41 cm, which takes the bookworm forty-one hours.

Coriolanus	1608
The Winter's Tale	1610
Cymbeline	1610
The Tempest	1611
Henry VIII	1611

Dates are estimated

LONGEST RIVERS (from page 179)

Nile	4,160
Amazon*	4,049
Chang (Yangtze)	3,964
Mississippi / Missouri	3,709
Ob / Irtysh	3,459
Yenisey / Angara / Selenga	3,448
Huang He (Yellow River)	3,395
Congo	2,900
Rio de la Plata / Parana	2,796
Mekong	2,749
Heilong Jiang / Argun	2,744
Lena / Kirenga	2,734
Mackenzie / Peace / Finlay	2,635
Niger	2,599
Murray / Darling	2,330
Volga	2,291
Purus	2,000
Madeira	1,988
Yukon	1,979
Indus	1,976
Syrdar'ya	1,913
St. Lawrence	1,900
Rio Grande	1,899
São Francisco	1,802
Danube	1,770
Brahmaputra	1,765
Salween	1,750
Euphrates	1,749
Tocantins	1,708
Tarim He	1,708
Zambezi	1,700
Araguaia	1,632

* The Amazon discharges somewhere between 10 and 30 million gallons of water into the Atlantic Ocean every second and contains about one-fifth of the world's fresh river water. The Amazon changes the salt content and color of the sea to a distance of about 200 miles from the coast.

Paraguay	1,615
Nelson / Saskatchewan	1,597
Nizhnaya Tunguska	1,590
Amudar'ya	1,578
Ural	1,575
Kolyma	1,562
Ganges	1,560
Orinocco	1,553

Figures are in miles and are approximate.

QUOTATIONS FROM POPULAR FILMS III (from page 182)

1. *Casablanca*; 2. *Bridget Jones's Diary*; 3. *Snakes on a Plane*; 4. *Lord of the Rings: The Fellowship of the Ring*; 5. *The Sound of Music*; 6. *Robin Hood: Prince of Thieves*; 7. *The Sixth Sense*; 8. *Psycho*; 9. *Finding Nemo*; 10. *The Incredibles*; 11. *Batman*; 12. *2001: A Space Odyssey*; 13. *Meet the Fockers*; 14. *Boogie Nights*; 15. *Pulp Fiction*; 16. *The Shawshank Redemption*; 17. *Airplane*; 18. *The Godfather, Part II*; 19. *The Graduate**; 20. *Butch Cassidy and the Sundance Kid*; 21. *The Stepford Wives*; 22. *Lawrence of Arabia*; 23. *Ace Ventura: Pet Detective*; 24. *Brief Encounter*.

COUNTRIES IN EUROPE†
(from page 185)

EUROPEAN CAPITAL CITIES
(from page 184)

Albania	Tirana
Andorra	Andorra la Vella
Austria	Vienna
Belarus	Minsk
Belgium	Brussels
Bosnia and Herzegovina	Sarajevo
Bulgaria	Sofia
Croatia	Zagreb
Czech Republic	Prague
Denmark	Copenhagen
Estonia	Tallinn
Finland	Helsinki
France	Paris
Germany	Berlin
Greece	Athens
Hungary	Budapest

---

* The film's poster features Dustin Hoffman framed by Mrs. Robinson's leg in an alluring pose. In reality the leg belonged to Linda Gray (rather than Anne Bancroft), who, an unknown model at the time, went on to play Sue Ellen in *Dallas* and later took on the role of Mrs. Robinson on the London stage.

† Note that Cyprus is sometimes considered to be in Europe. Geographically it is part of Asia, but politically it is closer to Europe. Also note that Turkey and Russia are part of both Europe and Asia.

Iceland	Reykjavik
Ireland	Dublin
Italy	Rome
Latvia	Riga
Liechtenstein	Vaduz
Lithuania	Vilnius
Luxembourg	Luxembourg
Macedonia	Skopje
Malta	Valletta
Moldova	Chisinau
Monaco	Monaco
Netherlands	Amsterdam
Norway	Oslo
Poland	Warsaw
Portugal	Lisbon
Romania	Bucharest
Russia	Moscow
San Marino	San Marino
Serbia and Montenegro	Belgrade
Slovakia	Bratislava
Slovenia	Ljubljana
Spain	Madrid
Sweden	Stockholm
Switzerland	Bern
Turkey	Ankara
Ukraine	Kiev
United Kingdom	London
Vatican City	Vatican City

AMERICAN STATES* (from page 188)

Alabama / Alaska[†] / Arizona / Arkansas / California
Colorado / Connecticut[F] / Delaware[F] / Florida / Georgia[F]
Hawaii[‡] / Idaho / Illinois / Indiana / Iowa / Kansas
Kentucky / Louisiana / Maine / Maryland[F]

---

* The U.S. also includes Washington, DC (District of Columbia), a district of sixty-eight square miles covering the city of Washington, the nation's capital. Washington, DC, is a federal area that is not part of any state. The district was formed on July 16, 1790, after disagreements arose over which state would contain the capital city. Consequently it was proposed to locate it on federal land rather, than in a state and the states of Maryland and Virginia ceded territory along the Potomac River for the new city, which took the name of George Washington, the first president.

† The United States purchased Alaska from Imperial Russia for $7 million in 1867. Alaska joined the Union in January 1959.

‡ Hawaii was the most recent state to join the Union, in August 1959.

Massachusetts[F] / Michigan / Minnesota / Mississippi
Missouri / Montana / Nebraska / Nevada
New Hampshire[F] / New Jersey[F] / New Mexico
New York[F] / North Carolina[F] / North Dakota / Ohio
Oklahoma / Oregon / Pennsylvania[F] / Rhode Island[F]
South Carolina[F] / South Dakota / Tennessee / Texas
Utah / Vermont / Virginia / Washington
West Virginia[F] / Wisconsin / Wyoming
[F] indicates a founding state

SCENTS (from page 194)

1. Chanel; 2. Ralph Lauren; 3. Calvin Klein; 4. Chanel; 5. Christian Dior; 6. Yves St. Laurent; 7. Calvin Klein; 8. Cacharel; 9. Christian Dior; 10. Lagerfeld; 11. Yves St. Laurent; 12. Calvin Klein; 13. Christian Dior; 14. Elizabeth Arden; 15. Lancôme; 16. Cartier; 17. Elizabeth Taylor; 18. Estée Lauder; 19. Givenchy; 20. Joop!; 21. Paco Rabanne; 22. Givenchy; 23. Gucci; 24. Guy Laroche.

COCKTAILS (from page 197)

Americano [BD] / Apple Martini [F] / B-52 [F] / Bacardi Cocktail [BD]
Banana Daiquiri [BD] / Bellini [L] / Black Russian [AD] / Bloody Mary [L]
Brandy Alexander [AD] / Brandy Egg Nog [L] / Bronx [BD] / Buck's Fizz [L]
Bull Shot [L] / Caipirinha [F] / Champagne Cocktail [L] / Cosmopolitan [F]
Cuba Libre [F] / Daiquiri [BD] / French Connection [AD] / Frozen Daiquiri [BD]
Gin Fizz [L] / God Father [AD] / God Mother [AD] / Golden Cadillac [AD]
Golden Dream [AD] / Grasshopper [AD] / Harvey Wallbanger [L]
Horse's Neck [L] / Irish Coffee [L] / Japanese Slipper [F] / Kamikaze [F]
Kir [BD] / Kir Royal [BD] / Long Island Iced Tea [F] / Mai-Tai [F]
Manhattan [BD] / Dry Manhattan [BD] / Medium Manhattan [BD]
Margarita [BD] / Dry Martini [BD] / Gibson Martini [BD] / Perfect Martini [BD]
Sweet Martini [BD] / Vodka Martini [BD] / Mimosa [L] / Mojito [F]
Negroni [BD] / Old Fashioned [BD] / Orgasm [F] / Paradise [BD] / Piña Colada [L]
Planter's Punch [L] / Porto flip [AD] / Rob Roy [BD] / Rose [BD] / Rusty Nail [AD]
Salty Dog [F] / Screwdriver [L] / Sea-Breeze [F] / Sex on the beach [F]
Singapore Sling [L] / Tequila Sunrise [L] / Tom Collins [L] / Whiskey Sour [BD]
White Russian [AD]
Cocktails indicated as: [BD] Before Dinner [AD] After Dinner [L] Long [F] Fancy

GREATEST FILMS (from page 201)

12 *Angry Men* [87] / *2001: A Space Odyssey* [15] / *The African Queen* [65]
All About Eve [28] / *All the President's Men* [77] / *American Graffiti* [62]
Annie Hall [35] / *Apart The Apartment* [80] / *Apocalypse Now* [30]
Ben-Hur [100] / *The Best Years of Our Lives* [37] / *Blade Runner* [97]
Bonnie and Clyde [42] / *The Bridge on the River Kwai* [36]
Bringing Up Baby [88] / *Butch Cassidy and the Sundance Kid* [73]
Cabaret [63] / *Casablanca* [3] / *Chinatown* [21] / *Citizen Kane* [1]

City Lights [11] / *A Clockwork Orange* [70] / *The Deer Hunter* [53]
Do the Right Thing [96] / *Double Indemnity* [29] / *Dr. Strangelove* [39]
Duck Soup [60] / *E.T. the Extra-Terrestrial* [24] / *Easy Rider* [84]
Forrest Gump [76] / *The French Connection* [93] / *The General* [18]
The Godfather [2] / *The Godfather Part II* [32] / *The Gold Rush* [58]
Gone with the Wind [6] / *Goodfellas* [92] / *The Graduate* [17]
The Grapes of Wrath [23] / *High Noon* [27] / *In the Heat of the Night* [75]
Intolerance [49] / *It Happened One Night* [46] / *It's a Wonderful Life* [20]
Jaws [56] / *King Kong* [41] / *The Last Picture Show* [95]
Lawrence of Arabia [7] / *The Fellowship of the Ring* [50]
The Maltese Falcon [31] / *MASH* [54] / *Midnight Cowboy* [43]
Modern Times [78] / *Mr. Smith Goes to Washington* [26] / *Nashville* [59]
Network [64] / *A Night at the Opera* [85] / *North by Northwest* [55]
On the Waterfront [19] / *One Flew Over the Cuckoo's Nest* [33]
The Philadelphia Story [44] / *Platoon* [86] / *Psycho* [14] / *Pulp Fiction* [94]
Raging Bull [4] / *Raiders of the Lost Ark* [66] / *Rear Window* [48] / *Rocky* [57]
Saving Private Ryan [71] / *Schindler's List* [8] / *The Searchers* [12]
Shane [45] / *The Shawshank Redemption* [72] / *The Silence of the Lambs* [74]
Singin' in the Rain [5] / *The Sixth Sense* [89]
Snow White and the Seven Dwarfs [34] / *Some Like It Hot* [22]
Sophie's Choice [91] / *The Sound of Music* [40] / *Spartacus* [81] / *Star Wars* [13]
A Streetcar Named Desire [47] / *Sullivan's Travels* [61] / *Sunrise* [82]
Sunset Boulevard [16] / *Swing Time* [90] / *Taxi Driver* [52] / *Titanic* [83]
To Kill a Mockingbird [25] / *Tootsie* [69] / *Toy Story* [99]
The Treasure of the Sierra Madre [38] / *Unforgiven* [68] / *Vertigo* [9]
West Side Story [51] / *Who's Afraid of Virginia Woolf?* [67]
The Wild Bunch [79] / *The Wizard of Oz* [10] / *Yankee Doodle Dandy* [98]

NEWTON'S LAWS OF MOTION (from page 6)

1. Any object will remain in a state of rest or continue at a uniform velocity unless acted on by an external force.
2. The rate of change of momentum of a body is equal to the force impressed upon it and in the same direction.*
3. For every action there is an equal and opposite reaction.

CAPITAL CITIES I (from page 8)

1. Thailand; 2. South Korea; 3. Finland; 4. Czech Republic; 5. Bulgaria; 6. Ethiopia; 7. Kenya; 8. Libya; 9. Bosnia and Herzegovina; 10. Zimbabwe; 11. Sri Lanka; 12. Myanmar (Burma); 13. Azerbaijan; 14. Ukraine; 15. North Korea; 16. United Arab Emirates; 17. Bahamas; 18. Bangladesh; 19. Armenia; 20. Democratic Republic of Congo; 21. Costa Rica; 22. Kazakhstan; 23. Montenegro; 24. Burkina Faso.

---

* Newton's Second Law may be expressed as the equation $f=ma$, where "f" is force, "m" is mass, and "a" is acceleration.

GHOSTS VISITING EBENEZER SCROOGE (from page 11)
The Ghost of Jacob Marley*
The Ghost of Christmas Past
The Ghost of Christmas Present
The Ghost of Christmas Yet to Come

U2 (from page 14)
Adam Clayton	Bass
Bono	Vocals
Larry Mullen Jr.	Drums
The Edge	Guitar

RECENT HISTORY I (from page 16)
1. 2003; 2. 2006; 3. 1997; 4. 1945; 5. 1999; 6. 1984; 7. 1939; 8. 1986; 9. 1993;
10. 1976; 11. 1971; 12. 1963; 13. 1918; 14. 1991; 15. 1985; 16. 1915; 17. 1967;
18. 1964; 19. 1974; 20. 1916; 21. 1955; 22. 1957; 23. 1919; 14. 1910.

NOVELS BY E. M. FORSTER (from page 75)
Where Angels Fear to Tread	published 1905
The Longest Journey	1907
A Room with a View	1908
Howards End	1910
A Passage to India	1924
Maurice†	1971
Arctic Summer‡	1980

MAJOR ACCOUNTING FIRMS (from page 24)
Deloitte / Ernst and Young / PWC / KPMG

MISCELLANY III (from page 25)
1. *Lady Chatterley's Lover* (D. H. Lawrence); 2. Beverly Hills; 3. *The Magic Flute*; 4. The nucleus; 5. Belly button; 6. Twenty; 7. Football§; 8. *The Jazz Singer*; 9. Orangutan; 10. France; 11. Horton; 12. The Adam's apple; 13. Alaska; 14. "Tonight I Celebrate My Love"; 15. Jordan; 16. White; 17. Frog; 18. 300; 19. Big Ben (the bell in the clock tower of the Palace of Westminster); 20. Watches at sea; 21. Rodgers and Hammerstein (from *Carousel*); 22. Taramasalata; 23. Canada; 24. The five baboons would win.¶

---

* Jacob Marley was Scrooge's miserly business partner. The story begins with the death of Marley; Marley's tortured ghost appears to Scrooge, dragging the heavy chains he is now forced to carry as a penance for the way he lived his life. Marley warns Scrooge a similar fate awaits him if he doesn't change his ways.

† Published posthumously, thought to be written in 1914.

‡ Unfinished, published posthumously.

§ Presented to the winners of the Super Bowl.

¶ Four baboons against two gorillas would result in a tie.

AMERICAN STATES BEGINNING WITH "A" (from page 30)
Alabama / Alaska / Arizona / Arkansas

FAMILY HOMINIDAE (from page 32)
Chimpanzees / Gorillas / Humans / Orangutans

MEANINGS OF PLACE NAMES (from page 35)
1. Rio de Janeiro; 2. Essex; 3. Argentina; 4. Nova Scotia; 5. Baton Rouge; 6. Soweto; 7. Costa Rica; 8. Casablanca; 9. Puerto Rico; 10. SoHo*; 11. Montenegro; 12. Munster; 13. Tripoli; 14. Sierra Nevada; 15. Belorussia; 16. Sierra Leone; 17. Bloemfontein; 18. Rajasthan; 19. Soho (London)†; 20. Hawaii; 21. Las Vegas; 22. Lagos; 23. Montreal; 24. Barbados.

NEW YORK CITY BOROUGHS (from page 37)
The Bronx / Brooklyn / Manhattan / Queens / Staten Island

COMMITTEE OF FIVE (from page 39)
John Adams	Massachusetts
Benjamin Franklin	Pennsylvania
Thomas Jefferson	Virginia
Robert R. Livingston	New York
Roger Sherman	Connecticut

EVENTS IN HISTORY II (from page 41)
1. 1789; 2. 1605; 3. 1812; 4. 1805; 5. 43; 6. 1789; 7. 1773; 8. 1807; 9. 1687; 10. 1506; 11. 1587; 12. 1600; 13. 476; 14. 1649; 15. 1653; 16. 1789; 17. 1519; 18. 79; 19. 122; 20. 1431; 21. 878; 22. 63; 23. 1065; 24. 312.

PILLARS OF ISLAM (from page 43)
The Testimony of Faith (Shahadah) / Prayer (Salah)‡
Giving of Alms (Zakah) / Fasting (Sawm)§
The Pilgrimage to Mecca (Hajj)¶

---

* Other New York acronyms are: NoHo (North of Houston), NoLIta (North of Little Italy), TriBeCa (Triangle below Canal), and DUMBO (Down Under the Manhattan Bridge Overpass).

† In medieval times, Soho was an area of private parkland owned by the king and used exclusively by royal hunting parties. The boundary of this area was marked by blue posts, which endures to this day in the many Soho pubs named "The Blue Posts."

‡ Muslims must pray five times per day, facing the direction of Mecca.

§ During Ramadan.

¶ All Muslims who are financially and physically able must make the journey to Mecca once in their lifetime.

"CIVILIZED" TRIBES (from page 46)

Cherokee / Chickasaw / Choctaw / Creek / Seminole

LINKED MISCELLANY IV (from page 49)

1. Madison Square Garden; 2. *Oklahoma!*; 3. *Harry Potter and the Order of the Pheonix*; 4. Concorde; 5. Olympia; 6. Helena Christensen; 7. Otto von Bismarck; 8. Columbia; 9. Baton; 10. Saint Paul.

The link is state capitals.*

NOBLE GASES† (from page 52)

Helium / Neon / Argon / Krypton / Xenon / Radon

MOON LANDINGS (from page 55)

Apollo 11	Landed on Moon July 20, 1969
Apollo 12	November 19, 1969
Apollo 14	February 5, 1971
Apollo 15	July 30, 1971
Apollo 16	April 20, 1972
Apollo 17	December 11, 1972

CAPITAL CITIES III (from page 58)

1. Canberra‡; 2. Oslo; 3. Warsaw; 4. Cairo; 5. Lisbon; 6. Buenos Aires; 7. Santiago; 8. Ankara; 9. Bogota; 10. Havana; 11. Quito; 12. Tunis; 13. Taipei; 14. San Salvador; 15. Tirana; 16. Belgrade; 17. Montevideo; 18. Bratislava; 19. Riga; 20. Dakar; 21. Tbilisi; 22. Dushanbe; 23. Antananarivo; 24. Vaduz.

NFL TEAMS YET TO REACH THE SUPER BOWL (from page 61; at the time of publishing)

Arizona Cardinals / Cleveland Browns / Detroit Lions
Houston Texans / Jacksonville Jaguars / New Orleans Saints

ACTORS IN *CASABLANCA* (from page 65)

Humphrey Bogart	Rick Blaine
Ingrid Bergman	Ilsa Lund
Paul Henreid	Victor Laszlo
Claude Rains	Captain Louis Renault

---

* Madison (Wisconsin), Oklahoma City (Oklahoma), Phoenix (Arizona), Concord (New Hampshire), Olympia (Washington), Helena (Montana), Bismarck (North Dakota), Columbia (South Carolina), Baton Rouge (Louisiana), and St. Paul (Minnesota)

† A seventh element in the series (temporarily called Ununoctium) was synthesized in 2006.

‡ Rivalry between Melbourne and Sydney led Australia to relocate its capital city from Melbourne to the neutral Canberra in 1913.

Conrad Veidt	Major Strasser
Sydney Greenstreet	Signor Ferrari
Peter Lorre	Signor Ugarte

QUOTATIONS FROM SHAKESPEARE I (from page 67)

1. *Hamlet* (Hamlet); 2. *Macbeth* (Three witches); 3. *Richard III* (King Richard); 4. *Hamlet* (Marcellus); 5. *Twelfth Night* (Orsino); 6. *Julius Caesar** (Soothsayer); 7. *Henry V* (King Harry); 8. *A Midsummer Night's Dream* (Puck); 9. *Hamlet* (Hamlet); 10. *Antony and Cleopatra* (Cleopatra); 11. *Macbeth* (Macbeth); 12. *Hamlet* (Horatio); 13. *Henry V* (King Harry); 14. *Romeo and Juliet* (Juliet); 15. *King Lear*† (Lear); 16. The Tempest (Prospero); 17. *Twelfth Night* (Malvolio); 18. *Romeo and Juliet* (Romeo); 19. *King Lear* (Lear); 20. *The Merchant of Venice* (Shylock); 21. *Hamlet* (Hamlet); 22. *King Lear* (Kent); 23. *Twelfth Night* (Feste); 24. *As You Like It* (Jacques).

CATHOLIC SACRAMENTS (from page 70)

Baptism / Confession / Confirmation / Eucharist
Matrimony / Ordination / Anointing the Sick

MERCURY SEVEN (from page 72)

Malcolm Carpenter / Leroy Cooper / John Glenn / Virgil "Gus" Grissom
Walter "Wally" Schirra / Alan Shepard / Donald "Deke" Slayton

MISCELLANY X (from page 75)

1. George Orwell (*Animal Farm*); 2. IBM; 3. Twelve; 4. Jaundice; 5. A star on the Hollywood walk of fame; 6. Decimate; 7. A wedding; 8. Nuclear Reactor; 9. Her right hand; 10. Hydrogen; 11. Twenty-four; 12. The jaw (or masseter); 13. UK; 14. Expressionism; 15. Philadelphia; 16. The Tet Offensive; 17. 1970 (to Brazil); 18. The Monty Python team (the spam sketch); 19. Michael Collins; 20. Mother's Day; 21. 8; 22. Contraceptive Pill; 23. *Rebecca*; 24. 28 ½ days.‡

NOVELS BY THE BRONTË SISTERS (from page 78)

Agnes Grey	(1847) Anne
The Tenant of Wildfell Hall	(1848) Anne
Jane Eyre	(1847) Charlotte
Shirley	(1849) Charlotte
Villette	(1853) Charlotte

---

* The "Ides" was the Roman name for the fifteenth day in March, May, July, and October and the thirteenth day of the other months. The Romans called the first day of the month the "Kalends" from which we get the word "calendar."

† *King Lear* is based on a mythical king who is thought to have ruled somewhere in the southwest of England in pre-Roman times. The story of Lear was first told by Geoffrey of Monmouth in his *Historia Regum Britanniae* (c. 1136).

‡ The snail reaches the top of the well halfway through the twenty-eighth day, that is, before nightfall on the twenty-eighth day.

COLORS OF THE VISIBLE SPECTRUM[†] (from page 80)

Red / Orange / Yellow / Green / Blue / Indigo[‡] / Violet

SPORTS GOVERNING BODIES II (from page 82)

1. Football Association; 2. World Boxing Council; 3. Union of European Football Associations; 4. United States Professional Golfers' Association; 5. National Football League; 6. Rugby Football Union; 7. International Olympic Committee; 8. International Rugby Board; 9. International Cricket Council; 10. International Rugby Football Board; 11. Ladies' Professional Golf Association; 12. Royal Yachting Association; 13. Rugby League; 14. *CON*federación Suda*ME*ricana de Fút *BOL*[§]; 15. Lawn Tennis Association; 16. International Judo Federation; 17. Fédération Internationale de Hockey sur Gazon[¶]; 18. International Baseball Association; 19. International Surfing Association; 20. World Bowls Board; 21. International Weightlifting Federation; 22. Fédération Internationale Des Echecs[**]; 23. Fédération Internationale de Volleyball; 24. Tug of War International Federation.

STATES BEGINNING WITH "M" (from page 85)

Maine / Maryland / Massachusetts / Michigan

Minnesota / Mississippi / Missouri / Montana

BASEBALL FIELDING POSITIONS (from page 88)

Battery

Pitcher (P) / Catcher (C)

Infield

First Base (1B) / Second Base (2B) / Third Base (3B) / Shortstop (SS)

Outfield

Left Field[††] (LF) / Center Field (CF) / Right Field (RF)

---

* Published posthumously in 1857. The novel was written before *Jane Eyre* but had been rejected by many publishers.

† Useful mnemonic: Richard Of York Gave Battle In Vain.

‡ The seven colors were originally cited by Sir Isaac Newton. The inclusion of indigo is questionable as most people cannot readily distinguish the color on the spectrum from either blue or violet. Newton believed that light exhibited symmetry with musical notes and therefore there were seven rather than six distinct colors. The word "indigo" is derived from a blue dye which came from India.

§ That is, the South American Football Confederation.

¶ Field hockey (as opposed to ice hockey).

** I.e. the International Chess Federation.

†† The phrase "out in left field" and "out of left field," meaning unexpected or seprated from reality, originate with baseball. They are thought to derive from the fact that in older ball parks, the left field was usually deeper than the right and the fielder would have to play further back against a right-handed batter.

CHARACTERS IN LITERATURE III (from page 94)

1. *Around the World in Eighty Days* (Jules Verne); 2. *Alice's Adventures in Wonderland* (Lewis Carroll); 3. *The World According to Garp* (John Irving); 4. *The Canterbury Tales* (Geoffrey Chaucer); 5. *A Christmas Carol* (Charles Dickens); 6. *Moby-Dick* (Herman Melville); 7. *David Copperfield* (Charles Dickens); 8. *The Picture of Dorian Gray* (Oscar Wilde); 9. *Lady Chatterley's Lover** (D. H. Lawrence); 10. *Anna Karenina* (Leo Tolstoy); 11. *Oliver Twist* (Charles Dickens); 12. *Wuthering Heights* (Emily Brontë); 13. *Heart of Darkness* (Joseph Conrad); 14. *Dr. Zhivago* (Boris Pasternak); 15. *American Psycho* (Bret Easton Ellis); 16. *Brighton Rock* (Graham Greene); 17. *Misery* (Stephen King); 18. *Rabbit* Series (John Updike); 19. *Mrs. Dalloway* (Virginia Woolf); 20. *A Clockwork Orange* (Anthony Burgess); 21. *One Hundred Years of Solitude* (Gabriel Garcia Marquez); 22. *Tom Sawyer* (Mark Twain); 23. *Treasure Island* (Robert Louis Stevenson); 24. *Mansfield Park* (Jane Austen).

CHARACTERS IN *CHEERS* (from page 96)

Sam Malone	Ted Danson
Diane Chambers	Shelley Long
Rebecca Howe	Kirstie Alley
Carla Tortelli	Rhea Perlman
"Woody" Boyd	Woody Harrelson
Norm Peterson	George Wendt
Cliff Clavin	John Ratzenberger
Frasier Crane	Kelsey Grammer
Ernie "Coach" Pantusso	Nicholas Colasanto
Lilith Sternin	Bebe Neuwirth

MEMBERS OF ASEAN (from page 99)

Brunei / Cambodia / Indonesia / Laos / Malaysia
Myanmar / Philippines / Singapore / Thailand / Vietnam

LINKED MISCELLANY VIII (from page 101)

1. *Kramer vs. Kramer*; 2. Couriers; 3. Austin; 4. Boris Pasternak; 5. Sarah Connor; 6. Venus; 7. *Graf Spee*; 8. Ash; 9. The Borg; 10. "Billie Jean."
The link is tennis players.[†]

---

* In 1960 Penguin Books were charged under the Obscene Publications Act over *Lady Chatterley's Lover*, a book that, according to the prosecuting counsel, "sets on a pedestal promiscuous intercourse, commends sensuality almost as a virtue, and encourages and even advocates coarseness and vulgarity of thought and language." Penguin won what would become a landmark case, as much for exposing the attitudes of the British judiciary as the legal precedent it set. During the trial, the crown prosecutor, Mervyn Griffiths-Jones asked, "Is it a book that you would even wish your wife or your servants to read?"

† Jack Kramer, Jim Courier, Tracy Austin, Boris Becker, Jimmy Connors, Venus Williams, Steffi Graf, Arthur Ashe, Björn Borg, and Billie Jean King.

THE WALTONS (from page 104)

Ben / Elizabeth / Erin / Grandma / Grandpa / Jason
Jim Bob / John Boy / John Sr. / Mary Ellen / Olivia

SIGNS OF THE ZODIAC (from page 108)

Aries ♈ Taurus ♉ Gemini* ♊ Cancer ♋
Leo ♌ Virgo ♍ Libra† ♎ Scorpio ♏
Sagittarius ♐ Capricorn ♑ Aquarius ♒ Pisces ♓

SOVIET HERO CITIES (from page 109)

Leningrad‡ / Odessa / Sevastopol / Stalingrad / Kiev / Moscow
Kerch / Novorossiysk / Minsk / Tula / Murmansk / Smolensk

APOSTLES (from page 112)

Andrew / Bartholomew§
James son of Alphaeus / James son of Zebedee
John / Jude¶ / Judas Iscariot** / Matthew††
Philip / Simon Peter / Simon the Zealot / Thomas

TAGLINES OF POPULAR FILMS II (from page 114)

1. *Apollo 13*; 2. *The Blues Brothers*; 3. *Groundhog Day*; 4. *Ocean's Twelve*; 5. *Schindler's List*; 6. *The Usual Suspects*; 7. *Deep Throat*; 8. *Shakespeare in Love*‡‡; 9. *Terms of Endearment*; 10. *Kill Bill: Volume 2*; 11. *Titanic*; 12. *Kindergarten Cop*; 13. *Gladiator*; 14. *The Truman Show*; 15. *Cool Runnings*; 16. *Westworld*§§; 17. *A Bug's Life*; 18. *Chicago* ; 19. *Trading Places*; 20. *Basic Instinct*; 21. *In the Line of Fire*; 22. *School of Rock*; 23. *There's Something about Mary*; 24. *The Talented Mr. Ripley*.

---

* Gemini represents Castor and Pollux, twin sons of Leda and the brothers of Clytemnestra and Helen of Troy.

† Libra is the only sign represented by a non-living thing (the scales).

‡ Leningrad (now St. Petersburg) was subjected to a siege by the German Army lasting thirty months, from September 1941 until January 1944. All food and power supplies were cut off and the city was subject to continual artillery bombardment. By the end of the siege an estimated 600,000 people had died of starvation or frozen to death, and 300,000 Russian soldiers were killed in the defense of the city and in efforts to relieve it. Leningrad was the first city to have the Hero City title bestowed upon it, in 1945.

§ Alternatively Nathaniel.

¶ Alternatively Thaddeus.

** After his suicide, Judas was replaced by Mathias as the twelfth apostle.

†† Alternatively Levi.

‡‡ The film was co-written by Tom Stoppard, who also wrote *Rosencrantz and Guildenstern Are Dead* (1990), another story in which the plot intertwines with an actual plot from Shakespeare.

§§ The script contains the first recorded use of the term "computer virus."

VITAMINS (from page 119; as at the time of publishing)

Vitamin A	Retinoids
Vitamin B1	Thiamine
Vitamin B2	Riboflavin
Vitamin B3	Niacin
Vitamin B5	Pantothenic acid
Vitamin B6	Pyridoxine
Vitamin B7	Biotin
Vitamin B9	Folic acid
Vitamin B12	Cyanocobalamin
Vitamin C	Ascorbic acid
Vitamin D	Ergocalciferol / Cholecalciferol
Vitamin E	Tocopherol / Tocotrienol
Vitamin K	Naphthoquinone

MARX BROTHERS FILMS (from page 121)

The Cocoanuts	1929
Animal Crackers	1930
Monkey Business	1931
Horse Feathers	1932
Duck Soup	1933
A Night at the Opera	1935
A Day at the Races	1937
Room Service	1938
At the Circus	1939
Go West	1940
The Big Store	1941
A Night in Casablanca	1946
Love Happy	1949
The Story of Mankind	1957

"ISMS" I (from page 122)

1. Vegetarianism; 2. Marxism; 3. Catholicism; 4. Atheism; 5. Anti-Semitism; 6. Feminism; 7. Sado-masochism; 8. Capitalism; 9. Nepotism; 10. Fascism; 11. Buddhism; 12. Federalism; 13. Materialism; 14. Anarchism; 15. Conservatism; 16. Judaism; 17. Confucianism; 18. Feudalism*; 19. Egalitarianism; 20. Utilitarianism; 21. Determinism; 22. Existentialism; 23. Nihilism; 24. Logical positivism.

MOST CAREER STRIKEOUTS BY A PITCHER (from page 127; as at the time of publishing)

Nolan Ryan	5,714

---

* Although feudalism disappeared in Britain around the start of the seventeenth century it endured in Japan until 1871 and in Russia until 1917. Slavery—feudalism by another name—persisted in the U.S. until 1865 and the Thirteenth Amendment of the Constitution.

Roger Clemens[A] 4,672
Randy Johnson[A] 4,616
Steve Carlton 4,136
Bert Blyleven 3,701
Tom Seaver 3,640
Don Sutton 3,574
Gaylord Perry 3,534
Walter Johnson 3,509
Phil Niekro 3,342
Greg Maddux[A] 3,273
Fergie Jenkins 3,192
Bob Gibson 3,117
Curt Schilling[A] 3,116
Pedro Martinez[A] 3,030

[A] indicates an active player

SUPER BOWL WINNERS (from page 130; at time of publishing)

Dallas Cowboys .... (5) VI, XII, XXVII, XXVIII, XXX
Pittsburgh Steelers .... (5) IX, X, XIII, XIV, XL
San Francisco 49ers .... (5) XVI, XIX, XXIII, XXIV, XXIX
Green Bay Packers .... (3) I, II, XXXI
Oakland / Los Angeles Raiders .... (3) XI, XV, XVIII
New England Patriots .... (3) XXXVI, XXXVIII, XXXIX
New York Giants .... (3) XXI, XXV, XLII
Washington Redskins .... (3) XVII, XXII, XXVI
Baltimore / Indianapolis Colts .... (2) V, XLI
Denver Broncos .... (2) XXXII, XXXIII
Miami Dolphins .... (2) VII, VIII
Baltimore Ravens XXXV
Chicago Bears XX
Kansas City Chiefs IV
New York Jets III
St. Louis Rams XXXIV
Tampa Bay Buccaneers XXXVII

MISCELLANY XVIII (from page 132)

1. Winston Churchill; 2. They both appear as ghosts; 3. Slavery; 4. 180; 5. Paisley;
6. Everest; 7. Impressionism; 8. Big Bird; 9. Red; 10. Meriweather and William; 11.
Four; 12. The FBI; 13. Frisbee; 14. They have each given their name to a dish*; 15.
Rhapsody in Blue (George Gershwin); 16. Azerbaijan, Afghanistan; 17. *High Society*;
18. Deputy Dawg; 19. *Brigadoon*; 20. Thomas Jefferson; 21. $250; 22. El Salvador
and Honduras; 23. Etiquette; 24. 50¢.†

---

* Caesar salad, mornay sauce, and pavlova.
† The wine costs $9.50 and the bottle 50¢.

LARGE BODIES OF WATER (from page 136)

Pacific Ocean 60,061,000
Atlantic Ocean 29,638,000
Indian Ocean 26,469,500
Southern Ocean* 7,848,500
Arctic Ocean 5,427,000
South China Sea 1,148,500
Caribbean Sea 971,500
Mediterranean Sea 969,000
Bering Sea 873,000
Gulf of Mexico 582,000
Arabian Sea 578,500
Sea of Okhotsk 537,500
Sea of Japan 391,000
Hudson Bay 282,000
East China Sea 256,500
Andaman Sea 218,000
Black Sea 196,000
Red Sea 175,000
North Sea 165,000
Baltic Sea 147,500

Figures are in square miles and are approximate.

LARGE ISLANDS (from page 138)

Greenland 840,000
New Guinea 312,000
Borneo 288,000
Madagascar 226,500
Baffin Island ^{Canada} 196,000
Sumatra ^{Indonesia} 183,000
Honshu ^{Japan} 88,000
Great Britain 84,500
Victoria Island ^{Canada} 84,000
Ellesmere Island ^{Canada} 76,000
Sulawesi ^{Indonesia} 73,000
South Island ^{New Zealand} 58,500
Java ^{Indonesia} 51,000
North Island ^{New Zealand} 44,500
Cuba 43,000
Newfoundland ^{Canada} 42,000
Luzon ^{Philippines} 40,500
Iceland 39,500

* The Southern Ocean (previously called the Antarctic Ocean) was defined in 2000 by the International Hydrographic Organization. It is now the fourth largest ocean.

Mindanao [Philippines]	....	36,500
Novaga Zemlya [Russia]	....	35,000

Figures are in square miles and are approximate

ETYMOLOGY OF ROCK AND POP NAMES I (from page 140)

1. Duran Duran; 2. Beastie Boys; 3. Dead Kennedys; 4. LL Cool J; 5. Iron Maiden;
6. The Bangles ; 7. Jethro Tull; 8. Hootie and the Blowfish; 9. Depeche Mode; 10.
Bauhaus; 11. The Thompson Twins; 12. Crowded House; 13 Limp Bizkit; 14. The
Propellerheads; 15. The Rolling Stones; 16. The Psychedelic Furs; 17. 10,000
Maniacs; 18. Marillion; 19. Chubby Checker; 20. The Orb; 21. Deacon Blue; 22.
T'Pau; 23. Kraftwerk; 24. Bachman Turner Overdrive.

JAMES BOND FILMS (from page 144; as at the time of publishing)

Dr. No [SC]	....	1962
From Russia with Love [SC]	....	1963
Goldfinger [SC]	....	1964
Thunderball* [SC]	....	1965
You Only Live Twice [SC]	....	1967
On Her Majesty's Secret Service [GL]	....	1969
Diamonds Are Forever [SC]	....	1971
Live and Let Die [RM]	....	1973
The Man with the Golden Gun [RM]	....	1974
The Spy Who Loved Me [RM]	....	1977
Moonraker [RM]	....	1979
For Your Eyes Only [RM]	....	1981
Octopussy [RM]	....	1983
A View to a Kill [RM]	....	1985
The Living Daylights [TD]	....	1987
License to Kill [TD]	....	1989
Goldeneye [PB]	....	1995
Tomorrow Never Dies [PB]	....	1997
The World Is Not Enough [PB]	....	1999
Die Another Day [PB]	....	2002
Casino Royale [DC]	....	2006
Quantum of Solace [DC]	....	2008

Bonds indicated as [SC] Sean Connery [GL] George Lazenby [RM] Roger Moore
[TD] Timothy Dalton [PB] Pierce Brosnan [DC] Daniel Craig

---

* *Thunderball* was originally written as a screenplay collaboration between Fleming,
filmmaker Kevin McClory, and writer Jack Whittingham, but the project stalled and
Fleming went ahead and released the story as a novel. The publication became the source
of a lengthy legal dispute between McClory and Fleming, and McClory was eventually
awarded the film rights to *Thunderball*. McClory wanted to make the film independently,
but after the success of Sean Connery and the first two films of the Broccoli/Saltzman
franchise, he was forced to cooperate and took a share of the profits when *Thunderball*
was made. McClory remade *Thunderball* as *Never Say Never Again* in 1983.

NICKNAMES OF STATES II (from page 149)

1. California; 2. Arizona; 3. Texas; 4. Kentucky; 5. Alaska; 6. Alabama; 7. Pennsylvania; 8. South Dakota; 9. Ohio; 10. Michigan; 11. Rhode Island; 12. Montana; 13. North Carolina; 14. North Dakota; 15. West Virginia; 16. Mississippi; 17. Georgia; 18. Iowa; 19. Indiana; 20. Louisiana; 21. Nevada; 22. Maryland; 23. Oregon; 24. New Jersey.

RUSHES OVER 10,000 YARDS (from page 152; as at time of publishing)

Emmitt Smith	18,355 career yards
Walter Payton	16,726
Barry Sanders	15,269
Curtis Martin	14,101
Jerome Bettis	13,662
Eric Dickerson	13,259
Tony Dorsett	12,739
Jim Brown	12,312
Marshall Faulk	12,279
Marcus Allen	12,243
Franco Harris	12,120
Thurman Thomas	12,074
Edgerrin James[A]	11,617
John Riggins	11,352
Corey Dillon	11,241
O. J. Simpson	11,236
Ricky Watters	10,643
Fred Taylor[A]	10,604
LaDainian Tomlinson[A]	10,487
Tiki Barber	10,449
Eddie George	10,441
Ottis Anderson	10,273
Warrick Dunn[A]	10,096

[A] denotes a currently active player

BUSIEST AIRPORTS (from page 155; as at time of publishing)

Atlanta Hartsfield-Jackson (ATL)	89,379,287
Chicago O'Hare (ORD)	76,159,324
London Heathrow (LHR)	68,068,554
Tokyo Haneda (HND)	66,671,435
Los Angeles (LAX)	61,895,548
Paris Charles de Gaulle (CDG)	59,919,383
Dallas-Fort Worth (DFW)	59,784,876
Frankfurt (FRA)	54,161,856
Beijing Capital (PEK)	53,736,923
Madrid Barajas (MAD)	52,122,214
Denver (DEN)	49,863,389

New York John F. Kennedy (JFK)	47,810,630
Amsterdam Schiphol (AMS)	47,793,602
Las Vegas McCarran (L.A.S)	47,595,140
Hong Kong (HKG)	46,995,000
Houston George Bush (IAH)	42,978,617
Phoenix Sky Harbor (PHX)	42,197,080
Bangkok Suvarnabhumi (BKK)	41,210,081
Singapore Changi (SIN)	36,701,556
Newark Liberty (EWR)	36,391,911
Orlando (MCO)	36,385,300
Detroit Metropolitan Wayne County (DTW)	36,126,555
San Francisco (SFO)	35,793,117
Tokyo Narita (NRT)	35,530,035
London Gatwick (LGW)	35,218,399

LINKED MISCELLANY XII (from page 163)

1. Montana; 2. The Moon; 3. Troy; 4. Baby Boomer; 5. Cunningham; 6. *Young Frankenstein*; 7. Sonny Bono; 8. Chandler; 9. Single In-Line Memory Module (SIMMs); 10. *The Brady Bunch*.

The link is NFL quarterbacks*

3,000 HIT CLUB (from page 167; as at time of publishing)

Pete Rose	4,256, scored 3,000th hit May 5, 1978
Ty Cobb	4,191, August 19, 1921
Hank Aaron	3,771, May 17, 1970
Stan Musial†	3,630, May 13, 1958
Tris Speaker	3,514, May 17, 1925
Carl Yastrzemski	3,419, September 12, 1979
Cap Anson	3,418, July 18, 1897
Honus Wagner	3,415, June 9, 1914
Paul Molitor	3,319, September 16, 1996
Eddie Collins	3,315, June 6, 1925
Willie Mays	3,283, July 18, 1970
Eddie Murray	3,255, June 30, 1995
Nap Lajoie	3,242, September 27, 1914
Cal Ripken, Jr.	3,184, April 15, 2000
George Brett	3,154, September 30, 1992
Paul Waner	3,152, June 19, 1942

---

* Joe Montana, Warren Moon, Troy Aikman, Boomer Esiason, Randall Cunningham, Steve Young, Sonny Jurgensen, Chris Chandler, Phil Simms, and Tom Brady

† Musial was one of the most consistent players in the MLB history. Scoring two hits in his final game, twenty-two years after he had scored two hits on his debut, caused one reporter to ironically observe: "He hasn't improved at all."

Robin Yount .... 3,142, September 9, 1992
Tony Gwynn .... 3,141, August 6, 1999
Dave Winfield .... 3,110, September 16, 1993
Craig Biggio[A] .... 3,060, June 28, 2007
Rickey Henderson .... 3,055, October 7, 2001
Rod Carew .... 3,053, August 4, 1985
Lou Brock .... 3,023, August 13, 1979
Rafael Palmeiro .... 3,020, July 15, 2005
Wade Boggs .... 3,010, August 7, 1999
Al Kaline .... 3,007, September 24, 1974
Roberto Clemente .... 3,000, September 30, 1972

[A] denotes currently active player

200 CAREER TOUCHDOWN PASSES (from page 170; as at time of publishing)

Brett Favre[A] 442
Dan Marino 420
Fran Tarkenton 342
Peyton Manning[A] 306
John Elway 300
Warren Moon 291
Johnny Unitas 290
Vinny Testaverde[A] 275
Joe Montana 273
Dave Krieg 261
Sonny Jurgensen 255
Dan Fouts 254
Drew Bledsoe 251
Boomer Esiason 247
John Hadl 244
Y. A. Tittle 242
Len Dawson 239
Jim Kelly 237
George Blanda 236
Steve Young 232
John Brodie 214
Terry Bradshaw 212
Jim Hart 209
Randall Cunningham 207
Jim Everett 203
Roman Gabriel 201

[A] denotes a currently active player

STATE CAPITALS II (from page 172)

1. Tennessee; 2. Georgia; 3. Massachusetts; 4. Arkansas; 5. West Virginia; 6. New York; 7. Connecticut; 8. Arizona; 9. Idaho; 10. Mississippi; 11. Delaware; 12. New

Mexico; 13. New Jersey; 14. Florida; 15. Virginia; 16. New Hampshire; 17. Missouri; 18. Wyoming; 19. Alabama; 20. South Carolina; 21. Montana; 22. Nevada; 23. Alaska; 24. South Dakota.

AMERICAN GLADIATORS (from page 175)
Atlas / Blaze / Bronco / Cyclone / Dallas / Diamond / Elektra / Gemini
Gold / Havoc / Hawk / Ice / Jade / Jazz / Lace / Laser / Malibu / Nitro
Rebel / Sabre / Siren / Sky / Slice / Storm / Sunny / Tank / Thunder / Titan
Tower / Turbo / Viper / Zap

SUPER BOWL MVPS (from page 177; as at time of publishing)
Joe Montana (3) . . . . San Francisco 49ers, XVI, XIX, XXIV
Terry Bradshaw (2) . . . . Pittsburgh Steelers, XIII, XIV
Tom Brady (2) . . . . New England Patriots, XXXVI, XXXVIII
Bart Starr (2) . . . . Green Bay Packers, I, II
Troy Aikman . . . . Dallas Cowboys XXVII
Marcus Allen . . . . Los Angeles Raiders XVIII
Ottis Anderson . . . . New York Giants XXV
Fred Biletnikoff . . . . Oakland Raiders XI
Deion Branch . . . . New England Patriots XXXIX
Larry Brown . . . . Dallas Cowboys XXX
Larry Csonka . . . . Miami Dolphins VIII
Terrell Davis . . . . Denver Broncos XXXII
Len Dawson . . . . Kansas City Chiefs IV
Richard Dent . . . . Chicago Bears XX
John Elway . . . . Denver Broncos XXXIII
Franco Harris . . . . Pittsburgh Steelers IX
Desmond Howard* . . . . Green Bay Packers XXXI
Chuck Howley† . . . . Dallas Cowboys V
Dexter Jackson . . . . Tampa Bay Buccaneers XXXVII
Ray Lewis . . . . Baltimore Ravens XXXV
Eli Manning . . . . New York Giants XLII
Peyton Manning . . . . Indianapolis Colts XLI
Harvey Martin . . . . Dallas Cowboys XII‡

---

* Desmond Howard is the only player from special teams to have been MVP with a ninety-nine-yard kickoff return for a touchdown, a Super Bowl record.

† Chuck Howley is the only player on a losing team to have been the MVP; he intercepted two passes and recovered a fumble. Super Bowl V (the Baltimore Colts beat the Cowboys by 16-13) was characterized by numerous errors made by both teams (a Super Bowl record of eleven turnovers were made in the game) and has been nicknamed the "Blunder Bowl."

‡ In Super Bowl XII Harvey Martin and Randy White were both awarded MVP in recognition of the role of the Cowboy's dominant defense.

Joe Namath	New York Jets III
Jim Plunkett	Oakland Raiders XV
Jerry Rice	San Francisco 49ers XXIII
John Riggins	Washington Redskins XVII
Mark Rypien	Washington Redskins XXVI
Jake Scott	Miami Dolphins VII
Phil Simms	New York Giants XXI
Emmitt Smith	Dallas Cowboys XXVIII
Roger Staubach	Dallas Cowboys VI
Lynn Swann	Pittsburgh Steelers X
Hines Ward	Pittsburgh Steelers XL
Kurt Warner	St. Louis Rams XXXIV
Randy White	Dallas Cowboys XII
Doug Williams	Washington Redskins XXII
Steve Young	San Francisco 49ers XXIX

WIT AND WISDOM III (from page 180)

1. "I don't care to belong to a club ..." .... Marx
2. "If you don't like your job you don't strike ..." .... Simpson
3. "I was raised in the Jewish tradition ..." .... Allen
4. "Weaselling out of things is important to learn ..." .... Simpson
5. "Outside of a dog, a book is man's best friend ..." .... Marx
6. "It's not easy to juggle a pregnant wife ..." .... Simpson
7. "I failed to make the chess team ..." .... Allen
8. "What's the point of going out ..." .... Simpson
9. "He may look like an idiot and talk like an idiot ..." .... Marx
10. "Getting out of jury duty is easy ..." .... Simpson
11. "I have had a perfectly wonderful evening ..." .... Marx
12. "Money is better than poverty ..." .... Allen
13. "Either he's dead or my watch has stopped." .... Marx
14. "I like my beer cold, my TV loud ..." .... Simpson
15. "I think crime pays ..." .... Allen
16. "A child of five would understand this ..." .... Marx
17. "I took a speed-reading course ..." .... Allen
18. "I never forget a face, but in your case ..." .... Marx
19. "No one asked me to volunteer." .... Simpson
20. "How can I believe in God when just last week ..." .... Allen
21. "Those are my principles ..." .... Marx
22. "Why was I with her? She reminds me of you ..." .... Marx
23. "I don't want to achieve immortality ..." .... Allen
24. "What if we chose the wrong religion ..." .... Simpson

LANDLOCKED COUNTRIES (from page 183)

Afghanistan / Andorra / Armenia / Austria / Azerbaijan[Casp]
Belarus / Bhutan / Bolivia / Botswana / Burkina Faso

Burundi / Central African Republic / Chad / Czech Republic
Ethiopia / Hungary / Kazakhstan^{Casp} / Kyrgyzstan / Laos
Lesotho / Liechtenstein ^{DL} / Luxembourg / Macedonia / Malawi
Mali / Moldova / Mongolia / Nepal / Niger / Paraguay
Rwanda / San Marino / Serbia / Slovakia / Swaziland
Switzerland / Tajikistan / Turkmenistan^{Casp} / Uganda
Uzbekistan ^{DL} / Vatican City / Zambia / Zimbabwe
^{Casp} indicates coastline on the Caspian Sea
^{DL} indicates doubly landlocked*

MISCELLANY XXV (from page 188)

1. Alcohol[†]; 2. 13 founding colonies; 3. Salmonella; 4. Jim Carrey; 5. *Madame Butterfly*; 6. Honolulu (Iolani Palace); 7. Green; 8. Hawaii; 9. Lemon and melon; 10. The Bronx; 11. Captain Flint; 12. Swahili; 13. 30%; 14. Oliver Cromwell; 15. They are not members of the United Nations; 16. Seven; 17. Table-tennis table; 18. They form the lethal injection used to execute prisoners in the U.S.; 19. Montana; 20. Six[‡]; 21. Valkyries; 22. The fourth day; 23. Jebediah Springfield; 24. 9 p.m.

COUNTRIES IN AFRICA (from page 194)

Algeria / Angola / Benin / Botswana / Burkina Faso
Burundi / Cameroon / Cape Verde / Central African Republic
Chad / Comoros / Congo / Congo, Dem. Republic
Côte d'Ivoire / Djibouti / Egypt / Equatorial Guinea
Eritrea / Ethiopia / Gabon / Gambia / Ghana / Guinea
Guinea-Bissau / Kenya / Lesotho / Liberia / Libya
Madagascar / Malawi / Mali / Mauritania / Mauritius
Morocco / Mozambique / Namibia / Niger / Nigeria
Rwanda / São Tomé and Príncipe / Senegal / Seychelles
Sierra Leone / Somalia / South Africa / Sudan
Swaziland / Tanzania / Togo / Tunisia / Uganda
Western Sahara} / Zambia / Zimbabwe

NOTORIOUS SHIPS I (from page 6)

1. *Titanic*; 2. *Rainbow Warrior*; 3. HMS *Bounty*; 4. HMS *Victory*; 5. *Mary Celeste*; 6. SS *Poseidon*; 7. *QEII*; 8. *Golden Hind*; 9. HMS *Pinafore*; 10. *Lusitania*[§];

---

* Bordered only by landlocked countries; two international borders must be crossed in order to reach the nearest coastline.

† It was repealed by the Twenty-first Amendment.

‡ 6–0 up in a tie-break.

§ Many of the victims of the sinking were American civilians; the event hastened the entry of the United States into the First World War.

11. Endeavour; 12. *Graf Spee*; 13. HMS *Beagle**; *14. African Queen*; 15. U.S.S *Enterprise*; 16. *Tirpitz*; 17. *Kon-Tiki*; 18. *Nautilus*; 19. U.S.S. *Yorktown*; 20. *Calypso*; 21. C.S.S. *Virginia*; 22. *Yamato*; 23. *Orca*; 24. *Mont-Blanc*.

STOOGES (from page 9)

Larry / Moe / Curly

GOLF MAJORS (from page 12)

The Masters / The U.S. Open
The Open / The U.S. PGA Championship

CHARACTERS IN LITERATURE I (from page 14)

1. *The Hobbit; Lord of the Rings* (J. R. R. Tolkien); 2. *Gone With the Wind* (Margaret Mitchell); 3. *Pride and Prejudice* (Jane Austen); 4. *Twenty Thousand Leagues Under the Sea* (Jules Verne); 5. *Treasure Island* (Robert Louis Stevenson); 6. *Tarzan of the Apes* (Edgar Rice Burroughs); 7. *Catch-22* (Joseph Heller); 8. *Bridget Jones's Diary* (Helen Fielding); 9. *The Count of Monte Cristo* (Alexandre Dumas); 10. *Don Quixote* (Miguel de Cervantes); 11. *A Streetcar Named Desire* (Tennessee Williams); 12. *The Graduate* (Charles Webb); *13. Sense and Sensibility* (Jane Austen); 14. *Brave New World* (Aldous Huxley); 15. *Persuasion* (Jane Austen); 16. *Middlemarch* (George Eliot); 17. *The Name of the Rose* (Umberto Eco); 18. *The Great Gatsby* (F. Scott Fitzgerald); 19. *Great Expectations* (Charles Dickens); 20. *Matilda* (Roald Dahl); 21. *Vanity Fair* (William Makepeace Thackeray); 22. *Alice's Adventures in Wonderland* (Lewis Carroll); 23. *A Confederacy of Dunces* (John Kennedy Toole); 24. *Shogun* (James Clavell).

---

* The first scientific weather forecasts were made by Robert Fitzroy (1805–65) after his appointment as director of the new meteorological service for the (British) Board of Trade in 1851. His reports (Fitzroy himself coined the term "weather forecasts") were the first to be published (in the *Times*) and he is also credited with the invention of the Fitzroy Barometer, a maritime barometer which became essential to nineteenth-century mariners. In spite of this, history remembers Fitzroy for an altogether different reason. In 1831, Fitzroy invited the twenty-one-year-old Charles Darwin on his round-the-world expedition on HMS *Beagle*, ostensibly for his company as a dining companion, as society etiquette frowned on gentlemen fraternizing with the lower ranks. It is a strange irony that Fitzroy's passion was creationism and his personal motivation for the voyage was to find evidence for the biblical interpretation of creation. He required a companion familiar with the scriptures to be able to discuss his ideas during the voyage and chose Darwin chiefly as he had just left Cambridge with a degree in divinity. Unsurprisingly, the two men quarrelled constantly throughout the five-year duration of the expedition. The publication of *On the Origin of Species* was to be a bitter blow to Fitzroy, from which he never recovered, and he committed suicide in 1865.

ROOSEVELT'S FOUR FREEDOMS (from page 20)

Freedom of speech / Freedom of worship
Freedom from want / Freedom from fear

THE GOLDEN GIRLS (from page 22)

Dorothy Beatrice Arthur
Sophia Estelle Getty
Blanche Rue McClanahan
Rose Betty White

NICKNAMES OF PEOPLE I (from page 24)

1. Jacqueline Kennedy Onassis; 2. Jane Fonda; 3. Joan of Arc; 4. Elle Macpherson; 5. George S. Patton; 6. Florence Griffith-Joyner; 7. Mohandas Gandhi; 8. Wilt Chamberlain 9. Arnold Schwarzenegger; 10. Sylvester Stallone; 11. Al Capone; 12. John McEnroe; 13. Babe Ruth 14. Mark Wahlberg; 15. Jim Morrison; 16. Charlie Parker; 17. Muhammad Ali; 18. John Wayne; 19. Marvin Hagler; 20. Simon Cowell; 21. Martha Jane Burke*; 22. Bette Midler 23. William Perry; 24. Billie Holiday.

BEAUTY PAGEANTS (from page 26)

Miss Universe / Miss World / Miss International / Miss Earth

CLASSICAL ELEMENTS† (from page 30)

Air / Earth / Fire / Water

ENTREPRENEURS I (from page 32)

1. Remington; 2. MySpace‡; 3. Virgin; 4. Apple computers; 5. Ben and Jerry's; 6. MGM; 7. Microsoft; 8. Yahoo; 9. Coca-Cola; 10. Amazon.com; 11. Sony; 12. Ikea; 13. Starbucks; 14. Sun Microsystems; 15. Penguin Books; 16. Kodak; 17. Nokia; 18. McDonald's; 19. Nike; 20. Google; 21. eBay; 22. General Motors; 23. Wal-Mart; 24. Oracle (computer software).

TRAVELING WILBURYS (from page 35)

Bob Dylan / George Harrison / Jeff Lynne
Roy Orbison / Tom Petty

---

* Martha Jane Burke was expelled from General George Crook's Black Hills force when an officer discovered she was a woman. Her nickname is thought to derive from her frontier lifestyle and her propensity to help people who were facing disaster.
† In China, there were five classical elements: metal, wood, earth, fire, and water. The five visible planets were associated with these: Venus (metal), Jupiter (wood), Saturn (earth), Mars (fire) and Mercury (water). The Moon represented Yin and the Sun represented Yang. These themes appear in the *I Ching*, a classical Chinese text.
‡ All new accounts created on MySpace have Tom as their default "friend."

SPICE GIRLS (from page 37)

Victoria Adams (now Beckham) .... Posh
Melanie Brown .... Scary
Emma Bunton .... Baby
Melanie Chisholm .... Sporty
Geri Halliwell .... Ginger

MISCELLANY V (from page 39)

1. Scholastic Aptitude Test; 2. Clint Eastwood; 3. Beefeaters; 4. First Lady of the United States; 5. Red; 6. Rudyard Kipling; 7. Noah Webster; 8. Opossum; 9. "The Owl and the Pussycat"; 10. Perry Masonry; 11. Jesse James; 12. Cyprus; 13. The New York Yankees; 14. $100; 15. The Suez Canal; 16. Vitamin D; 17. The two atom bombs dropped on Japan; 18. Dynamo; 19. Captain Ahab (*Moby-Dick*); 20. Jerusalem; 21. The America's Cup; 22. The structure and state representation under the U.S. Constitution; 23. (Large) diamonds; 24. 218.

DISNEY THEME PARKS (from page 42; as at the time of publishing)
Disneyland Resort (California)
Walt Disney World Resort (Florida)
Tokyo Disney Resort
Disneyland Resort Paris
Hong Kong Disneyland Resort

ATMOSPHERIC LAYERS (from page 44)

Troposphere* .... 0-20 km
Stratosphere .... 20-50 km
Mesosphere .... 50-85 km
Ionosphere[†] .... 85-690 km
Exosphere[‡] .... 690-10,000 km

PSEUDONYMS I (from page 46)

1. David Soul; 2. Andy Garcia; 3. Eminem; 4. Eric Clapton; 5. Fatboy Slim; 6. Jean-Claude Van Damme; 7. Marilyn Monroe; 8. 50 Cent; 9. Tiger Woods; 10. Nicolas Cage; 11. Woody Allen; 12. Elle Macpherson; 13. Fred Astaire; 14. George Michael; 15. John Wayne; 16. Seal; 17. Tina Turner; 18. Van Morrison; 19.

---

* The lowest portion of the troposphere is known as the peplosphere, where the atmosphere is subject to interaction with the surface of the earth. Notably at this level, the movement of air travels across isobars (lines of equal pressure) whereas at altitude air travels parallel to isobars.

† Or thermosphere.

‡ Beyond the exosphere is a region known as the magnetosphere or solar wind, which extends approximately 70,000 km away from the earth.

Meatloaf; 20. Bob Dylan; 21. Buffalo Bill; 22. Cary Grant*; 23. Jay Z; 24. Pablo Picasso.

GREAT LAKES (from page 49)

Lake Superior[†] / Lake Michigan / Lake Huron
Lake Erie / Lake Ontario[‡]

VOCAL RANGES (from page 52)

Soprano / Mezzo-soprano / Contralto (or Alto)
Tenor / Baritone / Bass

CURRENCIES (from page 55)

1. Russia or Belarus; 2. Japan; 3. India, Pakistan or Sri Lanka; 4. Thailand; 5. Israel; 6. Lesotho, South Africa or Swaziland; 7. Bolivia; 8. Poland; 9. Turkey, Malta or Cyprus; 10. Brazil; 11. Indonesia; 12. Iceland or Sweden; 13. Denmark or Norway; 14. China[§]; 15. Venezuela; 16. Guatemala; 17. North Korea or South Korea; 18. Albania; 19. Ecuador; 20. Latvia; 21. Morocco; 22. Costa Rica; 23. Peru; 24. Mongolia.

STATES OF MATTER (from page 58)

Bose-Einstein Condensate (0) / Solid (1) / Liquid (2)
Gas (3) / Plasma (4) / Filament (5)

NOVELS BY JANE AUSTEN[¶] (from page 61)

Sense and Sensibility	1811
Pride and Prejudice	1813
Mansfield Park	1814
Emma	1816
Northanger Abbey	1817
Persuasion	1817

SUPERMAJORS (from page 63)

ExxonMobil / BP / Royal Dutch Shell / Total S.A.
Chevron Corporation / ConocoPhillips

---

* Archibald Leach was the name of the character played by John Cleese in *A Fish Called Wanda*.

† Lake Superior is the largest freshwater lake in the world (by surface area).

‡ Lake Ontario is at the lowest elevation of all the Great Lakes. Water travels to Lake Ontario via the Niagara Falls.

§ In spoken Chinese the yuan is pronounced "kuai." Chinese currency is often referred to as renminbi (RMB)

¶ Dates of publications are supplied. *Northanger Abbey* and *Persuasion* were published posthumously.

LINKED MISCELLANY V (from page 65)

1. Emperor penguin; 2. Eve*; 3. Platoon; 4. "Daisy bell"; 5. *The Six Million Dollar Man*; 6. Africa; 7. Rebecca Howe; 8. Chicago; 9. Casablanca; 10. George S. Patton. The link is films which won the Academy Award for Best Picture[†]

AFRICAN COUNTRIES BEGINNING WITH "M" (from page 68)

Madagascar / Malawi / Mali / Mauritania
Mauritius / Morocco / Mozambique

WONDERS OF THE ANCIENT WORLD (from page 70)

The Pyramids of Giza[‡]
The Hanging Gardens of Babylon
The Temple of Artemis
The Mausoleum of Halicarnassus
The Colossus of Rhodes
The Pharos of Alexandria
The Statue of Zeus at Olympia

FIRST LINES OF POP SONGS II (from page 72)

1. "Stairway to Heaven" (Led Zeppelin); 2. "Crazy" (Gnarls Barkley); 3. "Whiter Shade of Pale" (Procol Harum); 4. "The Joker" (Steve Miller Band); 5. "Gangsta's Paradise" (Coolio featuring LV); 6. "Thriller" (Michael Jackson); 7. "Is There Something I Should Know?" (Duran Duran); 8. "I Got You Babe" (Sonny and Cher); 9. "Get the Party Started" (Pink); 10. "Once in a Lifetime" (Talking Heads); 11. "Honky Tonk Woman" (Rolling Stones); 12. "Crazy in Love" (Beyonce); 13. "Don't You Want Me" (Human League); 14. "Comfortably Numb" (Pink Floyd); 15. "Video Killed the Radio Star" (The Buggles); 16. "All Night Long (All Night)" (Lionel Richie); 17. "Stuck in the Middle With You" (Stealers Wheel); 18. "Walk This Way" (Run DMC); 19. "I Think We're Alone Now" (Tiffany); 20. "With or Without You" (U2); 21. "Dead Ringer for Love" (Meatloaf); 22. "Drive" (The Cars); 23. "Cry Me a River" (Justin Timberlake); 24. "You Ain't Seen Nothing Yet" (Bachman Turner Overdrive).

---

* Unlike nuclear DNA, there is no change in Mitochondrial DNA (mtDNA) from parent to offspring. This enables it to be used to track ancestry back through the female line.

† *The Last Emperor* (1987), *All About Eve* (1950), *Platoon* (1986), *Driving Miss Daisy* (1989), *Million Dollar Baby* (2004), *Out of Africa* (1985), *Rebecca* (1940), *Chicago* (2002), *Casablanca* (1943), and *Patton* (1970).

‡ The pyramids are the only one of the Seven Wonders that still exists today. The Great Pyramid at Giza took twenty years to construct and was completed around 2600 B.C. The pyramid, which stands 137 meters tall, was the world's tallest structure for nearly 4,000 years and was only superseded during the cathedral-building era of medieval Europe.

CHRONICLES OF NARNIA (from page 73)

WONDERS OF THE NATURAL WORLD (from page 76)

The Grand Canyon

Mount Everest

The Harbour of Rio de Janeiro

The Great Barrier Reef

Victoria Falls

Paricutin Volcano

The Northern Lights (*Aurora Borealis*)

SIGNS OF AGING (from page 78)

Lines and wrinkles

Uneven skin texture

Uneven skin tone

Appearance of pores

Blotches and age spots

Dry skin

Dullness

CHARACTERS IN LITERATURE II (from page 80)

1. *A Christmas Carol* (Charles Dickens); 2. *Nineteen Eight-four* (George Orwell); 3. *Tess of the d'Urbervilles* (Thomas Hardy); 4. *Pygmalion* (George Bernard Shaw); 5. *The Prime of Miss Jean Brodie* (Muriel Spark); 6. *Jane Eyre* (Charlotte Brontë); 7. *Emma* (Jane Austen); 8. *The Mystery of Edwin Drood* (Charles Dickens); 9. *To Kill a Mockingbird* (Harper Lee); 10. *Pride and Prejudice* (Jane Austen); 11. *Animal Farm* (George Orwell); 12. *A Room with a View* (E. M. Forster); 13. *Master and Commander* (Patrick O'Brian); 14. *Treasure Island* (Robert Louis Stevenson); 15. *Breakfast at Tiffany's* (Truman Capote); 16. *The Talented Mr. Ripley* (Patricia Highsmith); 17. *Lolita* (Vladimir Nabokov); 18. *His Dark Materials* trilogy (Philip Pullman); 19. *David Copperfield* (Charles Dickens); 20. *War and Peace* (Leo Tolstoy); 21. *To Kill a Mockingbird* (Harper Lee); 22. *Tom Sawyer* and *Huckleberry Finn* (Mark Twain); 23. *Anna Karenina* (Leo Tolstoy); 24. *Jeeves and Wooster* books* (P. G. Wodehouse).

---

* In *Right Ho, Jeeves*, Bertie offers his opinion that Gussie looks like a fish. Jeeves confirms that there is "something of the piscine" about him (p. 318).

IVY LEAGUE (from page 83)

Brown / Columbia / Cornell / Dartmouth
Harvard / Pennsylvania / Princeton / Yale

RESERVOIR DOGS (from page 85)

Mr. White .... Harvey Keitel
Mr. Orange .... Tim Roth
Mr. Blonde .... Michael Madsen
Mr. Pink .... Steve Buscemi
Mr. Brown ' .... Quentin Tarantino
Mr. Blue .... Edward Bunker
Joe Cabot .... Lawrence Tierney
"Nice Guy" Eddie Cabot .... Chris Penn

MISCELLANY XII (from page 88)

1. Nepotism; 2. "A dish best served cold"; 3. The Taj Mahal; 4. Lake Ontario; 5.
David Copperfield; 6. Six; 7. *Frasier*; 8. Atlantic Ocean; 9. Mount Everest; 10.
Strategic Arms Limitation Treaty; 11. A New York ticker-tape parade; 12. Maine; 13.
The U.S. National Debt*; 14. Sherlock Holmes; 15. Tungsten; 16. Bishop[†]; 17. Ernst
Stavro Blofeld; 18. Mikhail Gorbachev; 19. Albus Dumbledore; 20. The War of
American Independence; 21. Set both of the hourglass timers running. When the two-
minute hourglass has run out, start cooking the egg. When the five-minute hourglass
has run out, stop cooking the egg; 22. Haricot beans; 23. Elephant; 24. $45.

STATES PREFIXED BY ADJECTIVES (from page 95)

New Hampshire / New Jersey / New Mexico
New York / North Carolina / North Dakota
South Carolina / South Dakota / West Virginia

COUNTRIES WITH FOUR-LETTER NAMES (from page 97)

Chad / Cuba / Fiji / Iran / Iraq
Laos / Mali / Oman / Peru / Togo

POLITICAL QUOTATIONS (from page 99)

1. Richard Nixon; 2. Bill Clinton; 3. John F. Kennedy; 4. Martin Luther King Jr.;
5. Richard Nixon; 6. George H. W. Bush; 7. Lloyd Bentsen[‡]; 8. Winston Churchill;

---

* The debt was briefly paid paid off under Andrew Jackson, the only time this has
ever happened in a modern economy.

† A crosier is a bishop's crook.

‡ In a televised vice-presidential debate in 1988, Dan Quayle, keen to rebuff criticism
of his inexperience, compared his own congressional experience to that of John F.
Kennedy. This brought a swift (and now famous) rebuff from the Democratic
candidate, Lloyd Bentsen: "Senator, I served with Jack Kennedy. I knew Jack Kennedy.
Jack Kennedy was a friend of mine. Senator, you're no Jack Kennedy."

9. Horatio Nelson*; 10. John F. Kennedy; 11. Julius Caesar†; 12. Karl Marx; 13. Abraham Lincoln; 14. Queen Elizabeth I; 15. Harry S. Truman; 16. Abraham Lincoln; 17. Ronald Reagan; 18. George W. Bush; 19. Franklin D. Roosevelt; 20. Harry S. Truman; 21. Henry Kissinger; 22. Theodore Roosevelt; 23. Nikita Khrushchev; 24. Oliver Cromwell.

MOST VALUABLE SPORTING EVENTS (from page 102)

NFL Super Bowl

Summer Olympic Games

FIFA World Cup

NASCAR Daytona 500

Rose Bowl

NCAA Men's Final Four

Winter Olympic Games

Kentucky Derby

MLB World Series

NBA Finals

MINERALS (from page 104)

Calcium / Chromium / Copper / Fluorine / Iodine / Iron

Magnesium / Phosphorus / Potassium / Sodium / Zinc

NICKNAMES OF STATES I (from page 108)

1. Hawaii; 2. Florida; 3. New York; 4. Illinois; 5. Missouri; 6. Vermont; 7. Washington; 8. Connecticut; 9. New Mexico; 10. Colorado; 11. Maine; 12. Oklahoma; 13. New Hampshire; 14. Tennessee; 15. Virginia‡; 16. Wisconsin; 17. South Carolina; 18. Massachusetts; 19. Delaware; 20. Nebraska; 21. Wyoming; 22. Kansas; 23. Minnesota; 24. Utah.

PEOPLE ON DOLLAR BILLS (from page 109)

George Washington $1
Thomas Jefferson $2

---

* Nelson's famous nine-word signal was hoisted from HMS *Victory*, flagship of the British fleet, at 11:30 on the morning of October 21, 1805, as it sailed into action against the combined fleets of France and Spain at the Battle of Trafalgar. Nelson's intention had been to express his trust in his men but the word "expects" was rather easier to signal than the word "confides" and was substituted by Nelson's signal officer. The signal was therefore given a rather harder meaning (that it was unacceptable for any man to do anything but his duty) than the vote of confidence that Nelson had intended.

† "Veni, vidi, vici." Caesar said this after the Battle of Zela and the defeat of Pharnaces II of Pontus.

‡ Virginia is also known as the "Mother of presidents" because it has been the birthplace of eight U.S. presidents.

Abraham Lincoln $5
Alexander Hamilton $10
Andrew Jackson $20
Ulysses S. Grant $50
Benjamin Franklin $100
William McKinley .... $500^R
Grover Cleveland .... $1,000^R
James Madison .... $5,000^R
Salmon P. Chase .... $10,000^R
Woodrow Wilson .... $100,000^R

^{R} the denominations of $500 and above were retired in 1969; the $100,000 bill was never publicly issued.

DICTATORS (from page 112)

1. Adolf Hitler; 2. Joseph Stalin; 3. Saddam Hussein; 4. Fidel Castro; 5. Robert Mugabe; 6. Idi Amin; 7. Benito Mussolini; 8. Pol Pot; 9. Mao Tse-tung; 10. Ayatollah Khomeini; 11. Francisco Franco; 12. Slobodan Milosevic; 13. Augusto Pinochet; 14. Manuel Noriega; 15. Kim Jong-il; 16. Nicolae Ceausescu*; 17. Ferdinand Marcos; 18. Josip Tito (Marshall Tito); 19. Haile Selassie; 20. Laurent Kabila; 21. Charles Taylor; 22. George Speight; 23. Hastings Banda†; 24. Sani Abacha.‡

EUROZONE (from page 126; as at the time of publishing)

Austria / Belgium / Cyprus / Finland / France
Germany / Greece / Ireland / Italy / Luxembourg
Malta / Netherlands / Portugal / Slovenia / Spain

CHARACTERS IN *HAPPY DAYS* (from page 116)

Arthur "Fonzie" Fonzarelli .... Henry Winkler
Howard Cunningham .... Tom Bosley
Marion Cunningham .... Marion Ross
Joanie Cunningham .... Erin Moran
Warren "Potsie" Webber .... Anson Williams
Richie Cunningham .... Ron Howard

---

* Ceausescu was the only communist leader to suffer a violent death as a result of the fall of the Soviet Union in 1989. He was executed, along with his wife Elena, by firing squad.

† Banda managed to accumulate $320 million worth of personal assets during his rule, equivalent to about one-fifth of his country's GDP.

‡ It is thought that Abacha, who died of a heart attack at the age of fifty-four, had siphoned $3 billion of public funds into private bank accounts, much of which ended up in the control of family members. In 1999, Abacha's eldest son Mohammad was arrested for fraud, money laundering, embezzlement, and murder, but charges were dropped in exchange for the return of 80% of the family's assets. The Abacha family is still thought to be worth at least $100 million.

Ralph Malph	Donny Most
Alfred "Al" Delvecchio	Al Molinaro
Charles "Chachi" Arcola	Scott Baio
Lori Beth	Lynda Goodfriend
Roger Phillips	Ted McGinley
Jenny Piccalo	Cathy Silvers
Matsuo "Arnold" Takahashi	Pat Morita

COUNTRIES IN SOUTH AMERICA (from page 119)

Argentina / Bolivia / Brazil / Chile / Colombia
Ecuador / French Guiana / Guyana / Paraguay
Peru / Suriname / Uruguay / Venezuela

BRITISHISMS II (from page 121)

1. Confectionery or sweets or chocolate; 2. Lift; 3. Crisps; 4. Petrol; 5. Curriculum vitae; 6. Draughts; 7. Cupboard; 8. Curtains; 9. Tap; 10. Motorway; 11. Queue; 12. Pavement; 13. Underground; 14. Dinner jacket; 15. Courgette; 16. Jam; 17. Noughts & Crosses; 18. Sweet potato; 19. Cashier; 20. Refrigerator; 21. Braces; 22. Pushchair or buggy; 23. Budgerigar; 24. Undertaker.

PROLIFIC CHART-TOPPING FEMALE ARTISTS (from page 124, as at time of publishing)

Mariah Carey	17 number one hits
Madonna	12
Whitney Houston	11
Janet Jackson	10
Diana Ross	6
Paula Abdul	6
Barbra Streisand	5
Olivia Newton-John	5
Céline Dion	4
Cher	4
Donna Summer	4
Jennifer Lopez	4
Beyoncé	4
Christina Aguilera	4

FILMS BY DAVID LEAN (from page 127)

In Which We Serve	1942
This Happy Breed	1944
Blithe Spirit	1945
Brief Encounter	1945
Great Expectations	1946
Oliver Twist	1948
The Passionate Friends	1949

^O indicates Oscar for Best Director

LATIN PHRASES I (from page 130)

1. Ante meridiem (a.m.); 2. Anno Domini* (A.D.); 3. Post scriptum (PS); 4. Quod erat demonstrandum (QED); 5. Status quo; 6. Per annum; 7. Coitus interruptus; 8. Id est (i.e.); 9. Alma mater; 10. Prima facie; 11. Circa (*c.*); 12. Ad hoc; 13. Per pro (pp.); 14. Exempli gratia (e.g.); 15. Confer (cf.); 16. Annus mirabilis; 17. Magnum opus; 18. Quid pro quo; 19. Bona fide; 20. De facto; 21. Primus inter pares†; 22. Et alii (et al.); 23. In flagrante delicto; 24. Obiter dictum.

STORIES BY ROALD DAHL (from page 133)

---

* A.D. is an abbreviation of "Anni Domini Nostri Jesu Christi," meaning "The Years of Our Lord Jesus Christ." The Latin for the epoch prior to this—"Ante Christum Natum" ("Before the birth of Christ") has been dropped in favor of Before Christ (B.C.). The religiously neutral terms C.E. ("Common Era" or "Christian Era") and B.C.E. ("Before the Common Era") may alternatively be used for the periods after and before year 1 of the Gregorian calendar.

† Used to describe the leader of a republic, the phrase was employed as a piece of political spin by the first Roman emperors to give the impression they were not dictators (which they were).

Esio Trot	1989
The Minpins	1991
The Vicar of Nibbleswicke	1991

POPULAR LANGUAGES* (from page 136)

Mandarin Chinese / English / Spanish / Hindi and Urdu / Arabic[†]
Portuguese / Bengali / Russian / Japanese / German
Wu Chinese / Javanese / Korean / Punjabi / Telugu[‡]
French / Marathi / Tamil / Italian / Yue Chinese[§]

PSEUDONYMS II (from page 138)

1. Cher; 2. Engelbert Humperdinck; 3. Dr. Seuss; 4. George Orwell; 5. Jennifer Aniston; 6. Lenin; 7. Muhammad Ali; 8. Ringo Starr; 9. Audrey Hepburn; 10. Moby; 11. Demi Moore; 12. Elton John; 13. George Eliot; 14. Greta Garbo; 15. Prince; 16. Sophia Loren; 17. Vanilla Ice; 18. Walter Matthau; 19. Bing Crosby; 20. Bruce Lee; 21. Calamity Jane; 22. Charlie Sheen; 23. Bono; 24. Snoop Doggy Dog.

WEALTHY COUNTRIES (from page 140)

Luxembourg	$80,288
Norway	$64,193
Iceland	$52,764
Switzerland	$50,532
Ireland	$48,604
Denmark	$47,984
Qatar	$43,110
United States	$42,000
Sweden	$39,694
Netherlands	$38,618
Finland	$37,504
Austria	$37,117
United Kingdom	$37,023
Japan	$35,757
Belgium	$35,712
Canada	$35,133

---

* Note that estimates for the number of language speakers are unreliable because (i) quality of data sources varies from country to country; (ii) treatment of dialects can be ambiguous (Hindu and Urdu, treated here as a single language, could be separated); (iii) treatment of mother tongue, first-language and second-language speakers is often ambiguous; (iv) figures changes rapidly as populations grow. The languages listed here are accepted by most sources as the twenty most widely spoken and are spoken by roughly three-quarters of the world's population.

† Arabic has twenty-seven different varieties.

‡ Spoken in the Andhra Pradesh area of India.

§ Cantonese.

Australia	$34,740
France	$33,918
Germany	$33,854
Italy	$30,200

Figures for per capita Gross Domestic Product from the IMF, 2005

100 CAREER TOUCHDOWNS (from page 141; as at time of publishing)

Jerry Rice	208
Emmitt Smith	175
Marcus Allen	145
Marshall Faulk	136
Cris Carter	131
Terrell Owens[A]	131
LaDainian Tomlinson[A]	129
Jim Brown	126
Walter Payton	125
Randy Moss[A]	125
Marvin Harrison[A]	123
John Riggins	116
Lenny Moore	113
Shaun Alexander[A]	112
Barry Sanders	109
Don Hutson	105
Tim Brown	105
Steve Largent	101
Franco Harris	100
Curtis Martin	100

[A] indicates a currently active player

WORLD SERIES WINNERS (from page 144; as at time of publishing)

New York Yankees	26 titles (2000)
St. Louis Cardinals	10 (2006)
Oakland Athletics	9 (1989)
Boston Red Sox	7 (2007)
Los Angeles (Brooklyn) Dodgers	6 (1988)
Cincinnati Reds	5 (1990)
Pittsburgh Pirates	5 (1979)
San Francisco Giants	5 (1954)
Detroit Tigers	4 (1984)
Atlanta Braves (Boston, Milwaukee)	3 (1995)
Baltimore Orioles	3 (1983)
Chicago White Sox	3 (2005)
Minnesota Twins (Washington Senators)	3 (1991)
Chicago Cubs	2 (1908)
Cleveland Indians	2 (1948)

Florida Marlins	....	2 (2003)
New York Mets	....	2 (1986)
Toronto Blue Jays	....	2 (1993)
Arizona Diamondbacks	....	1 (2001)
Kansas City Royals	....	1 (1985)
Los Angeles Angels of Anaheim	....	1 (2002)
Philadelphia Phillies	....	1 (1980)

Date of most recent World Series win given in brackets.

MISCELLANY XX (from page 147)

1. Iceland; 2. Diamonds; 3. They are palindromes; 4. "Bohemian Rhapsody" (Queen); 5. Campbell's Soup; 6. The title character does not appear in the play; 7. Superman; 8. Houston*; 9. Minnehaha; 10. Freelance; 11. Wyoming; 12. Charles Bronson; 13. Mauna Kea; 14. With vinegar and brown paper; 15. Directly beneath it; 16. Four boys, three girls; 17. Italy and Switzerland; 18. Charles II; 19. The Extraterrestrial Highway; 20. CAT Scan; 21. Electricity; 22. 24; 23. Pulmonary artery; 24. Footballs.

500 HOME RUN CLUB (from page 150; as at time of publishing)

Barry Bonds[A]	....	762 career home runs
Hank Aaron	....	755
Babe Ruth	....	714
Willie Mays	....	660
Sammy Sosa[A]	....	609
Ken Griffey, Jr.[A]	....	593
Frank Robinson	....	586
Mark McGwire	....	583
Harmon Killebrew	....	573
Rafael Palmeiro	....	569
Reggie Jackson	....	563
Mike Schmidt	....	548
Mickey Mantle	....	536
Jimmie Foxx	....	534
Willie McCovey	....	521
Ted Williams	....	521
Alex Rodriguez[A]	....	518
Frank Thomas[A]	....	513
Ernie Banks	....	512
Mel Ott	....	511
Jim Thome[A]	....	507
Eddie Murray	....	504

[A] indicates a currently active player

---

* "Houston, Tranquillity Base here. The Eagle has landed."

GREEK ALPHABET (from page 152)

A Alpha / B Beta / Γ Gamma / Δ Delta / E Epsilon / Z Zeta / H Eta / Θ Theta / I Iota / K Kappa / Λ Lambda / M Mu / N Nu / Ξ Xi / O Omicron / Π Pi* / P Rho / Σ Sigma / T Tau / Υ Upsilon / Φ Phi / X Chi / Ψ Psi / Ω Omega

RECENT HISTORY III (from page 155)

1. 2004; 2. 2005; 3. 2002; 4. 1988; 5. 1992; 6. 1990; 7. 1977; 8. 1989; 9. 1940; 10. 1979; 11. 1980; 12. 1953; 13. 1981; 14. 1943; 15. 1983; 16. 1982; 17. 1912; 18. 1917; 19. 1929; 20. 1948; 21. 1946; 22. 1956; 23. 1922; 24. 1924.

COUNTRIES WITH FIVE-LETTER NAMES (from page 164)

Benin / Chile / China / Congo / Egypt / Gabon
Ghana / Haiti / India / Italy / Japan / Kenya
Korea† / Libya / Malta / Nauru / Nepal
Niger / Palau / Qatar / Samoa / Spain
Sudan / Syria / Tonga / Yemen

COURSES HOSTING THE U.S. OPEN (from page 167; as at time of publishing)

Atlanta Athletic Club	1976
Baltusrol Golf Club	1954, 1967, 1980, 1993
Bellerive Country Club	1965
Bethpage State Park	2002
Canterbury Golf Club	1946
Champions Golf Club	1969
Cherry Hills Country Club	1960, 1978
Congressional Country Club	1964, 1997
The Country Club	1963, 1988
Hazeltine National Golf Club	1970, 1991
Inverness Club	1957, 1979
Medinah Country Club	1949, 1975, 1990
Merion Golf Club	1950, 1971, 1981
Northwood Club	1952

---

* The ratio of the circumference of a circle to its diameter is represented by Pi and is equal to 3.14159265358979323846264338327950288419716939937510582097494 45923078164062862089986280348253421170679 (to 100 decimal places).

Mathematicians describe Pi as an irrational number, that is, a number that cannot be expressed as the ratio of any two integers. This was an irksome fact to the state of Indiana in 1897; so much so that legislation was drafted (based on the work of local mathematician Edward J. Goodwin) setting Pi alternative values of 3.2, 3.23, and 4. The bill passed its first reading, but, fortunately for Indiana, was held up at the second reading largely due to remarks made by a passing math professor, C. A. Waldo, questioning the mental health of the bill's authors.

† Korea is actually divided into North Korea and South Korea. There could also be an argument for the inclusion of East Timor and the Czech Republic in the list.

Oak Hill Country Club	1956, 1968, 1989
Oakland Hills Country Club	1951, 1961, 1985, 1996
Oakmont Country Club	1953, 1962, 1973, 1983, 1994, 2007
Olympia Fields Country Club	2003
Olympic Club	1955, 1966, 1987, 1998
Pebble Beach Golf Links	1972, 1982, 1992, 2000
Pinehurst Resort	1999, 2005
Riviera Country Club	1948
Shinnecock Hills Golf Club	1986, 1995, 2004
Southern Hills Country Club	1958, 1977, 2001
St. Louis Country Club	1947
Torrey Pines Golf Course	2008
Winged Foot Golf Club	1959, 1974, 1984, 2006

CATCHPHRASES II (from page 170)

1. Oliver Hardy; 2. Donald Trump (*The Apprentice*); 3.John McEnroe; 4. Fox Mulder (*The X-Files*); 5. Shaggy (*Scooby Doo*); 6. Harry Callahan (*Sudden Impact*); 7. Ross Geller (*Friends*); 8. *Wayne's World*; 9. Joan Rivers; 10. *The Waltons*; 11. Walter Cronkite (*CBS Evening News*); 12. Charlie Brown; 13. Michael Buffer; 14. Robot (*Lost in Space*); 15. Bob Eubanks (*The Newlywed Game*); 16. Mr. Burns (*The Simpsons*); 17. The Soup Nazi* (*Seinfeld*); 18. Eric Idle (*Monty Python's Flying Circus*); 19. Dan Aykroyd† (*Saturday Night Live*); 20. Bender Bending Rodriguez (*Futurama*); 21. Arnold Jackson (*Diff'rent Strokes*); 22. Ed Sullivan (*The Ed Sullivan Show*); 23. Tattoo (*Fantasy Island*); 24. Ralph Kramden (*The Honeymooners*).

LONGEST AMERICAN RIVERS (from page 173)

Mississippi	2,348 miles
Missouri	2,315
St. Lawrence	1,900
Yukon	1,979
Rio Grande	1,899
Arkansas	1,459
Colorado	1,450
Red	1,290
Columbia	1,243
Snake	1,038
Platte	990
Ohio	981
Pecos	926
Brazos	923
Canadian	906

---

* The Soup Nazi has a strict code of conduct in his kitchen. When characters are in breach of this code, he delivers his famous catchphrase.

† to Jane Curtin

Colorado	862
North Canadian	800
Kansas	743
Green	730
Kuskokwim	724
White	722
Cumberland	720
James (Dakota)	710
Yellowstone	692
Pearl	661
Tanana	659
Tennessee	652
Gila	649
Milk	625
North Platte	618
Ouachita	605

LINKED MISCELLANY XIII (from page 178)

1. Brazil; 2. The Hunter; 3. The Bronx; 4. Ziggy Stardust; 5. Jacqueline Kennedy;
6. *Casino Royale*; 7. Heat; 8. Cape Town; 9. A driver; 10. A bull market.

The link is Robert De Niro films.*

AMERICAN PRESIDENTS (from page 181)

George Washington	1789–97
John Adams [Fed]	1797–1801
Thomas Jefferson [DR]	1801–9
James Madison [DR]	1809–17
James Monroe [Rep]	1817–25
John Quincy Adams [DR]	1825–9
Andrew Jackson [Dem]	1829–37
Martin Van Buren [Dem]	1837–41
William Henry Harrison [Wg]	1841
John Tyler [Wg]	1841–45
James K. Polk [Dem]	1845–49
Zachary Taylor [Wg]	1849–50
Millard Fillmore [Wg]	1850–53
Franklin Pierce [Dem]	1853–57
James Buchanan [Dem]	1857–61
Abraham Lincoln [Rep]	1861–65
Andrew Johnson [DNU Imp]	1865–69
Ulysses S. Grant [Rep]	1869–77
Rutherford B. Hayes [Rep]	1877–81

---

* *Brazil, The Deer Hunter, A Bronx Tale, Stardust, Jackie Brown, Casino, Heat, Cape Fear, Taxi Driver*, and *Raging Bull.*

James A. Garfield [Rep] 1881
Chester A. Arthur [Rep] 1881–85
Grover Cleveland* [Dem] 1885–89; 1893–97
Benjamin Harrison [Rep] 1889–93
William McKinley [Rep] 1897–1901
Theodore Roosevelt [Rep] 1901–9
William H. Taft [Rep] 1909–13
Woodrow Wilson [Dem] 1913–21
Warren G. Harding [Rep] 1921–23
Calvin Coolidge [Rep] 1923–29
Herbert C. Hoover [Rep] 1929–33
Franklin D. Roosevelt[†] [Dem] 1933–45
Harry S. Truman [Dem] 1945–53
Dwight D. Eisenhower [Rep] 1953–61
John F. Kennedy [Dem] 1961–63
Lyndon B. Johnson [Dem] 1963–69
Richard M. Nixon [Rep] [Res] 1969–74
Gerald Ford [Rep] 1974–77
Jimmy Carter [Dem] 1977–81
Ronald Reagan [Rep] 1981–89
George H.W. Bush [Rep] 1989–93
Bill Clinton [Dem] [Imp] 1993–2001
George W. Bush [Rep] 2001–present

Parties are indicated as: [Dem] Democrat; [Rep] Republican; [DR] Democrat-Republican; [DNU] Democrat/National Union; [Wg] Whig; [Imp] Impeached; [Res] Resigned

SINGERS AND BACKERS III (from page 186)

1. Adam; 2. KC; 3. Gloria Estefan; 4. Gladys Knight; 5. John Lennon; 6. Bob Marley; 7. Kool; 8. Huey Lewis; 9. Bruce Springsteen; 10. Kid Creole; 11. Freddie; 12. Nick Cave; 13. Buddy Holly; 14. Gary Numan; 15. Joey Dee; 16. Frank Zappa; 17. Sheila E; 18. Smokey Robinson; 19. Duane Eddy; 20. Jimmy Gilmer; 21. Billy J. Kramer; 22. Brian Poole; 23. Georgie Fame; 24. Bobby Angelo.

OLYMPIC DISCIPLINES (from page 194; as at the time of publishing)
Alpine Skiing[Ski] / Archery / Artistic Gymnastics[Gym]
Athletics[‡] / Badminton / Baseball / Basketball

---

* The only president to serve two non-consecutive terms Cleveland was the twenty-second and twenty-fourth president of the United States.

† Franklin Roosevelt was the only president to serve more than two terms in office—he was elected four times and died one year into his fourth term. The Twenty-second Amendment to the U.S. Constitution, restricting presidents to two terms in office, became law in 1951.

‡ Athletics is the highest-profile sport at the Olympics. There are twenty-six track-and-field events.

Beach Volleyball^{Vol} / Biathlon / BMX^{Cyc} / Bobsled^{Bob}
Boxing / Cross-country Skiing^{Ski} / Curling
Diving^{Aq} / Dressage^{Eq} / Eventing^{Eq} / Fencing
Figure Skating^{Ska} / Flatwater^{Can} / Football
Freestyle Skiing^{Ski} / Freestyle Wrestling^{W}
Greco-Roman Wrestling^{W} / Handball / Hockey / Ice Hockey
Indoor Volleyball^{Vol} / Judo / Luge / Modern Pentathlon
Mountain Bike^{Cyc} / Nordic Combined^{Ski} / Road Racing^{Cyc}
Rowing / Rhythmic Gymnastics^{Gym} / Sailing / Shooting
Short Track Speed Skating^{Ska} / Showjumping^{Eq}
Skeleton^{Bob} / Ski Jumping^{Ski} / Slalom^{Can} / Snowboard^{Ski}
Softball / Speed Skating^{Ska} / Swimming^{Aq}
Synchronised Swimming^{Aq} / Table Tennis / Taekwondo
Tennis / Track^{Cyc} / Trampoline^{Gym}
Triathlon / Water Polo^{Aq} / Weightlifting
Sports with multiple disciplines indicated as ^{Aq} Aquatics ^{Bob} Bobsleigh ^{Can} Canoeing ^{Cyc} Cycling ^{Eq} Equestrian ^{Gym} Gymnastics ^{Ska} Skating ^{Ski} Skiing ^{Vol} Volleyball ^{W} Wrestling

OLYMPIANS II (from page 197)

1. Jesse Owens*; 2. Mark Spitz[†] 3. Bob Beamon[‡]; 4. Edwin Moses; 5. Florence Griffith-Joyner; 6. Gwen Torrence; 7. Justin Gatlin; 8. Alonzo Babers; 9. Dan O'Brien; 10. Dick Fosbury[§]; 11. Evelyn Ashford; 12. Jim Hines; 13. Jo Frazier; 14. Joanna Hayes; 15. Johnny Weissmuller; 16. Kristi Tsuya Yamaguchi; 17. Matt Biondi; 18. Michael Phelps; 19. Quincy Watts; 20. Shawn Crawford; 21. Alfredrick Joyner; 22. Nancy Kerrigan; 23. Scott Hamilton; 24. Wyomia Tyus.

FIRST LINES OF POPULAR NOVELS I (from page 3)

1. *The Hobbit* (J. R. R. Tolkien); 2. *The House at Pooh Corner* (A. A. Milne); 3. *Pride and Prejudice* (Jane Austen); 4. *A Tale of Two Cities* (Charles Dickens); 5. *The Lion, the Witch and the Wardrobe* (C. S. Lewis); 6. *Adventures of Huckleberry Finn*

---

* In winning his four gold medals, Jesse Owens embarrassed Hitler's attempts to make the Berlin Olympics a show case of Aryan superiority. The previous year, on May 25, Owens broke three world records and equalled a fourth in a 45-minute period.

† Mark Spitz holds the record for the most gold medals won at a single Olympics (seven).

‡ Bob Beamon smashed the Men's Long Jump record with a jump of 8.90 m (29 ft. 2 in.) at Mexico City, beating the previous record by 55 cm (it was the first jump over 29 ft as well as over 28 ft). Beamon's record stood for twenty-three years.

§ Dick Fosbury won the gold at Mexico City with a pioneering style which became known as the Fosbury Flop. Prior to Fosbury, high jumpers went headfirst or used the straddle technique.

(Mark Twain); 7. *I, Robot* (Isaac Asimov); 8. *Nineteen Eighty-four** (George Orwell); 9. The Mill on the Floss (George Eliot); 10. *Rebecca* (Daphne du Maurier); 11. *One Hundred Years of Solitude* (Gabriel Garcia Marquez); 12. *Little Women* (Louisa May Alcott); 13. *Captain Corelli's Mandolin* (Louis de Bernières); 14. *Emma* (Jane Austen); 15. *Charlotte's Web* (E. B. White); 16. *Wuthering Heights* (Emily Brontë); 17. *The Exorcist* (William Peter Blatty); 18. *The Time Machine* (H. G. Wells); 19. *Lord of the Flies* (William Golding); 20. *2001: A Space Odyssey* (Arthur C. Clarke); 21. *The Da Vinci Code* (Dan Brown); 22. *The Maltese Falcon* (Dashiell Hammett); 23. *Fear of Flying* (Erica Jong); 24. *Paul Clifford* (Edward George Bulwer-Lytton).†

MUSKETEERS‡ (from page 7)

Aramis / Athos / Porthos

SONS OF ADAM AND EVE (from page 9)

Cain§ / Abel / Seth

FILMS AND THEIR STARS I (from page 5)

1. *Titanic*; 2. *Star Wars*; 3. *Dr. No*; 4. *Some Like It Hot*; 5. *Psycho*; 6. *Butch Cassidy and the Sundance Kid*; 7. *As Good As It Gets*; 8. *An Officer and a Gentleman*; 9. *Breakfast at Tiffany's*; 10. *Alexander*; 11. *Crash*; 12. *Planet of the Apes*; 13. *Sideways*; 14. *Saving Private Ryan*; 15. *Fargo*; 16. *Diner*; 17. *Guess Who's Coming to Dinner*; 18. *Little Miss Sunshine*; 19. *Field of Dreams*; 20. *Mars Attacks!*; 21. *Papillon*; 22. *Dr. Strangelove*; 23. *The Last Temptation of Christ*; 24. *Who's Afraid of Virginia Woolf?*

---

* Originally titled *The Last Man in Europe*, the book introduced the phrases "Big Brother," "Room 101," and "Thought Police."

† This oft quoted opening line inspired the Bulwer-Lytton Fiction Contest, sponsored by the English Department of the State University of San Jose, which annually awards the worst opening line in fiction. Previous winners of the $250 prize have included:

"Gerald began—but was interrupted by a piercing whistle which cost him ten percent of his hearing permanently, as it did everyone else in a ten-mile radius of the eruption, not that it mattered much because for them 'permanently' meant the next ten minutes or so until buried by searing lava or suffocated by choking ash—to pee." (Jim Gleeson)

and:

"As he stared at her ample bosom, he daydreamed of the dual Stromberg carburetors in his vintage Triumph Spitfire, highly functional yet pleasingly formed, perched prominently on top of the intake manifold, aching for experienced hands, the small knurled caps of the oil dampeners begging to be inspected and adjusted as described in chapter seven of the shop manual." (Dan McKay)

‡ D'Artagnan, the protagonist of the novel, is not one of the musketeers of the title.

§ Cain killed Abel.

GRAND SLAM TENNIS TOURNAMENTS (from page 14)
Australian Open / French Open / U.S. Open / Wimbledon

CLASSICAL COLUMNS (from page 20)
Tuscan / Ionic / Doric / Corinthian

HOBBIES AND PROFESSIONS I (from page 22)
1. One skilled in folding paper; 2. A candle maker or vendor of nautical supplies; 3. A collector of stamps; 4. One who makes carts and wagons; 5. A beekeeper; 6. One who embroiders; 7. A worker on a drilling rig; 8. Wine expert; 9. A textile dealer; 10. One who makes bells or metal castings; 11. A butcher specializing in pork; 12. A dealer of stocks and shares; 13. One who works leather; 14. One who makes archery bows; 15. A freelance journalist; 16. A bell ringer; 17. One who makes barrels; 18. A butterfly and moth collector; 19. Tree surgeon; 20. A coin collector; 21. One who analyzes minerals and ores; 22. A collector of cigarette cards; 23. A peddler of cheap books and pamphlets; 24. One who distributes charity.

BIG FOUR TROPHIES (from page 24)
Commissioner's Trophy World Series Winner
Vince Lombardi Trophy Super Bowl Winner
Stanley Cup NHL Champion
Larry O'Brien Trophy NBA Finals Winner

LED ZEPPELIN (from page 26)
John Bonham* .... Drums
Jimmy Page .... Guitar
Robert Plant .... Vocals
John Paul Jones .... Bass Guitar, Keyboards

SPORTS GOVERNING BODIES I (from page 30)
1. Marylebone Cricket Club; 2. Fédération Internationale de Football Association; 3. Professional Golfers' Association; 4. World Boxing Organization; 5. National Hockey League; 6. Test and County Cricket Board; 7. Fédération Internationale de l'Automobile; 8. International Association of Athletics Federations; 9. World Boxing Association; 10. Confederation of North, Central American and Caribbean Association Football; 11. British Amateur Gymnastics Association; 12. All England Lawn Tennis Club; 13. National Basketball Association; 14. International Ice Hockey Federation; 15. Fédération Internationale de Ski; 16. International Tennis Federation; 17. Fédération Internationale de Motocyclisme; 18. British Darts Organisation; 19. Fédération Internationale de Basketball Amateur; 20. International Table Tennis Federation; 21. World Professional Billiards and Snooker Association; 22 World Water Skiing Union; 23. Fédération Internationale de Gymnastique; 24. World Karate Federation.

---

* Led Zeppelin disbanded following the death of Bonham in 1980.

FACES OF MOUNT RUSHMORE (from page 33)

George Washington / Thomas Jefferson
Abraham Lincoln / Theodore Roosevelt

POSITIONS IN A BASKETBALL TEAM (from page 35)

Point Guard / Shooting Guard
Centre
Small Forward / Power Forward

HOLY PLACES (from page 37)

1. Christianity; 2. Catholicism; 3. Islam*; 4. Christianity; 5. Anglicanism; 6. Catholicism†; 7. Islam; 8. Mormonism (Church of Jesus Christ of Latter-Day Saints); 9. Sikhism; 10. Judaism‡; 11. Buddhism or Shinto; 12. Judaism; 13. Islam§; 14. Hinduism; 15. Eastern Orthodox¶; 16. Buddhism**; 17. Hinduism; 18. Buddhism (Tibetan); 19. Christianity; 20. Eastern Orthodox; 21. Buddhism or Taoism; 22. Eastern Orthodox; 23. Jainism; 24. Buddhism††

NOVELS BY F. SCOTT FITZGERALD (from page 40)

This Side of Paradise (1920) / *The Beautiful and Damned* (1922)
The Great Gatsby (1925) / *Tender Is the Night* (1934)
The Last Tycoon (unfinished, 1941)

OLYMPIC RINGS (from page 42)

Blue / Yellow / Black / Green / Red

BATTLES I (from page 44)

1. American Civil War (1863); 2. Second World War (1642); 3. American War of Independance (1775); 4. Second World War (1945); 5. Vietnam War (1969); 6. Texan Mexican War (1836)‡‡; 7. American War of Independence (1781); 8. Norman Conquest of Britain (1066); 9. American Civil War (1862); 10. First World War (1916); 11. American Civil War (1862); 12. Crimean War (1854); 13. American Civil War (1863); 14. American War of Independence (1777); 15. Second World War (1941–44); 16. American War of Independence (1775); 17. Hundred Years' War (1415); 18. American Civil War (1861); 19. First World War (1916); 20. Greco-Persian Wars (480

---

* Mecca is the birthplace of Muhammad and the direction Muslims must face to pray five times a day.

† Where the Virgin Mary appeared to St. Bernadette in a vision in 1858.

‡ Where Moses received the Ten Commandments from God.

§ Where Muhammad ascended into heaven in AD 621.

¶ The Seat of the Ecumenical Patriarchate of Constantinople.

** Where the Buddha reached enlightenment.

†† Where the Buddha died.

‡‡ In which Colonel Travis, Jim Bowie, Davy Crockett, and 180 other Texans were killed by Mexican troops.

B.C.)*; 21. English Civil War (1644); 22. Seven Years War (1757); 23. Wars of Alexander the Great (333 B.C.)†; 24. Hundred Years' War (1428–29).

THE A-TEAM (from page 47)

Col. John "Hannibal" Smith .... George Peppard
Lt. Templeton "Faceman" Peck .... Dirk Benedict
Sgt. Bosco "B. A." Baracus .... Mr. T
Capt. H.M. "Howling Mad" Murdock .... Dwight Schultz
Amy Amanda "Triple A" Allen .... Melinda Culea

TIME ZONES (from page 49)

Eastern Standard Time / Central Standard Time
Mountain Standard Time / Pacific Standard Time
Alaska Standard Time / Hawaii-Aleutian Standard Time

MISCELLANY VII (from page 52)

1. Fifteen; 2. The ace of spades; 3. Ronald Reagan; 4. Refraction; 5. Debra Messing; 6. Eddie "The Eagle" Edwards; 7. A piece of text that includes every letter in the alphabet‡; 8. He sold his soul to the devil; 9. Q; 10. It was the shortest on record—he died approximately one month into office; 11. Mexico City§; 12. 1888 (MDCCCLXXXVIII); 13. Spaghetti; 14. Palm reading; 15. The letters are in alphabetical order; 16. Loch Ness; 17. Ireland; 18. Mercury; 19. Either side of the Strait of Gibraltar; 20. Venezuela (Venice); 21. Drew Barrymore (in *E.T. the Extra Terrestrial*); 22. The Siegfried Line; 23. Fold a single piece of paper; 24. Nine miles.

VILLAGE PEOPLE (from page 56)

Biker / Construction Worker / Cowboy
Indian / Motorcycle Cop / Soldier

MONTY PYTHON (from page 58)

John Cleese / Eric Idle / Graham Chapman
Michael Palin / Terry Gilliam / Terry Jones

---

* Salamis is a small island in the Saronic Gulf near Athens. The battle was fought between Persian and Greek fleets numbering approximately 1,200 and 400 ships respectively and was recorded by Herodotus. The Greek Triremes were fitted with an "embolon"—a bronze pole which was effective at ramming and causing damage to opposing ships. The decisive factor in the Greek victory was probably the agility of the smaller Greek fleet, fighting in a small and enclosed expanse of water against a larger, less manoeuvrable Persian force.
† In which Alexander defeated Darius III leading to the fall of the Persian Empire. The battle altered the course of Asian and European history.
‡ For example "Cozy sphinx waves quart jug of bad milk," "Brick quiz whangs jumpy veldt fox," "Woven silk pyjamas exchanged for blue quartz," "The quick brown fox jumps over the lazy dog."
§ September 14, 1847, during the Mexican War.

FOREIGN WORDS AND PHRASES I (from page 62)

1. Déjà vu; 2. Kindergarten; 3. Zero; 4. Robot; 5. Mogul; 6. Intelligentsia; 7. Tariff; 8. Angst; 9. Almanac; 10. Dolce vita; 11. Bungalow; 12. Tycoon; 13. Guru; 14. Vis-à-vis; 15. Verboten; 16. Kowtow; 17. Bonanza; 18. Doppelgänger; 19. Aficionado; 20. Husting; 21. Kitsch; 22. Hazard; 23. Tundra; 24. Checkmate.

HARRY POTTER NOVELS (from page 65)

DWARFS (from page 68)

Bashful / Doc / Dopey / Grumpy / Happy / Sleepy / Sneezy

HOBBIES AND PROFESSIONS II (from page 70)

1. Person who shapes hedges; 2. Person who sells sewing-related articles; 3. Wine merchant; 4. Person who sells stockings; 5. Coffee purveyor*; 6. Amateur radio operator; 7. Person who sells cloths and fabrics; 8. Member of royal household responsible for horses; 9. Person who makes or sells hats; 10. Mechanic; 11. Teacher; 12. Dealer in rare books; 13. Army officer below the rank of captain; 14. Person who makes arrows; 15. Person who shoes horses; 16. Shorthand typist; 17. Horse handler; 18. Clock collector; 19. Fortune teller who uses cards; 20. Tightrope walker; 21. Matchbox collector; 22. Striptease artist; 23. Street seller of fruit and vegetables; 24. Magician skilled in sleight of hand.

CATHOLIC CHURCH HIERARCHY (from page 73)

Pope / Cardinal / Archbishop / Bishop
Monsignor[†] / Priest / Deacon

---

* Coffee is thought to have been discovered in Ethiopia in A.D. 950, from where it quickly became popular throughout the Arab world (especially as alcohol is forbidden to Muslims). European traders brought it back in the seventeenth century and London coffee houses came into being, quickly establishing themselves as places to exchange news and gossip and conduct business. The Arab monopoly on coffee was broken when the Dutch smuggled coffee seedlings from the Arab port of Mocha to the East Indies. Thirty years later, in 1723, coffee was introduced to the New World. Coffee (in terms of dollar value) is now the second most important legally traded commodity after oil, and is notable for being the primary export of many of the world's developing countries. Some 25 million farmers around the world are dependent on income from coffee.

† Monsignor is an honorary title that may be conferred upon a priest by the Pope at the request of a bishop.

COUNTRIES IN CENTRAL AMERICA (from page 76)
Belize / Costa Rica / El Salvador / Guatemala
Honduras / Nicaragua / Panama

LINKED MISCELLANY VI (from page 78)
1. Cleveland; 2. Calvin Klein; 3. *The Bridges of Madison County*; 4. *Garfield*;
5. Johnson & Johnson; 6. *Ulysses*; 7. *The Mary Tyler Moore Show*; 8. Wilson Pickett;
9. Marilyn Monroe; 10. Abraham.

The link is U.S. presidents*

TAXONOMY OF LIVING THINGS† (from page 81)
Kingdom
Phylum (animals) or Division (plants or fungi)
Class
Order
Family
Genus
Species

PRESIDENTS WHO DIED IN OFFICE (from page 83)
William Harrison / Zachary Taylor / Abraham Lincoln
James Garfield / William McKinley / Warren Harding
Franklin D. Roosevelt / John F. Kennedy

QUOTATIONS FROM POPULAR FILMS I (from page 85)
1. *Star Wars*; 2. *The Silence of the Lambs*; 3. *Gladiator*; 4. *Back to the Future*; 5. *The Hunt for Red October*; 6. *Top Gun*; 7. *Some Like It Hot*; 8. *Forrest Gump*; 9. *The Wizard of Oz*; 10. *Shrek*; 11. *A Fish Called Wanda*; 12. *The Terminator*; 13. *The Italian Job*; 14. *Marathon Man*; 15. *The Great Escape*; 16. *Apollo 13*; 17. *Pirates of the Caribbean: The Curse of the Black Pearl*; 18. *Fight Club*; 19. *Toy Story*; 20. *My*

---

* Grover Cleveland, Calvin Coolidge, James Madison, James A. Garfield, Andrew Johnson, Ulysses S. Grant, John Tyler, Woodrow Wilson, James Monroe, and Abraham Lincoln.

† For example, Homo sapiens is classified as Kingdom: Animalia, Phylum: Chordata, Class: Mammalia, Order: Primates, Family: Hominidae, Genus: Homo, Species: Homo sapiens. Note that sub-classifications are used in order to help classify diverse organisms such as insects. This taxonomy is known as the Six-kingdom System with the top level consisting of Protista, Archaebacteria, Eubacteria, Fungi, Plantae, and Animalia. A recent taxonomy has added an eighth level, Domain, to the top of the hierarchy. The Three-domain System was introduced by Carl Woese, a microbiologist, in 1990 and re-drew taxonomy based on genetic relationships rather than physical characteristics. Under Woese's system the top level consists of the domains of Bacteria, Archaea, and Eucarya, the last of which contains plants, animals, and fungi.

Big Fat Greek Wedding; 21. *The Jerk*; 22. *My Fair Lady*; 23. *American Beauty*; 24. *Midnight Cowboy*.

COUNTRIES ENDING WITH " ~ LAND"* (from page 89)

Finland / Iceland / Ireland / Netherlands / New Zealand
Poland / Swaziland / Switzerland / Thailand

MOST OSCAR-NOMINATED ACTORS (from page 95; as at the time of publishing)

Jack Nicholson	12 nominations (3 wins)
Laurence Olivier	10 (1)
Spencer Tracy	9 (2)
Paul Newman	9 (1)
Marlon Brando	8 (2)
Jack Lemmon	8 (2)
Al Pacino	8 (1)
Peter O'Toole	8 (0)
Dustin Hoffman	7 (2)
Richard Burton	7 (0)

ARTISTS (from page 97)

1. Leonardo da Vinci; 2. Vincent Van Gogh; 3. John Constable; 4. Michelangelo; 5. Claude Monet; 6. Alessandro Botticelli; 7. Pablo Picasso; 8. Andy Warhol; 9. Edvard Munch[†]; 10. Salvador Dalí; 11. J. M. W. Turner; 12. Jan Vermeer; 13. Èdouard Manet; 14. Pierre-Auguste Renoir; 15. Titian; 16. Roy Lichtenstein; 17. Henri Matisse; 18. Gustav Klimt; 19. Edgar Degas; 20. Jan van Eyck[‡];

---

* Examples of non-sovereign countries with this name ending are England and Scotland (UK) and Greenland (Denmark).

† The painting was inspired by an experience that Munch described in his diary on January 22, 1892: "I was walking along the road with two friends. The sun was setting. I felt a breath of melancholy. Suddenly the sky became blood-red. I stopped, and leant against the railing, deathly tired. I looked out across the flaming clouds that hung like blood and a sword over the blue-black fjord and town. My friends walked on but I stood there, trembling with fear. I sensed a great, infinite scream pass through nature."

‡ The painting celebrates the marriage of Giovanni Arnolfini and Giovanna Cenami, a wealthy Italian couple who had settled in Bruges. It is renowned, not only for the skill with which van Eyck employed the very latest painting techniques (he was the leading exponent of painting with oils), but also for the symbolism with which the painting is packed. Fertility and childbirth are alluded to by the presence of the bed behind the couple and by Giovanna's dress and posture which give the appearance that she is pregnant (she was not). Discarded shoes were a symbol for religious ceremony, an indication that the painting was perhaps meant to be a visual wedding certificate.

21. Rembrandt; 22. Hans Holbein*; 23. Hieronymus Bosch; 24. Pieter Bruegel the Elder.

EVENTS IN THE DECATHLON (from page 100)

100 m / Long jump / Shot put / High jump / 400 m
110 m hurdles / Discus / Pole vault / Javelin / 1,500 m

STATES NAMED AFTER PEOPLE (from page 102)

Georgia	King George II of England
Hawaii	Hawaiiloa†
Louisiana	King Louis XIV of France
Maryland	Queen Henrietta Maria, wife of King Charles I of England
North Carolina	King Charles I of England
Pennsylvania	Admiral William Penn
South Carolina	King Charles I of England
Virginia	Elizabeth I of England
Washington	George Washington
West Virginia	Elizabeth I of England

MISCELLANY XIV (from page 104)

1. Light Emitting Diode; 2. Florida; 3. Queen Victoria; 4. 41—Cleveland counted twice; 5. Sumo wrestling; 6. Kaleidoscope; 7. Tamagotchi; 8. Australia; 9. Tarzan; 10. Paul Revere; 11. Billiard Balls; 12. Cleopatra's Needle; 13. Fingers; 14. Dylan Thomas; 15. It was non-speaking; 16. Three; 17. Lighning; 18. Libya (green); 19. Stealth Bomber; 20. I/eye, you/ewe; 21. The War of Jenkins' Ear; 22. Glenn Miller‡; 23. Bedlam; 24. The palm.

CHARACTERS IN *M*A*S*H* (from page 106)

Hawkeye Pierce	Alan Alda
Trapper John McIntyre	Wayne Rogers
B. J. Hunnicut	Mike Farrell
Henry Blake	McLean Stevenson
Sherman T. Potter	Harry Morgan
Frank Burns	Larry Linville
Margaret "Hot Lips" Houlihan	Loretta Swit
Charles Winchester	David Ogden Stiers
Radar O'Reilly	Gary Burghoff

---

* Holbein was artist to the court of Henry VIII but fell out of favor with the King over a portrait of Anne of Cleves. Henry had agreed to marry Anne (his fourth wife) on the basis of Holbein's portrait which he had liked, but was rather disappointed when he met Anne for the first time on their wedding day; he likened her to a "fat Flanders mare."

† Who, according to Hawaiian legend, discovered and colonised the islands.

‡ "Chattanooga Choo Choo" in 1941.

Father Mulcahy	William Christopher
Maxwell Klinger	Jamie Farr

GREEK GODS (from page 109)
Zeus / Hera / Poseidon / Ares / Hermes / Hephaestus
Aphrodite / Athena / Apollo / Artemis / Demeter / Hades

MISCELLANY XV (From page 110)
1. Texas; 2. Acting; 3. "The Star Spangled Banner"*; 4. High Street; 5. The CIA; 6. *Gone With the Wind*; 7. A fan's right to keep a baseball hit into the stands; 8. Sioux[†]; 9. Gerald Ford; 10. Elton John; 11. Elvis has left the building[‡]; 12. Jet fighters (MiG); 13. Tobacco; 14. Asthma and isthmus; 15. National Association of Securities Dealers Automated Quotations; 16. Graceland; 17. Lake Erie and Lake Ontario; 18. One (the ship floats on the tide); 19. Ridley Scott; 20. S; 21. The orchid; 22. George Bernard Shaw[§]; 23. Sex test; 24. Fill the three-gallon jug and pour this into the five-gallon jug. Fill the three-gallon jug again and pour into the five-gallon jug, leaving one gallon of water remaining in the three-gallon jug. Empty the five-gallon jug and then pour the one gallon of water from the three-gallon jug into the five-gallon jug. Finally, fill the three-gallon jug and empty this into the five-gallon jug, giving four gallons.

SATURDAY NIGHT LIVE "5 TIMERS" (from page 113, as at time of publishing)
Steve Martin	14 appearances as host
Alec Baldwin	13
John Goodman	12
Buck Henry	10
Chevy Chase	9
Tom Hanks	8
Elliott Gould	6
Danny DeVito	6
Christopher Walken	6
Candice Bergen	5
Bill Murray	5
Drew Barrymore	5

COUNTRIES WITH NAMES CONTAINING ADJECTIVES (from page 116)
Central African Republic / Dominican Republic / East Timor

---

* Originally a poem by Francis Scott Key.
† They were members of the Lakota, the westernmost of the Sioux tribes.
‡ "Ladies and gentlemen, Elvis has left the building. Thank you and good night."
§ Shaw was awarded the Nobel Prize in Literature in 1925, and the Oscar for Writing Adapted Screenplay in 1938 for the same work, *Pygmalion*. Note that Al Gore shared the Nobel Peace Prize in 2007 and wrote and presented the Oscar-winning documentary, *An Inconvenient Truth*.

Equatorial Guinea / New Zealand / North Korea
Papua New Guinea / South Africa / South Korea
United Arab Emirates / United Kingdom
United States of America / Western Sahara

IMPERIAL UNITS (from page 119)

1. Foot; 2. Yard; 3. Pound; 4. Inch; 5. Pint; 6. Stone; 7. Mile; 8. Gallon; 9. Ton;
10. Fluid ounce; 11. Acre; 12. Furlong; 13. Ounce; 14. Hand; 15. Fathom; 16.
Hundredweight; 17. League; 18. Chain; 19. Quart; 20. Gill; 21. Nautical mile; 22.
Hide; 23. Cubit; 24. Bushel.

BRITISH NOBILITY (from page 122)

King / Queen / Prince / Princess
Marquess / Marchioness / Duke / Duchess
Earl / Countess / Viscount / Viscountess
Baron / Baroness

CAREER GRAND SLAMS (from page 124, as at time of publishing)

Fred Perry
Don Budge (1938)
Rod Laver (1962, 1969)
Roy Emerson
Andre Agassi
Maureen Connolly (1953)
Doris Hart
Shirley Fry
Margaret Court (1970)
Billie Jean King
Chris Evert
Martina Navratilova [Non-Cal 83/83]
Steffi Graf (1988*) [Non-Cal 93/94]
Serena Williams [Non-Cal 02/03]

Dates in brackets indicate players who completed the feat in a calendar year
[Non-Cal] indicates all four titles held simultaneously but not in the same calendar year

METRIC UNITS (from page 128)

1. Temperature; 2. Sound intensity; 3. Electric current; 4. Energy; 5. Absolute
temperature; 6. Frequency; 7. Power; 8. Pressure; 9. Resistance; 10. Force; 11.
Potential difference; 12. Luminous intensity; 13. Electric charge; 14. Amount of
substance; 15. Angle within a plane; 16. Radioactivity; 17. Luminance; 18. Angle
within a solid; 19. Magnetic flux density; 20. Electrical capacitance; 21. Radiation
exposure; 22. Inductance; 23. Magnetic flux; 24. Electrical conductance.

---

* Steffi Graf also won the Olympic singles title in 1988.

NOVELS BY THOMAS HARDY (from page 131)

^{SS} indicates short stories

CHART-TOPPING SINGLES BY ELVIS PRESLEY (from page 133; as at time of publishing)

---

* Hardy became disillusioned with literature after the negative reaction he received from the publication of *Jude the Obscure* (and earlier from *Tess of the d'Urbervilles*), which outraged Victorian morality. From 1897 he wrote only poetry.

FIRST LINES OF POP SONGS IV (from page 136)

1. "The House of the Rising Sun" (The Animals); 2. "Get Up (I Feel Like Being) A Sex Machine" (James Brown); 3. "Baby One More Time" (Britney Spears); 4. "Candle in the Wind" (Elton John); 5. "Love Shack" (B52s); 6. "Hotel California" (The Eagles); 7. "Justify My Love" (Madonna); 8. "Hay Ya!" (Outkast); 9. "Hard to Handle" (Otis Redding); 10. "Born to Be Wild" (Steppenwolf); 11. "Sledgehammer"*(Peter Gabriel); 12. "The Boys of Summer" (Don Henley); 13. "Every Little Thing She Does Is Magic" (The Police); 14. "You Can't Hurry Love" (The Supremes); 15. "Thank You" (Dido) or "Stan" (Eminem); 16. "End of the Road" (Boyz II Men); 17. "California Girls" (The Beach Boys); 18. "Mickey"† (Toni Basil); 19. "Pretty Vacant" (The Sex Pistols); 20. "Where the Streets Have No Name" (U2); 21. "California Love" (2Pac feat. Dr. Dre); 22. "Hung Up" (Madonna); 23. "Times They Are A-Changing" (Bob Dylan); 24. "Lust for Life"‡ (Iggy Pop).

FREQUENTLY OCCURRING WORDS (from page 139)

the / of / and / to / a / in / is / that / was / it
for / on / with / he / be / I / by / as / at / you

CHARACTERS IN *DALLAS* (from page 143)

Miss Ellie	Barbara Bel Geddes 1978-84, 1985-1990 / Donna Reed	1984-1985
Jock Ewing	Jim Davis	1978-1981
Bobby Ewing	Patrick Duffy	1978-1985, 1986-1991
J. R. Ewing	Larry Hagman	
Pamela Ewing	Victoria Principal	1978-1987
Sue Ellen Ewing	Linda Gray	1978-1989
Lucy Ewing	Charlene Tilton	1978-1985, 1988-1990
Cliff Barnes	Ken Kercheval	
Ray Krebbs	Steve Kanaly	1978-1988
Donna Krebbs	Susan Howard	1979-1987
Clayton Farlow	Howard Keel	1981-1991
Jenna Wade	Priscilla Beaulieu Presley	1983-1988
Jack Ewing	Dack Rambo	1985-1987
April Stevens	Sheree J. Wilson	1986-1991
Stephanie Rogers	Lesley-Anne Down	1990
Michelle Stevens	Kimberly Foster	1989-1991
Carter McKay	George Kennedy	1988-1991
James Beaumont	Sasha Mitchell	1989-1991

---

* The innovative Claymation video for "Sledgehammer" revived Gabriel's career and remains the most aired video on MTV.

† "Mickey" became a hit in the U.S. and worldwide after first entering the charts in the UK. Toni Basil's real name is Antonia Basilotta.

‡ The song, whose lyrics celebrate giving up alcohol, was the theme to *Trainspotting*, a film about heroin addiction.

Cally Harper Ewing .... Cathy Podewell 1988-1991
Liz Adams .... Barbara Stock 1990-1991

INNOVATIONS II (from page 144)

1. Television; 2. Airship; 3. Helicopter; 4. Jumbo jet*; 5. Pasteurization; 6. Wheel;
7. Penicillin; 8. Revolver; 9. Mechanical lift; 10. Centigrade thermometer; 11. Motor
car (petrol engine); 12. Aqualung; 13. World Wide Web (HTTP); 14. Computer
(difference engine); 15. Phonograph[†](or gramophone); 16. Vaccination; 17. Food
processor; 18. Catseye (reflective road marker); 19. Photographic film; 20. Paper; 21.
Bicycle; 22. Submarine; 23. Washing machine; 24. Spreadsheet.[‡]

TAROT CARDS (from page 148)

0 Fool / I Magician / II High Priestess / III Empress / IV Emperor
V Hierophant / VI Lovers / VII Chariot / VIII Justice / IX Hermit
X Wheel of Fortune / XI Fortitude / XII Hanged Man / XIII Death
XIV Temperance / XV Devil / XVI Tower / XVII Star / XVIII Moon
XIX Sun / XX Judgement / XXI World

LANGUAGES OF THE EUROPEAN UNION (from page 150; as at the time of publishing)

Bulgarian / Czech / Danish / Dutch / English / Estonian / Finnish
French / German / Greek / Hungarian / Italian / Irish / Latvian
Lithuanian / Maltese / Polish / Portuguese / Romanian / Slovak
Slovenian / Spanish / Swedish

OFFICER RANKS IN THE U.S. MILITARY (from page 151)

Five Star Ranks[§]:
General of the Army / Fleet Admiral / General of the Air Force

---

* The Boeing 747 was developed after intense lobbying of Boeing by Pan Am, who
wanted a jet airliner twice the size of the popular Boeing 707. Unsure of the
passenger market for such a large aircraft, the company hedged their bets and
designed the 747 so that it could be adapted into a freighter. The cockpit was raised
to the top of the aircraft so that a payload door could be added to the nose cone,
creating the recognisable bulge. The production schedule for the new aircraft was so
ambitious that the engineers who worked on it became known as "The Incredibles."
Having almost bankrupted the company, the 747 was a massive success and led to
Boeing virtually monopolising the passenger aircraft market for the next thirty years.
† Edison famously recorded the nursery rhyme "Mary Had a Little Lamb" on his
new invention. Edison became known as "The Wizard of Menlo Park" and was one
of the most prolific inventors in history, eventually holding 1,097 U.S. patents in his
name.
‡ They created VisiCalc, the first spreadsheet software.
§ Five star ranks are held only in exceptional situations such as periods of war. Only
ten appointments have been made to this rank in the U.S. military.

U.S. Army / U.S.A.F. rank	U.S. Navy rank
General	Admiral
Lieutenant General	Vice Admiral
Major General	Rear Admiral (upper half)
Brigadier General	Rear Admiral (lower half)
Colonel	Captain
Lieutenant Colonel	Commander
Major	Lieutenant Commander
Captain	Lieutenant
First Lieutenant	Lieutenant, Junior Grade
Second Lieutenant	Ensign

UNTIMELY DEATHS (from page 153)

1. Elvis Presley; 2. Sid Vicious; 3. John Lennon; 4. Marilyn Monroe; 5. Glenn Miller; 6. Michael Hutchence; 7. Grace Kelly; 8. James Dean; 9. Vincent Van Gogh*; 10. Jimi Hendrix; 11. Kurt Cobain; 12. Tupac Shakur; 13. Judy Garland; 14 Karen Carpenter; 15. Marvin Gaye; 16. Kirsty MacColl; 17. Sylvia Plath; 18. Gianni Versace†; 19. Sonny Bono; 20. Notorious BIG‡; 21. Virginia Woolf; 22. River Pheonix; 23. Heath Ledger; 24. Janis Joplin.

POPULOUS COUNTRIES (from page 161; as at the time of publishing)

China	1,317
India	1,125
United States of America	301
Indonesia	234
Brazil	186
Pakistan	166
Bangladesh	145
Russia	142
Nigeria	134
Japan	127
Mexico	110
Philippines	91
Vietnam	85
Germany	82
Egypt	80
Ethiopia	77
Turkey	73

* Van Gogh died two days after shooting himself. His last words were: "The sadness will last forever."

† Versace was murdered by Andrew Cunanan, who killed four other people during a three-month killing spree in 1997 before committing suicide aboard a Miami yacht.

‡ The deaths of Notorious BIG and Tupac Shakur may possibly be linked, although nobody has ever been convicted of either crime.

Figures represent millions of people and are approximate.

TRACK-AND-FIELD-EVENTS (from page 164)

100 m / 200 m / 400 m / 800 m / 1,500 m / 5,000 m / 10,000 m
Marathon / 100 m hurdles ^{W} / 110 m hurdles ^{M} / 400 m hurdles
Steeplechase ^{M} / High jump / Long jump / Pole vault
Triple jump / Shot / Discus / Hammer / Javelin
Decathlon ^{M} / Heptathlon ^{W} / 20km walk
50 km walk ^{M} / 4 × 100m relay / 4 × 400m relay
^{M} indicates male-only events ^{W} indicates female-only events

MISCELLANY XXII (from page 167)

1. Crimean War; 2. The White House; 3. Ronnie Wood; 4. "You do not talk about Fight Club"; 5. A Russian Big Mac; 6. *A Clockwork Orange*; 7. Cindy; 8. The Khyber Pass; 9. They feature ghosts; 10. Charles Yeager; 11. Pole vault; 12. The first televised presidential debate[*]; 13. The Panama[†] Canal; 14. Nine days; 15. Maine; 16. *Star Trek*[‡]; 17. Al Capone; 18. Baroque; 19. The Sargasso Sea; 20. Twelve; 21. Angostura bitters; 22. Carbon dioxide and water; 23. The Ministry of Truth; 24. A few seconds after twelve o'clock.[§]

---

[*] Between Richard Nixon and John F. Kennedy. Kennedy was considered to have won the debate largely because he was better prepared for the medium of television. Nixon was perceived unfavorably largely because his poor make-up led him to perspire under the lights. Those who listened to the debate on the radio considered Nixon to have performed the better.

[†] The Panama Canal Authority decides the tolls for each use of the canal based on vessel type, size, and cargo, although smaller vessels are charged based on length only. The toll of $249,165 levied for the container ship *Maersk Dellys* in May 2006 is at the time of writing the highest toll ever levied for using the Panama Canal. Richard Halliburton swam the canal in 1928 and was charged a toll of 36 cents.

[‡] Captain Kirk (William Shatner) and Lieutenant Uhura (Nichelle Nichols) shared a kiss in the 1968 episode "Plato's Stepchildren," albeit under the influence of a controlling alien mind.

[§] Martin hears the last chime of twelve o'clock as he arrives home.

NHL TEAMS (from page 171; as at time of publishing)

Eastern Conference

New Jersey Devils[A] / New York Islanders[A] / New York Rangers[A]
Philadelphia Flyers[A] / Pittsburgh Penguins[A] / Boston Bruins[NE]
Buffalo Sabres[NE] / Montreal Canadiens[NE] / Ottawa Senators[NE]
Toronto Maple Leafs[NE] / Atlanta Thrashers[SE] / Carolina Hurricanes[SE]
Florida Panthers[SE] / Tampa Bay Lightning[SE] / Washington Capitals[SE]

Western Conference:

Chicago Blackhawks[C] / Columbus Blue Jackets[C] / Detroit Red Wings[C]
Nashville Predators[C] / St. Louis Blues[C] / Calgary Flames[NW]
Colorado Avalanche[NW] / Edmonton Oilers[NW] / Minnesota Wild[NW]
Vancouver Canucks[NW] / Anaheim Ducks[P] / Dallas Stars[P]
Los Angeles Kings[P] / Phoenix Coyotes[P] / San Jose Sharks[P]

[A] Atlantic   [NE] Northeast   [SE] Southeast   [C] Central   [NW] Northwest   [P] Pacific

NFL TEAMS	**NFL STADIUMS** (from page 173)
Arizona Cardinals [NFC West]	University of Phoenix Stadium
Atlanta Falcons [NFC South]	Georgia Dome
Baltimore Ravens [AFC North]	M&T Bank Stadium
Buffalo Bills [AFC East]	(seven games per season) Ralph Wilson Stadium
	(1 game per season) Rogers Centre*
Carolina Panthers [NFC South]	Bank of America Stadium
Chicago Bears [NFC North]	Soldier Field
Cincinnati Bengals [AFC North]	Paul Brown Stadium
Cleveland Browns [AFC North]	Cleveland Browns Stadium
Dallas Cowboys [NFC East]	Texas Stadium[†]
Denver Broncos [AFC West]	Invesco Field at Mile High
Detroit Lions [NFC North]	Ford Field
Green Bay Packers [NFC North]	Lambeau Field
Houston Texans [AFC South]	Reliant Stadium
Indianapolis Colts [AFC South]	Lucas Oil Stadium
Jacksonville Jaguars [AFC South]	Jacksonville Municipal Stadium
Kansas City Chiefs [AFC West]	Arrowhead Stadium
Miami Dolphins [AFC East]	Dolphin Stadium
Minnesota Vikings [NFC North]	Hubert H. Humphrey Metrodome[‡]
New England Patriots [AFC East]	Gillette Stadium
New Orleans Saints [NFC South]	Louisiana Superdome
New York Giants [NFC East]	Giants Stadium[§]
New York Jets [AFC East]	Giants Stadium

* Toronto, Canada.

† Due to be replaced by New Cowboys Stadium in Arlington, Texas, in 2009.

‡ Probably to be replaced by Vikings Stadium in or around 2012.

§ To be replaced in 2010 by New Meadowlands Stadium, which will be shared with the NY Jets.

Oakland Raiders ^{AFC West} .... McAfee Coliseum
Philadelphia Eagles ^{NFC East} .... Lincoln Financial Field
Pittsburgh Steelers ^{AFC North} .... Heinz Field
San Diego Chargers ^{AFC West} .... Qualcomm Stadium
San Francisco 49ers ^{NFC West} .... Monster Park
Seattle Seahawks ^{NFC West} .... Qwest Field
St. Louis Rams ^{NFC West} .... Edward Jones Dome
Tampa Bay Buccaneers ^{NFC South} .... Raymond James Stadium
Tennessee Titans ^{AFC South} .... LP Field
Washington Redskins ^{NFC East} .... FedExField

FIRST LINES OF POP SONGS V (from page 175)

1. "Son of a Preacher Man" (Dusty Springfield); 2. "(Sittin' on) the Dock of the
Bay" (Otis Redding); 3. "Rappers Delight (Sugarhill Gang); 4. "Lola" (The Kinks);
5. "Torn" (Natalie Imbruglia); 6. "Tainted Love" (Soft Cell); 7. "I Feel Love
(Donna Summer); 8. "Push It" (Salt-N-Pepa); 9. "Addicted to Love" (Robert
Palmer); 10. "Like a Virgin" (Madonna); 11. "Yellow" (Coldplay); 12. "Heart of
Glass" (Blondie); 13. "Take Me Out" (Franz Ferdinand); 14. "Dreamlover" (Mariah
Carey); 15. "The Real Slim Shady" (Eminem); 16. "Light My Fire" (The Doors);
17. "Aquarius (Let the Sun Shine In)" (Fifth Dimension); 18. "Faith" (George
Michael); 19. "Born to Run" (Bruce Springsteen); 20. "That Don't Impress Me
Much" (Shania Twain); 21. "I Want to Hold Your Hand" (The Beatles); 22. "The
Tracks of My Tears" (The Miracles); 23. "Israelites" (Desmond Dekker and the
Aces); 24. "Nuthin' But a 'G' Thang" (Dr. Dre).

FIRST SPOUSES (from page 178; as at time of publishing)

Martha Washington .... wife of George Washington
Abigail Adams .... wife of John Adams
Dolley Madison .... wife of James Madison
Elizabeth Monroe .... wife of James Monroe
Louisa Adams .... wife of John Quincy Adams
Anna Harrison .... wife of William Henry Harrison
Letitia Tyler .... first wife of John Tyler
Julia Tyler .... second wife of John Tyler
Sarah Polk .... wife of James K. Polk
Margaret Taylor .... wife of Zachary Taylor
Abigail Fillmore .... wife of Millard Fillmore
Jane Pierce .... wife of Franklin Pierce
Mary Lincoln .... wife of Abraham Lincoln
Eliza Johnson .... wife of Andrew Johnson
Julia Grant .... wife of Ulysses S. Grant
Lucy Hayes .... wife of Rutherford B. Hayes
Lucretia Garfield .... wife of James A. Garfield
Frances Cleveland Preston .... wife of Grover Cleveland
Caroline Harrison .... wife of Benjamin Harrison

Ida McKinley	wife of William McKinley
Edith Roosevelt	wife of Theodore Roosevelt
Helen Taft	wife of William H. Taft
Ellen Wilson	first wife of Woodrow Wilson
Edith Wilson	second wife of Woodrow Wilson
Florence Harding	wife of Warren G. Harding
Grace Coolidge	wife of Calvin Coolidge
Lou Hoover	wife of Herbert C. Hoover
Eleanor Roosevelt	wife of Franklin D. Roosevelt
Bess Truman	wife of Harry S. Truman
Mamie Eisenhower	wife of Dwight D. Eisenhower
Jacqueline Kennedy Onassis	wife of John F. Kennedy
Claudia "Lady Bird" Johnson	wife of Lyndon B. Johnson
Thelma "Pat" Nixon	wife of Richard M. Nixon
Betty Ford	wife of Gerald Ford
Rosalynn Carter	wife of Jimmy Carter
Nancy Reagan	wife of Ronald Reagan
Barbara Bush	wife of George H. W. Bush
Hillary Clinton	wife of Bill Clinton
Laura Bush	wife of George W. Bush

FIRST LADIES (from page 187; as at time of publishing)

The thirty-nine first spouses above plus:

Martha Jefferson Randolph	daughter of Thomas Jefferson
Emily Donelson	niece of Andrew Jackson
Sarah Yorke Jackson	daughter-in-law of Andrew Jackson
Angelica Singleton Van Buren	daughter-in-law of Martin Van Buren
Jane Irwin Harrison	daughter-in-law of William Henry Harrison
Priscilla Cooper Tyler	daughter-in-law of John Tyler
Harriet Lane	niece of James Buchanan
Mary Arthur McElroy	sister of Chester A. Arthur
Rose Cleveland	sister of Grover Cleveland
Mary Harrison McKee	daughter of Benjamin Harrison

MASTERS CHAMPIONS (from page 184; as at time of publishing)

Jack Nicklaus (6)	1963, 1965, 1966, 1972, 1975, 1986
Arnold Palmer (4)	1958, 1960, 1962, 1964
Tiger Woods (4)	1997, 2001, 2002, 2005
Jimmy Demaret (3)	1940, 1947, 1950
Nick Faldo (3)	1989, 1990, 1996
Gary Player (3)	1961, 1974, 1978
Sam Snead (3)	1949, 1952, 1954
Seve Ballesteros (2)	1980, 1983
Ben Crenshaw (2)	1984, 1995
Ben Hogan (2)	1951, 1953

Bernhard Langer (2)	1985, 1993
Phil Mickelson (2)	2004, 2006
Byron Nelson (2)	1937, 1942
José María Olazábal (2)	1994, 1999
Horton Smith (2)	1934, 1936
Tom Watson (2)	1977, 1981
Tommy Aaron	1973
George Archer	1969
Gay Brewer	1967
Jack Burke Jr.	1956
Billy Casper	1970
Charles Coody	1971
Fred Couples	1992
Raymond Floyd	1976
Doug Ford	1957
Bob Goalby	1968
Ralph Guldahl	1939
Claude Harmon	1948
Trevor Immelman	2008
Zach Johnson	2007
Herman Keiser	1946
Sandy Lyle	1988
Cary Middlecoff	1955
Larry Mize	1987
Mark O'Meara	1998
Henry Picard	1938
Gene Sarazen	1935
Vijay Singh	2000
Craig Stadler	1982
Art Wall Jr.	1959
Mike Weir	2003
Craig Wood	1941
Ian Woosnam	1991
Fuzzy Zoeller	1979

LATIN PHRASES II (from page 184)

1. Post meridiem (p.m.); 2. Et cetera (etc.); 3. Post mortem; 4. Persona non grata; 5. Vice versa; 6. Per capita; 7. Modus operandi (MO); 8. Nota bene (NB); 9. Alter ego; 10. Compos mentis; 11. Ceteris paribus; 12. Versus (vs.); 13. Pro tempore (p.t.); 14. Curriculum vitae (c.v.); 15. In loco parentis; 16. Habeas corpus*;

---

* The Habeas Corpus Act was introduced by Charles II in 1679 to prevent false arrest or false imprisonment; it demands that a prisoner be brought before a judge and that evidence be presented justifying why he or she has been detained. Prior to this, prisoners could be held indefinitely without charge.

17. Mea culpa; 18. Sub poena; 19. A priori; 20. Non sequitur (non seq.); 21. Deus ex machina*; 22. Ipso facto; 23. Infra dignitatem (infra dig.); 24. Inter alia.

U.S.A. FOR AFRICA (from page 186)

Dan Aykroyd / Harry Belafonte / Lindsey Buckingham [FM]
Kim Carnes / Ray Charles / Mario Cipollina[HL&N] / Johnny Colla
Bob Dylan / Sheila E. / Bob Geldof / Bill Gibson[HL&N]
Daryl Hall / John Oates / Sean Hopper [HL&N] / James Ingram
Jermaine Jackson / Jackie Jackson / LaToya Jackson
Marlon Jackson / Michael Jackson / Randy Jackson / Tito Jackson
Al Jarreau / Waylon Jennings / Billy Joel / Cyndi Lauper
Huey Lewis [HL&N] / Kenny Loggins / Bette Midler / Willie Nelson
Jeffrey Osborne / David Paich To / Steve Perry [Jo] / Anita Pointer [PS]
Ruth Pointer [PS] / Issa Pointer [PS] / Steve Porcaro [To] / Kenny Rogers
Diana Ross / Lionel Richie / Smokey Robinson / Paul Simon
Bruce Springsteen / Tina Turner / Dionne Warwick / Stevie Wonder
Groups indicated as: [FM] Fleetwood Mac [HL&N] / Huey Lewis & the News
[To] Toto [Jo] Journey [PS] The Pointer Sisters

POPULOUS AMERICAN CITIES (from page 191; as at time of publishing)

New York City (New York)	8,214,426
Los Angeles (California)	3,849,378
Chicago (Illinois)	2,833,321
Houston (Texas)	2,144,491
Phoenix (Arizona)	1,512,986
Philadelphia (Pennsylvania)	1,448,394
San Antonio (Texas)	1,296,682
San Diego (California)	1,256,951
Dallas (Texas)	1,232,940
San Jose (California)	929,936
Detroit (Michigan)	871,121
Jacksonville (Florida)	794,555
Indianapolis (Indiana)	785,597
San Francisco (California)	744,041
Columbus (Ohio)	733,203
Austin (Texas)	709,893
Memphis (Tennessee)	670,902
Fort Worth (Texas)	653,320

---

* The phrase is commonly used in the television and film industry to describe a resolution of a plot in a way that is external to the plot line and therefore not a logical consequence of it. It originates in early Greek dramas where a stage hand would often lower a character representing a god on to the stage to settle a hopeless situation. Deus ex machina resolutions of plots are generally unsatisfying as they appear artificial or contrived.

Baltimore (Maryland) 631,366
Charlotte (North Carolina) 630,478
El Paso (Texas) 609,415
Boston (Massachusetts) 590,763
Seattle (Washington) 582,454
Washington (District of Columbia) 581,530
Milwaukee (Wisconsin) 573,358
Denver (Colorado) 566,974
Louisville/Jefferson County (Kentucky) 554,496
Las Vegas (Nevada) 552,539
Nashville-Davidson (Tennessee) 552,120
Oklahoma City (Oklahoma) 537,734
Portland (Oregon) 537,081
Tucson (Arizona) 518,956
Albuquerque (New Mexico) 504,949
Atlanta (Georgia) 486,411
Long Beach (California) 472,494
Fresno (California) 466,714
Sacramento (California) 453,781
Mesa (Arizona) 447,541
Kansas City (Missouri) 447,306
Cleveland (Ohio) 444,313
Virginia Beach (Virginia) 435,619
Omaha (Nebraska) 419,545
Miami (Florida) 404,048
Oakland (California) 397,067
Tulsa (Oklahoma) 382,872
Honolulu (Hawaii) 377,357
Minneapolis (Minnesota) 372,833
Colorado Springs (Colorado) 372,437
Arlington (Texas) 367,197
Wichita (Kansas) 357,698

LINKED MISCELLANY XIV (from page 195)

1. Michelle Pfeiffer; 2. Raccoon; 3. Norwegian; 4. Pepper; 5. Lockheed SR-71
Blackbird; 6. Madonna; 7. USSR; 8. Sixty-four; 9. *Diamonds Are Forever*; 10. "The
Walrus and the Carpenter."

The link is songs by the Beatles.*

---

* "Michelle," "Rocky Raccoon," "Norwegian Wood (This Bird Has Flown)," "Sgt
Pepper's Lonely Hearts Club Band," "Blackbird," "Lady Madonna," "Back in the USSR,"
"When I'm Sixty-Four," "Lucy in the Sky with Diamonds," and "I Am the Walrus."

SEAS* (from page 205)

Adriatic Sea / Aegean Sea / Alboran Sea / Amundsen Sea
Andaman Sea / Arabian Sea / Arafura Sea / Aral Sea / Aru Sea
Balearic Sea / Bali Sea / Baltic Sea / Banda Sea / Barents Sea
Beaufort Sea / Bellingshausen Sea / Bering Sea / Bismarck Sea
Black Sea / Bo Hai Sea / Canarias Sea / Caribbean Sea
Caspian Sea / Celebes Sea / Celtic Sea / Ceram Sea / Chukchi Sea
Coral Sea / East China Sea / East Siberian Sea / Flores Sea
Greenland Sea / Halmahera Sea / Hebridian Sea / Iceland Sea
Inland Sea of Japan / Ionian Sea / Irish Sea / Java Sea / Kara Sea
Labrador Sea / Laccadive Sea / Laptev Sea / Ligurian Sea
Lincoln Sea / Mediterranean Sea / Mindanao Sea / Molucca Sea
Natuna Sea / North Greenland Sea / North Sea / Norwegian Sea
Philippine Sea / Red Sea / Ross Sea / Savu Sea / Scotia Sea
Sea of Azov / Sea of Japan / Sea of Marmara / Sea of Okhotsk
Solomon Sea / South China Sea / Sulawesi Sea / Sulu Sea
Tasman Sea / Timor Sea / Tyrrhenian Sea / Weddell Sea
White Sea / Yellow Sea

LAST LINES OF POPULAR FILMS II (from page 201)

1. *Alien*; 2. *Gone With the Wind*; 3. *The Godfather*; 4. *Four Weddings and a Funeral*; 5. *Apollo 13*; 6. *Erin Brockovich*; 7. *Who Framed Roger Rabbit*; 8. *Goodfellas*; 9. *Lord of the Rings: The Fellowship of the Ring*; 10. *Blade Runner*; 11. *A Fish Called Wanda*; 12. *It's a Wonderful Life*; 13. *Raging Bull*; 14. *My Fair Lady*; 15. *Footloose*; 16. *Rebecca*; 17. *Gandhi*; 18. *White Christmas*; 19. *Love Story*; 20. *Some Like It Hot*; 21. *The Prime of Miss Jean Brodie*; 22. *The Big Lebowski*; 23. *Die Hard*; 24. *Memento*.

---

* Note that the IHO does not currently recognize the Sargasso Sea, the Dead Sea, or the Sea of Galilee.

GAMES

"Whoever undertakes to set himself up as
a judge of Truth and Knowledge is
shipwrecked by the laughter of the gods."

Albert Einstein

NOTES ON THE GAMES

1. Settle any disputes or tied games by posing a quiz question from elsewhere in the book.

2. To avoid time-wasting, players may wish to agree a time limit for responses.

3. Certain games will be better suited to certain types or sizes of quiz.

4. Some games are better suited to individual play (for example *Round Robin*, *Bluff and Subterfuge*, and *Nominate*) and some for team play (for example *Auction* and *Contract*).

5. Adjudicators may wish to read out any footnotes accompanying the questions for clarity or to assist the players.

6. If selecting a list, shorter lists are found towards the beginning of the Quizzes section and longer lists towards the end of it. If selecting a list for an elimination game, choose a list that has at least as many items as the number of players.

7. All *Linked Miscellanies* contain ten questions; otherwise all other quizzes (those which are composed of questions rather than a list) have twenty-four questions. In the main, the questions will get harder as you go through.

8. If the end of a list in an elimination game is reached with more than one player or team remaining in the game, the player or team to name the last item is declared the winner. A winner in an elimination game is otherwise the last player or team remaining. The winner does not need to provide any further response after the penultimate player or team has been eliminated.

9. Readers are encouraged to devise their own games.

ROUND ROBIN The players elect an adjudicator and divide themselves either into teams or individual players. The adjudicator selects a quiz that is to their personal liking and poses it to the players (or teams of players). Moving clockwise from the adjudicator, players or teams respond alternately either to name a single item from the chosen list or respond to a single question (depending on the type of quiz that has been chosen). If a player or team responds incorrectly or is unable to respond, that player or team is eliminated. The game is won when only one player or team remains. For longer lists, the adjudicator may allow players to commence the game with three "lives."

DON'T MISS THE TARGET Players divide themselves into two teams: an inquisitive team and an answering team. The inquisitive team select a quiz and presents it to the others, stating the associated target number. The answering team, depending on the type of quiz that has been chosen, either attempts to name as many items or respond to as many questions as they can with the objective of achieving the target number. If they fail to achieve this, the game is won by the inquisitive team; if they succeed, the teams exchange roles and another quiz is selected. The game is won as soon as a team fails to hit the target. For quizzes that contain lists, the answering team may have as many attempts to answer as there are items of the list but no more.

AUCTION The players elect an adjudicator and divide themselves either into teams or individual players. The adjudicator selects a quiz of their liking and reads the title and description out to the players (or teams of players) as well as the associated target number. Moving clockwise from the adjudicator, teams lodge bids according to either the number of items they expect to be able to name or the number of questions they expect to be able to answer (depending on the type of quiz that has been chosen). Each bid must be greater than the previous bid; if a team or player is unable to bid they drop out of the bidding and the bid passes clockwise to the next team or player. The bidding concludes when only one team or player remains. This team or player must then attempt to honor their bid by naming their predicted number of items or answering their predicted number of questions. If the bid is achieved this team or player is awarded five points. If the bid is not achieved the remaining teams or players are awarded two points. Play continues with another selected quiz. The game is won when a team or player reaches ten points. In constructing their bids, players should use the target numbers as a guide. Adjudicators may opt to give players a few minutes in consideration of their bids.

CONTRACT The game is played in the same way as *Auction*, except that instead of a bidding round, the competing players or teams submit unseen written bids to the adjudicator. When all of the bids have been received, the adjudicator announces the results. The team or player with the winning bid then attempts to honor their bid and play continues in the same way as in auction.

BLUFF AND SUBTERFUGE The game is played in the same way as *Round Robin*, except that the adjudicator does not respond to any of the answers. Players supply responses in the normal way and at any time one of the remaining players may challenge this response. The adjudicator will then declare the correct answer and therefore the success of the challenge. If a challenge is successful, that is, the original response was wrong, the player making this response is eliminated (or loses a life). If the challenge is unsuccessful, that is, the original response was correct, the challenger is eliminated (or loses a life).

NOMINATE This game is played in the same way as *Round Robin* except that instead of passing clockwise, after providing a successful response the successful player nominates a player to provide the next response. If the nominated player offers a correct response, they in turn nominate the next player to respond. If the nominated player cannot offer a correct response they are eliminated (or lose a life) and play passes clockwise to the next player.

INCREMENTAL This game is played in the same way as *Don't Miss the Target* except that the game is played only with those quizzes containing lists. The game also always begins with a list containing three items and is incremented on each successive round. So, if in the first question the target number (out of three) is reached, the two teams swap roles and a list is selected containing four items. Play continues with the number of items in the list incremented by one each time until a team fails to hit the target.

QUIZ This game is played with the quizzes containing multiple questions. The players elect an adjudicator and divide themselves into teams. The adjudicator selects four quizzes from the book and announces the titles to the teams (for example *Miscellany*, *Linked Miscellany*, *Films and Their Stars*, and *First Lines of Pop Songs*). Starting with the first of the four, the adjudicator poses the questions to the teams, who write down their answers. After the teams have had some thinking time, the answers are marked and scores recorded. This is repeated for the three further rounds. The team with the highest score at the end is declared the winner.

ROUND ROBIN ROUND ROBIN This game is played in the same way as *Round Robin* except that at the outset it is agreed to play the same number of games as there are players. Play commences as normal but at the end of the first game, the players are awarded points in the reverse order of how they were eliminated (for example with four players the winner gets four points, the first player eliminated gets one point; the adjudicator receives no points for that game). The role of adjudicator then passes clockwise from the player who was previously the adjudicator and a new game commences. The player with the most points on completion of the agreed cycle of games is the winner.

SPOT THE LINK The players elect an adjudicator and divide themselves either into teams or individual players. The adjudicator selects a *Linked Miscellany* and reads out each question in turn, pausing after each. The players write down the answers. The game is won by the first player to shout out the correct link.

SPLOSH Players agree on a forfeit to be carried out by the loser of each round. A player is elected to adjudicate for the first round and selects a list from the book which has at least as many items as there are players. The adjudicator then writes down one of the items from the list but keeps this out of the view of the other players. Players take turns, starting to the left of the adjudicator, to name items from the list. When a player names the item the adjudicator has written down, or is unable to respond in a timely fashion, that player is declared the loser and must pay the forfeit.* Further rounds are played with the role of adjudicator passing clockwise until each player has had a turn as the adjudicator.

---

* A suggested forfeit is for the adjudicator to pour an eggcup full of water over the unwitting loser. For added drama, keep the eggcup in view of the players for the duration of the round. The author can not accept responsibility for any damage to personal effects, property, or personal pride incurred in the course of this game.

A NOTE ON THE AUTHOR

David Gentle is a self-confessed factaholic, who, since losing to his sister in a trivia contest on a childhood car trip, vowed to one day write this book. David splits his time between composing quizzes and consulting for the computer industry. He lives in Wandsworth, England, with his oft-tested wife and young son.